# THE RAKKASANS

# THE
# RAKKASANS

## The Combat History of the 187th
## Airborne Infantry

Lt. Gen. E. M. Flanagan Jr. USA (Ret.)

PRESIDIO

*To the valiant Rakkasans—past, present, and future*

Copyright © 1997 by E. M. Flanagan Jr.

Published by Presidio Press
505 B San Marin Drive, Suite 300
Novato, CA 94945-1340

**Library of Congress Cataloging-in-Publication Data**

Flanagan, E. M., 1921–
     The Rakkasans : the combat history of the 187th Airborne Infantry
/ E. M. Flanagan.
         p.   cm.
     Includes bibliographical references (p. 375) and index.
     ISBN 0-89141-604-8 (hc)
     1. United States. Army. Airborne Infantry, 187th. 2. United States.
Army—Airborne troops—History. I. Title.
     UD483.F58   1197
     356'.166'0973—dc21                                96-49009
                                                              CIP

Photos courtesy the United States Army.
Printed in the United States of America

# Contents

Foreword     vii

Preface     ix

PART 1: WORLD WAR II     1
    1: Birth and Youth of the Regiment     3
    2: The Attack on Manila and the Genko Line     90
    3: Mount Macolod     108
    4: Occupation of Japan     126

PART 2: THE KOREAN WAR     145
    5: On to Korea     147
    6: Bloody Inje—Wonton-ni     207
    7: Japan—and Korea—Third Time     245
    8: Army Reorganization Turmoil     255

PART 3: THE VIETNAM WAR     267
    9: On to Vietnam     269
    10: The Battle for Dong Ap Bia     283
    11: Vietnamization     302
    12: Between the Wars     316

PART 4: DESERT STORM     321
    13: The Outbreak of the Persian Gulf War     323
    14: Covering Force Mission—Desert Shield     333
    15: Cobra to the Euphrates     353
    16: Cease Fire—The Road Home     370

Bibliography     375

Index     381

# Foreword

There are many American combat battalions that have shared the fighting in the four major military commitments to the battlefield during the latter part of the twentieth century. But there are few that carried the fight to the enemy as did the 187th Airborne Infantry—the only airborne infantry unit to fight in all four of those conflicts: World War II, Korea, Vietnam, and Desert Storm. Therefore, the role of the 187th Airborne Infantry is an important part of the combat history of the U.S. Army. General Flanagan's book will take its place on the shelves of the military libraries of our nation.

To put the role of the 187th Regimental Combat Team and its battalions in perspective, one must appreciate that a major innovation of World War II was the ability to transport combat units to the immediate battlefield through the air by the use of parachutes and gliders. In Vietnam, the helicopter served that purpose. The 187th Infantry battalions were pioneers of such development during World War II and the conflict in Korea and helped significantly in perfecting the tactical use of the helicopter in Vietnam. Battalions of the 187th have served initially as glidermen and paratroopers and then as air assault troops in Vietnam and Iraq, launching their attacks in those two conflicts on and above the battlefield in assault helicopters. As fate would have it, three of the actions in which the 187th Infantry were involved were in the Far East, first as a regiment of the 11th Airborne Division in combat in the Philippines and in the occupation of Japan and later in Korea in Japan as a separate airborne combat team. During its stay in Japan, the Japanese referred to the 187th as the Rakkasans, a translation of the Japanese term for "Umbrella Man." Since those days, the Regiment has retained that nickname. During the war in Vietnam, the battalion of the Rakkasans fought many battles as part of the 101st Airborne Division (Air Assault), and in Desert Storm the Rakkasans made the longest and largest helicopter air assault in military history. Stateside, elements of the 187th have been posted at Fort Benning with the 11th Airborne Division and at Fort Campbell as a part of the 101st Airborne Division (Air Assault).

As a former commander of the Rakkasans in Korea and Japan, I welcome the publication of General Flanagan's book and salute a distinguished regiment.

William C. Westmoreland
General, U.S. Army (Ret.)

# Preface

This is a story of a unit, unique in the annals of the United States Army. It began as a glider regiment of two infantry battalions in the 11th Airborne Division in World War II. By the end of the war, it had become "airborne," another term for paratrooper. In the Korean War it was an airborne regimental combat team (RCT), complete with a direct support artillery battalion and other support units. All its men were parachute qualified. Among other noteworthy achievements during the Korean War, the RCT made two combat jumps. During the Vietnam War, the Rakkasans were represented in the 101st Airborne Division by only one battalion, the "air mobile" 3d of the 187th Airborne Infantry Regiment. But that battalion made history at the bloody and ferocious battle for Ap Bia Mountain. During Desert Shield and Desert Storm, the 187th Regiment was the 3d Brigade of the 101st Airborne Division (Air Assault). And in Desert Storm, the Rakkasans made the longest and largest helicopter assault in military history when it air-assaulted from Saudi Arabia over 150 miles to hostile territory along the Euphrates River.

The Rakkasans are brave: four of its soldiers were awarded the Medal of Honor, twenty-six the Distinguished Service Cross, four hundred and eleven the Silver Star, and three thousand eight hundred and forty the Purple Heart. To its credit, the Rakkasans fought in three World War II, nine Korean, twenty-one Vietnam, and two Persian Gulf campaigns.

Today, the Rakkasans are a proud, well-disciplined, highly trained, combat-ready, and vital part of the 101st Airborne Division (Air Assault), stationed at Fort Campbell, Kentucky.

# Acknowledgments

Gathering the material for a book about a regiment whose history spans over fifty years and four major wars required the assistance of a number of people. A partial list is included in the bibliography, particularly under the sections "Author Interviews, Private Papers, Letters and Personal Communications." I am especially indebted to Generals Westmoreland, Peay, Shelton, Mackmull, Cleland, Gorwitz and Scholes; Colonels Miley, Weber, Charles, Boyle, Costello, Peck and Thomas; and Major Chester. The monographs written by former members of the 187th at the Advanced Course of the Infantry School right at the end of World War II were detailed and fortunately still fresh in the minds of the authors.

The staff of Presidio Press was more than helpful. E. J. McCarthy, the Executive Editor, was patient, discerning, and most helpful. Craig Schneider, the copy editor, caught a number of mistakes with a sharp eye. And I am grateful that publisher Bob Kane has consented to publish *The Rakkasans,* my fifth book with Presidio Press.

# WORLD WAR II

# 1: Birth and Youth of the Regiment

Hoffman, North Carolina, was no metropolis. Before World War II, it was a small southern hamlet with one main, wide, dusty street lined along both sides with a series of dingy, flat-topped, red-bricked buildings and stores, none more than two stories high. Included among the stores were only the necessary ones, a grocery, a drugstore, a clothing store specializing in farmers' wear, a gas station, a furniture store, a barber shop, a diner, and a hardware store. But at the end of the main street there was a small railroad station, usually a minor stop on the main north-south, East Coast railroad line.

Because of the proximity of Hoffman to Camp Mackall, North Carolina (in the first couple of months of 1943 Camp Mackall was actually called Camp Hoffman), the railroad station made the town memorable to men of the 187th Glider Infantry Regiment and the 11th Airborne Division. For, beginning at 0200 on 2 March 1943, it was at this station that train after train stopped and spilled onto its platform groups of newly drafted eighteen- and nineteen-year-old boys, bedraggled, confused, and apprehensive, lads from the farms and streets of the nation who were soon to become men before their time. For the most part, after minimum processing to include only classification, clothing issue, shots, and physical examinations but no basic training, they came from reception centers like Fort Dix, New Jersey; Fort Lewis, Washington; Camp Wolters, Texas; Fort Sill, Oklahoma; and Fort Benjamin Harrison, Indiana. So the Hoffman railroad station, drab though it was, with its few lights blinking feebly through the cold North Carolina mist, was a singular transition point for these striplings: At the station, they lost their last link with the civilian world and their previous identity and were thrust, willing or not, into the strangling grip of the U.S. Army.

As each trainload of men debarked from the relative security of the stuffy, smoky railroad coach cars and gathered haphazardly and uncertainly on the railroad-station platform, it was met by a group of sharp-voiced sergeants who immediately tried to organize the shuffling mob into some semblance of a military formation. Then the sergeants herded the men toward a line of two-and a-half-ton trucks parked alongside the railroad tracks. The sergeants told their charges, dressed in just recently issued uniforms and heavy GI overcoats, to toss their over-stuffed barracks bags into the trucks, climb aboard, and sit down on the benches along the sides of the truck beds. When the sergeants deemed that their men were safely aboard, they climbed into the front seats next to the driver, and the lead sergeant in the first truck ordered the convoy to move out. A short, dusty ride led to Camp Mackall.

The recruits' first look at their new homes, "barracks" to the initiated, startled a number of the more sophisticated among them who reasoned, naively and optimistically, that the tar-paper-covered shacks they saw were only temporary and that more permanent barracks would be built later. Others saw signs indicating that Mackall was the home of the 11th Airborne Division and wondered by what chance of fate and legerdemain had they been detoured into this outfit. Infantry and tanks they had heard rumors about—but airborne seemed futuristic and out of the question. They had not volunteered for airborne; there must have been a mistake back at the induction station. Some of them mumbled sarcastically that the army induction system was as blunder-prone as they had heard.

The convoy stopped on a dusty street alongside the barracks of the 11th Airborne Division Casual Detachment, an ad hoc unit of some ten officers and forty-five men, headed by Lt. Col. Ernie Massad of University of Oklahoma football fame, formed to process the recruits as they arrived at all hours of the day and night. The Casual Detachment had taken over numbers of barracks and mess halls in the 511th Parachute Infantry Regimental area at the western end of Camp Mackall to house, feed, and process the new arrivals. (The 511th was in Taccoa, Georgia, undergoing the physical rigors of preparachute training under a demanding regimen authored and directed by a stern disciplinarian, Col. Orin D. "Hardrock" Haugen, commander of the 511th.)

Once the convoy had arrived at the detachment, the seemingly omnipotent and omnipresent sergeants ordered the recruits to dismount, gather their barracks bags, and "Fall in," one of the commands with which they would become increasingly and unpleasantly familiar in the weeks ahead. After the sergeants were satisfied that the column was in some semblance of order, they turned it over to the Casual Detachment cadre for housing, classification, and a meal. After processing, which took a day or so, the detachment NCOs assigned the recruits to specific units of the division. If by some chance they had volunteered for parachute duty, they were assigned to a parachute unit of the division. All others went to the glider units—whether they wanted to or not. At the first organizational sign, 188TH GLIDER INFANTRY REGIMENT, the sergeants halted the column and called out some names. The future infantrymen of the 188th fell out of the column and came under the control of the 188th cadremen who were waiting for them. The next stop was the 187th Glider Infantry Regiment. The sergeant called out another list of names, the anointed fell out of the column, and preliminary life began for the 187th. It was not exactly Genesis; but it was a start. Then the column moved on to the 127th Engineers, the glider artillery battalions, and the other units of the division. The final halt was at Special Troops.

If some of the 187th recruits had blanched at the word *airborne,* they must have been mystified at the word *glider* hidden in the title of their new outfit, prominently displayed on a sign in front of the 187th Regimental headquarters. But since they had not volunteered, there was no backing out now. They would learn later that paratroopers "volunteered" for the privilege of jumping out of airplanes and received extra pay (in 1943, fifty dollars per month for enlisted men and one hundred dollars for officers) for that so-called hazardous duty and, if the paratrooper "froze" in the door before a jump or decided on the ground that parachuting was not for him, he could sign a "quit slip" and be reassigned to a "leg" outfit. Glidermen, on the other hand, were given no "hazardous duty pay" and no choice about whether or not they wanted to be tugged aloft in rickety, motorless aircraft made of frames of pipe, covered with canvas. They would learn later that they had gotten into an outfit that was destined to be "roped into" combat.

The 11th Airborne Division was activated on 25 February 1943; the 187th Glider Infantry Regiment, however, was constituted in the War Department files on 12 November 1942. But it, too, was activated on 25 February 1943.

The diary of the 11th Airborne Division for 25 February 1943 made a simple statement: "Activation Day, Flag raised." It did elaborate that the day was cool, and the sky overcast. On Activation Day, Maj. Gen. E. G. Chapman Jr., commanding general of the Airborne Command, whose headquarters was also at Camp Mackall, was the luncheon guest of Maj. Gen. Joseph M. Swing, the commanding general of the 11th Airborne Division. General Swing, slender, tall, prematurely white haired, and possessed of piercing blue eyes, an inquisitive mind, and an innate command presence, graduated from West Point with the famous class of 1915, the class that spawned Generals Eisenhower, Bradley, Beukema, Ryder, Irwin, McNarney, and Van Fleet, among others. General Swing, although to the young men of the division he seemed old and mature, would celebrate his forty-ninth birthday only three days after the activation of his division.

After lunch, the two generals toured the division area. Their jeep raised clouds of dust along the unfinished, sandy roads. They stopped occasionally to check the work of the contractors whose men were still hammering and sawing in and on the flimsy, tar-paper-covered, one-story "Theater of Operations" type barracks, mess halls, supply rooms, hospitals, theaters, and headquarters buildings. In other areas, they watched bulldozers push over pine trees and scrub growth and shove piles of roots, branches, and debris into bigger piles for burning or removal. Clearings appeared where just a day or so ago pines and scrub oaks had flourished.

General Swing, as was his wont, had a number of comments later for the chief contractor. One of the most important had to do with troop accommodations such as latrines, showers, and mess halls. The contractor had planned on double bunks in barracks but had built the ancillary buildings to support the number of barracks, not the number of men who would occupy them. General Swing pointed out that the supporting structures would have to be increased proportionately. He directed his assistant division commander, Brig. Gen. Albert Pierson, recently transferred from the War Department, to contact the chief of engineers in Washington. Between them, they rectified the situation to the extent possible—but not totally. Some officers and men lived in winterized pyramidal tents during their tour at Mackall.

Most of the men who joined the 187th Glider Infantry Regiment in those cold North Carolina days of the spring of 1943 were unaware of the uniqueness of the division and the regiment. The division strength was small: 506 officers, 29 warrant officers, and 7,970 men, just over half the strength of a standard infantry division of World War II. The division's infantry strength was spread out in one parachute regiment of three battalions and two glider regiments of two battalions each. The 187th had 73 officers, 3 warrant officers, and 1,602 men. The original Table of Organization and Equipment (T O and E), of the 187th included such basic transportation as 29 bicycles, 18 jeeps, 10 two-and-a-half-ton trucks, and 76 handcarts. The weapons included 635 carbines, 23 machine guns of various calibers, 36 60mm and 81mm mortars, 136 pistols, 42 BARs (Browning automatic rifles), 8 37mm antitank (AT) guns, and 672 M1 and 120 M1903 rifles. A realistic and pessimistic observer might have concluded, after looking at the 187th Table of Equipment, that except for the jeep and the M1, relatively little progress had been made in arms and transportation since the end of World War I.

Colonel Harry Hildebrand, the first commander of the 187th, was present with his cadre when the first fillers for the regiment arrived in his area at Mackall. He was a courtly gentleman, apparently not in top physical condition, and forty-nine years old, a relatively advanced age in World War II for the commander of an infantry regiment, particularly an airborne one. He had been assigned to the division in November of 1942 and had gone through preliminary training and orientation with the division staff and other commanders in Washington, where they met with Gen. Leslie McNair, the commander of Army Ground Forces; at Fort Holibird where they learned, for some unknown reason, to drive trucks in convoy through the streets of Baltimore; at Aberdeen Proving Grounds, where they had a look at the Army's current weapons, to include the folding-stock carbine, with which many of the airborne troopers would be armed, and the pack 75mm howitzer, a holdover from the days of mule artillery and the undersized artillery piece with which the airborne artillerymen would harass the enemy. Then Gen. Albert Pierson, Col. Robert "Shorty" Soule, the designated CO of the 188th Glider Infantry, and Colonel Hildebrand went to Fort Benning for a three-week special infantry course that emphasized the relatively new and, to date, relatively unsuccessful use of U.S. airborne forces in combat. By late February, they were all back at Mackall to begin the task of training from scratch for combat as a division, and a unique airborne one, at that.

Lieutenant Colonel Lucas E. Hoska Jr., class of 1937 at West Point and twenty-nine years old in the spring of 1943, was the first commander of the 674th Glider Field Artillery Battalion. Though he had been a Corps squad boxer at West Point, he walked with a loose, long, gangling stride. A perpetual half-smile belied his penchant for discipline and demand for hard work and training in his battalion. In early 1943, Brig. Gen. Wyburn D. Brown, the 11th Airborne Division Artillery commander, went to Fort Sill, Oklahoma, where he met his artillery battalion commanders, among them Douglass P. Quandt, who would command the 457th Parachute Field Artillery Battalion, and Colonel Hoska. At Sill, they received an orientation on the peculiarities of airborne artillery. In those days, for example, there was no way to parachute a whole artillery piece from the C-47, so the airborne artillery had to resurrect the 75mm howitzer, a weapon that could be broken down into seven two-hundred-pound loads for transportation by mules, as the prime artillery piece of the airborne artillery. The group then returned to Mackall to make artillery "red legs" of the fillers arriving daily.

In training the 11th Airborne, General Swing had two distinct advantages; one, he would not be required to furnish cadres to form other divisions, as was the case with almost every one of the ninety-one divisions on the army's rolls by the end of World War II; and, two, the men who formed the division were of exceptional quality: the average age was just under twenty years, and sixty percent of the enlisted men had at least a score of 110 on the Army General Classification Test, the minimum intelligence standard for admission to officer candidate school.

The 187th went through basic training from 15 March to 21 June 1943. General Swing placed special emphasis on physical training for all officers and men, paratrooper and glider-rider alike. Runs, push-ups, sit-ups, stretches, and chin-ups were part of the daily early-morning routine. Then, for the rest of the day, came weapons cleaning and training; weapons qualification; foxhole digging; field fortifications; close order marching; squad drills; close-combat, infiltration, and transition courses; full field and barracks inspections; and long hikes—twelve-, eighteen-, and finally, twenty-five-milers in less than eight hours—with full field equipment.

The officers of the division were not spared the physical training. One Friday afternoon, 19 March 1943, General Swing ordered all officers to assemble near division headquarters for a "short, brisk walk." The short walks became runs of some three or four miles duration and were dubbed "Swing sessions" by the division officers. The sessions continued every Friday afternoon that the division was not in the field, during the Mackall phase of training.

By 29 March, General Swing felt that the division was well enough trained to appear in public. On that date, he scheduled the first full division review with the troops "Passing in Review" down the gravelly road in front of the division headquarters. Later in its training, the division held reviews on the runways of Mackall for such visiting dignitaries as Lt. Gen. Ben Lear, Gen. Henri Giraud of the French Army, and for General Chapman of the Airborne Command. On 1 May, the division formed on the Mackall runway to formally dedicate the post in honor of Pvt. John T. "Tommy" Mackall, a young paratrooper from Wellsville, Ohio, killed in Africa with the 509th Parachute Infantry Battalion. In actuality, General Swing did his best to restrict the number of division reviews, feeling that they detracted from his primary mission of training the division for combat.

The troops in the division reviews usually wore wool uniforms or khaki shirts and trousers, helmet liners, slung rifles, web belts, and leggings. The leggings were worn by paratrooper and gliderman alike and illustrated General Swing's attempt to homogenize and "desegregate" the division. Even though General Swing was himself a qualified paratrooper, he wanted no obvious distinction between paratrooper and gliderman. His basic policy, which he developed during training at Mackall, was that the entire division should eventually be dual qualified, able to enter combat either by parachute or glider. To this end, he set up jump schools wherever the division was located and encouraged the glidermen to become jump qualified.

That the proud and swaggering paratroopers were forbidden to wear their highly polished and symbolic jump boots in Camp Mackall was difficult for them to understand and to accept. But General Swing was determined to rein in the cocky paratroopers. In the spring of '43 while the 511th was at Taccoa and Fort Benning undergoing jump training, reports filtered back to General Swing that the 511th troopers were "full of hell," "rowdy," "hell-raisers," and somewhat undisciplined. At the time, Henry Muller was a young captain with the 511th. When the 511th joined the rest of the division at Mackall after jump qualification, Henry Muller remembers: "It was quite a shock to us. General Swing, who had heard terrible reports about the alleged rowdyism and unprofessionalism [of the 511th], determined to 'make us over right.' The first thing to go were the leather jackets, [air corps 'bomber jackets' issued to flight crews] worn [and authorized] by paratrooper officers. Next were the beloved boots for all ranks! We were in a state of shock. That dreadful morning when we all had to put on 'leggins' . . . nearly broke our spirit—but not for long. The old horse artilleryman [General Swing] knew what it would take to bring a high-spirited horse under control. In the long run, it was good for us too-cocky paratroopers and helped prevent unhealthy rivalry between the paratroopers and the glidermen."

The 187th Glider Infantry Regiment and its direct support artillery, the 674th Glider Field Artillery Battalion, were finished with basic training. The bewildered "boys" who had gotten off the train in Hoffman had taken a large step toward becoming soldiers, and "airborne" ones at that. But they were still largely neophytes; the harder and more dangerous training was yet to come. Involuntary glider-riding would grab their attention.

### The Knollwood Maneuver and Camp Polk
On the twenty-first of June, the 187th and the other units of the 11th Airborne Division entered a new phase of training—unit training. Squad training shortly gave way to platoon and company training and longer, ten-day tactical problems in the field. In July, the 674th, the direct support battalion for the 187th, went to Fort Bragg for live firing on Bragg's artillery ranges. (Even though Mackall had some 51,971 acres, the triangle of runways consumed a great deal of space, and there were no areas large enough for firing artillery weapons even at the limited range of the pack 75s—some eight thousand yards.)

In late July, the 187th started formal glider training at Maxton Air Base and studied the intricacies of glider loading, rope tying, slide-rule manipulation, and the proper lashing of vehicles, equipment, ammunition, and supplies into the fragile CG-4A gliders. On 16 September, the men who feared that flying in gliders was risky were proved right— one of the 674th gliders crashed at Mackall during an airborne exercise and cost the lives of the two glider pilots and four men from the 674th.

By the fall of 1943, the 11th Airborne Division and its subordinate organizations were beginning to coalesce as units. But within the hierarchy of the army, there were senior commanders and staff officers who doubted the viability and combat practicality of the airborne division as an entity. True, the Germans had successfully used airborne forces, paratroopers and glidermen, in the invasion of the Netherlands during the early morning hours of 10 May 1940 and in Crete on 20 May 1941. But the American use of airborne forces in Africa on 7 November 1942 and in Operation Husky in Sicily on 7 July 1943 were disastrous, because of poor aerial navigation, mixed-up air and ground communications, shoot-down of 23 U.S. paratrooper planes by "Friendly Fire," wide-spread dispersion of troops, and unusually high landing casualties.

In the aftermath of the airborne debacle in Sicily, General Eisenhower wrote to General Marshall that "I do not believe in the airborne division. I believe that airborne troops should be reorganized into self-contained units, comprising infantry, artillery, and special services, all of about the strength of a regimental combat team. . . . To employ at any time and place a whole division would require a dropping over such an extended area that I seriously doubt that a division commander could regain control and operate the scattered forces as one unit. . . ."

The commander of Army Ground Forces, Gen. Leslie J. McNair, who had earlier been a staunch proponent of the airborne division, took General Eisenhower's words seriously. Other senior officers in Army Ground Forces, particularly armor officers, had expressed similar doubts about the value of the airborne division. Air corps senior officers found it difficult to plan the allocation of money and resources on hundreds of transport aircraft for airborne divisions when bombers and fighters, whose losses in the air war campaigns were prodigious, were in such great demand.

In the fall of 1943, General McNair convened a board of officers, headed first by General Pierson and then by General Swing, to study and recommend the future mission and scope of U.S. airborne forces. The board, later informally known as the "Swing Board," recommended the continuation of the airborne division and the publication of War Department Training Circular 113, which became the bible for future airborne operations. In spite of the Swing Board's recommendations, General McNair still doubted the practicality of the airborne division and decided to test the concept before he made a decision. Consequently, he ordered General Swing to plan an airborne division operation for December 1943 in which the entire 11th Airborne Division, with the 501st Parachute Infantry Regiment attached, would mount up in transports and gliders, fly for three to four hours out over the Atlantic, then return to North Carolina, parachute and glider-land during the hours of darkness at precise times and locations, resupply itself by air for three to four days, and accomplish its missions on the ground. General McNair also told General Swing that the future of the airborne division concept rested upon the result of that operation. Accordingly, General Swing and his staff planned the Knollwood Maneuver in accordance with General McNair's order and the precepts of WD Circular 113.

On 4 December the division trucked to departure airfields at Pope Field at Fort Bragg; Camp Mackall; Lumberton; and Laurinburg-Maxton, North Carolina; and Florence, South Carolina. The 187th and the 674th loaded their equipment aboard the CG-4As, bivouacked near their aircraft, and awaited the order to mount up. Foul weather prevented the launch of the operation as planned on 5 December. Undersecretary of War Robert Patterson and General McNair were present on the fourth but returned to Washington when the operation was held up. They considered it so vital, however, that they were back in time for the launch on the evening of the sixth. So were General Ridgway, commanding general of the 82d, already deployed to Europe, and a number of ground force and air corps staffers, many of whom doubted the worth of the airborne division.

The Knollwood maneuver was a great success. After a long flight out over the Atlantic, the long columns of transports and gliders swung around and headed back to drop and landing zones in and around Southern Pines and Pinehurst, including famed golf courses. The paratroopers began dropping and the gliders cut loose at 2300 hours. There were few difficulties. The lights on the pararack bundles of the 457th Parachute FA Battalion cut loose unexpectedly with opening shocks and cascaded to the ground in a brilliant display that looked like luminescent hailstones. But the division assembled with speed, attacked a composite combat team from the 17th Airborne Division and the 541st Parachute Infantry Regiment, and seized its objective, the Knollwood Airport. The division then set up an airhead around the airfield and resupplied itself by air. After three days, the division returned to Mackall in a cold, driving rain.

The Knollwood maneuver climaxed the training period for the 187th and the 11th Airborne. On the second of January 1944, the division started its move by train to Camp Polk, Louisiana. By the fifth of February, the 187th was in the field near Hawthorn, Louisiana, for two weeks of testing by Army Ground Force teams to determine the regiment's readiness for deployment to a combat zone. The tests were a series of four three-day tactical flag exercises (the enemy was a group of flags) over a period of two weeks. The exercises involved approach marches, attack of an objective, defense of a piece of ground, and then a tactical withdrawal. The incessant rain, cold weather, and sodden ground ingrained the Calcasieu Swamps near Camp Polk indelibly into the minds of the troopers of the 187th. In late February, the regiment returned to Polk for reequipping, showdown inspections, physical examinations, shots, and processing for overseas movement.

In the interim, General Swing established a jump school at DeRitter Army Air Corps Base, the first of four division-run jump schools he would establish in the next few years. Others would be in New Guinea, Luzon, and Japan. For this first jump school, the 187th and the 674th furnished a number of volunteers who were less than enchanted with the prospects of further glider rides and were eager to collect jump pay. Thus began the first and as yet limited transformation of the 187th and 674th from purely glider outfits to airborne units.

The tests at Camp Polk represented the graduation exercises for the 11th Airborne and the 187th. The War Department had alerted General Swing to be ready to leave Camp Polk of the fifteenth of March but delayed the move for a month. By 15 April, all units were restricted to the post, and commanders readied their units for an overseas move. The division would go incognito. This meant removal of 11th Airborne shoulder patches, cap emblems, and the storing of jump boots. The troops went through a series of inoculations for a variety of exotic diseases, lectures on censorship and security, physical inspections, Inspector General checks, Table of Equipment audits, and the initiation of taking the daily Atabrine pill, which caused all men in a few months to have yellow eyes and tawny-colored skin.

### New Guinea

The division started the train trip on 20 April to Camp Stoneman, California, where it would spend about six days in final preparation for overseas movement, to include, among many other things, the first censorship of enlisted men's mail by unit officers. On the second of May, the first units of the division marched out of Camp Stoneman, moved to nearby Pittsburg, California, and then boarded inland boats for the trip to the port of embarkation, San Francisco. The ships tied up at the Oakland Mole, near the ships on which the division was to sail, and the troops debarked. They marched, laden down with duffel bags, into a large wharfside shed where young and smiling Red Cross girls dispensed coffee and doughnuts. The irony of the "condemned man" syndrome was not lost on the troopers. Then the troops mounted the gangplanks of their ships for the next phase of their trip to war. They did not know specifically where they were headed, but since they were leaving from California, they reasoned, not illogically, that their destination must be the Pacific Theater. Australia? New Guinea? Burma? Only time would tell. The division staff, even if it knew, would not.

The merchant marine troop transports were hot, crowded, and slow. The food was only marginal even at the beginning of the trip and degenerated rapidly thereafter. Spam would never again be a food of choice for the men of the 187th. Finally, after about three weeks, but what seemed an eternity to the men of the 187th jammed into the stuffy and airless triple- and quadruple-decked holds of the troopships, the troops spotted land. The ships sailed up the winding, jungle-bordered channel of Milne Bay, and the men got their look at the lush, verdant growth that they would come to know and hate. But Milne Bay was a water stop only; no troops debarked. The ships then moved up the east coast of New Guinea, pulled into Oro Bay, and the men began to unload into a fleet of DUKWs, (though not an acronym, a DUKW is an all-wheel drive utility vehicle) that had pulled up alongside the ship. After a trip to the beach and then a ride along a few miles of dusty roads, the DUKWs halted at a cleared area around an abandoned airstrip. The regiment and the division were in their new home for the next six months —Dobodura, New Guinea.

When the DUKWs stopped, the troops unloaded and felt for the first time the heat and heavy humidity of New Guinea. The humidity was so overpowering that it almost drove the men to the ground. But in a few minutes, the regiment formed up into company units and marched, laden with duffel bags, to company areas that had already been laid out by advance crews. The 187th's jungle phase of training and acclimatization to the tropics was about to begin.

The 187th spent the first month in New Guinea building up its area—mess halls, framed pyramidal tents, showers and latrines, dayrooms, and chapels. Native laborers used ingenious designs and local vegetation and lumber to construct thatch-roofed chapels, dayrooms, and mess halls, and they supplied them with wicker furniture and bamboo decorations. One project of some note was the huge, slope-roofed four-hundred-man division chapel built by New Guinea natives by hand and without nails.

Once the regiment was settled in its area, training began again in earnest. The jump school reopened, and a large majority of the men and officers of the 187th qualified as paratroopers. They remained in the 187th and would later provide the men who would make a combat jump from L-4s and L-5s in Leyte. At one point, 75 percent of the enlisted men and 82 percent of the officers of the division were jumpers—a result of General Swing's determination to make his division dual qualified. In August and September, the division operated a glider school with the 54th Troop Carrier Wing at Nadzab, New Guinea, for the late arrivals in the glider units and for some of the paratrooper outfits.

From July to September, the division and the 54th TC Wing conducted combined airborne–troop carrier training for a different troop carrier squadron each week. The squadrons had been merely cargo haulers to this point. Pilots learned to fly in multiship formations, and paratroopers learned to jump into innocent-looking kunai grass, and then find themselves engulfed up to their necks in the razor-sharp grass. In August and September, the 187th underwent amphibious training at Oro Bay with the 4th Engineer Special Brigade. The 187th also sent a cadre of men to the jungle training course conducted by ANGAU (the trade name for the Australian organization governing New Guinea) near Higatura. The cadre then set up courses in the nearby jungles for the rest of the regiment. The regiment also underwent live fire training exercises for combined infantry-artillery-engineer battalion combat teams at an abandoned airstrip at Soputa. The 674th practiced its artillery skills on the ranges at Embi Lake and Soputa.

In September 1944, the War Department authorized jump pay to all qualified jumpers regardless of unit assignment. (In 1944, monthly jump pay was fifty dollars for enlisted men and a hundred dollars for officers. There was still no extra pay for glider-riders. In 1985, however, the Department of the Army finally rectified the discrepancy between officers' and enlisted men's jump pay; today all jumpers receive $110 per month jump pay.)

The division actually received authorization for battle honors for participation in the New Guinea Campaign because the division had been placed in reserve for the Hollandia operation but was not committed. Probably no one but the division staff and some of the major commanders knew of the alert. The official authorization was General Orders No. 26, Headquarters United States Army Forces in the Far East (US-AFFE), dated 11 February 1945.

By October, rumors of the division's move to combat abounded. On 12 October, General Swing received an order from Southwest Pacific Command to move his division "administratively" (not combat-loaded) to Leyte to prepare for an operation in Luzon. At the time, General MacArthur's headquarters apparently had no intention of using the 11th Airborne as a "ground outfit" in combat on Leyte.

General Pierson and a segment of the division staff flew ahead of the division to Leyte and selected and set up a campsite. In New Guinea, the division prepared to move out. John Conable, the division quartermaster, wrote recently: "The next three weeks [after 13 October] were spent waterproofing the equipment, deciding which unit went on which ship, and actually loading the ships. This time (as opposed to the move across the Pacific, when the division moved in merchant marine vessels) we had Navy ships, seven APAs (personnel carriers) and two AKA cargo carriers. In an administrative move, the howitzers were packed in the bottom of the holds, and the parachutes were packed on top. Our theory was that we would get the parachutes off first and under shelter, since we needed to keep them dry. The ships were loaded this way."

The battalions of the 187th loaded much the same way. The 187th Regimental Headquarters and the 1st Battalion loaded aboard the APA *Canbria* in Oro Bay. But the 2d Battalion had a unique departure plan. It flew to Finschaven by C-47s and there boarded the troop transport *Calvert.* Eli Bernheim of the 187th remembers that the *Calvert,* in the invasion of Sicily, was one of the U.S. ships that fired on the planes of the 82d Airborne Division by mistake and brought down a number of them. One of the *Calvert* crew told Bernheim that they thought they were shooting down the Germans. The captain of the *Calvert* remarked that the men of the battalion were "lean—lean with the leanness of the fine-drawn and fit." Bernheim attributed the health of the 187th, after the rigors of the jungle training, the various diseases which abounded, and the heat of the tropics, to "the nagging care of our medical officers and General Swing." The regiment was "remarkably free of malaria, dengue, scrub typhus, and many other tropical diseases." And because the battalion on his ship looked so hungry, the captain of the *Calvert* went out of his way to ensure that the troops were well fed.

By 11 November, the division had loaded its nine ships, the troops were aboard in the crowded holds, and the navy announced that it was ready to sail. Later that day the nine-ship convoy pulled out of Oro Bay, escorted by nine U.S. Navy destroyers.

The trip to Leyte was uneventful. One Japanese submarine did venture within detecting range, but a navy DE drove it off. Aboard ship, life was calm. John Conable remembers that he spent most of his time "playing bridge and drinking coffee in the wardroom. The navy knew how to eat. We were through with the Australian rations."

The division historian recorded that "underneath the surface gaiety aboard the ship, we were tense. We had thought for a long time about combat. We could look around and know that within a short time some of the faces we saw would be gone. This was a time for thought and mental preparation for what lay ahead. . . . We didn't know then—no one knew—how soon we were to be committed to combat, but it came sooner than any of us expected."

Leyte would prove to be a tougher-than-expected proving ground for the 11th Airborne and the 187th. For the unknowing men aboard the transports steaming toward Leyte, combat was just a few days away.

## Leyte Landing

On the morning of 11 March 1942, General MacArthur, in starched khakis and wearing a tie, sat at his desk in his small, makeshift office in one of the side corridors of Malinta Tunnel on Corregidor. Outside the tunnel, constant Japanese air and artillery bombardments had reduced to rubble all buildings aboveground, had scorched the rock of the island, had burned the foliage, shrubs, and trees, and had infused the laterals and tunnels of Malinta with smoke, dust, and haze.

General MacArthur called to his office Gen. Jonathan M. Wainwright, his successor in command of all forces in the Philippines. "Jim," he said, "hold on till I come back for you." General MacArthur later wrote: "I was to come back, but it would be too late—too late for those battling men in the foxholes of Bataan, too late for the valiant gunners at the batteries of Corregidor, too late for Jim Wainwright."

At 1715 that evening, General MacArthur, his wife, his son, his son's amah, Ah Cheu, and seventeen very carefully selected officers and men left bomb-blasted South Dock of Corregidor and boarded four "battle-scarred" PT boats commanded by Lt. John D. Bulkeley.

The trip was hazardous, not only because the boats were driving through waters controlled by the Japanese Navy but also because the weather had deteriorated rapidly, causing towering waves that buffeted the four, seventy-seven-foot-long plywood boats and caused them to break formation and scatter. General MacArthur and his party in PT-41 finally arrived at Cagayan Port on Mindanao Island in the southern Philippines at 1600 on the twelfth.

Brigadier General William F. Sharp, commander of the Visayan-Mindanao force, was on hand to meet them. He told General MacArthur that four B-17s from Australia, scheduled to meet his party, had not yet arrived. Sharp put General MacArthur and his party in the Del Monte Club house and guest cottages to wait for the B-17s.

On March 16, two war-weary B-17s landed, and, shortly after midnight on the seventeenth, General MacArthur and members of his party took off from the Del Monte strip for Australia, using the cover of darkness to help protect them in the Japanese-controlled airspace. General MacArthur's plane landed at Batchelor Field in Australia; he and his party then made their way by an ancient, slow train to Adelaide. When MacArthur arrived at the Adelaide railroad station, he was met by re-porters who pressed him for a comment. He was ready. He read a state-ment from the back of an envelope, the last three words of which were to become the most quoted, controversial, and famous of the Pacific Campaign: "The President of the United States ordered me to break through the Japanese lines and proceed to Australia for the purpose, as I understand it, of organizing the American offensive against Japan, a primary objective of which is the relief of the Philippines. I came through and I shall return."

After two and a half years of combat, intermixed with high-level de-bate on Pacific strategy ("the relief of the Philippines" as the "primary objective" of "the American offensive against Japan" was by no means certain in March of 1942), General MacArthur was about to make good his presumptuous boast, "I shall return." (A number of his critics thought that he should have said, "We shall return." Stubbornly, he refused to change it.)

His Southwest Pacific Area (SWPA) forces had driven up the coast of New Guinea, the southern prong of an enormous pincers movement that brought the Allied forces back through the vast stretches of the western Pacific to the Philippines. The northern prong of the pincers was the Pacific Ocean Area force of Adm. Chester W. Nimitz, which had, in close coordination with the forces of General MacArthur, forged across the western Pacific from island group to island group, invading and defeating the Japanese successively in the Solomons, the Gilberts, the Marshalls, and the Marianas, at the same time crippling the formerly potent air arm of the Japanese Navy and dealing serious blows to the Japanese surface fleet. By September of 1944, both forces were poised some three hundred miles from Mindanao, the southernmost island of the Philippine archipelago.

MacArthur and Nimitz, coequal commanders in the Pacific and each responsible directly to the Joint Chiefs of Staff, had disagreed on the next strategic move in the Pacific Ocean arena. Nimitz, strongly supported by Adm. Ernest J. King, the chief of naval operations and a member of the Joint Chiefs, wanted to use the Philippines only as a stepping-stone to Formosa. The navy was not interested in totally freeing the Philippines before moving on to Formosa, six hundred miles south of Japan. Nimitz reasoned that Formosa in U.S. hands would block the Japanese ocean lanes from its southern source of raw materials and permit the Allies to move on to China, where they could build airfields for the aerial subjugation of Japan.

MacArthur, on the other hand, "was in total disagreement with the proposed plan, not only on strategic but psychological grounds," he wrote later. In July of 1944, President Roosevelt flew to Hawaii to hear the Pacific commanders' opposing points of view. General MacArthur, with his usual grandiloquence, told the president that the United States not only had a moral commitment to free the Philippines, an American territory, as rapidly as possible, but also that Luzon would be easier to capture than Formosa because of the widespread support of guerrillas and the civilian population and that Luzon would serve the same strategic purpose as Formosa. The president did not make a decision in Hawaii. In early September the Joint Chiefs did order the Pacific forces to invade Mindanao on 15 November and Leyte on 20 December. But that decision failed to settle the larger question of Formosa versus Luzon.

During the second week of September, Adm. William F. "Bull" Halsey, commander of the Third Fleet under Nimitz, helped decide the issue. Halsey launched a series of air raids on the Philippines preliminary to invading the Palau Islands, 550 miles from Mindanao. His planes hit Japanese installations on Mindanao, and returning pilots reported that they had destroyed 478 planes, most on the ground, and had sunk some 59 ships. They also reported that they had met no serious opposition either from the ground or from the air. Admiral Halsey found this report "unbelievable and fantastic" and deduced that the Japanese position in the Philippines was a hollow shell with weak defenses and skimpy facilities," a conclusion that would later prove to be overly optimistic. He recommended to Nimitz that the invasion of Mindanao be scratched and that the date for the invasion of Leyte be accelerated.

Nimitz approved the recommendation and passed it to the Joint Chiefs, who were conferring at the time in Quebec with Roosevelt and Churchill. The Joint Chiefs queried MacArthur for his opinion; immediately he cabled a recommendation for approval. On 14 September, the Joint Chiefs canceled the Mindanao invasion, moved up the Leyte invasion to 20 October, and assigned Halsey's Third Fleet to cover the invasion. MacArthur then told the Joint Chiefs that, with the accelerated timetable for the invasion of Leyte, he would be ready to invade Luzon before the end of the year. With this rejoinder, on 3 October the Joint Chiefs made the strategic decision: Invade Luzon, not Formosa, after freeing Leyte.

On 20 October 1944, four army divisions landed abreast on Leyte's eastern beaches in the largest amphibious operation so far in the Pacific. The ground forces were two corps of the Sixth Army, under Gen. Walter Krueger. The X Corps, to the north, under Maj. Gen. Franklin C. Sibert, landed the 1st Cavalry Division and the 24th Division on beaches south of Tacloban with the objective of capturing the Tacloban airfield and then moving along the northern part of the island through

Tacloban to Carigara; the XXIV Corps, to the south, commanded by Maj. Gen. John R. Hodge, landed with the 96th and 7th Divisions abreast between Dulag and San Jose with the immediate mission of establishing a beachhead and capturing the Dulag airfield, about two miles inland.

A few hours after the initial landings, which were made against light opposition, General MacArthur, in his traditional khakis and gold-encrusted cap (but with no tie—his condescension to battle dress) and his entourage of generals, newsmen, and Philippine President Sergio Osmena, waded ashore through some thirty-five yards of knee-deep surf, an event duly recorded for posterity by many photographers. On the beach, General MacArthur traded greetings with some of the commanders onshore and then moved to a hastily set-up Signal Corps radio microphone. He broadcast an emotion-filled two-minute speech to the people of the Philippines." I have returned," he said, with his voice uncharacteristically quivering and his hands shaking. "Rally to me. . . . Let no heart be faint. . . . Let every arm be steeled." He had indeed returned—albeit accompanied by a number of troops.

By evening of the twentieth, X Corps had overrun an abandoned Tacloban airstrip, and XXIV Corps had taken the town of Dulag against very light opposition. The initial attack had been a great success, but the real battles were yet to come. Opposition had been light on the beaches because most of the Japanese 10,500-man 16th Division and another 11,000 troops had moved inland to escape the preinvasion naval and aerial bombardment.

The prime initial mission of Sixth Army was to secure Leyte Valley, a broad plain stretching from the invasion beaches to the ridge of jungled mountains that ran down the spine of the island. On this plain, General MacArthur intended to build large American air bases from which his planes could strike not only the entire Philippine Archipelago but Formosa and the China coast as well. But the terrain and the abominable weather—during a three-week period an abnormally heavy monsoon dumped thirty-five inches of rain on the valley—slowed progress of the troops on the ground, mired construction equipment, sank trucks up to their hubcaps on so-called roads, and delayed the reconstruction of even Tacloban and Dulag strips.

In addition to the soggy terrain and the incessant rains, General MacArthur had another unexpected problem that his intelligence team had not prepared him for. General Tomoyuki Yamashita, the Japanese commander in the Philippines, decided to make his major Philippine stand on Leyte, a move that would confound General MacArthur's intelligence officers. They had estimated that the Japanese would bring only about 12,000 more men to Leyte and that their major stand would be on Luzon; in fact, Yamashita doubled his strength within two weeks of the American landings and by the end of the campaign had infiltrated, through Ormoc on the west coast, about 45,000 troops, some, like his 1st Division, from as far away as Manchuria. He also had made a misjudgment: He had estimated that the Americans had landed only two divisions, and he thought that his four-division force could hurl them back into the sea.

By the fourteenth of November, General Krueger had the bulk of his four divisions spread along a fifty-mile front, which ran southeast from Pinamopoan on Carigara Bay in the north to Abuyog, just south of Bito Beach in the south. The area of Leyte in U.S. hands was a small fraction of the island. And Yamashita's reinforcements continued to land, although with difficulty, and his depleted air arm continued to harass the U.S. forces on a limited basis. The weather kept both sides' planes grounded for long periods. General MacArthur's ambitious time-table for an invasion of Luzon before the end of the year was in jeopardy.

On the eighteenth of November, the 11th Airborne Division "joined the King II operation [the code name for the battle of Leyte] by landing unopposed on Bito Beach," according to the division periodic report for that date.

The *Calvert*, carrying the 2d Battalion of the 187th, arrived in Leyte Gulf early on the morning of the eighteenth. One of the men of that battalion recorded later his thoughts of that trip. "So now we were aboard a ship, one of dozens which made up our convoy, and headed for battle. By now every man knew how to sustain himself in the jungle. Each was proficient at snap-shooting at unexpected targets, and in throwing grenades in dense kunai grass, growing to eight feet. Squads and platoons had been taught to crowd in close behind mortar and artillery barrages, thus taking advantage of the enemy's momentary shock to administer the coup-de-grâce with grenade and bayonet. All knew the efficiency of demolition and flamethrower technique in reducing enemy pillboxes and similar installations. The regiment had been well grounded in amphibious operations, and 90 percent of its personnel had been qualified as paratroops."

The two ships carrying the 187th anchored about a thousand yards off Bito Beach on the morning of 18 November. Three Zeros attacked the tail of the convoy but missed the 187th's ships. Kamikaze pilots also harassed the hundreds of ships jammed into the bay. The navy, most anxious to unload its ships and get out of the combat zone, pressed the 187th to unload its transports before evening and the cargo ships, the AKAs, as soon as possible.

From the *Calvert*, small naval landing craft taxied the troops and their individual duffel bags, weapons, ammunition, and rations to the beach as fast as the troops could clamber over the sides, down the landing nets, and into the craft. Then the troops piled out on the beach, and the landing craft made another trip. LCTs carried heavier equipment ashore, and a two-hundred-man crew from the 187th worked in shifts around the clock, sometimes in chest-deep surf, to unload their regimental supplies and equipment. A hundred yards or so behind the beach, other work crews erected pyramidal tents for sleeping quarters, messes, supply rooms, orderly rooms, and headquarters for all commands.

A small advance party from division headquarters, Brig. Gen. Albert Pierson, Lt. Col. Glenn J. "Chief" McGowan, the G1, and Lt. Col. Bill Crawford, the G4, had flown up from New Guinea via Biak to select an area for the division. By a process of elimination, because most desirable areas along the east coast had already been occupied, Bito Beach became the choice.

Bito Beach is a long, narrow spit of land, bounded on the north and south by swift, unfordable rivers, on the front by Leyte Gulf, and in the rear by a bottomless swamp. About a hundred-yard strip of sand fronted the bay, and in the rear of the sand was a coconut grove about 150 yards deep. Once ferried ashore, no vehicle could leave the beach until days later when the 127th Engineers had built bridges across the swamp and the two rivers. Soon the beach in front of the 187th bivouac area was piled high with rations, ammunition, gasoline and oil, vehicles, bundles of clothing, and crew-served weapons.

On the second day after the 187th landed at Bito, a lone kamikaze flew south along the water's edge and scattered the troops working along the beach to the shelter of the palm trees behind the tents. But the kamikaze did not strafe troops on the beach; he was after larger game. Halfway down the beach, he turned left and dived on a transport that was in the process of unloading about a thousand yards offshore. Antiaircraft rounds fired from the beach and from ships in the area bounced off the bottom of the plane. The pilot held grimly to his diving course and rammed straight into the bridge of the transport. The plane blew up in a cloud of flames, and the ship caught fire and sank. But the water was not deep at that point, and the ship's hull remained above the surface. Men of the 187th helped the survivors as they came ashore in life jackets and small boats. The sunken hull of the transport was a reminder thereafter to the men of the 187th that that ship might easily have been one of theirs.

The 187th set up its first bivouacs near the Filipino villages of Abuyog and Balay Baban. Overhead, an occasional dogfight between a Zero and P-38 livened the day. But for the first few days on Leyte, the 187th simply cleared and policed the beach by moving the supplies to dumps in the coconut grove in the rear, built a base camp out of pyramidal tents, cleaned weapons, enjoyed the waves on Bito, and readied itself for its first taste of combat. It would not be long in coming.

### Combat on Leyte

General Krueger formally attached the 11th Airborne Division to XXIV Corps on 22 November. But a day or so earlier, just after the division came ashore, General Swing had reported to General Hodge at XXIV headquarters near Dulag. General Hodge told General Swing to relieve the 7th Division along the line Burauen–La Paz–Bugho and destroy all the enemy in that area, protect and secure all corps and air corps installations in his zone of responsibility, protect the Leyte Gulf supply bases and shipping, and coordinate operations with the 96th Division on his northern flank, which would run generally on an east-west line through the village of Dagami. General Swing went back to his pyramidal tent CP on Bito, briefed his staff, and alerted the units of the division to be ready to deploy. He was more than ever aware that the fighting strength of the division was seven small infantry battalions supported by three field-artillery battalions with a total of twenty-four 75mm pack howitzers and twelve sawed-off 105s. But he took the order in stride and put the division in motion piece by piece as the situation demanded.

Overnight, the 11th Airborne Division went from a theater reserve role to direct combat.

By the time the 11th Airborne entered the fight on Leyte, the 24th and 1st Cavalry Divisions were attacking south from the Pinamopoan-Carigara area; the 96th and 7th Divisions were in scattered contact with the Japanese in the foothills around Dagami and Burauen, inland from their original landing beaches. When the 11th relieved the 7th in the Burauen area, the 7th swung south, crossed the mountain spine by the Abuyog-Baybay Road, which was clear of the enemy, and, after reaching the west coast, began to attack due north, compressing the Japanese between its forces and those of the 24th and 1st Cavalry attacking south. The 11th Airborne was left with the task of attacking across the center of the jungled, soggy mountains from the Burauen area to Albuera on the west coast. It was raining the day the 11th debarked on Bito Beach, and it rained constantly and heavily almost every day until the end of the battle. In Leyte during the last two months of 1944, monsoonal rain was a constant.

At 0700 on 21 November, the 511th Parachute Infantry Regiment, the first element of the 11th Airborne to be committed to combat, left Bito Beach by LCT and moved to Dulag, where it loaded into trucks for its move inland to Burauen. After a ride along the boggy Burauen road, the regiment unloaded and assembled in the mud flats next to the Daguitan River, occupying the "carabao wallows as the 7th Division evacuated them," according to the division historian. Colonel Rock Haugen's mission was to move the 511th west across the uncharted mountains and link up with the 7th Division on the west coast. A couple of days later, Colonel Soule moved the 188th north from Bito to protect the southern flank of the 511th as it moved to the west, and to clear the enemy from the area—a sector on which little intelligence had been developed and whose maps and charts were virtually useless blanks.

Initially, General Swing left the 187th on the beach and placed Colonel Hildebrand in command of all the division forces remaining there. On 24 November, General Swing moved his headquarters to San Pablo, a barrio outside Burauen, and occupied the former headquarters of the 7th Division. To protect the Fifth Air Force Headquarters of Gen. Ennis C. Whitehead near Burauen, General Swing stripped the 674th and 675th Glider Field Artillery Battalions of their pack 75s, moved them from Bito Beach, and assigned them the mission. The glider field artillerymen, armed mainly with folding-stock carbines, became infantrymen overnight. Lieutenant Colonel Lucas E. Hoska Jr., the commander of the 674th, acted like a young man with a new car; he was now an infantry battalion commander and, true to the spirit that had made him an outstanding boxer at West Point, he accepted the new assignment with relish and verve.

To protect the base at Bito Beach and to provide additional protection to the 511th's pending move to the west, Colonel Hildebrand told Lt. Col. George Pearson to move his 1st Battalion of the 187th to the vicinity of Balinsayao along the mountain-pass road from Abuyog to Baybay through the narrow waist of central Leyte. From that base, for the next week, Colonel Pearson sent out patrols to the west and the south by foot, jeep, and boat. "Contact patrols," according to one of the 187th's troopers, "continually worked through the Baybay Pass to keep abreast of the 7th Division's situation, and some of these witnessed their first banzai attacks, which the seasoned 7th always stopped, sometimes with canister fired point-blank from 37mm guns.

"Meanwhile patrols from the 2d Battalion of the 187th gained no contact with the enemy but kept up routine jaunts yielding nothing more interesting than a wide variety of bananas and coconuts. Comparatively free from war and woe, the 2d Battalion, and Regimental Headquarters, industriously spooned up the housekeeping," wrote a 187th trooper.

But, for the 187th, those easy, enemy-free days on the beach and along the Baybay Pass would shortly be over. Surprisingly enough, the 187th would have their counterparts in the Japanese Army, its airborne forces, to thank for its initial entry into combat.

With the arrival of American forces on Leyte and the potential buildup of air power based there, the Japanese Imperial General Headquarters foresaw the aerial threat to the line of communications between the Japanese homeland and the South Pacific area. General Headquarters, therefore, directed Gen. Tomoyuki Yamashita, the commanding general of the Fourteenth Area Army with headquarters on Luzon, to neutralize the airfields at Dulag and Tacloban and to seize the airfields in the southern Leyte Valley before the American air force could establish itself in strength on the island. In the latter part of November, Yamashita ordered Lt. Gen. Sosaku Suzuki, commander of the Thirty-fifth Army on Leyte with headquarters at Ormoc to "occupy Burauen airfield as soon as possible and at the same time neutralize Tacloban and Dulag airfields. Moreover," he said, "we must annihilate the enemy's air power."

The Japanese plan to carry out the edict of General Headquarters and seize the airfields on Leyte was more courageous than sensible. The plan was to be a coordinated effort by both the ground and the air forces. In Phase 1, a four-day effort beginning on 23 November, the air force would launch an all-out campaign to wipe out the American air power. In Phase 2, slated for the night of the twenty-sixth, four transport aircraft, U.S. code-named Topsy and looking much like C-47's, carrying specially trained demolitionists, were to crash-land on the Dulag and Tacloban airstrips and blast them out of commission. In Phase 3, on the night of 5 December, the 3d and 4th Airborne Raiding Regiments from Luzon would parachute onto the three Burauen airfields of Buri, Bayug, and San Pablo. In coordination with the parachute attack, the Japanese 26th and 16th Divisions were to infiltrate east through the central mountains, deploy down out of the hills, and attack and seize the Burauen airfields on 6 December. Then, if all went well with the plan, the ground forces were to continue the attack to the east and capture the Dulag airfield on the shores of the Leyte Gulf.

The execution of the plan was less successful than the High Command or General Yamashita, both still confident of ultimate victory, envisioned. Phase 1 barely got under way because the constant rains and low clouds grounded both the Japanese and the American planes for long stretches. Phase 2 at least showed some semblance of activity. At 0245 on 27 November, three Japanese transports with their lights on flew at fifty feet altitude over Leyte Gulf. Ten minutes later, one of the transports crash-landed on the beach two miles south of Rizal near the 728th Amphibian Tractor Battalion. One of the battalion guards, who thought that the transport was a C-47 and friendly, climbed on the wing of the plane and asked if he could help them. A couple of Japanese came out of the plane and threw a grenade at the guard. The noise alerted some other men of the battalion, who rushed out to the plane and killed two Japanese with small-arms fire. Three other Japanese, however, escaped into a swamp west of the crash site. Ten or more of the enemy moved south along the surf and also disappeared into the swamp.

A second transport crash-landed at Buri; all the men aboard were killed.

A third plane landed across the river that formed the northern boundary of the division area on Bito Beach. According to the division history, "An antiaircraft machine-gun crew was in position on the alert for enemy aircraft. When the third plane landed and came to a halt, one of the crew called across the small river: 'Need any help?' 'No, everything's okay,' someone yelled back, and the machine-gun crew went back to watching the skies for enemy aircraft. As the sun came over the horizon of Leyte Gulf, the red sun on the side of the aircraft gradually became more visible, and an excited machine-gun crew cautiously stalked a now deserted Topsy. Only one of the passengers was ever found, and he was found and killed by a division patrol about an hour after dawn." The patrol also found many abandoned demolitions kits in the plane, giving credence to the idea that the Topsy carried demolitionists and not pathfinders.

On 27 November, the 511th started its move into the hills to the west of Burauen. To replace Lt. Col. Norman Shipley's 2d of the 511th, General Swing ordered Lt. Col. Harry Wilson, West Point class of 1937, to move his 2d Battalion of the 187th into defensive positions on the heights just to the west of Burauen. Chief Warrant Officer William G. Nelson, personnel officer of the 2d of the 187th, wrote of the battalion's trip to Burauen: "En route, we stared like yokels at a starlet, as we crossed the coastal plain between Dulag and Burauen, for up to this time, we had no idea of the magnitude of the American effort on Leyte. . . . The job of the 2d Battalion was to protect this whole gigantic, and confused, mélange, and, accordingly, it occupied positions about eight hundred yards west of the town on a low hill dominating the surrounding flatland."

The 2d Battalion of the 187th did not stay there long. On 2 December, General Swing ordered Harry Wilson to move his battalion into the hills and follow the 511th across the narrow, treacherous, unmapped, jungle-covered trails, which wound around ridges and up and down cliffs. In the mountains of Leyte, the Japanese were only part of the problem. CWO Nelson wrote that "we moved off light, each man carrying his own weapon, with ammo and two days K rations. In our wake moved Lieutenant Bernheim's supply train; its rolling stock was a herd of sluggish, patient carabao loaded with heavy weapons, spare ammo, and the heavier signal equipment. Such was life in the 'modernized war.'"

Eli Bernheim, the 2d Battalion's S4, remembers the move into the mountains. "I won't go into the details on the horrors of the march through the mountains; I can recall more than one night spent in a hole with water up to my chin or places where you couldn't dig a hole and tried to sleep on the mud covered by a poncho. Eventually, we could take the carabao no farther. We lost two heavy-machine-gun cradles when a carabao fell off a ridge. We finally turned the carabao loose, and the herders tried to backtrack. I don't know whatever happened to them, but if we had known what was ahead, we might have considered a slaughter-and-butcher operation."

To replace the 2d Battalion of the 187th around Burauen, General Swing ordered Lt. Col. George Pearson to bring up his 1st of the 187th from its patrol positions to the north and west of Bito, where, along with elements of the 503d Parachute Infantry Regiment, it had been patrolling deep into the area behind the beach, more intensely after the crash landing of the Japanese transports. On its patrols, the battalion had succeeded in killing a number of the Japanese who had survived the crash landings. On 2 December, the battalion moved up by amtracs and occupied positions on the east end of the San Pablo airstrip, across the road and about a mile east of the 11th Airborne Division headquarters.

Lieutenant Charles "Pop" Olsen was the commander of C Company of the 187th. He had taken over command of the company when the previous commander, Captain Ferrelly, had been killed in New Guinea during a demonstration of a Japanese hand grenade. The morning after the 1st Battalion moved into San Pablo, Colonel Pearson told him to meet him at division headquarters. There, they met with General Swing, who told Colonel Pearson to send C Company into the hills behind the 2d of the 187th, which had already left. But he also startled them when he told them he wanted one platoon of C Company to make a combat jump into Manarawat. Manarawat was a deserted barrio in the central mountains of Leyte, halfway between Burauen and Albuera, on Ormoc Bay, on the west coast of Leyte. It was a flat, tabletop clearing in the jungle rising about 150 feet above a streambed, surrounded on three sides by sheer, brush-covered cliffs, and on the fourth by a more gentle slope. The clearing at Manarawat was about six hundred feet long by two hundred feet wide, and fringed by coconut trees. Across the stream, which made a rectangular island out of this oasis, jungle-covered mountains rose high and forbiddingly.

The need for speed in sending a platoon of C Company to Manarawat was this: The 1st Battalion of the 511th (less C Company), under the command of Lt. Col. Ernie LaFlamme, West Point class of 1937, was currently at Manarawat, which was becoming the hub for command, communications, logistical, and medical support for the division's operations along the mountain trails to the west. But C Company of the 511th was in difficulty. A treacherous Filipino guide had led the company under the command of Capt. Tom Mesereau, West Point class of January 1943, plus the regimental headquarters group including Col. Rock Haugen, into an ambush near Lubi on the north trail toward Manarawat. They were completely surrounded by the Japanese, and their ammunition and rations were running low. On the second day of the ambush, a group of Japanese, led by the Filipino guide, approached C Company's perimeter with a surrender offer. A C Company rifleman killed the guide, and the Japanese departed in some haste. That night, Colonel Haugen and a patrol of two men crawled out of the ambush and headed for the division headquarters. Two days later, they arrived. When General Swing became aware of C Company's situation, he ordered Colonel LaFlamme to leave Manarawat and rescue C Company. Fortunately, Colonel Haugen had already sent an eight-man patrol to Manarawat to guide LaFlamme's battalion back to the ambush site.

After General Swing had explained the situation to them, Colonel Pearson and Lieutenant Olsen did not question the somewhat unexpected and unusual order. They did not mention that C Company of the 187th was a glider unit, nor ask where the aircraft, parachutes, and drop containers were coming from. They simply said, "Yes, sir," saluted, and left.

For the 187th Glider Infantry Regiment, the Leyte campaign was heating up.

### The Battle for the Airfields

Olsen returned to his company position, simply a relatively dry area where the men had taken off their packs and gear, sprawled out on the ground in groups, lit up their K-ration cigarettes, and waited to find out their next move. Olsen sent for his first sergeant and his platoon leaders. He briefed them on their new mission. He told Lt. Chester J. Kozlowski, who had transferred into the 187th from the 503d Parachute Infantry Regiment after the 503d's hazardous and trouble-laden parachute operation on Noemfoor Island, that he and his platoon would remain behind and would not go into the hills on foot with the rest of the company but would parachute ahead of them into an obscure place called Manarawat. He also told a perplexed Kozlowski to report immediately to General Swing at the division command post. Lieutenants, reasoned Kozlowski correctly, were not in the habit of reporting to major generals; his mission must be unusual.

Kozlowski and his platoon of C Company of the 187th made the first unit combat jump of the 11th Airborne Division—albeit one jumper at a time from artillery observation aircraft. And in those days the 187th was still designated a glider regiment.

On the afternoon of 4 December, A Battery of the 457th Parachute Field Artillery Battalion also parachuted into Manarawat. But Lt. Col. Nick Stadtherr, commander of the 457th, had been fortunate to find an air-sea rescue C-47 whose pilot was willing to attach pararacks to the bottom of his plane and make thirteen trips to Manarawat, dropping one-thirteenth of A Battery on each trip. Colonel Stadtherr personally jumpmastered each drop into the tiny, jungle-surrounded clearing. On that same afternoon, a division staff group consisting of Lt. Col. Douglass Quandt, the division G3, Capt. Wells Albade, assistant G3, Capt. Jack Atwood, and a section of the 511th Signal Company with an SCR-694 radio also arrived in Manarawat parachuting from L-4s. Manarawat was rapidly becoming the hub of the division operations west of Burauen, and the division artillery fleet of L-4s and L-5s, designed for aerial observation of artillery, were being put to a totally unexpected, but imaginative and valuable, use.

General Swing, however, was not yet satisfied with the Manarawat setup. He foresaw the need there for medics and a strip long enough to land the Cub aircraft, permitting them to fly out the wounded to avoid the long, hazardous trek down the muddy, winding jungle trails. General Swing directed his division engineer, Lt. Col. Douglas C. Davis, to build the strip at Manarawat. On the afternoon of 4 December and the morning of the fifth, a platoon of the 127th Airborne Engineer Battalion, led by Lts. Jack T. Clift and Walter L. Brough, using the same liaison Cub aircraft that Kozlowski had used, jumped into Manarawat. The platoon also dropped bundles of shovels, saws, axes, and picks for clearing off the plateau and carving out a strip long enough for the Cubs to land and take off. This was an engineering effort in a most primitive sense—manpower for bulldozer power.

But even before the strip was ready, the Cubs also dropped into the small clearing at Manarawat three surgeons and ten medics from a portable surgical hospital of the division's 221st Airborne Medical Company. *Portable* took on a new meaning for the surgeons. They built a nipa-thatched, silk-parachute-lined "hospital" out of what materials were available and provided medical and surgical care for the wounded carried into the area by patrols from the infantry units fighting out in the jungle. As soon as the walking wounded could make it back to their companies from Manarawat, they caught a patrol going in that direction. If the wounded could not walk out but had to be evacuated, they had to wait in the "hospital." In a few days, the engineers had cleared a strip long enough for the L-4s, but not the slightly more powerful L-5s, to land and take off (even though there was a curve near the end of the runway, which the pilots learned to negotiate without accident). The medics fitted a piece of plywood over the backseat of the L-4 long enough to accommodate a wounded man on a mattress, and long enough to bump the pilot in the front seat on the back of his neck. With the crude but effective medevac in operation and with the medics performing miracles in their "hospital," the wounded of the 11th were receiving unexpectedly good medical care deep in the rain-soaked Leyte mountains.

Sixth Army had alerted the 11th Airborne staff to the possibility of a Japanese parachute attack somewhere on Leyte. "On the evening of December fourth or fifth, at this point I can't recall the exact date," Hank Burgess, the acting G3 at the time, wrote recently, "I was the duty officer in the evening when a coded message entitled 'Alamo Report' was received by the communications section advising that a force of Japanese paratroopers had left Formosa the day before for airfields in Luzon, which were then in Japanese possession. It was believed that they would jump in Leyte to recapture the airfields at Burauen. Not knowing what 'Alamo Report' was but sensing that it must be important, I took it to Swing, who immediately came into the operations tent and spent a great deal of time looking at the maps of the area and determining what might be done if the Japanese did attack our areas of responsibility. He was excited and related that an 'Alamo Report' was top secret and reliable. "The only combat infantry unit quickly available to the division at either Bito Beach or Burauen was the 1st Battalion of the 187th . . . which was the Division reserve. A 155mm artillery battalion of marines and a battalion of tanks that had been stuck in the mud were within several miles of Division Headquarters and close to Fifth Air Force Headquarters. All of the troops in the area were under the command of Colonel Hildebrand."

The Japanese generals were having a difficult time coordinating their attack on the Leyte airfields. General Sosaku Suzuki, the commander of the 35th Army on Leyte, with his headquarters at Ormoc, requested from General Tomoyuki Yamashita, the commander of the Fourteenth Area Army in Manila, a forty-eight-hour delay in the attack because he had not had enough time to make adequate preparations. General Yamashita denied the request but, because of a forecast of bad weather, he did delay the parachute jump on the airfields for twenty-four hours until the night of 6 December.

General Suzuki considered the battle for the airfields so important that he personally took command of the Burauen operation and, on 1 December, he and part of his staff trudged over the mountain trails from Ormoc to a position in the hills to the west of Burauen. On 2 December, General Makino and the remnants of the 16th Division, about 500 men out of the original strength of 8,800, assembled in the foothills southwest of Dagami. The men rested, ate what few rations they had, and moved out toward the Buri airfield. En route, U.S. artillery and tank fire killed about two hundred men of the 16th Division. The remainder of the force moved into a deep gorge about 6,500 yards to the southwest of Dagami, prepared to move out on 5 December to join the paratroopers in a combined assault on the Buri airstrip. From later interrogation of captured Japanese, the Americans learned that the morale of the 16th Division was nonexistent, that they were living on coconuts and bananas because the officers had taken the few remaining rations, and they were abandoning their wounded where they were hit.

To compound their problem, General Makino was unaware that the parachute drop had been postponed for twenty-four hours. Therefore, following his original orders, he planned to attack the Buri strip on the night of 5–6 December. The U.S. troops working at the Buri strip were 47 men from the 287th Field Artillery Observation Battalion and 157 men from various service units attached to the U.S. 5th Bomber Command. Some small elements of engineer troops and a signal company were at the foot of a bluff, near the northern edge of the Buri strip.

Paradoxically, by 5 December, XXIV Corps G2 felt that the three Burauen airfields were relatively secure. The 2d Battalion of the 511th and the 1st Battalion of the 187th had moved west into the mountains. The 3d Battalion of the 306th Infantry which had been northwest of the airfields, had reverted to the 77th Division for the amphibious landings near Ormoc. The 5 December XXIV Corps G2 periodic report on the situation in the Burauen–Dagami–Mount Alto area read: "An examination of reports of action in this area since 1 November may well warrant the assumption that organized resistance had about ceased." But early in the black hours of the next morning, what was left of the Japanese 16th Division attacked out of the hills. The attack may not have been organized in the U.S. Army's sense of the word, but it caused many casualties and widespread confusion on the airstrips for a number of days.

At 0600 on the morning of the sixth, men from the 287th saw some Japanese cross the main road south of the battalion's position and head east toward the Buri strip. The 287th immediately radioed the information to the XXIV Corps headquarters. After the Japanese crossed the main road, they moved into a swamp near the strip. One fifteen-man Japanese squad set up a machine gun in a Filipino shack about three hundred yards west of the road. At 0630, the Japanese launched a surprise attack on the Buri strip. It was led by a traitorous Filipino who was later captured and turned over to the Filipino guerrillas—for swift justice.

The Japanese broke into the service units' bivouac area around Buri while most of the men were still in their tents asleep. The enemy bayoneted some of the sleeping men in their bunks or before they could get to their weapons. Some of the Americans, clad only in their shorts, did manage to grab weapons and hold off the Japanese until they could run out of the area. The Americans ran wildly up the bluff to the road or to the headquarters of the 5th Bomber Command. After the 11th Airborne Division headquarters found out about the attack, it radioed XXIV

Corps that the service troops "were firing at everything that moves . . . and probably inflicting casualties among our troops." What was left of the Japanese 16th Division entrenched themselves in the woods north of the Buri strip.

General Hodge, commanding general of the XXIVth Corps, meantime had ordered the CG of the 96th Division to turn over the 1st Battalion of the 382d Infantry to the operational control of General Swing and to send the battalion south along the Dagami-Burauen road. A reinforced company of the 382d was already in the area north of Buri.

Early on the morning of the 6th, after General Swing had become aware of the situation around Buri, he sent for Col. George Pearson and briefed him on the situation around Buri. He directed Colonel Pearson to take one of his platoons and fly it from San Pablo to the Buri strip in the artillery's Cub planes and to have the rest of his battalion follow on foot to Buri. General Swing told Henry Burgess, the acting G3 because Doug Quandt was at Manarawat with General Pierson, to fly up to Buri to check on the situation there.

The Cub planes made three round trips to ferry Burgess and a platoon from the 1st of the 187th to Buri. At the strip, they were met by a "very excited" group of disorganized engineer, service, and air corps troops. Colonel Pearson, meanwhile, was leading his battalion on a muddy march from San Pablo to the airstrip.

Colonel Pearson and the rest of his battalion arrived at Buri at about 0900. He talked to Henry Burgess, who had already learned, from the troops on the ground, about the extent of the attack and the general situation. Colonel Pearson told Capt. Sterling R. Nesbitt to leave one of his squads on the strip to give it some security and to use the rest of his platoon (the one which had flown to Buri) as patrols to comb the area west of the Dagami-Burauen road. He told the patrol leaders to assemble in the Engineer Battalion area after they had completed their sweeps.

Occasionally, Colonel Pearson could hear firing from the direction in which he had sent the patrols. In about half an hour, the patrols reported back to him in the Engineer Battalion bivouac area. Lieutenant Paul G. Bashore reported that his patrol had killed eighteen of the enemy while another patrol had accounted for eight more. Colonel Pearson was now convinced that the Japanese attack in the area had been made by more than a "small combat patrol" and that a large number of the enemy remained in the area around Buri. Even with his entire battalion at Buri, Colonel Pearson had only a total of 180 men present to wipe out the remnants of the Japanese 16th Division. He prepared to attack.

"None of us," wrote CWO Nelson, "will ever forget the denseness of the jungle growth to the north and east of our rendezvous. Tall, thick bamboo; dense rain forest —in fact all the lush, treacherous vegetation of the tropics covered the area and the [Japanese] could have concealed a very large force indeed within its depths.

"The battalion formed in a line of skirmishers, two yards interval between men, and advanced to the northeast. Not five minutes after we entered the jungle, we flushed our quarry and a series of gunfights ensued at point-blank range. Occasionally we'd break through the underbrush into the open of flooded rice paddies, where we'd see the Japanese floating face downward in the water, apparently dead. Prodded with bayonets, most of them would prove plenty lively until we ran them through and they became real corpses."

For two hours, the battalion continued to grope and fight its way through, the steaming jungle to the north of the strip, attacking the enemy troops in their defensive positions, often in hand-to-hand combat and at close ranges where grenades and bayonets were the weapons of choice. Finally, Colonel Pearson called a halt to check his men and their situation. The company commanders reported a total kill of eighty-five of the enemy while suffering only two wounded of their own. This battle was the 1st of the 187th's first combat mission.

### Clearing the Airfields

General Swing, a man who was to prove in combat that he never missed a good fight if he could possibly get to it, flew from San Pablo to Buri in a Cub. When he landed, Captain Nesbitt reported to him and gave him a rundown on the battalion's battle to date. General Swing told Nesbitt to find Colonel Pearson and tell him to "take up positions along the Dagami-Burauen road and keep it open and to look to his west, from which he should soon expect a lot of trouble." Carrying out these orders, Colonel Pearson deployed his small battalion along the road, with

A and B Companies on line. He moved the battalion command post, covered by a section of heavy machine guns, to a nearby mound in the Engineer Battalion bivouac area.

Colonel Pearson had a problem. He had moved to Buri under the mistaken notion that his mission was one of reconnaissance, would last only a few hours, and required speed in getting there. Therefore, he had ordered the battalion to leave heavy equipment, packs, and mess equipment at San Pablo. Thus Lieutenant Carlson, the mortar platoon commander, had no mortars. But Carlson did not sit around bemoaning his situation. He took his platoon down the road to an ordnance depot and borrowed two mortars and ammunition. It turned out to have been a fortuitous move.

At 1500, Colonel Pearson sent Lieutenant Hanna and a patrol to contact the 1st Battalion of the 382d Infantry of the 96th Division to the north of Buri. "An hour later," according to CWO Nelson, "a great deal of activity was noted on the hill to our west. Observers from the companies along the road estimated that there were several hundred men in that area and believed them to be [Japanese]. Later it was found that the force numbered between a thousand and twelve hundred men. When a patrol from B Company determined definitely that the observed force was Japanese, the battalion commander called for and got artillery fire on the [enemy]." Unfortunately, the fire soon lifted because someone at division headquarters told Colonel Pearson's S3 the artillery "was landing smack on the boundary between divisions and there was a probability that the target area was occupied by troops of the 96th Division."

All afternoon, Japanese snipers harassed the men of the 1st of the 187th along the Buri-Burauen road. By 1800, though, Pearson's men had driven most of the enemy back from the Buri strip, although a few pockets of Japanese remained around its edges. "Soon it was twilight," wrote CWO Nelson, "and except for the raucous chorus of night birds and insects, inevitable in the tropics, all was quiet. No packs and no rations and we didn't know when we'd get them up. Grimly we eyed those hills toward the west and dug our slit trenches deeper. Squad leaders circulated around and were free with their advice. "Don't get trigger happy—don't advertise your positions with tracer bullets—you men on the perimeter, use your grenades—you men inside, don't use grenades—if the [enemy] comes inside the perimeter, use your knives and bayonets." The 1st of the 187th settled in for the night. Its false sense of security and tranquility were soon to be shattered.

A mile or so south of Buri was the Bayug strip. After supper on the evening of the sixth of December, Michael J. Kalamas, a member of the division's aerial resupply team, and another member of the team were washing their mess kits near the mess tent on the north side of Bayug strip, about halfway between the ends of the runway, which ran east and west. "The next moment," he wrote after the war, "the peaceful, warm evening erupted in complete bedlam. Incendiary bombs were exploding all around us. The noise was deafening, and pieces of white hot magnesium were flying through the air and covering the ground like so many hailstones.

"We stood in our tracks, not knowing what to do, and as I looked skyward, I could see several bombers overhead," Kalamas wrote. "I expected them to return and make another run, possibly with something harder this time. I yelled to my friend, and I took off running to my tent to get my carbine and steel helmet. Trying not to step on any of the burning fragments, we discovered that the roof of the tent was filled with holes from the hot magnesium and it was all over the dirt floor.

"I couldn't locate my web belt, so I grabbed my carbine and helmet and I went out the back way, with my friend on my heels. I was heading for the safety of the trees, but before we got there, we heard a loud whine of an aircraft engine. Out of the corner of my eye, I saw a fighter plane diving in our direction, with guns belching fire. I dove into a nearby ditch, and my friend landed on top of me. The barrel of my carbine dug into the ground, so I tried to find a stick to unplug it. Seconds later, the fighter zoomed back into the sky from where it had come, and by then I was able to clear the barrel.

"We stood up to see what else was happening. Two men were near our tent, looking at the trees at the far end of the airstrip, and they were yelling that they had seen a lot of parachutes coming down in that area. I asked who they were, and he said he thinks they may have been Japanese. And with that, they took off across the runway running as fast as they could."

Kalamas and his friend ran into an officer on the north side of the strip. They got into a jeep and tried to make it across the runway. Just as they broke into a clearing near the strip, they could see men coming down the strip in their direction. "They were singing and shouting and carrying on, and we knew all at once that they were not our guys." The officer driving the jeep put it into reverse and headed back into brush north of the strip. Then the jeep bogged down in a marsh. The officer jumped out and yelled to Kalamas and his friend, "Let's go." With that, they headed out toward the runway.

"Stumbling through the brush," Kalamas wrote, "we emerged into the clearing, very close to where most of the aircraft were sitting. The three of us stood still in silence, watching as we tried to catch our breath. Everything was on fire. The drums of gasoline were burning. Also two supply tents on the other side of the runway. The planes farther away from us were also on fire, and a couple of Japanese soldiers were tossing hand grenades into the cockpits, as they were heading in our direction."

Kalamas and the other two men headed west toward Burauen and ran into a guard from a U.S. unit. They spent the night with that outfit. The next morning Kalamas and his two friends made their way to the 11th Airborne Division CP in Burauen. They went immediately to the operations tent and reported what they had seen and where they had been, thinking that they were bringing surprising news to the staff at division. In fact, the men around the division CP has seen more of the Japanese airborne attack than had the men around the Bayug strip.

At dusk on the sixth of December, some of the division staffers were just sitting down to supper in the staff mess tent when they heard, overhead, the drone of aircraft. They all raced outside and saw a number of transport planes—C-47s, they thought—flying low, almost directly overhead. They saw that the cabin lights were on in the planes and, ominously, that each plane had a man standing in the door. Major Henry Burgess, the acting G3, had the presence of mind to say to the officer standing next to him, "You count the planes and I'll count the jumpers." Burgess estimated immediately that about 250 paratroopers had jumped on the San Pablo strip.

What the men of the 11th Airborne had been witnessing from various locations around the three Burauen airstrips was the airborne phase of General Yamashita's operations plan to recapture the airfields in the Burauen-Dulag area. His operations order required the transports to begin dropping paratroopers at 1840 on the sixth accompanied by an escort of fighters to neutralize the defenses around the airstrips. In addition, just before the drop, Yamashita's plan ordered medium bombers to strafe the Buri, San Pablo, and Bayug strips. At the same time, he called for light bombers to hit the AA positions between Dulag and Burauen. Yamashita assigned a total of fifty-one aircraft to the operation.

Just before dark, on schedule, thirty-nine enemy transports, with fighter and bomber escort, roared over the Burauen area. The bombers dropped several incendiary bombs on the San Pablo strip, setting a gasoline dump and a liaison plane on fire. Fighters, with machine guns blazing, raced up and down the strips. U.S. antiaircraft guns shot down eighteen enemy planes. The commander of the Japanese 3d Parachute Regiment managed to jump with about 60 of his men on the Buri strip; between 250 and 300 of his men landed on or near the San Pablo runway. But the Japanese transports assigned to drop paratroopers at Tacloban were shot down; the one targeted for Dulag crash-landed, killing all the paratroopers.

At the San Pablo strip, the Japanese paratroopers landed and unsnapped their parachute harnesses equipped with a quick release that was apparently not totally trustworthy. Some of the men of the 11th reported that they had seen a few paratroopers falling to the ground without benefit of their parachutes when the quick releases broke on opening shock. Later, the 11th troopers found another anomaly; in the packs of dead paratroopers were bottles of liquor whose labels indicated that they were for use only in flight.

Once on the ground, the Japanese used a system of bells, whistles, horns, and even distinctive songs for assembling their small units. At the San Pablo strip, 11th troopers heard the Japanese shouting and yelling slogans, to include: "Everything is resistless. Surrender. Surrender. The great Japanese Army is descending. Everything is resistless." And, "Hello. Where are your machine guns?"

The Japanese who landed to the west of the San Pablo strip were in between San Pablo and Bayug. After landing, they spread out; some moved down both sides of the San Pablo strip and others moved off to the west toward Bayug, where they set fire to a number of the Cub planes that the 11th needed so desperately to supply the troops in the mountains. The Japanese then moved into the bivouac area of the men who manned the resupply site and destroyed the camp. On Bayug at the time were seventy-five U.S. officers and men. Most of them dug in and defended the south side of the strip until morning. Captain Felix Coune of 11th Division Artillery was killed when he tried to move across the runway. Another patient but thoroughly frightened pilot spent fourteen hours lying in a drainage ditch while the enemy paratroopers walked above and around him. For Captain Davy Carnahan, the commander of the resupply team on Bayug, his greatest loss was his prized air mattress.

At San Pablo, the Japanese ran around and across the runway, and assembled on the north side. They burned three or four more Cub aircraft, a jeep, several tents, and a gasoline dump, on which, for some peculiar reason, they threw ammunition. The only troops in the area were small units from the 127th Engineers, the 511th Signal Company, Headquarters Battery of Division Artillery, 408th Quartermaster Company, the 711th Ordnance Company, and some air corps service troops. According to Capt. Charles Bellows, who made a report to the G3 of XXIV Corps, "There was uncontrolled and disorganized firing and much difficulty arose in establishing a coordinated command." Perhaps he did not realize how much he understated the situation.

During the night of 6–7 December, Lt. Paul J. Pergamo and a platoon from the 127th Engineers, armed with three machine guns, succeeded in scattering a group of the enemy and then dug in on the southwest corner of the San Pablo strip on some slightly higher ground. Three times during the night, the Japanese charged Pergamo's position; three times Pergamo and his engineers threw back the Japanese "with heavy loss to the attackers" in spite of the fact that one of the Japanese charges got to within fifteen feet of the position. At dawn, perhaps according to the overall operations order, the Japanese at San Pablo assembled and moved northwest to the northern edge of the Buri strip and joined the remnants of the Japanese 16th Division.

At Buri, Sgt. Jack S. Blessing and an assistant were just getting out of Cubs when the Japanese paratroopers landed. Blessing was bringing much needed radio gear to the 1st of the 187th west of the strip. Sergeant Blessing was killed, but his assistant managed to make it to the 187th's perimeter. At daybreak, Pfc. Joe E. Rangel, B Company of 187th, was found dead under two of the enemy, one of whom he had knifed.

The other had apparently held a grenade to Rangel's back, killing both of them.

After dawn on the seventh, the Japanese increased their sniper fire on elements of the 1st of the 187th deployed along the highway. Toward the Buri strip, the troopers of the 187th killed three of the enemy in a supply tent near the battalion CP. In the medical aid station, Capt. Hans Cohn, the battalion surgeon, was working on a wounded man when a sniper shot a plasma bottle out of his hand. Dr. Cohn calmly lowered his patient into a slit trench and carried on his work.

Sometime late in the night of the sixth of December, it became clear to General Swing and his staff that the Japanese airborne and air attacks were something more than a reconnaissance in force or a rather elaborate suicidal demolition mission. But General Swing's seven small infantry battalions were already committed either in the hills beyond Burauen or deployed near Buri. Accordingly, he diverted his other troops from primary missions to that of acting infantry. He ordered Lt. Col. Lucas E. Hoska Jr., commanding officer of the 674th Glider Field Artillery Battalion, to leave his pack 75s on the beach at Bito and to move his battalion as rapidly as possible to San Pablo. General Swing charged Lt. Col. James Farren, CO of the 152d Antiaircraft Battalion, to use what men he had left around Burauen to defend the division command post. And he ordered Lt. Col. Douglas C. Davis, CO of the 127th Airborne Engineer Battalion, to protect the San Pablo strip.

At daylight on the seventh, Colonel Davis, with a diverse group of soldiers from his own battalion and from other service units of the division, started to attack across the San Pablo strip to clear the enemy from it and relieve some beleaguered division troops, some from his own A Company, who had been trapped all night by the roaming, shouting, shooting, grenading Japanese paratroopers. Just as Davis was about to launch his frontal attack, Colonel Hoska and his carbine-wielding artillerymen arrived in DUKWs. The 674th dismounted hastily and moved on line to the right of Colonel Davis's composite unit.

In the interim, General Swing arrived on the scene. "To anyone familiar with Civil War battles," wrote the 11th Airborne Division historian, "the similarity of this morning's fight will immediately become apparent. On the left were the engineers, drawn up along the southern edge of the strip. On the right was the artillery, similarly drawn up in battle formation. . . . In the center, between the two outfits, was General Swing, shouting as he directed the two commanders in the attack. They in turn bellowed at their units, and the attack moved off. The Japanese were holed up all around the strip, but initially the strongest resistance was met in front of the engineers. However, by maneuvering his companies, Colonel Davis succeeded in pushing across . . . three hundred yards to the north of the airstrip. . . . Behind them, dead Japanese were removed from the strip, and the few L-4 planes remaining after the Japanese attack immediately took off, harassed by sniper fire, to deliver much needed supplies to the mountain troops."

After advancing across the runway, the engineers ran out of ammunition. The 674th moved quickly forward to a coconut grove to the north of the strip. Colonel Davis closed the gap between the units with a strong patrol. That evening, the two ersatz infantry units went into a tight perimeter and remained in that area for the next few days in defense of San Pablo.

Near Buri, the 1st of the 187th had moved west along the Dagami-Burauen road on the sixth. By the middle of the morning of the seventh, the Japanese who had jumped near Buri had completely occupied the undefended strip and had reinforced their own arms with the weapons and ammunition of the air corps and service troops who had abruptly fled the area. The CO of the 767th Tank Battalion, which had been in the area, had charged 2d Lt. Rudolph Mamula with recovering the abandoned weapons but, given the number of Japanese roving about the area, the task was beyond him.

Late on the night of the sixth, General Swing got word to Colonel Pearson that he wanted the 1st of the 187th to clear the Buri strip as soon as possible. During the morning of the seventh, the battalion, still northwest of the Bayug strip, had taken machine-gun fire from about a platoon of Japanese west of the Dagami-Burauen road. The battalion held this force in check while Colonel Pearson organized an attack on the Buri strip to the east. At about 0930, the 1st of the 382d from the 96th Division arrived in the area. (General Hodge had ordered the commanding general of the 96th to turn over a battalion to the operational control of General Swing and to send the battalion south along the Dagami-Burauen road.) At 0945, the two battalions attacked toward the Buri airfield. Twice, Lieutenant Pickle's platoon of A Company fought its way to a precarious foothold on the northwest corner of the strip; twice they were blasted off by heavy enemy fire. Companies A and B of the 382d also advanced aggressively but faltered when the company commander of A Company was hit. Colonel Pearson decided to withdraw both battalions to the north and consider another scheme of maneuver.

He made a personal reconnaissance around the west end of the Buri strip and crawled to within fifty yards of the enemy position. He decided that he could move a couple of platoons up a ravine on the west and then south to a clearing on the south side of the strip. In this position, Lt. Clayton B. Farnsworth's heavy machine guns and Lieutenant Carlson's mortars could bring in supporting fire.

The 1st of the 187th moved out at 1400 through the ravine, but the lead men ran into booby traps that the Japanese had already set. Colonel Pearson directed the lead elements of the battalion to turn to the south. Farnsworth and his men set up their machine guns a few feet from the edge of the landing strip.

While Farnsworth's men were setting up their machine guns, three Japanese jumped up from the grass about thirty feet to their front. Fortunately, they did not have their rifles ready to fire. Farnsworth told his men to continue setting up the machine guns and that he would "take care of the three Japanese." At the sound of his first shot, three more of the enemy popped up out of the grass. None of them had a weapon ready, either, and Farnsworth, a superb shot, took them under fire. "These six shots were the fastest six that I have ever fired at anything," he recalls. "In a matter of less than a minute, the crews had the machine guns operating. As to how effective their fire was, I cannot say. They may have only scored on a couple of dozen or so, or it could easily have been several times that many. I did catch the first burst out of the corner of my eye and it was directly in line with a bunch of Japanese hurrying across the strip. The tracer bullets showed the fire a little low but the bullets ricocheting from that hard air-strip floor should have been more deadly than if it had been directly into the enemy."

Farnsworth left the machine-gun firing up to his crews and crawled over to a nearby foxhole dug earlier by the men who had first defended the strip. The hole was deep enough for him to stand and to rest his arms on the top, making a perfect platform from which he could shoot well-aimed single shots. In the next three minutes, he got off five shots. From his position in the hole, he could spot the enemy soldiers through the scope of his rifle as soon as they raised their heads. But his luck did not hold. He took a Japanese rifle round through the stock of his rifle that not only shattered the stock but also a bone in his right arm. He used his belt as a tourniquet to stop the flow of blood.

In about fifteen minutes, the machine-gun crews ran out of ammunition. Two men crawled to the rear to get more and came back with the orders for Farnsworth to withdraw his two guns to the rear. "After having a clear look across the strip, this seemed like a heartbreaking thing to do," he said later, "but we lifted the guns from their cradles and started to drag them back. That is, the men did it. I had all I could do to drag myself."

On their way back, the Japanese took them under fire from the rear. Private Miller, crawling along with a tripod on his back, found a palm log forming a barrier across his path. Instead of crawling around it, he stood up and tried to make a dash across it. A Japanese burst of fire picked him off. The bullets continued to kick up dirt around him after he had fallen.

The machine-gun crews suffered the loss of Miller, four others wounded, and, Farnsworth thought, Sergeant McKenna, whose helmet had been penetrated with fifty-caliber bullets. McKenna had fallen in the mud some distance away, apparently dead. Farnsworth had to leave him where he lay.

As Farnsworth and his men tried to rejoin the rest of the battalion, the Japanese closed in around them. Farnsworth told his men to strip the guns and "destroy their vital parts to keep them from falling into the hands of the Japanese." Then Farnsworth signaled his men to continue the withdrawal. They dragged their wounded with them and finally made it back to the battalion.

To the west of Buri, the 1st of the 187th and the 1st of the 382d regrouped. Colonel Pearson ordered his A and B Companies to attack abreast to the northeast and Company A of the 382d to attack due east. The three battalions ran into heavy enemy fire but continued their advance. By 1600, they were holding the southwest corner of the Buri strip but their ammunition was low, water was scarce, and the troops were "dog-tired." About that time a Cub flew over. The pilot cut his engine, leaned out, and shouted: "Japanese—over there." The soldiers on the ground were not surprised.

That afternoon, a very tall Japanese soldier, undoubtedly a paratrooper who was selected for his size, walked into the 1st Battalion 187th's CP with his hands in the air. About fifteen feet from where the command group was standing, he leaped into a ditch. Lieutenant Ace Parker shot him between the eyes. The soldier had three hand grenades strapped to his belt.

At about 1630, the 1st of the 187th made contact with the 1st of the 149th at the western end of the Buri strip. By dusk, the remainder of the 1st of the 382d had arrived and had taken up a position near the 1st of the 149th. By 2000, the sector was apparently quiet.

During the night, the Japanese brought up two machine guns and dug them in directly in front of A Company of the 382d. At dawn, the enemy started firing the well-emplaced guns. Grazing fire pinned down the company. Private First Class Warren G. Perkins, with bullets flying past him, slithered out of his hole, searched the area, and found the guns. His call for mortar fire fifty yards from his position silenced the guns temporarily. When they started to fire again, Pvt. Ova A. Kelly rose up out of his foxhole, charged the two guns, and killed eight of the enemy before he was killed. Later, he was awarded the Medal of Honor posthumously. The rest of A Company, emboldened by Kelly's charge, ran out of their position and secured the edge of the runway where it went into a perimeter defense.

With the arrival of the 1st of the 149th in his area, Colonel Pearson felt that he could now attack and secure the length of Buri. But that was not yet to be the case.

Late on the afternoon of the seventh General Swing sent word to Colonel Pearson to move his battalion from the Buri area to Burauen to defend the Fifth Air Force Headquarters, which was located in Burauen a few miles from the 11th Airborne command post along the Burauen-Dulag road. The Fifth Air Force Headquarters was a critical CP. "For," according to Henry Burgess, "it was from this location that all of the orders were prepared for the daily bombing and fighter flights over all the Philippines. The office worked twenty-four hours a day with lights on inside the buildings and with floodlights shining on the outside. . . ." It was obviously an inviting target for the Japanese 26th Division descending out of the hills to the west of Burauen.

Colonel Pearson thought that there must be some mistake; he still had not taken Buri. He radioed the division G3, who confirmed the order. Colonel Pearson duly ordered his staff to make the move, realizing that the security of the Fifth AF Headquarters was more important at the moment than the final capture of Buri. In the bustle of moving out for Burauen, Sergeant McKenna, who had been left for dead by Farnsworth's machine gunners, walked into the CP of the 1st of 187th under his own power.

By midnight of the seventh, the 1st of the 187th (less C Company, which was at Manarawat), trudged into the area of the Fifth AF Headquarters. The infantrymen found the staff of Fifth AF Headquarters walking guard "cadet style," with flashlights blinking on and off all around the buildings. "The flyboys were right happy to see us," reported Mr. Nelson. "They fed us coffee and Spam." The 1st of the 187th then moved into positions previously occupied by the 2d of the 187th, about eight hundred yards west of Burauen, on a rise in the foothills of the mountains. From this height, they could see a large portion of the Leyte Valley and watch the 149th battle the stubborn Japanese for control of the Buri airstrip. They were also in position to block remnants of the Japanese 26th Division from attacking east toward the Fifth Air Force Headquarters.

On the tenth of December, the 1st of the 149th, after a half-hour artillery concentration, attacked north across the Buri strip with A and C Companies abreast and B Company in the rear. In their advance, the 1st of the 149th cleared the airfield and wiped out some remaining pockets of Japanese. At 1700, the battalion went into a perimeter defense; Buri was finally clear.

But the Japanese were still not finished with their attack on the Burauen area. On the evening of the tenth, a battalion of the 26th Division attacked out of the hills to the west of Burauen toward the various U.S. installations in and around Burauen. A battalion was the maximum force that the 26th could muster and it was four days late in arriving at its line of departure for the planned combined assault on the Burauen airfields. One major reason for the 26th's difficulties was that it was trying to move east in the mountains along the same trails the 511th was using to move to the west.

At 1930 that evening, the 26th troops began firing at the buildings of the Fifth AF Headquarters. XXIV Corps Headquarters called the 11th

Airborne CP and notified its staff that the enemy was attacking the Fifth
AF Headquarters and the 44th Station Hospital close by. "Rumors were
rampant," according to one of the 11th Airborne staffers. "We heard that
the [enemy] had gotten into the hospital, were going down the aisles
of the wards butchering the patients with sabers, and ruthlessly killing
the doctors."

As it turned out, the rumors were highly exaggerated. Lieutenant
John G. Hurster, mess officer of the 1st of the 187th, had set up his
kitchen near the 44th Hospital from where he could carry hot meals to
the troops dug in the foothills to the west. The CO of the 44th, deeply
concerned about the safety of his hospital and its patients, had earlier
asked Lieutenant Hurster to set up a perimeter around the hospital.
Lieutenant Hurster had complied, using his cooks, supply men, and
drivers from headquarters of the 1st of the 187th. These relatively untrained infantrymen dug and manned the perimeter, with foxholes
about five yards apart.

On the night of the Japanese 26th Division attack, Lieutenant Hurster
and his odd assortment of converted infantrymen held their position.
The next morning, they found nineteen dead enemy soldiers around the
perimeter. That same morning, Colonel Pearson sent out patrols from
his position in the foothills. The patrols killed another seventeen of the
enemy in the rice paddies in front of the 44th. This small battle marked
the end of the attack by the remnants of the 26th and was the last gasp
in General Suzuki's effort to regain control of the Burauen airstrips.

On the 7th of December, the 77th Division had landed amphibiously
just below Ormoc on Leyte's west coast. About the tenth, General
Suzuki learned of the landings and recognized the importance of holding Ormoc at all costs. He was in the area of Burauen, where he had gone
to coordinate the attacks on the airfields. When he heard of the 77th
operation, he canceled all operations against the airfields and ordered
all troops who had been involved with the failed attack to move west
across the mountains to the Ormoc Valley. The move was difficult: The
Japanese had lost all command control, the trails were muddy and precipitous, and the 511th was operating in the same area. The Japanese
who ran this gamut of obstacles did so individually.

"The Japanese had failed to achieve any major objective," wrote historian M. Hamlin Cannon. "The air transports allotted to Tacloban were

destroyed by antiaircraft fire, while those destined for Dulag crash-landed, killing all their occupants. Though they had destroyed minor fuel and supply dumps and a few American aircraft, delayed airfield construction, and isolated Fifth Air Force Headquarters for five days, they had not appreciably delayed the Letye operation."

General Swing recognized that the division's final effort on Leyte would be to push to the west and link up with the 7th and the 77th Divisions on the west coast. On the ninth of December, he told General Pierson, the assistant division commander, and Col. Doug Quandt to return to Burauen, ostensibly so that he could move to the Manarawat location and direct the division's push to the west from that advanced command post. "Quandt and I and a small patrol made the return trek along awesome trails to the division CP," according to General Pierson. "We returned to the division CP about three days after the Japanese attack. . . . General Swing flew up to Manarawat shortly after our return . . . and just before Haugen made his final push at Anas."

The 11th Airborne and the 187th had had their baptism of fire under circumstances that were at times hectic—certainly not unusual in a combat environment. The 187th had landed on Leyte not expecting to be committed to combat on the island. Under those circumstances, coupled with the abysmal weather and the surprise Japanese parachute attack on relatively thinly defended installations, the 187th, committed to combat unexpectedly and in haste, performed superbly. But further tests of their fighting skills were in the immediate offing.

### Clearing the Mountains

The 11th Airborne Division diary for most of December 1944 starts off each day with the same entry: "Frequent heavy showers during the day, with the weather mostly cloudy. Periods of good visibility were limited."

The abysmal, soggy weather in the mountains of Leyte not only made life miserable for the constantly soaked men slogging through the dripping jungles but also frequently grounded the division's fleet of L-4s and -5s, the "Biscuit Bombers," the lifeline of supplies from the Burauen airfields to the hungry men in the hills. The grounding of the "Biscuit Bombers" caused a shortage of food, medicine, ammunition, new boots, and fatigues to the beleaguered troops fighting across the mountains. For many days, three men made do with one K ration per day, and platoon leaders were forced to ration ammunition by the bullet rather than by the clip.

In the grimy and clinging mud, fatigues became soaked and rotten, and mud sloshed over the tops of boots whose soles rotted off in a matter of a few days. During the night, the air was cold and damp, and the troops not on foxhole alert rolled up in their ponchos in their muddy foxholes and tried to steam-dry their fatigues during the night. When it came their turn to be on guard, they roused themselves and quietly moved to the forward edge of their muddy foxholes, shared with two, three, or four other men. They kept their weapons pointed toward the outside of the perimeter and their steel helmets handy to throw over any grenade that a Japanese might lob into the hole. Under these conditions, some men went for days without ever taking off their fatigues or their boots. Dry socks, a clean shave, and a hot bath were luxuries men only dreamed of in the mud of the Leyte mountain jungles and foxholes.

While the battle for the airstrips near Burauen was under way, elements of the 511th were trudging along a path southeast of Mahonag. Lieutenant Colonel Harry Wilson's 2d of the 187th had climbed from the Burauen heights to relieve Lt. Col. Norman M. Shipley's 2d of the 511th north on Anonang. Haugen ordered Shipley to follow the north trail to Anas. Lieutenant Colonel Muller, G2 of the 11th, thought that the north trail might lead to the long-sought main Japanese supply trail. The mission of the 11th was now to fight its way through the mountains to the west coast and link up with the other elements of Sixth Army fighting along the west coast, north of Albuera and generally along the Talisayan River.

The 2d of the 187th, like the battalions of the 511th that had preceded it, had the terrain to fight as well as the Japanese in its march to Anonang. There was just one trail after the battalion left the relatively flat ground west of Burauen. Chief Warrant Officer Nelson, writing a history of the 187th just after the war, recorded: "The battalion was strung out in single file. Every inch of the trail was slippery and the going was hot and tough as we crossed the flooded rice fields west of Burauen. This part of the move was pleasant strolling compared to the mountain trails we were about to encounter.

"Once in them, it was a nightmare of climbing straight up the sides of sheer cliffs, cutting footholds as we went, pulling ourselves up by the vines along the trail. Foot by foot we scaled the greasy heights and a slip would have plunged one to his death on the rocks below. Reaching the crests, we'd catch our breath, then slip and slide down the other face of the height only to be met with the necessity of crossing a raging mountain river in the canyon below."

Late on the afternoon of 3 December, the 2d of the 187th reached Anonang, a simple clearing in the jungle with a small, overgrown camote and corn patch and one abandoned, dilapidated shack in the middle of the clearing. Colonel Wilson ordered Capt. George Ori and his F Company to occupy an old 511th outpost, on a hill two thousand yards to the northwest of the battalion perimeter at Anonang. Once his company climbed up there, after a three-hour struggle, Ori found that the position commanded a clear view of a strong Japanese position on a plateau beneath it. He also found an old, still-workable 511th telephone line. On the night of the third, the Japanese climbed up from their plateau and hit Ori's position. Using the phone, Ori brought in mortar fire from Anonang and drove off the enemy attack. F Company suffered no casualties.

The next day, Captain Ori decided to probe the Japanese position with a platoon commanded by Lieutenant Kneebone. Kneebone and his men headed north through the forest and shortly broke out into a clearing stretching to the north. As soon as the platoon was in the clearing, the Japanese opened up with machine guns that had been sighted along taped-out lanes. Kneebone and two of his men, including Sergeant Newsome, who died that night, were hit. The enemy tried to counterattack, and Ori ordered the platoon to withdraw. F Company had run up against a very strong Japanese force on a hill that, sometime later, would become known as "Purple Heart Hill."

Butch Muller, the division G2, had fairly well determined the locations of the main Japanese forces still remaining within the division sector. One force, of unknown size, that F Company had just found, was just north of Anonang; the other was west of Mahonag, size also unknown. And there were more Japanese retreating to the west after their failure to seize the Burauen, Tacloban, and Dulag Airfields.

But even after the debacle at the airfields, the stubborn Yamashita was still determined to make Leyte the major battlefield. On the seventh of December, he sent a convoy of fourteen ships to San Isidro in northwest Leyte. Planes of the Fifth Air Force sank all of the ships and shot down sixty-four Japanese planes. In spite of those losses, some two to three thousand enemy troops managed to make it to shore on Leyte. On the eleventh of December, Fifth Air Force planes intercepted a Japanese convoy off Palompon and sank five of the transports, damaged the remaining six, and shot down thirteen Japanese planes. The enemy air assets were rapidly declining.

From the fourth until the eleventh, the 2d of the 187th had had a number of firefights with the enemy around Anonang while the 511th was fighting its way west toward Mahonag. On the eleventh Gen. Albert Pierson and Col. Doug Quandt arrived at Anonang. After reviewing the situation, General Pierson ordered Colonel Wilson to attack the main Japanese position below Ori Hill, the hill from which Captain Ori and F Company had been repulsed on the fourth.

On the twelfth, F and G Companies of the 187th launched the attack. G Company moved up the riverbeds to strike the position from the north while F Company moved through its old perimeter to hit it from the southwest—a small pincers movement. A Battery of the 457th, the battery that had parachuted into Manarawat, supported the drive, but A Battery's forward observers with F and G Companies could hardly find their adjusting rounds through the thick jungle overhang that limited visibility to a few yards. The Forward Observers reverted to adjustment by sound—which proved not entirely accurate.

By 1300, F Company had cleared Ori Hill and had worked down the slope toward the main enemy position. "Presently, F Company was stymied by our own artillery, whose shells were bursting in the trees, above and behind it," reported CWO Nelson. "High-angle fire was unfeasible when sensings were so inaccurate. Lead scouts reported that when an 'over' did land in the [Japanese] positions, it had absolutely no effect on their coconut-tree revetments.

"The only light along the trail was a strange macabre phosphorescent glow from the jungle debris lining the streambed. Holding on to each others' belts, we slipped and fell, tumbled into holes, bumped our heads on our lead files' weapons, tripped over logs as we felt our way through the black pitch. At hourly halts, the surgeon administered blood plasma to the wounded. Private First Class Cleo Harrell, who had been wounded in the abdomen and had walked back up to Ori Hill holding his intestines in with his hands, died en route, and his last words were to his company commander: 'Sir, did we do what you wanted?'"

Early on the thirteenth, a detachment of the 152d Airborne Antiaircraft Battalion, manning a radio relay station at Catabagan, radioed the 2d of the 187th that it was surrounded by a large enemy force and needed help. Colonel Wilson immediately dispatched E Company to handle the problem. As the company neared the 152d's position, it ran into and killed about ten Japanese. But the main enemy force had apparently pulled back to the northeast. On the return to the battalion perimeter, Private Shadden, one of the lead scouts, shot two more of the enemy. But another Japanese soldier jumped him and wrestled him for his rifle. Shadden pulled his knife and stabbed him in the chest, killing him. His company commander, recognizing sheer bravery when he saw it, made Shadden a Pfc. on the spot.

On the same day, Lt. Harrison I. Merritt, a platoon leader in G Company, led his platoon out of the company perimeter on a routine reconnaissance patrol. About 1,500 yards northeast of Anonang, the platoon butted headlong into a large enemy force, well dug in. Merritt and his platoon attacked, but the Japanese held the platoon off with rifle and machine-gun fire and grenades. Merritt radioed his situation to Captain George Walters, who immediately moved out with the rest of G Company to help him. When the company attacked the position, Captain Walters was killed and several other men wounded. Merritt took charge of the company, called in heavy mortar fire from Anonang, and scattered the enemy force. G Company returned to Anonang carrying its wounded and its dead company commander.

Late on the afternoon of the thirteenth, Lt. Col. George Pearson and the 1st Battalion of the 187th arrived at Anonang with orders to relieve the 2d of the 187th. On the fourteenth, General Swing ordered Colonel Wilson and his 2d of the 187th to move west to Mahonag "to protect the drop zone at Mahonag and to block the Japanese supply trail between Mahonag and Anas."

"It was time we moved," wrote CWO Nelson. "We were completely out of rations and the camote and green corn patches had been picked clean. Moreover, the wild pigs had become wary of the area. By now, we were subsisting on the nourishing but tough buffalo steaks. It was slim picking we turned over to our brother battalion."

The trail that the 2d of the 187th followed to the west ran first south along the streambeds, past Lubi. Then it turned west over a series of towering ridges. "The going was the toughest yet and we had to hand-carry our heavy equipment because carabao not already slaughtered were simply spent," remembered CWO Nelson. "They and their drivers were abandoned to make their way home as best they could.

"We were continually harassed along the trail by [Japanese] delaying forces, with mortars and machine guns, who retired from ridge to ridge as we advanced. Four of our lead scouts, whose lives were downright poor insurance risks on that route, were wounded. We formed no perimeter that night but simply lay on the sides of the trail and trusted ourselves to God."

At 1500 on the fifteenth, Lieutenant Siegel and his platoon were leading the march of the 2d of the 187th. At one point on the trail, he received fire from what he thought was a Japanese ambush site. Siegel moved his platoon off the trail and tried to outflank the ambush by moving through the jungle. Again, he received fire. Fortunately, no one was injured. A few minutes later, he heard what was, unmistakenly, American profanity from a position farther up the trail. Siegel soon discovered that the Americans were part of the 511th who had been attacking the ambush site from one side while Siegel had been hitting it from the other. In the meantime, the enemy had abandoned the site.

When the battalion finally struggled into Mahonag, it found a rather strange and desolate sight. "Mahonag was a field on a hillside, about three hundred yards long by two hundred wide," wrote the 187th historian. "It was studded with stumps and fallen trees, packed with hundreds of slit trenches, littered with boxes and cans and debris of spent ration packs. Permeating the atmosphere was the horrible sickening odor of unburied, decomposing bodies. At once, we were assaulted by the largest, most prosperous swarm of flies we'd ever seen.

"This forlorn bit of real estate blossomed with green and yellow and white cargo parachutes which the men had set up tentwise for shelter. Color and cloth for a circus. . . . Those chutes had brought in ammo and rations and the men squatted around campfires, boiling the coffee and cooking stew in helmets, of the excellent ten-in-one rations. Many of us have since paid bucks for meals that couldn't match the taste of that hot chow, the first we'd eaten in days."

The free-fall "biscuit bombing" from the liaison planes and C-47s was not without casualties. Throughout the division, fourteen men were killed and a number wounded by boxes and crates dropped into small clearings. Included were two men from the 2d of the 187th—1st Sgt. Teddy Sowards, who was injured, and Private Bircheler, who was killed. At Mahonag, the 187th medics improvised imaginative facilities. In one corner of the clearing, they set up a field hospital shack with bamboo sides and a parachute roof. Stretchers were hospital beds, and nearby slit trenches provided protection for both the doctors and patients during Japanese attacks.

For the next few days after it had arrived at Mahonag, the 2d of the 187th dug a perimeter, incorporating some of the holes left by the 511th. Colonel Wilson immediately sent out patrols and set up and baited ambushes along the trails. "Ambush duty was interesting and fruitful," wrote the 187th historian. "A squad or half-squad would take up positions along the trails, like hunters near a deer run, and wait until the [Japanese] walked into the line of fire. As the kills diminished at one 'blind,' new positions would be set up and the hunt would go on. Of course, the Japanese had their own blinds and we lost men to them too."

The men not on ambushes or patrols found time at Mahonag to clean themselves in streams, wash their clothes, and maintain their weapons. But their bodies overall were rapidly deteriorating due to lack of medical supplies, food, and the constant rains. Some men had one or more of various jungle fevers, almost all of them had dysentery, and many men had "jungle rot" on their feet and around their ankles. When they took off their boots and socks, the outer layer of skin peeled off. The Japanese suffered from dysentery, too, as evidenced by the fact that many of them, found dead along the trails, had cut out the entire seat of their trousers.

In the middle of December, General Swing relocated his infantry forces. The 188th moved from the south, relatively free of Japanese, to a new location near Manarawat. Colonel Hildebrand and a skeleton forward echelon of the 187th regimental headquarters moved to Anonang by way of Manarawat and took over command of the central section of the mountains from Anonang to Mahonag. On the twentieth, F Company of the 188th relieved the 2d of the 187th of its security mission at Mahonag. General Swing ordered the 2d of the 187th to move west, passing through the 2d of the 511th en route.

On the twenty-first of December, General Swing and Colonel Quandt flew into Manarawat in Cub planes. From there, they marched up to Mahonag, escorted by a four-man patrol of men who had been wounded and were returning from the makeshift hospital at Manarawat to their units at Mahonag. They arrived late in the afternoon. General Swing was as "muddy as any dogfaced private," a 187th trooper recalled. "He was accorded the honor of sleeping in the position's only nipa hut, a one-day privilege as it was demolished the next day by a salvo of misdirected ration boxes."

C-47s occasionally airdropped supplies to the 2d of the 187th at Mahonag by parachute. But many of the bundles hung up in trees or drifted over into enemy territory. To increase the accuracy of the drops, Lieutenant Eli Bernheim remembers that "we erected a platform and fashioned some crude semaphore flags. My platoon sergeant, Ernie Stringham, on the platform, would signal the planes as they swooped low over the area and give them a wave at the precise moment as directed by General Swing. He took a vigorous part in this operation, and there was no doubt as to who was running the show."

At 0400 on the morning of the twenty-third, the 2d of the 187th left Mahonag for a two-hour march to Rock Hill, near Anas. General Swing had ordered Colonel Wilson to "make contact with the 511th Infantry on Rock Hill and to be prepared to aid in the breakthrough attack to the coast." The 2d of the 187th moved out with General Swing near the head of the column. On the march, "we shot a few groups of Japanese who insisted on dying," CWO Nelson reported. "Once we passed through a canyon reeking with the smell of decomposing bodies. It was the end of the trail for the ambitious Japanese 26th Division, which once had planned to overrun Burauen."

In the march to Rock Hill, G Company was in the lead. "The trails were treacherous, muddy, and slippery," recalls Lt. Joseph Giordano, the platoon leader of the 2d Platoon of G Company. "However, the battalion made its way along the difficult route without incident, and at approximately 0600 the approaches along the slopes of Rock Hill were reached." The 2d of the 187th then passed through the 2d of the 511th, which had assaulted and defeated a large enemy force on Hacksaw Ridge, near Mount Mahonag. The route past Hacksaw Ridge was "lined with enemy dead."

"The battalion went forward to overtake the lead elements of the 511th who were pushing forward at breakneck speed along the Japanese supply trail that ran along the razorback ridge in the direction of Ormoc," Giordano continued. "It was difficult to understand how a unit engaged in bitter fighting could keep up the terrific rate of march forward. The trails were littered with enemy dead, as were the slopes of the ridge (named after the gallant commander of the 2d of the 511th, Lt. Col. Frank S. 'Hacksaw' Holcombe)." At 1200, the 2d of the 187th passed through Holcombe's battalion and took over the lead in the march to the west. Lieutenant Giordano and his platoon led the 2d of the 187th.

Colonel Rock Haugen, the CO of the 511th, stopped Giordano and told him, "You must keep going as fast as possible. Run if you have to, but don't give the [enemy] a chance to set up their weapons. We've got them with their pants down. You can't even stop to kill them all. Just push through. We are behind you and will take care of them as we come to them. Just keep going fast. Any questions?" Giordano remembers that he had no questions.

Giordano and his platoon had gone less than a hundred yards down the trail when they were fired on by a machine gun about twenty yards to their front where the trail turned abruptly to the left. One of his BAR men sprayed the area, and one of the lead scouts tossed a white phosphorous grenade toward the Japanese position. Giordano enveloped the enemy location by sending his lead squad to the left in the jungle and a four-man assault team to the right. In a few minutes the leader of the assault team was back with the report that "the machine gun and the three men manning it are out of action."

In another 150 yards, the trail disappeared into a deep gorge. At the lip of the gorge, the platoon scouts fired on a number of the enemy below them on the trail. The Japanese returned the fire ineffectively. Giordano happened to look to the bottom of the gorge, where a small stream passed through it. He saw two Japanese along the sides of the stream blow their heads off with hand grenades.

Giordano checked the gorge carefully and decided that the far bank, above his position, would make an excellent defensive position for the enemy. He attacked with a time-tested small-unit maneuver: he established a base of fire with one squad, sent a second squad to the right, and the third to the left. When the platoon was in position and ready, he gave the signal to attack. In short order, the platoon overran the Japanese, who put up only "feeble resistance."

At about that time, Colonel Wilson arrived on the scene and asked Giordano, "What's holding up the parade?" Giordano pointed out thirteen dead enemy, two of whom were part of the security force on the right bank who had jumped off a 150-foot cliff when the second squad assaulted the position.

The platoon moved out and headed up the far side of the gorge without further delays, thanks to the third squad, which had knocked out two snipers who would have been firing down at the platoon column. The platoon plodded on and in a couple of hours reached a point high on the western slope of a mountain, from where the men could plainly see their goal: the west coast of Leyte. Here Giordano stopped the platoon and fired a violet smoke grenade, "which was the signal for friendly forces intended to attract elements of the 77th Infantry Division that might be in the vicinity." On a ridge four or five hundred yards to the west, Giordano saw violet smoke. He had at last made visual contact with the U.S. forces on the west coast.

Giordano and his platoon continued to follow the Japanese supply trail and soon reached the approaches to "an extremely dangerous-looking position to the front." Here he stopped the column, put out security, and sent a patrol to reconnoiter the position. Halting the platoon brought forward the chain of command, this time with General Swing in the group. He had been marching near the head of the battalion column. Giordano's recon patrol soon returned with a report that the position to the front was honeycombed with caves and deeply dug-in foxholes, that it appeared to have been heavily shelled, judging by the condition of the camouflage, and that the area was littered with dead Japanese.

Giordano led his platoon up the steep side of the hill to the top of the peak. He found that the position was "well laid out, camouflaged, and dug in almost solid rock. The battered trees and number of enemy dead found on top of this position, which was long and narrow in shape, served as mute evidence of heavy gunfire. Among the dead were two American soldiers that appeared to have been dead less than twenty-four hours."

When he reached the west end of the ridge, Giordano could see Ormoc and the seacoast. And to his front, about two hundred yards away, he saw dug-in emplacements. That position, he said, was "soon alive with members of the 2d Battalion, 32d Infantry. They were amazed to see fellow Americans on the same strong enemy position that had given them so much trouble. 'Oh, yes,' said one of the members of the 32d, 'we expected you. Saw the violet smoke. But we didn't think that you were coming over that hill. Why, only last night it was solid with Japanese. We lost two of our boys on it.' Thus physical contact was made with the Ormoc Corridor, and the trail between this point and Rock Hill was covered with approximately 750 enemy dead. The road was finally opened between Burauen and Anas, and the area west of Mahonag was cleared." That night the battalion spread out on clean grass beside a stream near Albuera.

After the 11th had completed its push across the Leyte mountains, General Bruce, the commander of the 77th Division near Ormoc, radioed General Hodge, the XXIV Corps commander, "Have rolled two sevens in Ormoc. Come seven, come eleven."

General Swing ordered the 511th, after the 2d of the 187th had passed through it near Hacksaw Ridge, to secure the route from Mahonag to the coast and to collect all the litter patients and the wounded from Mahonag and Rock Hill. By Christmas Day, the 511th had cleared the mountains and completed its mission. General Swing ordered the 511th back to its base camp at Bito Beach and ordered the 2d of the 187th, from its base at the head of the Talisayan River, to secure the western end of the Japanese supply trail. But the fighting in the mountains was still not over for the 11th Airborne Division and the 187th.

The Japanese pocket about 1,400 yards northwest of Anonang had still not been wiped out. The 1st and 2d Battalions of the 511th and the 2d and 1st Battalions of the 187th had, in turn, butted against this formidable enemy force. Each battalion had sent recon patrols to feel out the position, and each probe had been hit hard with Japanese sniper and machine-gun fire and was forced to turn back. Early on in the campaign, General Swing realized that the Anonang position was substantial and that it would take a well-coordinated, multibattalion force to knock it out. General Swing decided that he would not attack it in strength initially while the major portion of his infantry was fighting across the mountains to the west. His major mission, ordered by Sixth Army, was to get to the west coast as rapidly as possible; a halt to attack the enemy stronghold at Anonang would unduly delay him. But now that he had joined up with the 77th Division, he felt that he could deal with the final, stubbornly held redoubt in his area of responsibility.

The Japanese defenses near Anonang were on two parallel ridges. On the first ridge, the Japanese had dug sixty-four "spider holes," each eight to ten feet deep, for individual riflemen. They had also dug in machine guns, both light and heavy, on both ridges with overhead cover and interlocking fields of fire. All faces of the slopes were studded with caves that overlooked and controlled the narrow trails and from which the Japanese had rolled grenades at some of the probing American patrols. In the rear of the defensive position was a bivouac area, cached with ammunition, rations, and other supplies, large enough to accommodate a regiment. The division G2 decided that the area was a "rallying point" for all the enemy in the area and that at least a thousand of the enemy were dug in and concentrated along the ridges and gorges.

The enemy had camouflaged the entire area with the "devilish" ingenuity so typical of Japanese groundworks. They had cut the centers out of bamboo thickets, inserted a machine gun and a couple of men, and then restored the thicket with such precise care that a U.S. soldier could walk within two feet of the nest and not know it—until it started firing—and then it was too late. In another gambit of camouflage, the Japanese would tie bushes around themselves, climb into trees, stay there motionless for endless hours, and blend so well with the foliage that a soldier directly under the tree did not know that a sniper in the tree above had him in his sights—until he was shot. The rear ridge, where the Japanese had concentrated the bulk of their defenses and their strength, became known among the 11th Airborne troopers, for obvious reasons, as Purple Heart Hill.

Lieutenant "Pop" Olsen had had his C Company of the 187th at Manarawat from the time that it had jumped and walked into that area. On the fourteenth of December, a Japanese force of about company size had tried to infiltrate the Manarawat strip, presumably to knock out the pack 75s of A Battery of the 457th and to halt the operation of Manarawat's strip. Just before dawn, the enemy burst into the northeast corner of the perimeter yelling, "Banzai, banzai, banzai." In coordination with the ground attack, mortar rounds exploded within the perimeter and machine-gun fire grazed the area.

The attack was well planned and surprised the 187th troops initially. But the men of C Company, by now in their perimeter defensive positions, returned the fire. "Several of the [enemy] gunners were hit," CWO Nelson reported, "but in a twinkling they were replaced by their determined buddies. Fire streaked through the nipa hospital, but the surgeons had rolled their patients into the slit trenches beneath. Lieutenant Olsen and another man crawled under the fire to the vicinity of the hospital and opened up on the attackers with BARs. The action lasted two hours, until some twenty-one Japanese were annihilated at a cost to us of two wounded."

On 18 December, C Company rejoined the 1st of the 187th in the Anonang area.

In that area, Colonel Tommy Mann and his 2d of the 188th had been probing the ridges for three days, searching for some undefended or weakly held approach into the position. The answer was always the same: there was none. The Japanese fired on every patrol he sent, no matter from which direction. In the meantime, Colonel Pearson had pulled the 1st of the 187th back from Anonang and, circling the enemy stronghold on a wide arc, moved to the north, above the Japanese defenses. To the west of the 1st of the 187th was the division reconnaissance platoon commanded by Lieutenant Jim Polka. Captain Bud Ewing, from the divisional staff, was with them. The recon platoon had traveled along the slopes of Mt. Lobi to try to find how far to the north the Japanese stronghold extended; the platoon found instead that the position extended to the west. Consequently, the platoon dug in on the northwest corner of the Japanese defensive network.

Colonel Robert Soule, CO of the 188th, was in overall command of the assault on Purple Heart Hill. He planned his attack for the morning of the 26th. For the assault, he had the 2d of the 188th and the 1st of the 187th plus the recon platoon under his command. First, he moved his F Company from Mahonag down the trail to the east to set up an ambush. Then, he used the 2d of the 188th, first as a ploy, and then as a part of the attack. The 2d of the 188th was on a hill southwest and across a gorge from the objective. Colonel Soule directed Colonel Mann to move to the southwest, away from the hill, leading the Japanese to believe that, like the four other battalions that had moved out of the area, the 2d of the 188th would also back out.

But the battalion moved into a narrow, steep-sided river bottom that hid it from the Japanese, then doubled back and moved up along the wooded side of a ridge, and climbed east up a rock gully onto the southern slope of Purple Heart Hill. Then the battalion turned left and moved up on the enemy's flank. The south slope of the hill was so steep that the men had to pull themselves up hand over hand on vines and bushes. As soon as they were within range and vision of the Japanese on the ridge, the Japanese took the lead troops under heavy fire from deep entrenchments.

Private First Class John Chiesa was in E Company of the 188th. "We just got to the top of the hill when all hell broke loose," he wrote recently. "The Japanese opened up with their woodpeckers and rifles. Duncan got hit in the rump and he went tumbling down the hill. I hit the ground and prayed.

"While we waited, I got hungry so I turned around facing down the hill and got out one of my K rations. I was opening up the can when twenty feet from me this Japanese jumped out of the bushes. He looked at me and I looked at him. I think he was as surprised as I was. I had an M1 rifle laying across my lap. Everything was done automatically. I grabbed the rifle, turned, and pulled the trigger. He was doing the same thing but I was luckier. I hit him smack in his Adam's apple....The thing that will always be on my mind is that if I didn't stop to eat, those Japanese would have killed all five of us."

The Japanese on Purple Heart Hill were so well entrenched and so numerous that Colonel Soule decided to blast them first with as much artillery fire as he could muster before he ordered any more ground attacks. Part of the fire came from A Battery of the 457th, which had earlier parachuted into Manarawat. During most of the night of the twenty-sixth, the artillery from Manarawat and Burauen and Colonel Mann's mortars pounded the Japanese defenses. Finally, after a strong artillery preparation, on the morning of the 27th, the 2d of the 188th stormed Purple Heart Hill and, after intense, close-in firefights and hand-to-hand fighting, struggled to the top of the Hill and stayed there. The entire battalion closed in at dusk but had no time to dig in. The exhausted men simply moved into the old holes and revetments from which they had so recently blasted the enemy.

The Japanese who had not been killed in the assault scattered to the north and the west. Those in the north ran into the 1st of the 187th, which was attacking south along the gorge and up the other ridge. "Three minutes before 1400 [H-hour for the 1st of the 187th]," reported one of the 1st of the 187th troopers, "we felt the mighty shock of the 'Long Toms' landing on the crest of the ridge, and at 1400, with a cheer, we clambered up to the plateau in assault, and it was like shooting ducks in a rain barrel. The concussion of the tremendous projectiles had shocked the defenders into impotence, and all we had to do was give them a dose of assault fire. Hundreds, we never knew how many, had been buried in the subterranean galleries." The Japanese fleeing to the west ran into the recon platoon and the F Company ambush along the Japanese supply trail.

The bloody battle for Purple Heart Hill was over after almost five weeks of containment followed by the final attack. The troops searched the area and found 238 dead Japanese and many fragments of bodies mangled by the artillery fire. They also found that the elusive Japanese supply trail, which wound from Ormoc Bay, ended at Anonang. Colonel Muller, the division G2, reasoned that, because of its extensive defenses, the fact that Purple Heart Hill was the eastern terminal of the supply trail, and because earlier recon patrols had seen Japanese sentries walking post with fixed bayonets, Anonang was probably the command post of the Japanese 26th Division.

During December, the morale and the physical condition of the Japanese on Leyte sank to an unbelievable low. The Japanese Thirty-fifth Army had begun to disintegrate. Desertions were common. The wounded refused to return to their basic units. Because the Japanese had scant medical facilities or medicine for treating their wounded, the problem of what to do with them became acute. The enemy resorted to drastic measures. General Tomochika, chief of staff of the Thirty-fifth Army, later said, "Commanders employing persuasive language frequently requested seriously wounded soldiers at the front to commit suicide; this was particularly common among personnel of the 1st Division and it was pitiful. However, the majority died willingly. Only Japanese could have done a thing like this and yet I could not bear to see the sight."

After the first of December, the Japanese on Leyte "were on a starvation diet and had to live off the land," according to Col. Junkichi Okabayashi, chief of staff of the 1st Division. "The men were forced to eat coconuts, various grasses, bamboo shoots, the heart fibers of coconut tree trunks, and whatever native fruits and vegetables they could forage. They were literally in a starved condition."

As they retreated, the Japanese abandoned equipment, weapons, and ammunition along the roads and trails. General Tomochika said that when the Americans captured his headquarters site, he "left without any clothing." However, he picked up "a new uniform and sufficient food while on the road."

After the success at Purple Heart Hill and the juncture of the 511th and the 1st of the 187th with other American forces on the west coast, the main battles of the 11th Airborne on Leyte were finished. Most of the division, including the 187th, withdrew to the Bito Beach base camp. The 674th and 675th Glider Field Artillery Battalions, however, still bereft of their howitzers and acting as infantry, stayed in the hills outside Burauen scouting and patrolling the eastern approaches to the Leyte hills. The 457th Parachute Artillery Battalion remained in position outside Burauen to support the other artillerymen still in the mountains. But by the fifteenth of January, all units of the 11th had returned to Bito Beach.

Life improved immeasurably on the beach. Each man had a cot in a pyramidal tent, he ate fresh meat and vegetables in mess tents with stand-up tables fashioned from pierced steel runway planks. He could dip in the ocean in front of the division area, loll and play ball on the sandy beach, put on dry fatigues and new boots, drink his ration of beer—even sometimes cold—get mail and write letters, and go to outdoor movies. But just so that he would not forget the "spit and polish" of an 11th Airborne soldier, he could dig out his khakis and take part in a division parade and awards ceremony, reviewed by Lt. Gen. Robert Eichelberger, commander of Eighth Army, on the twenty-first of January 1945 along the Bito Beach.

At lunch that day, General Eichelberger told General Swing that he was "elated" that General MacArthur had given him the "go-ahead" to invade Batangas, Luzon, with the 11th Airborne Division. He also gave General Swing a top priority: Get to Manila ahead of the Sixth Army.

The battle for Leyte was over. The Americans had established a base on the island from which medium bombers could strike Luzon, the heart of the Philippine archipelago. Ahead was more intense fighting for the Allies, but even before the invasion of Luzon, the Japanese High

Command had lost confidence. After the war, Gen. Tomoyuki Yamashita, the commander of all the Japanese forces in the Philippines, said, "After the loss of Leyte . . . I realized that decisive battle was impossible."

For the past three years, the Allies had fought through jungles and over soggy, rocky mountain chains, in torrid temperatures and monsoon rains, at the end of a supply system that spewed out the necessities for battle but no luxuries. Ahead lay more hard battles, more casualties, more discouragement, and more frustrations.

In the pyramidal tents on Bito, on the sandy beach, in the mess lines, and wherever else the troops gathered, the main topic of conversation centered on the location of their next fight. Rumors abounded. The troops did know that Sixth Army had invaded Luzon at Lingayen Gulf on the ninth of January. They had heard that the paratroopers of the 11th had been alerted for a jump ahead of Sixth Army at Nichols Field outside Manila. But toward the end of the month, unit commanders received a supply of handbooks describing the terrain and geography of southern Luzon. Company commanders lectured their soldiers on the vegetation, climate, and the road network of Luzon. Staffs built sand tables of the area from Nasugbu east to Batangas and north to Manila. Rumors became reality. Shortly, the 11th Airborne received orders for an operation in southern Luzon.

## Mounting Up for Luzon

While the 11th Airborne Division was healing its wounds, both human and logistical, on Bito Beach, and while the Eighth Army was mopping up Leyte with the forces left behind by Sixth Army, Sixth Army had invaded Luzon at 0930 on 9 January with the Ist and XIVth Corps, a force of some 68,000 men. The enemy forces, under General Yamashita, numbered about 275,000; among other units, he had one armored and six infantry divisions. The strength of the enemy was misleading: many of the units, hastily thrown together with poor equipment and marginal leaders, were formed from survivors of other outfits. In addition, there were 16,000 naval troops in and around Manila, but Yamashita had no control over them. The 11th and the 187th would learn a lot more about these renegade sailors in the weeks to come.

To defend the island, Yamashita withdrew most of his troops from the coastal regions and ordered them to prepare for a lengthy delaying action in the interior of the island. His objective was to hold Luzon as long as possible to prevent the Allies from using it as a base for final operations against his homeland. He deployed his main force of about 152,000 men into a number of mountain strongholds in the north of the island; he sent another 50,000 to defend southern Luzon and the hills east of Manila; and he stationed a third group of 30,000 west of the Luzon Plain in the hills dominating the huge Clark Field complex.

Yamashita considered Manila too flat and, because of the thousands of thatch-roofed houses, too "flammable to defend." He also knew that he could not support the 600,000 civilians in Manila during an extended siege. He planned, therefore, to move his troops out of Manila, except for a small group who would protect his supply lines and blow up bridges as the Americans advanced. Yamashita clearly wanted to make Manila an "open city" as MacArthur had done in the dark days of 1942. But the 16,000 naval troops in Manila under the command of the stubborn and hard-nosed RAdm. Sanji Iwabuchi had no intention of leaving the city "open." As the 11th Airborne attacking Manila from the south and Sixth Army attacking from the north were to learn to their horror, Iwabuchi and his men would fight savagely to the last man; burn, blast, and pillage every possible business facility, hospital, and home in Manila; and rape, ravage, and kill thousands of civilians savagely, indiscriminately, and wantonly.

Back on Bito Beach on the twenty-second of January, General Swing received Field Order Number 17 from Eighth Army, which alerted the division for a two-phased operation on Luzon and directed that the "11th A/B will land one regimental combat team on X-Day at H-Hour in the Nasugbu area, seize and defend a beachhead; 511th Parachute Regimental Combat Team will be prepared to move by air from Leyte and Mindoro bases, land by parachute on Tagaytay Ridge, effect a junction with the force of the 11th A/B moving inland from Nasugbu; the 11 A/B Div, reinforced after assembling on Tagaytay Ridge, will be prepared for further action to the north and east as directed by Commanding General, Eighth Army."

On the 25th of January, General Swing wrote a letter to his father-in-law, Gen. Peyton C. March, the army's chief of staff during the latter months of World War I. "Dear General," he wrote, "I've won somewhat of a victory over the air corps and the Big G3. We're going in half airborne and half amphibious. The plan is one I've advocated for four months, only I was to go whole hog by air with another division seaborne. As you can imagine, it's an end run with a forward pass." (This was nearly fifty years before the celebrated "Hail Mary" play in Desert Storm.)

"As a climax, Eichelberger is going in with me to take over as soon as more troops arrive, and as there is no love lost between him and Krueger, he's going to give me all the support he can muster from the 'leavings' of the Lingayen convoy. If he isn't standing at the bar in the Army-Navy Club when Krueger walks in the door, it won't be for lack of trying. . . ."

General Swing was annoyed at the "big G3," General MacArthur's operations officer, because from 9 January until shortly before 22 January, General Swing was under a directive from General Headquarters to drop the 511th Regimental Combat Team in two-hundred-man (or reinforced company-sized) units "all over southern Luzon." GHQ reasoned, presumably, that paratroopers scattered all over the southern Luzon landscape would confuse the enemy as to the size and location of the airborne forces and cause General Yamashita to keep his units south of and out of Manila searching for the dispersed paratroopers. General Swing was so livid at the suggestion that he is alleged to have said to GHQ, "If you want to take my division from me, relieve me of command. But give my men a fighting chance."

The field order galvanized the entire division into action. The staff worked with the navy to arrange shipping to move the division, less the 511th RCT, from Leyte to Luzon and, with the air corps, to provide planes for the 511th RCT drop on Tagaytay Ridge. The quartermaster worked overtime to bring all units up to full Table of Equipment strength, a formidable task because 90 percent of the backup supply of individual equipment and clothing and many of the crew-served weapons had been lost in the jungles or destroyed by the 6 December Japanese parachute attack near the division supply dumps at Burauen. All of the division's vehicles, of which there were a scant few in comparison with other standard divisions, had to be completely overhauled because of their continuous use for over two months in the hubcap-deep mud of Leyte. For the units going in amphibiously, their vehicles had to be waterproofed. For the parachute units, their few vehicles had to be loaded with the units landing amphibiously and reclaimed later. All weapons went through a rigorous rehab program and inspection.

Many units, including the division staff, went through staff and command changes as a result of losses to KIAs, WIAs, and combat shakedown. In the 187th, Lt. Col. George Pearson took over as executive officer of the regiment from Lt. Col. Bob MacCleave, who had suffered an almost fatal heart attack at Patog, Leyte, and was flown back to Walter Reed Hospital in Washington. Lieutenant Colonel Harry Wilson moved from the 2d Battalion to replace Colonel Pearson, and Lt. Col. Norman Tipton returned from the 511th to take over his old battalion, the 2d of the 187th. The regimental surgeon, both battalion executive officers, and many company officers were also switched.

On the twenty-fourth of January, Division Headquarters issued its Field Order No. 10 that outlined in detail the division's plan for executing Eight Army's Field Order No. 17. In addition to telling unit commanders precisely how many days of supplies they would load aboard the ships, the field order also ordered an amphibious dry run for glider units that were more prepared to enter combat by landing in a field in a glider than they were in wading ashore from a navy amphibian. On the twenty-sixth of January, as directed, the first three waves loaded, pushed out into Leyte Bay, and then came churning back at Bito Beach. The division commander deemed the dry run a success, and ordered the amphibians to mount their ships for the cruise to Nasugbu, Luzon.

The 187th, glider and parachute trained, was now going to emulate the marines—storm across the beaches from the sea.

### The Landing on Southern Luzon

On 26 January, the amphibious elements of the division, of which the 187th was a part, loaded onto the ships of Task Group 78.2, under the command of RAdm. William M. Fechteler. TG 78.2 numbered some 120 ships and landing craft of all types, with 4 APDs (high speed transport) and 6 LSTs (landing ship, tank), the largest. There were also 32 LCIs (landing craft, infantry) and 8 LSMs (landing ship, medium). An additional 8 LCIs carried the 511th to Mindoro. Admiral Fechteler was aboard the command ship *Spencer*. Naval support for the amphibious landing was provided by Task Unit 77.3.1, a light cruiser and two destroyers. Planes of the 310th Bombardment Wing provided air support. Admiral Fechteler commanded what one trooper called "this shoestring task force" and gained the affection and gratitude of the division through his capable planning and operation of the mission." Task Group 78.2 sailed from Leyte on 27 January.

But before this two-phased amphibious and parachute operation came to pass, the planning staffs at echelons above the 11th Airborne had developed a number of other scenarios for the employment of the 11th on Luzon. The division was lightly equipped and scantily manned, about 8,200 men with only seven small infantry battalions, just a little more than half the size of a standard World War II division. But it was a division by title and so treated by higher headquarters when it came to assigning missions.

One of the original "higher headquarters" schemes for employing the division on Luzon was for an airborne—parachute and glider—attack on Clark Field. This was ruled out when it became apparent that there were insufficient troop carrier planes in the theater and when a surprised staff officer found that all the CG-4A gliders were boxed and stored on an island somewhat removed from the Philippines. Another plan had the 503d Parachute Infantry Regimental Combat Team attached to the 11th for operations on Luzon. Both General Swing and Col. George Jones, the CO of the 503d, favored this option. But this possibility evaporated when the GHQ staff began to plan for retaking Corregidor and the likely use of the 503d in a parachute assault on that small, rocky, windswept island in Manila Bay. Another plan, the scattering of the 511th all over southern Luzon in groups of two hundred or so men, collapsed under General Swing's vehement disagreement. Still another possibility had the 188th and the 187th landing on different beaches in southern Luzon. The latter plan was such a strong contender that the 187th staff spent a couple of weeks in January studying the maps and photos of the Lucena area.

What finally evolved was Operation Mike VI, the combined parachute-amphibious assault in southern Luzon, essentially a reconnaissance in force, to be exploited at the discretion of the Eight Army commander. General MacArthur told General Eichelberger before the attack that he wanted him to "undertake a daring expedition against

Manila with a small mobile force using tactics that would have delighted
Jeb Stuart."

With those guidelines, Generals Eichelberger and Swing developed
Operation Mike VI, an operation that other, more traditional military
planners might consider unorthodox. The plan directed the 188th
Glider Infantry Regimental Combat Team to lead the amphibious assault
on the beach at Nasugbu followed, on order, by the 187th Glider Regimental Combat Team with the mission of protecting the south flank and
blocking the enemy approach from the Balayan Bay–Santiago Peninsula
area. The plan ordered the 511th Parachute RCT (including the 457th
Parachute Field Artillery Battalion) to drop on Tagaytay Ridge when
General Swing could assure General Eichelberger that the amphibious
elements could link up with the parachute force in less than twenty-four
hours. Eighth Army designated 31 January as X-Day and 0831 as H-Hour.
(The precision of H-Hour—at one minute past 0830—is, admittedly,
somewhat baffling.) Seventh Fleet would shell the beaches for one hour
prior to the landing and the Thirteenth and Fifteenth Air Forces would
provide assault and supporting fires.

Lieutenant Colonel Butch Muller, the division G2, had gathered intelligence data on the climate, geography, and enemy situation from
higher headquarters, guerrillas, air corps photos, and Sixth Army's
Alamo Scouts, a behind-the-lines reconnaissance unit of uncommon daring and inestimable value. Muller put it all together in great detail on
a sand table in the division war room. He also made available terrain
handbooks and maps of the area down to battalion level.

To gather still more precise intelligence, General Swing sent Lt.
Robert L. Dickerson and SSgt. Vernon W. Clark, both from the 188th,
to meet with guerrillas in southern Luzon to reconnoiter the beaches
and the Japanese defenses near Nasugbu. Dickerson and Clark traveled
from Leyte to Mindoro and then to Luzon by PT boat. On 20 January,
they landed in Loac Cove, north of Nasugbu, met with a guerrilla unit,
and for four days Dickerson and the guerrillas patrolled the area, determining enemy troop strength, defensive positions, gun emplacements, road network, buildings, and the depth of the water at designated
landing sites. Dickerson made map overlays of all the information, including guns in the vicinity of San Diego Point. In the early-morning

hours of the twenty-third, he and Clark returned by *barca* and PT boat to San Jose on Mindoro, where, because of the importance of their mission, they were met by Generals Eichelberger and Swing. Dickerson turned over his maps to General Swing and the group returned to Leyte by C-46.

The S2 of the 187th also made a sand table of the landing area. One of the men from the 187th said that "all platoons were briefed on the terrain from aerial photographs and around sand-table relief mock-ups so realistic that when we reached our destination the area seemed positively familiar."

What the maps, aerial photos, and sand tables pointed out was that the terrain and approaches to Tagaytay Ridge from Nasugbu dictated that the division's advance would be canalized along Highway 17. This road ran east from Nasugbu through valleys, between high mountains, along crests of ridges, and over rolling to flat terrain. Behind Nasugbu were rice and cane fields, which would restrict vehicular traffic to the roads. Six miles behind the city, the highway began to rise gradually, cross several rivers, and pass through a defile between Mount Cariliao and Mount Batulao. At this point, the road was 700 feet above sea level; the mountains on either side were about 2,500 feet high.

The terrain in the area was heavily to slightly wooded and, rather ominously for the attacker, the highway snaked through easily defended embankments in most of the area. Beyond the mountains, Highway 17 ran east and up gently rising slopes to the top of Tagaytay Ridge. Here the ridge formed the northern edge of Lake Taal, a spectacularly scenic lake formed in the blown-out crater of an extinct volcano. The northern slope of Tagaytay Ridge was gentle, but its southern slope dropped precipitously to the lake, fourteen miles long and eight miles wide, surrounded by a steep rim of rocky ridges and gullies, like spokes on a huge wheel.

Near the eastern edge of Tagaytay Ridge, the road turned north and began a slow descent to a plain area and Bacoor City on Manila Bay. From Bacoor, the highway passed through Las Pinas, and Paranaque, and edged past Nichols Field before reaching Manila proper. From Nasugbu to Tagaytay Ridge was about thirty miles; from Tagaytay Ridge to Manila was about thirty-seven miles. In the weeks ahead, these names and distances would become vividly familiar to the troopers of the 187th.

Colonel Muller estimated that the Nasugbu-Tagaytay area held about eight thousand enemy soldiers, including a regiment of mixed units manning the defenses in southern Luzon, all amalgamated into a composite group commanded by Col. Masatoshi Fujishige. The bulk of the Japanese troops came from the 17th and 31st Infantry Regiments of the 8th Infantry Division and other miscellaneous outfits. Muller also estimated that about five hundred Japanese defended the shores of Nasugbu Bay and that the main Japanese force, about five thousand strong, held Highway 17 at Tagaytay Ridge and a defile west of the ridge where the highway passed between the peaks of two extinct volcanoes.

The Japanese in southern Luzon were reasonably well equipped with normal infantry weapons and light and medium artillery pieces. Following the usual defensive Japanese tactics in the Philippines, the commander of the Fuji Heiden concentrated his major units inland in central locations and defended the beaches with light holding forces, intending to conduct his defense in the first critical terrain feature to the rear of the beaches, probably near Aga. In addition, the hills to the rear of the beaches, heavily overgrown, offered excellent cover and concealment and high ground for dug-in defensive tactics.

The guerrillas reported that the Japanese were defending the Nasugbu beach area with only two 75mm guns and several machine guns emplaced on the high ground at Nasugbu Point, Wawa, and San Diego Point.

The enemy air force posed an insignificant threat. One corps after-action report held that "recent air raids by Admiral Halsey's fleet had reduced the enemy air force [on Luzon] to an estimated nominal figure of 160 fighters and 170 bombers." Other reports estimated that the serviceable Japanese aircraft were far fewer than those numbers.

Another part of the G2 report had to do with the climate on Luzon in the early months of 1945. The troopers of the 187th were delighted to learn that, after enduring the severity of the Leyte monsoons, the weather in Luzon in February was "fairly dry with moderate temperatures."

Major Hoppenstein summed up the loading and voyage of the amphibious elements of the division, including the 187th, this way: "The catch to the whole plan was the uncertainty of what ships the navy would send, and this was not definite until the ships came in at approximately 2000 hours on 25 January. Most of the supply ships were completely loaded within twenty-four hours, except for the great bulk of engineer supplies, ammunition, and gasoline. The LCIs for the troops arrived at 0700 hours on 27 January, and soon thereafter, the troops went aboard. The assault convoy of almost a hundred ships (LSMs, LSTs, LCIs, APDs, and escort destroyers) pulled out to sea late that afternoon."

General Eichelberger and his staff and General Swing and a scaled-down 11th Airborne Division staff traveled to Luzon on Admiral Fechteler's command ship, the *Spencer*. (As was the combat custom in the 11th, General Pierson and another small staff traveled separately so that if one command group were knocked out, the other would be ready to take over command.)

During the four-day trip, General Eichelberger had ample time to write to his wife, "Dearest Emmaline" or simply "Miss Em." On 29 January, he wrote: "I might try a fast drive to Manila . . . almost dark. . . . Have been selling Joe [Swing] the idea of a rapid advance—will back him up if he gets his pants shot off. . . ." On the thirtieth, he wrote: "Tomorrow morning about this time we land ourselves. . . . We are not expecting any air attacks, but of course one never can tell with people as unpredictable as the [Japanese]. They are just liable to pass up a good target and attack a rowboat.

"Joe Swing is grand to deal with. . . . He spent quite a long time in Africa and in the Sicily landing on a very peculiar mission. . . . He saw a great deal of interplay of personalities and from what I judge we get it rather lightly out here. . . . Billie Bowen and I are standing here now talking about what we may run into tomorrow. There is always a big gamble. One always gets surprises."

At dawn of 31 January, the convoy arrived off Nasugbu. The sea was calm, the sky was clear, and the visibility was superb. On the landing craft, the troops could get a glimpse of the white beaches, the town of Nasugbu, and, beyond that, the green mountains of southern Luzon. From all of their briefings, the soldiers knew that the seemingly beautiful landscape was a deceitful mirage that hid thousands of the enemy, dug in, with weapons poised, ready and more than willing to kill them.

Combat reality returned at 0700 when eighteen A-20s and nine P-38s appeared overhead, roared down on the deck and strafed the beaches. At 0715, the Navy LCIs and destroyers shelled and rocketed the landing area, Red Beach. At 0815, the shelling ceased, and the beach party headed for shore. At 0822, the party radioed back that they had landed without opposition. At 0825, the first wave of eight LCVPs (landing craft vehicle personnel) chugged toward the shore. When the craft ran up on the beach, the ramps splashed down and the glider riders turned amphibians hurried down the ramps, waded through the surf sometimes up to their waists and chests, and waddled ashore through soft sand sometimes up to their ankles. The first assault troops, members of Lt. Col. Ernie LaFlamme's 1st of the 188th, headed for their first objective— Nasugbu—1500 yards away. Some Japanese, in caves on Nasugbu Point to the north and near San Diego Point on the south flank of the beach-head, fired machine guns sporadically and scattered a few artillery rounds along the beach. Colonel LaFlamme immediately sent patrols to the flanks to silence the opposition.

At 0830 on the thirty-first, General Eichelberger wrote: "Landings going according to schedule—no opposition so far as I can tell from here— lots of rocket bursts from our rocket ships—air strafing, bombardment, etc. Afraid they have knocked down the building I want to have. Can see Corregidor with the naked eye although it is some distance away."

General Pierson remembers the landing at Nasugbu this way: "Each staff [his and General Swing's] transferred to LCVPs [General Pierson and his staff had traveled aboard an LST from Leyte] to reach the beach and the two landing craft arrived simultaneously, just behind the second wave of the 188th. We had moved only about ten yards when we were taken under fire by a Japanese machine gun to our left. Fortunately, the position of the gun in a cave was picked up by gunners on an LCI that had discharged the 188th and was quickly silenced. The only casualty to our group was the compass which was deflected hanging from my belt."

Colonel Muller was a part of the division staff landing with General Swing. He remembers: "I was also pinned down for a spell alongside General Swing and Bill Crawford [the G4]. Crawford became exasperated because the naval gunners would not man their guns and return the enemy fire. He announced that he was going to run back across the beach and man the gun of one LCI himself. General Swing grabbed his boot and tumbled him to the sand again, yelling, 'You keep down, I need a G4.'"

While the two command groups were lying in the sand, Col. Irving R. Schimmelpfennig, West Point class of 1930 and a Rhodes scholar, the division chief of staff, retrieved from the sand a bullet that had landed next to him. He immediately dropped the bullet with the comment: "Gee, it's hot." General Swing, lying next to him, remarked rather coldly, "Well, Shimmy, what did you expect?"

At 0930, General Eichelberger wrote: "Everything is going very nicely so far. There is no opposition and I know Joe Swing will make fast time. I must make the decision after I hear from him whether to put any more troops ashore. The first landing is called a 'reconnaissance in force'. . . . The picture right now is very favorable. Lots of friendly planes overhead lots of power in the harbor. After they all go back, however, there won't be so much, but I like Joe's outfit. They look like they'll fight plenty. . . ."

By 0945, the 188th had moved through Wawa, Nasugbu, and its airstrip. Nasugbu had been relatively untouched by the war and was the first town of any consequence that most of the troops had seen since they left the United States. Nasugbu was complete with a village square and bandstand—the site of the first 11th Airborne Division CP on Luzon.

Originally, the landing of the glider elements of the 11th had been designed as a strong reconnaissance by one regimental combat team to be exploited only if that unit found little resistance. At about 1000, General Eichelberger decided that the time was propitious for the landing of the remainder of the amphibious force of the 11th and so ordered.

At 1030, Lt. Col. Harry Wilson led the 1st of the 187th ashore. His battalion, part of the division's floating reserve, was attached to the 188th on landing. The battalion quickly assembled on the beachhead and moved up to the Sugar Central, just behind the beach, to reorganize. After the 2d of the 188th had taken Lian and the Japanese had been driven back into the hills, the 1st of the 187th joined the rest of the 188th in the march inland and up hill on the road to Tagaytay Ridge. The remainder of the 187th followed the 1st ashore, relieved two companies of the 188th on flanking missions, and assumed responsibility for the operation of the beachhead and the defense of Nasugbu. One battery of the 674th remained on the beach to support the 187th in the defense of the port. By 1300, all combat elements of the two glider regiments were ashore and moving inland. General Eichelberger and a small Eighth Army command group had landed and joined General Swing near the head of the column marching and fighting up Highway 17.

### The Attack Inland

By the thirty-first of January, General MacArthur was becoming testy and frustrated with the pace of Sixth Army's advance on Manila from the north. General Eichelberger wrote to his wife that "the commander in chief is very impatient" and that he had to "speed up your palsy-walsy [General Krueger]" and that "Krueger doesn't radiate courage."

General MacArthur played his commanders off against one another. "Get to Manila," he ordered his field commanders. "Go around the Japanese, bounce off the Japanese, save your men, but get to Manila. Free the internees at Santo Tomas. Take Malacanan and the legislative buildings."

General Eichelberger reacted with imagination and dash. He realized that if he could bluff the Japanese into thinking that he commanded a large force moving up Highway 17 across Tagaytay Ridge and heading for Manila, he would have a tactical advantage and a relatively unopposed run to the southern limits of the capital. He ordered General Swing to move both the 187th and the 188th as fast as their legs or shuttle trucks could move them, making as much dust and firing as many weapons and artillery as possible. Eichelberger called the tactic a "monumental bluff."

At 1400 on the afternoon of the thirty-first, General Swing radioed Admiral Fechteler that he was prepared to assume command of the operation and his forces ashore. The 187th and the rest of the division didn't know it, but they had been under the command of an admiral for a number of hours.

Colonel Soule led his force, including the 1st of the 187th, inland at a rapid pace—even though that pace was a walking one. By 1430, the lead unit of the regiment was eight miles from the beach and at the Palico River Bridge, a steel-trussed bridge with a wooden roadway that spanned a gorge some 85 feet deep and 250 feet wide. Colonel Soule had led the force inland so rapidly that the Japanese guarding the bridge were taken by surprise.

The lead element of the 188th raced up the road toward the bridge, down a small hill to the west of it, dashed across the bridge, routed a squad of the enemy who were about to blow it, killed six of them, and scattered the remainder to the east. If the Japanese had succeeded in blowing the bridge, they would have seriously delayed the 11th's advance, because the lightly equipped 127th Airborne Engineer Battalion did not have the material to replace it. Even so, the Japanese had partially cut some of the wooden stringers and supports. The 127th inactivated the charges and reinforced the weakened sections. By 1530, the 188th and the 1st of the 187th had secured the bridge and the area around it.

From the Palico River Bridge, Highway 17 wound eastward past Tumalin, through the defile between the high peaks of Mount Batulao on the south and Mount Cariliao on the north, through Aga, and up onto the Tagaytay Ridge plateau. On the east end of Tagaytay, it turned north and started gently downhill to Imus, where it turned northeast through Paranaque into the southern outskirts of Manila. The area from Nasugbu to Tagaytay Ridge was mountainous and cut by many deep, heavily wooded gorges. Once off the road, only foot travel was possible, which made fast advances impossible. Highway 17 itself was suitable for two-way vehicle traffic, although the roadbed from Nasugbu to Tagaytay was rough and rocky.

By 1800 on the thirty-first, Colonel Soule and his reinforced regiment were at Tumalin, about eight miles inland, still moving forward. Beyond Tumalin, Highway 17 rose more sharply. The regiment found itself marching cautiously through narrow defiles, bordered by steep wooded banks, ideal spots for enemy ambushes.

At the intersection of the Nasugbu road and Highway 17, the lead company of the 188th was halted by fire from the right flank. About that time, General Pierson arrived, and Colonel LaFlamme told him that his point men could see enemy activity on high ground to the right. General Pierson went back to the road junction just as Colonel Soule rode up in his jeep. "He then spread his map on the hood of the jeep," General Pierson remembers, "when all hell broke loose. Artillery, machine-gun, and rifle fire. I was younger then and my reflexes were quicker. I jumped into the roadside ditch and Soule jumped in on top of me. He received a piece of shrapnel in his buttocks and commented that he had been hit. He then got out of the ditch and talked to O'Kane, the regimental executive officer. We had answering artillery fire in short order, and then the 188th moved in on Shorty Ridge (named after Colonel 'Shorty' Soule)."

The normal sunset tactic of most units fighting the Japanese in the Pacific was to halt just before dark, set up a perimeter defense of three- to four-man foxholes about five yards apart all around the perimeter, eat whatever rations were on hand, and bed down for the night with at least one man in each foxhole or machine-gun position awake and on guard. Every few hours, the guard changed silently. No one left the hole during the hours of darkness. Many men, wandering out of their holes in the dark, had been killed by their own buddies.

General Eichelberger realized that if the 11th kept moving at night, the enemy would be thrown off balance and would be unable to practice their customary night probes. General Eichelberger felt that he had momentum with the 11th and told General Swing to keep pushing. General Swing needed no prodding. His aggressiveness was legendary among his men.

A full moon on the night of the thirty-first made the trek of the 188th up Highway 17 considerably easier. Lieutenant Colonel Harry Wilson and his 1st of the 187th had been following the 188th. The battalion had had a small skirmish with the Japanese in the vicinity of the Sugar Central near Nasugbu, killed a few of the enemy, and then moved onto Highway 17 at about 1500. At midnight, the battalion moved through the 188th to lead the attack. It kept marching until 0400 on the first of February, when Colonel Wilson halted the march. The men dug in and slept for two hours and then were off again down the road at 0600.

At daybreak, the advance elements of the 1st of the 187th approached the Mount Cariliao–Mount Batulao defile. Mount Cariliao rises 2,100 feet on the north side of the road, and Mount Batulao 2,700 feet on the south side. At the foot of Mount Cariliao was Mount Aiming, some 1,200 feet high. It was a mound separate and distinct from Cariliao and, like the two higher mountains, was densely wooded. Captain Albert F. Leister described Mount Aiming as being "like a thimble at the base of an overturned teacup." The three peaks gave the Japanese a perfect defensive position that dominated the highway.

The Japanese, when they saw the point of the 1st of the 187th advancing up the highway, opened up with machine guns, mortars, and artillery, the heaviest barrages that the division had encountered since its landing. In some instances, the enemy dropped hand grenades onto the troops on the road from caves and tunnels above them.

The first enemy fire from the peaks around the road had slowed the division's advance in front of what appeared to be the Japanese outpost line of resistance. As the troops advanced, they ran into the MLR (main line of resistance) across Highway 17, hinged on Mount Aiming and anchored on Mounts Cariliao and Batulao. The MLR was a string of caves, dugouts, and tank traps all interconnected by a zigzag line of trenches. The MLR was backed up with one 155mm gun, seven 105s, six 75mm howitzers, and several 37mm antitank guns, manned by some 250 soldiers, emplaced north and east of Mount Aiming. Artillery rounds from these weapons bracketed Highway 17. The defenses into which the division had now run appeared to be the line to which the enemy had been falling back; it was also obvious from the volume of fire that the Japanese were now ready to fight.

There were about four hundred Japanese infantrymen in caves and trenches on Mount Aiming and across the highway. They were members of the 2d Battalion, 31st Infantry, and of the 3d and 4th Battalions, 8th Field Artillery Regiment, all organic units of the 8th Japanese Infantry Division. According to the division G2, these were the best combat troops in the sector, and, according to one of the 187th troopers near the point, "They could see us coming."

General Swing gave Colonel Soule the mission of reducing the enemy stronghold. Colonel Soule left the 1st of the 187th in the lead and ordered Colonel Wilson to lead the attack; he sent the 1st of the 188th to the left and north of the highway; he sent the 2d of the 188th to the right and south of the road. Lieutenant Colonels Luke Hoska and Mike Massad had brought their 674th and 675th Glider Field Artillery Battalions forward and in position to support the attack. The forward air observer with the 188th laid on air support.

The attack got under way at 0900 on the morning of the first. Air corps fighters and A-20s bombed and strafed the positions on the hills. The artillery fired concentrations on defensive and artillery positions. At about noon, A Company of the 188th, led by Capt. Raymond Lee, charged up the hill and, using bayonets, rifles and grenades, broke through the Japanese on Mount Aiming. But the company became separated from the rest of the 1st Battalion and dug in. The Japanese attacked Lee's position all afternoon but failed to dislodge the company. One man from the 187th remembered that "we were to learn later that Captain Lee lost but one man from the company because he'd used the [enemy's] own caves on the west (reverse) slope. . . ." For four hours, Lee and his company withstood continuous counterattacks and one banzai attack.

Seizing Mount Aiming pierced and split the Japanese defenses in the area. While the 1st of the 188th held its position on the north flank, the 2d of the 188th moved quickly south of the road, crossed a deep gorge, deployed, and, on the right flank of the regiment, attacked the enemy strong point between Mount Batulao and the highway. The 1st of the 187th moved in between the two 188th battalions, and, as the center battalion on the line, attacked eastward astride the highway.

On the morning of the second, the regiment launched an all-out attack to the east. At 0830, P-38s and A-20s and the division's two glider artillery battalions hit the main enemy positions in the vicinity of Aga between the two mountains. The concentrations of air and artillery finally knocked out a Japanese artillery battery at Kaytitinga. The 1st of the 187th and the 2d of the 188th continued the assault toward the east and passed the 1st of the 188th on Mount Aiming, protecting the regiment's left flank. Progress down the highway was slow initially, but the pace quickened as the Japanese were forced to withdraw.

Major Hoppenstein wrote that "the assault was so vigorous and fast that the enemy was driven back in a complete rout. This was verified by the capture of an enemy regimental command post (later found to be the headquarters of the Japanese 31st Infantry Regiment—Colonel Fujishige's CP) at Aga at 1300 hours, which showed the haste in which their personnel had departed. Large stores of ammunition, food, clothing, engineer equipment and cigarettes were captured. Several cases of liquor, many documents, weapons, and a Japanese saber were also found by the writer. The documents and saber were turned in to division headquarters. Another indication of the hasty retreat of the Japanese were the numerous individual soldier packs found containing food and clean clothing."

In the Aga-Caylaway area, the 188th found between seventy-five and one hundred tons of ammunition. In the defense of their regimental CP, the Japanese had built three deep tank traps across the highway. The ditches were trapezoidal in shape, twenty feet long across the top, four feet long across the bottom, and twenty-five feet deep. Subsequently, the 127th Engineer Battalion built bridges across the ditches, which could not be bypassed.

The 1st of the 188th moved north through Kaytitinga; the 2d of the 188th continued to attack the Japanese in the coconut groves in the northern foothills of Mount Batulao. So far, the division had lost sixteen men killed and forty-one wounded and had killed about ninety-one of the enemy. By dusk of the second, the division had butted up against the third and strongest position of the enemy MLR across Highway 17. Throughout that night, the Japanese harassed the forward units with artillery, mortars, and small arms. They located the firing position of the 675th and forced Colonel Massad to order a hasty displacement of his guns.

As the division advanced to the east, it bypassed a number of Japanese formations, large and small. The task of nullifying these pockets fell to the guerrillas in the area. Fortunately, these guerrillas were well organized and armed, unlike some other Filipino guerrilla bands, which were simply the foraging gangs of sectional warlords, extracting taxes and subsistence from innocent civilians and fighting for "turf" with other warlords—not the Japanese. The southern Luzon guerrillas were vital to the division's efforts because they permitted the division to advance rapidly in a narrow front without having to halt, deploy, and defeat the enemy to its flanks.

After the division landed, General Swing gave Colonel Hildebrand, the CO of the 187th, the mission of organizing and controlling all of the guerrilla units in the area. Captain Leister wrote that "during the later stages of the operation, the division had the assistance of more than 5,000 guerrillas and they were credited with killing more than 2,300 Japanese."

The fight at the defile, which was by no means over, had slowed the 11th's advance up to Tagaytay Ridge and had ruined General Eichelberger's hopes of bringing in the 511th Regimental Combat Team a day early, on the second, instead of the originally planned third.

Eichelberger was under a restriction from General MacArthur: He could not bring in the 511th until he was certain that the amphibious units of the division could link up with the paratroopers in less than twenty-four hours. Because of the delay at the Aga defile, General Eichelberger reluctantly ordered General Swing to bring in the 511th on the third. General Eichelberger also ordered a second battalion of the 19th Infantry of the 24th Division to move from Leyte to Nasugbu to operate and protect the port and the MSR (main supply route) up Highway 17. When this battalion of the 19th arrived, it would free up the 2d of the 187th to join the rest of the division in its march to Manila.

The division had accomplished a number of missions in the few days since it had come ashore. It had unloaded all of its combat equipment, established a port, cleared an airstrip to handle C-47s, (the first plane to land on the thirty-first was an L-5 flown by Capt. John H. McLeod from Leyte to Mindoro to Luzon), had advanced inland on foot a total of nineteen miles, and had penetrated the enemy's MLR.

The 2d of the 187th had moved up Highway 17 after the 19th Infantry had come ashore to protect the base at Nasugbu. Colonel Tipton, CO of the 2d of the 187th, had his headquarters men dig in the command post on one side of the road; one of his rifle companies dug in on the other side. Just before dark, a rifle company of the 19th moved up and relieved a company of the 188th in the same area. Colonel Tipton told the new company commander that there did not appear to be many of the enemy in the area and he did not want any unnecessary shooting. Lieutenant Bernheim was Tipton's S4. He and his platoon had relocated the battalion's supply and ammo dump into the area just before dark but had to leave outside the perimeter a quarter-ton trailer loaded with 81mm, white phosphorous rounds, with four loaded flamethrowers lashed to the top. Colonel Tipton wisely did not want that potential bomb inside his troop area.

Bernheim remembers that, after he had moved the supplies forward, he was exhausted and, at dark, "I spread a poncho on the ground in the middle of the CP and foolishly did not dig in. I can recall, as I fell asleep, the chattering of a monkey mascot we had acquired. In the middle of the night I was awakened by bursts of small-arms fire from across the highway, and the bullets were snap-cracking through our area. Colonel Tipton yelled: 'You trigger-happy bastards, stop that goddamn shooting.'

"No sooner were the words out of his mouth than what sounded like a thousand Japanese started yelling and screaming. What turned out to be about twenty [of them] were moving down the highway toward Nasugbu and the 19th Infantry perimeter spotted them first. Our people opened fire and the flamethrowers were hit and started burning. The monkey was up in a tree screaming away. Some of the WP started exploding. I was so scared over my exposed position that I can recall vibrating off the ground. I thought I heard Japanese voices coming closer and just as I raised up on my elbows, a 2.36 bazooka round came whizzing end over end and hit me in the left side. I can recall that I saw or sensed it before it hit me. The pin was still in, fortunately, because a Japanese hand grenade had exploded in a bazooka position and set off the propelling charge. It felt like Ted Williams hitting me with a bat and the wind was knocked completely out of me. In the morning [the medic] strapped my ribs, and some months later X-rays indicated that I had five cracked ribs, although I was never evacuated."

At 0730 on the morning of the third of February, the 188th, with the 1st of the 187th attached, attacked the third and final Japanese position in the stubbornly defended Cariliao-Batulao defile. The three battalions advanced rapidly against little resistance until about 1100. Then the lead squads began rounding a bare ridge-nose on the north side of a sharp bend in Highway 17 at the western edge of Tagaytay Ridge. The enemy was holding another steep, bare ridge-nose south of the bend. When the point of the advance units rounded the curve, the Japanese opened up with heavy artillery, machine-gun, and small-arms fire. The southern ridge from which they were firing was the highest ground on Tagaytay Ridge and would be known thereafter as Shorty Ridge, named after the diminutive but feisty and belligerent Colonel "Shorty" Soule.

The accuracy of the Japanese fire along the road had confounded the 11th's infantrymen, who noted that, at least in this area, the Japanese did not seem to need to adjust their artillery fire. The infantrymen soon learned the secret: Prior to the landing of the 11th at Nasugbu, the Japanese gunners had placed large white crosses in trees bounding Highway 17. These markings were targets on which they had previously adjusted and recorded the firing data. When the troopers of the 11th reached a certain cross, the Japanese gunners simply set the correct data and fired accurately.

Not only were men of the 187th and 188th pinned down by the enemy artillery fire, but so were a number of high-ranking officers who formed what the troops called the "tip" of the "spearhead tipped with brass." On the morning of the third, the "brass" contingent consisted of General Eichelberger, General Pierson, Gen. Frank Farrell, the commanding general of the 11th Airborne Division Artillery, and a number of colonels and lieutenant colonels on their staffs. In one of the barrages that hit the lead elements that morning, among others, Col. Rinaldo Coe, Eighth Army Headquarters commandant, and the commander of a supporting tank destroyer unit were killed; Col. Harry Wilson and Capt. William Lyman, of the 1st of the 187th, were wounded. In all, the barrage killed eight men and wounded another twenty-one men.

The artillery barrages forced everyone on the road to take cover. Colonel Soule was with his point men and immediately took over control of the ensuing attack on the Japanese position. He crawled under the artillery fire some fifty yards to his jeep and its radio but was wounded slightly en route. His driver, Pius Corbett, was lying alongside the jeep. Lieutenant Gabe Allen, the communications officer of the 1st of the 188th, remembers that Colonel Soule crawled up to the jeep and said, "Corbett, do you want to hand me that radio?" Corbett replied, "No, sir, I don't even want to move." But he did, and Colonel Soule got to his radio and then to a telephone whose wire had just been strung forward to his location. He sent orders to his regimental XO, Lt. Col. Mortimer J. O'Kane to send up the lead battalion, Harry Wilson's 1st of the 187th.

Captain Hanna commanded the lead company of the 1st of the 187th. Colonel Wilson ordered Hanna to swing behind the position and try to take it from the rear. Tommy Mann led his 2d of the 188th off the road to the south and onto Shorty Ridge. By 1300, troops of the 187th and 188th, using flamethrowers and hand grenades, supported by the howitzers of the 674th and 675th Glider Field Artillery Battalions, wrested Shorty Ridge from the enemy, killing over three hundred in the battle.

The march to Manila continued.

### The Jump on Tagaytay Ridge

The position was obviously an important one in the Japanese defensive scheme. It was honeycombed with enormous supply tunnels, reinforced-concrete caves, and strong gun and individual firing positions.

With the reduction of Shorty Ridge, the units of the 11th that had landed amphibiously and fought their way along a difficult uphill route of attack were ready to make contact with the paratroopers of the 511th, who, since 0815 on the morning of the 3d, had been landing on Tagaytay Ridge.

Because of a shortage of transport aircraft, only about a third of the 511th RCT could be dropped in one lift. The first group consisted of the regimental command group, the 2d Battalion, and half of the 3d Battalion—about 915 men in all.

The ridge, which had been swept of most of the Japanese by local guerrillas, made an excellent drop zone for a mass drop. The area selected for the DZ on top of the ridge was flat, some two thousand yards wide and over four thousand yards long. It was open, plowed in some places, and even though cut by a number of small streams and dotted with a few scattered nipa huts, there were few major obstacles to the paratroopers. The only dangerous feature of the jump was the possibility of being blown off the ridge and down into Lake Taal. But that did not happen to any of the jumpers.

What did happen was that the first wave of eighteen C-47s jumped properly over the "Go" point. But the next wave, 570 men in thirty planes, for some still obscure reason, jumped prematurely about eight thousand yards east of the "Go" point. At about 1210, the rest of the regiment—one half of the 3d Battalion and the entire 1st Battalion—came in over the ridge. Unfortunately, some of the planes dropped on the parachutes from the previous lift that dropped prematurely. In all, 425 men landed on the proper DZ; 1,325 landed between four and six miles to the east and northeast.

In spite of the scattered landings, the 511th was assembled into companies and battalions in about five hours. By 1300 on the afternoon of the 3d, the lead elements of the 188th, including parts of the 187th, had moved up the ridge and had made contact with the 511th. (Another echelon of the 511th RCT, the 457th Parachute Field Artillery Battalion, would not jump on Tagaytay until the following morning.)

Both Generals Eichelberger and Swing were with the forward elements of the 188th and, at 1330, they contacted Colonel Haugen, the 511th CO, near the Manila Hotel Annex atop the ridge overlooking Lake Taal. General Eichelberger ran into a reporter for the *Chicago Times* and remarked, "The 11th Airborne Division was the fightingest god-damn troops I ever saw."

That afternoon, the 2d of the 511th secured the drop zone area. After Colonel Lahti had assembled his 3d Battalion, he took over the DZ defensive mission for Col. Hacksaw Holcombe and the 2d Battalion that then moved to the junction of Highways 17 and 25B to take up defensive positions and await further orders.

The division command post moved up from the Palico Barracks to the Manila Hotel Annex, a prewar model of opulence. During the war it had been neglected and looted of its furnishings. But it was in a central position on the ridge and made a convenient CP and supply point for the troops moving east and north.

From the Manila Hotel Annex, General Eichelberger could see Manila shining brightly in the distance and could make out the curved forefinger of Cavite Peninsula hooking into Manila Bay. The "Pearl of the Orient" was aptly named when one viewed, from a distance, its thousands of white buildings laid out along the curve of the bay. It acted like a magnet on General MacArthur moving south and on General Eichelberger moving north. General Eichelberger was motivated by a keenly felt competitive urge to beat General Krueger's Sixth Army to Manila, the major prize of the Pacific War to date, with his Eighth Army (consisting mainly of the 11th Airborne Division).

Highway 17 from Nasugbu to Tagaytay was gravel and usually only one lane; as it turned and sloped gently to the north and toward Manila, it became concrete and two lane. It was a harbinger of good fortune and easy going, thought General Eichelberger; he might yet beat Krueger to Manila. He wrote to his wife on the evening of the third: "The guerrilla reports make me laugh. The report tonight is that Manila is being burned by the Japanese, and yet I can look right down into the town and see lights and one little fire. . . ." He did not yet know it, but for Manila and its inhabitants the worst, far worse, was yet to come.

Generals Eichelberger and Swing had hoped that the 511th could move to the north and on to Manila on the afternoon of the third, but there were simply not enough trucks nor gasoline in the Nasugbu dump to permit it. Late on the afternoon of the third, however, the division quartermaster managed to unload seventeen two-and-a-half-ton trucks from landing craft and sent them to the Manila Hotel Annex. And by the fourth, ten C-47s had landed at Nasugbu's dirt strip, widened and cleared by the 127th Engineers, with a cargo of gasoline that the QM immediately sent forward to the Annex.

Generals Eichelberger and Swing were anxious to start the move toward Manila. To reconnoiter the road to Manila, General Swing sent Lt. George Skau and twenty-one men of the division recon platoon, mounted in jeeps, down the road after dark on the evening of the third. Before he sent him on his way, General Swing cautioned Skau that he was going into unknown territory and to radio his observations as soon as he ran into the Japanese defenses. At 0400 the next morning, Skau radioed back to Colonel Muller that the road was secure as far as Imus, where the Japanese had blown the bridge and had set up a defensive position. But, said Skau, he and his platoon had found a dirt road that bypassed the blown-out bridge. It, too, had a bridge ready to be blown but the recon platoon men had removed the charges.

At 0530 on the morning of the fourth, the point of the 2d Battalion of the 511th moved out in two jeeps. Two hours later, the rest of the battalion began its move down the road with D Company, commanded by Capt. Steve Cavanaugh, mounted in two-and-a-half-ton trucks in the lead. After a heavy firefight at an old Spanish barracks with thick stone walls, the entire 2d Battalion moved out toward Manila on foot. Holcombe sent the two-and-a-half-ton trucks back to shuttle forward other units of the 511th that had started out on foot from Tagaytay Ridge.

Holcombe and the 2d Battalion secured the Imus River Bridge and moved on another three miles to Zapote, where Highway 17 ended at a juncture with Route 25, which led another half mile northeast across the Zapote River to a junction with Route 1, a mile south of a bridge over the Las Pinas River at the town of Las Pinas. The Japanese had prepared to demolish the bridge, but Holcombe's men caught them by surprise and, after a hard fight, took the bridge intact.

The rest of the 511th, by truck and by foot—the 1st Battalion walked the entire thirty-six miles from Tagaytay to the cathedral in Paranaque— had moved forward and were now pushing against the southern defenses of Manila. The regiment, however, was not yet within the Manila city boundary.

Back along Tagaytay Ridge on the fourth, the 188th and the 1st of the 187th, having cleaned out Shorty Ridge, left one company to secure the area. Colonel Soule led the rest of his command on foot toward Manila. At 0815, the third serial of the 511th RCT, the 457th Parachute Field Artillery Battalion, dropped on Tagaytay Ridge just opposite the Manila Hotel Annex. With the division on a new and very tough mission, and with his supply tail strung out over nearly seventy miles, General Swing altered the missions of some of his units. He gave Colonel Hildebrand and the 187th the mission of securing the MSR (main supply route). It was a formidable task. Colonel Hildebrand used guerrillas to assist the 187th, putting him in virtual command of all the guerrillas in the provinces of Batangas and Cavite. By the beginning of February, almost two thousand guerrillas had been assembled. But coordinating their activities, supplying them, and sorting out who ran what section of the province, was distinctly different from commanding an American outfit.

To assist in the vast task of covering the large area that the division had liberated, General Eichelberger brought ashore the 19th Infantry, less one battalion, which he assigned to Colonel Hildebrand. Colonel Hildebrand accomplished his far-flung mission by patrolling the area thoroughly and by establishing outposts along the entire MSR. His force was not large enough to take on large concentrations of the Japanese, but the active patrols of the 187th drove the enemy farther and farther back into the surrounding hills. One Japanese concentration was around Mount Pico de Loro; another was on Mount Sungay. In future weeks, the entire 11th Airborne would be back in the area to wipe out the pockets. But first it had to assist in the subjugation of Manila. And in a few days, both battalions of the 187th would move to the area south of Manila and join the division in what would prove to be one of its bloodiest fights.

General MacArthur was very much the optimist when he wrote about the capture of Manila. "In the morning hours of February 1," he wrote, "the 1st Cavalry Division started down toward Manila, its exposed left flank guarded by marine air units. Simultaneously, the 37th Division from the XIV Corps and the 11th Airborne Division of the Eighth Army closed in on the city. A flying column from the cavalry under Brig. Gen. William C. Chase entered Manila on February 4, and relieved the prisoners at Santo Tomas and Bilibid. For all strategic purposes, Manila was now in our hands."

General MacArthur may have been right in his strategic assessment. But the troops were fighting in a tactical environment and would suffer heavy losses as they bashed themselves against the interlocking, deep defenses of the Genko Line. And Manila, before its final liberation, would suffer unimaginable devastation of its buildings and its people. Manila was far from free and hardly "in our hands" on the fourth of February.

# 2: The Attack on Manila and the Genko Line

### The Attack on Manila and the Genko Line

By 2130 on the night of the fourth of February, the 511th had advanced as far as the Paranaque River Bridge, the southern boundary of the metropolitan area of Manila. And it was here that the division ran into well-planned and heavily manned enemy defenses that the paratroopers could not by pass. They had found the Genko Line.

The Paranaque River Bridge had not been completely destroyed, and the Japanese had the north bank studded with machine-gun emplacements and pillboxes enclosing larger-caliber automatic weapons. And it was here that the division first ran into ground-mounted Japanese naval gunfire.

In December 1941, the population of Manila was about 625,000; until September 1944, and the Allied invasion of the Philippines, it grew rapidly until it reached over 800,000. But with the advent of new battles in early 1945, the people evacuated the city in droves and moved to what they felt was the safer countryside. Manila was made up of nipa-thatched huts in the slums in some areas and exquisite mansions in others; it had movie theaters, racetracks, cockpits, gas stations, beautiful cathedrals, grim back alleys, and broad tree-lined boulevards; hospitals and colleges; yacht clubs and opulent hotels; pony-drawn carts, streetcars, and buses; monasteries and breweries. It was a lot of things to a lot of diverse people.

The Japanese who halted the 11th Airborne at the Paranaque River Bridge were part of the Southern Force's 3d Naval Battalion, reinforced by a company of the 1st Naval Battalion and artillery units armed with an assortment of naval, ground, and antiaircraft weapons. The 3d Naval Battalion's position in Manila was the strongest because it had been there the longest. Reinforced-concrete pillboxes dotted the street intersections in the suburb south of the city limits, and many were covered with thick layers of dirt, which in months past had overgrown with weeds and plants and gave them a natural camouflage. Other defensive positions were hidden in clumps of trees. North of Paranaque was Nichols Field, from which the Japanese Naval Air Service operated; it was defended by a part of the 3d Battalion. Nichols Field was studded with antiaircraft weapons that could fire either vertically at planes or horizontally at troops on the ground.

On 4 February, the enemy had few troops on Neilson Field, two miles to the north-northeast of Nichols, but the 4th Naval Battalion held Fort McKinley, which was just two miles from Neilson. Other Japanese units manned a group of AA guns midway between Fort McKinley and Nichols in support of the 3d Naval Battalion. These defenses formed part of the Genko Line.

Rear Admiral Sanji Iwabuchi, who commanded the defenses of Manila, had twenty thousand men under his command—sixteen thousand naval troops and four thousand soldiers who had been trapped by the American pincers movement on Manila from the north and the south. Before the invasion at Lingayen, Iwabuchi believed that the main American effort against Manila would come from the south, and therefore had prepared the strongest defenses of the city south of the Pasig River. He integrated into these defenses the reinforced-concrete buildings of prewar construction and heavy naval guns from damaged or sunken ships. He interlaced into the defensive line a tremendous number of automatic weapons, mortars, and AA field artillery pieces.

The Genko Line consisted of a series of mutually supporting concrete pillboxes extending in depth six thousand yards through the Manila Polo Club. It stretched east across Nichols Field and anchored on the high ground of Mabato Point along Laguna de Bay. The rear of the line was based on the high ground of Fort McKinley. Five- and six-inch guns and 150mm mortars were set in concrete emplacements, facing south, and 20-, 30-, 40-, and 90mm AA guns sited to fire horizontally were tactically located to assist in the defense. Many of the concrete pillboxes were two and three stories deep. Some of the forts were stone and had dome-shaped roofs piled high with sod and dirt and so overgrown with weeds that they could only be recognized from a few feet away. Embrasures in the pillboxes were narrow but controlled a wide field of fire. Most of the pillboxes were defended by two men and either a .50-caliber machine gun or a 20mm automatic weapon.

The Genko Line held some 6,000 Japanese in over 1,200 pillboxes supported by 44 heavy artillery pieces, 164 AA weapons, over 500 machine guns, and 245 hundred-pound bombs and 35 antisubmarine depth charges rigged as land mines. All roads leading to the line were heavily mined with five-hundred-pound aerial bombs armed with low-pressure detonators.

The enemy defenses stopped the 511th at the Paranaque River Bridge. The 674th (which after the war would become part of the 187th Regimental Combat Team) had by this time moved up into positions from which it could support the advance of the 511th. General Swing had set up his CP in the cathedral near Paranaque. Lieutenant Colonel Luke Hoska, CO of the 674th, reported to General Swing there and told him that he believed that he and his pack 75s could neutralize the heavy enemy fire coming from across the bridge. General Swing gave him permission to try.

Colonel Hoska crawled to the riverbank with his radio, went down to the water's edge, and, between midnight and 0500 on the fifth, directed seven hundred rounds from one howitzer in a precision attack on the Japanese defensive positions. He knocked out five machine-gun emplacements and two 20mm high-velocity guns embedded in the concrete breakwater wall thirty yards across the Paranaque River from his observation point.

Iwabuchi's men had also fortified the city with such expedients as overturned trucks and trolleys, houses converted into machine-gun nests with their entrances sandbagged, stairways barricaded, and walls sliced open for firing ports. Iwabuchi ordered his men to blow up all the city's military installations and the port area, the bridges, and the municipal water and electrical supply systems. His men carried out the order with a vengeance. On the fifth of February, they dynamited the northern port area and fled south across the Pasig River, blowing all the bridges behind them. The blasts ignited fires that quickly engulfed a section of bamboo houses near the port. In a short time, much of the northern half of the city was in flames, visible for fifty miles, which hampered the 37th Division as it fought its way south, street by street.

General Eichelberger wrote to his wife: "The view of Manila last night was a terrible thing as the whole part of the city seemed to be on fire. Smoke and flames were going way up in the air. . . . What a shame it is. This is particularly true since the Filipinos are going to have their independence and it is really the destruction of a neutral city. . . . It is something which I shall never forget. . . ."

From the fourth to the sixth of February, the 511th fought its way north about two thousand yards in house-to-house and pillbox-to-pillbox fighting. It was a radical change from the Leyte-type fighting that bloodied the division in its first battles. In fighting through the increasingly more devastated and destroyed streets and buildings of Manila, the 511th had to depend on the infantryman's weapons—rifles, grenades, flamethrowers, mortars, bayonets, and occasionally 75mm pack artillery. In two days, the regiments lost six men KIA and thirty-five WIA and killed about two hundred of the enemy.

On the sixth, General Swing called a halt to the 511th's advance; that afternoon, the 188th and Lieutenant Colonel Tipton and the 2d of the 187th arrived near Nichols Field. General Swing planned to send the 188th and the 2d of the 187th against Nichols Field from the south and southeast while the 511th continued its drive into Manila in the west, on the left flank of the division. Under cover of darkness on the night of the sixth to the seventh, the 188th and the 2d of the 187th moved up to a line of departure about a mile and a half southeast of Nichols, ready to launch its attack on the morning of the seventh. The attack, across fairly open terrain, gained little ground in the face of heavy, concentrated, and accurate field artillery, mortars, and machine guns.

By the eleventh, the division had consolidated its advances. It had established a solid line from the northwest to the southeast corners of Nichols Field, slicing diagonally across the NW–SE runway, and had eliminated the last enemy resistance on the west end of the field. In the 511th sector, the front lines extended from Dewey Boulevard along Libertad Avenue and east to Taft Avenue Extension. Division permitted patrols beyond this line, and one patrol made contact with a 1st Cavalry patrol on the eleventh in the vicinity of the Philippines Racing Club.

The division had been unable to reduce substantially the volume of enemy fire from the Nichols Field defensive complex. A20s from Mindoro and the pack howitzer of 75s of the division had failed to knock out enough of the enemy guns to permit the infantry to advance without severe losses. "The Japanese defended Nichols Field," wrote the division historian, "as if the emperor's palace itself were sitting on the center runway."

The airfield was the center of the Genko Line. This part of the line was an interconnecting network of concrete pillboxes and gun emplacements linked together by underground tunnels. The hundred-foot revetments used to protect aircraft were hollowed for defensive positions, and aprons of barbed wire ringed the area. In general, the terrain around Nichols Field was open, providing the Japanese with excellent fields of fire for their flat-trajectory machine guns and innumerable dual-purpose AA weapons. On the outer rim of the field, the Japanese had embedded in concrete a number of five-inch naval guns. Their months of occupying Manila had obviously not been wasted.

One air corps crew was, unfortunately, unaware of the ownership of Nichols Field in the early stages of the battle for its control. Eli Bernheim, S4 of the 2d of the 187th, remembers that, when the 2d of the 187th was headed into the southern part of Manila, he and some of the battalion staff were kneeling on the ground looking at a map and being oriented by Colonel Tipton on the situation. They heard an airplane and looked at Nichols Field in time to see a C-47 shot down as it was making its final landing run on one of the runways. Bernheim later learned that the pilot thought that Nichols Field was in U.S. hands.

On the eleventh of February, the 511th was strung out along the shore of Manila Bay north to Libertad Avenue and east toward Nichols Field. "At the time, the 2d of the 187th was attached to the 511th," Bernheim remembers. "Our battalion CP was in a Spanish-style house with a thick wall surrounding it. We were getting harassed by low-trajectory 20mm AA fire.... General Swing, Colonel Haugen (CO of the 511th), Colonel Tipton, and, I believe, Capt. Dick Barker, the battalion S3, were in a second-floor room discussing the situation. There was a small hexagonal-shaped window on one wall. I was going up the stairs to report to Colonel Tipton when there was a loud explosion that caused me to trip on the stairs. A 20mm shell had penetrated the window and exploded in the room. Colonel Haugen received a sucking chest wound. Miraculously, no one else was wounded." Colonel Haugen died later on the air evac flight from Mindoro to Hollandia, New Guinea.

On the twelfth of February, General Griswold authorized General Swing to launch a full-scale attack on Nichols Field. The 2d of the 187th attacked generally east from the northwest corner of the field; the 188th and the 1st of the 187th drove in from the south and southeast. The preattack artillery and air had softened some of the defenses, and, under cover of continuing artillery barrages, the infantry moved forward by rushes to assault the pillboxes and emplacements with their rifles, grenades, and bayonets. In the afternoon, the Japanese launched a strong counterattack, but the infantrymen beat it off. By dusk, the 187th and the 188th had cleared most of the field.

The division continued the attack the next day. The 511th advanced east astride the Manila–Fort McKinley road to come up on line with the remainder of the division's infantry along the Laguna extension of the Manila Railroad. The 187th and the 188th continued to fight across Nichols. But the field was by no means in shape to accept American planes. The runways and taxiways were cracked open and pockmarked with bomb craters. The Japanese guns at Fort McKinley occasionally dropped artillery rounds at random on the field.

On the eleventh of February, General Eichelberger wrote to his wife: "Sir George [Kenney, MacArthur's air commander] thinks that I should have dropped the 511th on Nichols Field, but in view of those concrete emplacements I believe they would have been murdered. I do not think I could have gotten a corporal's guard out alive. No one will take a bigger risk than I will if I feel I have a reasonable chance, but I do not believe it would have been a fair show. I would not have minded dropping them in the vicinity of Imus, which is almost down to Manila, because there were practically no Japanese there. My force was so ridiculously small because I only landed with four battalions and one of these . . . had to hold the base, which left me with three battalions, and one had to hold Tagaytay Ridge, which was a very commanding terrain feature, so I would only have two battalions to march toward Manila if I had not dropped the three battalions from the air on Tagaytay Ridge. There were only seven [infantry] battalions in the whole division. Personally, I think we pulled one of the most daring feats of the war." In another letter, he said that "Joe Swing is going to be very sorry to come under any other unit. I am going to recommend the 11th Airborne Division for a Presidential Citation."

On the morning of the fifteenth, the division continued its attack across Nichols and toward Fort McKinley. The division plan directed the 188th, with the 2d of the 187th attached, to pivot and strike toward Fort McKinley and for the 511th to continue its attack to the east—with all six battalions converging at the Carabao Gate of Fort McKinley.

The plan of attack for the 2d of the 187th was "simple as there was no choice except to push straight to the front and keep going," wrote Captain Harrison Merritt, commander of G Company of the 187th,

after the battle. When Colonel Tipton briefed his company commanders on the battle plan, he said, "Don't give the little bastards a chance
to get set. I ran a good many problems over this same ground when stationed here as a lieutenant. It is a damned good defensive terrain and
so I repeat—hit hard and keep moving. Don't stop for anything. What
you bypass, E Company will take care of."

The line of departure (LOD) was the south line of the Manila Railroad that ran north and south at the base of the ridge the battalion occupied. The bed of the railroad was about six feet above the level of
the ground. Just beyond the railroad and running parallel to it was a
dry streambed. The terrain to the east rose gradually to form a grass-
covered east-west ridge with its highest point about a thousand yards
east of the LOD. At 1215 on the fifteenth, following an intense artillery
and mortar barrage coupled with an air strike, G Company, 187th,
jumped off in the attack. Merritt's first platoon scrambled over the railroad tracks in its sector and started moving forward. No enemy reaction. The platoon crossed a dry streambed, started up the other side,
and kept moving—first a hundred yards, then two hundred—"and still
not a target appeared or a casualty suffered as the platoon crossed the
dry streambed and started up the barren slopes," wrote Merritt. The
platoon moved forward cautiously but quickly. Still no enemy reaction.
"Something was wrong," said Merritt. "Suddenly the unexpected happened again. Machine guns located in the streambed that the platoon
had just crossed opened up on the right rear of the first platoon. . . .
Every man in G Company was a veteran of the Leyte campaign and
battle-wise. As a result, the platoon was well dispersed. . . . Before any
fire could be brought to bear on the general location of the machine
guns, a shouting, screaming mass of [Japanese] climbed out of the
creekbed and charged toward the platoon. . . . The machine gunners
who had been following close behind had their weapons mounted and
firing within seconds. Their firing, combined with the fire of the BARs
and individual weapons, began knocking the [Japanese] over like
'tenpins.' Still they came on in seemingly endless streams. Soon the
leading enemy closed into the first platoon and all semblance of organization vanished. It was every man for himself."

Merritt knew that, because the enemy was so close to and intermingled with his own troops, he could not use his mortars. He decided in-

stead to commit his second platoon and ordered the platoon leader to move into the draw. The platoon leader was one step ahead of him. He had already led his platoon over the railroad tracks and into the draw on the other side. The second platoon moved down into the draw and knocked out several enemy machine guns while suffering only two casualties. "This had been fairly simple," said Merritt, "as the creekbed was empty except for the enemy machine gunners who had ceased firing, because their fire was masked by their own troops, and were engrossed in watching the battle. The platoon leader ordered one squad to continue up the creekbed for another hundred yards and hold up. Leading the other two squads, he left the creekbed and headed into the melee.

"Everything was really confused at this time," Merritt wrote. "The [Japanese], for some unknown reason, did not attempt to fight it out, but tried to pass through the platoon and reach the shelter of their holes. Screaming like a flock of frightened chickens, they were running right through the first platoon and up the ridge toward their bunkers and pillboxes."

Merritt realized that the enemy in the bunkers would soon start firing even if it meant killing their own men. Merritt tried to move the first platoon up the hill. The second platoon leader and two squads joined Merritt, and together they started up the hill. "The platoon leader of the first platoon," wrote Merritt, "was quick to understand what was taking place and with the help of his platoon sergeant began pushing his platoon forward.

"Help now arrived on the scene. F Company on the left flank of G Company had swung to their right and reached the crest of the hill. This put the remaining [Japanese] between the two companies and cut off the route to their positions."

Within a few minutes, firing ceased, and both companies moved to the top of the hill. F Company then moved to the left back into its own zone. Merritt told a few men to drop grenades into the firing apertures of the position on top of which they stood. Suddenly, and without warning, a muffled explosion shook the area, and "the earth on top of the hill rose and settled." Most of the men on top of the hill were knocked to the ground, but none was injured. "Preferring death to the disgrace of capture, he had blown his position while the enemy was on top of it,"

Merritt concluded. "Without doubt, he expected the whole hill to be destroyed, killing everyone on it. Fortunately, the charge was too small or all of it did not explode, and his last attempt turned out to be a failure also."

The division had now seized two-thirds of the Genko Line. The 511th, with the 2d of the 187th attached, had pushed through the left end of the line, battering its way through block after block of the crumbled, burning, debris-littered streets of Manila, then turned east to join the attack on Nichols Field. The 188th and the 1st of the 187th had swung north across pillbox-studded, defense-heavy Nichols Field and joined with the 511th and the 2d of the 187th coming east. The 674th and 675th Glider Field Artillery Battalions had been firing ceaselessly in support of the infantry assaults, and brass shells, cases, and fiber boxes were piled in high heaps behind the gun positions. Gun crews, abetted by clerks, cooks, and drivers, fired in shifts around the clock and occasionally took out an overheated howitzer for cooling off, oiling, and barrel replacement.

The artillery, unlike their counterparts in the European War, were often subject to ground attacks from the Japanese, who, in the hours of darkness, infiltrated through the infantry to try to blow up the guns that blasted them so incessantly. Around Manila, banzai attacks against the artillery positions were commonplace. Each battery set up a perimeter around its guns. The morning after, the 675th, in position south of Nichols Field, warded off three Japanese charges during the night. Colonel Massad, the commander, sent a requisition to division for "12 each, bayonets, for howitzer, 105mm." (The 675th was the only artillery battalion in the division artillery armed with the 105; the others had the pack 75s.)

Robert R. Smith summed up the division's attack around Manila and Nichols Field: "With the seizure of Nichols Field, the 11th Airborne Division substantially completed its share in the battle for Manila. Since its landing at Nasugbu, the division had suffered over 900 casualties. Of this number, the 511th lost approximately 70 men killed and 240 wounded; the 187th and 188th Infantry Regiments had together lost about 100 men killed and 510 wounded. The division and its air and artillery support had killed perhaps 3,000 Japanese in the metropolitan area, destroying the 3d Naval Battalion and isolating Abe Battalion."

Following the fall of Nichols Field, the division regrouped for the assault on the last bastions of the Genko Line: Fort McKinley and Mabato Point, the high ground on Laguna de Bay about two thousand yards south of Fort McKinley. General Swing used conventional tactics: Blast the defenses with air strikes and artillery, attack from the blind and vulnerable sides, squeeze the enemy tighter and tighter, and, if they tried to escape, attack the escape routes with air, artillery, or from previously set ambush sites.

On the fourteenth of February, General Swing formed a special task force under the command of Brig. Gen. Albert Pierson, the assistant division commander, to reduce Mabato Point and to attack Fort McKinley from the south. The Pierson Task Force was composed of Harry Wilson's 1st of the 187th, the 3d of the 19th Infantry, A Company of the 44th Tank Battalion, a platoon from C Company of the 127th Engineers, and a platoon from the 221st Medical Company.

The next day, the Pierson Task Force advanced north toward McKinley along the east side of the Manila Railroad that ran parallel to the shore of Laguna de Bay. The 188th, reinforced by the 2d of the 187th, and the 511th attacked east in the face of heavy Japanese automatic-weapons and artillery fire from Fort McKinley. They formed a line, facing east, above the left flank of the Pierson Task Force.

"Between the fifteenth and the seventeenth, we consolidated our gains but the [enemy] were by no means docile," wrote Lt. Eli Bernheim after the war. "They tried several abortive counterattacks and a number of night infiltrations. On the night of the fifteenth, one enterprising [enemy] soldier penetrated clear into the battalion command post where Lieutenant Colonel Tipton and Captain Barker were sleeping. Both officers awoke to find him poking at them with his bayonet. Barker shot the assailant dead but not before he'd taken several wounds in the leg and Tipton a badly lacerated hand."

On the sixteenth, Tipton sent Lt. James W. Roberts with his platoon from E Company to reconnoiter the approaches to the eastern side of Fort McKinley. Roberts found that the area was studded with land mines and barbed-wire obstacles. He and his platoon tried to cut a swath through the fortifications. At one point, there was an enormous explosion from the eastern end of the fort that demolished one side of a hill. The concussion knocked some of the platoon flat. One explosion followed another as the enemy tried to destroy their ammunition dumps.

General Griswold gave General Swing permission to launch his attack on Fort McKinley on the seventeenth. Meanwhile, unit commanders issued ammunition, checked the condition of their troops, briefed the operation down the line of commanders—to the platoon and squad level—and then moved their outfits into the most favorable locations for the assault.

On the seventeenth of February, on schedule, the 11th Airborne launched its attack on Fort McKinley. From the west, the 1st of the 511th, under the command of Maj. Henry Burgess, led the attack. "The closer we got to Fort McKinley the more artillery, ack-ack fire, small-arms fire, and mortar fire from emplacements and pillboxes were encountered," Burgess wrote later. "At one time in the open rolling country one could see seven infantry battalions attacking on a line supported by tanks and self-propelled guns. . . .

"As we approached Fort McKinley, its presence became more ominous. Built of brick, the buildings were beautiful, and the fort dominated the surrounding terrain for hundreds of yards. Streets were paved and the grounds immaculate. Approach routes to the fort itself were open and devoid of any cover. The 1st Battalion of the 511th had been designated as the lead battalion in taking Fort McKinley, an assignment which was going to be expensive in troopers.

"That morning, as we came closer to McKinley, Lieutenant Colonel Tipton, CO of the 2d of the 187th, was on our right. Colonel Tipton's first assignment had been at Fort McKinley upon graduation from West Point. He came to see me and told me of his love for McKinley, the good years he had spent there, and that he would deem it a great achievement to retake his first post. I couldn't believe my ears! Here was a tough nut to crack, and he wanted the assignment. We had telephone wire from battalion to Division Headquarters through the intermediate switchboards, and in a few minutes Colonel Quandt, the G3, authorized Colonel Tipton and his battalion to take McKinley. It immediately deployed and commenced the approach on the fort."

Tipton attacked with Company E in the assault, with Roberts and his platoon in the lead. "Suicide parties [Japanese] fought desperate delaying actions but our casualties were comparatively light," wrote Bernheim. "Just inside the Carabao Gate our attack was halted by Division order. The First Cavalry Division had crossed the Pasig River and were working toward us from the northeast corner of the post.

"The rest of the day was spent in killing snipers and watching the Japanese burn the buildings of the old fort. Lieutenant Colonel Tipton was mightily pleased to see some of his braves drop a Japanese just as he was about to set fire to the very house that the CO had occupied when he was stationed there before the war. A tank destroyer's 75mm gun knocked a sniper off a cupola with one round.

"'Seems a helluva way to kill just one little Japanese with such a big shell,' someone commented.

"'We just want to show you it can be done,' purred the TD's commander.

"Aside from local patrolling, the Nichols Field–Fort McKinley fight was over. The kitchens came up and we enjoyed hot meals again. Some of us once more experienced the thrill of American motoring, for we had captured several fine passenger cars in perfect condition. For the next several days we rested but our 1st Battalion was busy, for the [enemy] had withdrawn to a new concentration area in the vicinity of Mabato Point and they were disposed to be very stubborn indeed."

### Mabato Point

Lieutenant Colonel George O. Pearson, 41, was the executive officer of the 187th Glider Infantry Regiment. Before the war, he had been an architectural engineer; in combat, he somehow retained the look of the prototype Wyoming rancher. In 1920, he had enlisted in the 1st Cavalry Regiment of the Wyoming National Guard and served with the Guard until his unit at the time, 115th Cavalry, was mobilized in 1941. On the seventeenth of February, he took over command of the Pierson Task Force, and General Pierson, as he wrote later, "went back to my regular tasks of visiting the different units and making myself available to members of the general and special staffs."

Mabato Point was on high ground on the western shore of Laguna de Bay about two thousand yards south of Fort McKinley. The terrain in front of it was rolling and open. From their well-fortified strong point on the top of Mabato Point, the Japanese had perfect observation and wide, grazing fields of fire. As they had on the rest of the Genko Line, the Japanese, along with indentured Filipinos, had been preparing the defenses of Mabato Point since 1942. The workers had burrowed tunnels through the hill that wound for hundreds of yards underground, occasionally opening into large rooms used for living quarters, hospitals, supply rooms, kitchens, communications centers, headquarters, and even shrines. The entire mass of subways was interconnected so that a Japanese soldier could move from one position to another hundreds of yards away without ever surfacing. All avenues of approach to the catacomblike position were covered by machine-gun, mortar, and artillery fire. Included in the defenders' weapons were quadruple-mounted heavy antiaircraft artillery and two carefully hidden 150mm mortars. The division G2 estimated that the redoubt was manned by about eight hundred Japanese of the Abe Battalion.

One member of the Pearson Task Force wrote that the tactics in reducing Mabato Point were simple: "Blast with air strikes and artillery, attack from vulnerable sides, squeeze the [Japanese] tighter and tighter, and if they tried to escape, slaughter them on their escape routes. Speed was essential. We had no time to bemoan our casualties or lick our wounds. There were times when we could have used a few more trucks or some bigger artillery pieces, but not much time to think about the deficiency."

To attack and reduce Mabato Point, Colonel Pearson held the 3d Battalion of the 19th Infantry on the heights south of Fort McKinley and sent Lt. Col. John L. Strong and his 3d of the 511th to control the southern exits of the area. He put Lt. Col. Harry Wilson and the 1st Battalion of the 187th to the west along the Manila Railroad, which ran from the northwest to the southeast across the area and a few hundred yards from Mabato Point. He assigned Maj. Jay D. Vanderpool and his guerrilla contingent a line across the south road. Colonel Pearson had deployed his Force in an arc surrounding Mabato Point. The 457th Parachute Field Artillery was ready to support the attack with its pack 75s from a position a few hundred yards behind the infantry.

When all of his units were in position, Colonel Pearson launched his attack. Midmorning of the eighteenth, Company B of the 187th, with a Sherman tank and an M-18 tank destroyer, struck due east. Company A also went partially up the hill, but the Japanese mortars drove both companies back. Colonel Pearson reassessed the situation and decided to call in air strikes and all the indirect fire he could to bring to bear on the targets.

That afternoon, P-38s, P-51s, and Marine SBDs blasted the area with thousand-pound bombs and strafing machine-gun fire, and the artillery and tanks fired hundreds of rounds, direct and indirect. But the ground around the Japanese defensive positions was so hard that the aerial bombs merely chipped off pieces of the fortification; the artillery, mortars, and tanks were even less effective. Finally, Colonel Pearson asked for and got napalm attacks. The napalm did two things: it seared off the camouflage of the cave and tunnel entrances, and when a firebomb landed near the tunnel openings, it burned up so much oxygen so rapidly that the enemy soldiers suffocated in the tunnels.

The task force attacked again on the morning of the nineteenth. In the 1st Battalion 187th area, C Company led the assault, aided by a platoon of Sherman tanks and tank destroyers. C Company under Captain Schick made its way partially up the hill but was blasted by the huge mortars. For days, the 1st Battalion 187th had been trying to locate the mortar observers who could bring in fire so accurately. Finally, Capt. Davy Carnahan, the battalion XO, spotted several Japanese in trees. He brought up some riflemen, who knocked them off their perches. The mortar fire subsequently abated.

By 21 February, the enemy was surrounded and cut off from all routes of escape. Colonel Pearson sent patrol boats out on Laguna de Bay to block the Japanese from escaping over the water.

That morning, a group of guerrillas and a young Filipino girl appeared near Colonel Pearson and his command group in the field west of Mabato Point. According to Eli Bernheim, a "comely Filipino phone girl from the barrio of Hagonoy was ushered into Colonel Pearson's presence, where she asked if it were possible for a Japanese medical officer to surrender. Colonel Pearson asked the whereabouts of the officer and she pointed to one of the 'guerrillas,' a nondescript little individual in white shorts and blue sweatshirt." The man promptly surrendered and, through a Nisei interpreter, said that there were perhaps four hundred more Japanese in the Mabato Point area who would surrender unconditionally if given the chance. Colonel Pearson decided that it would be worth a trial and ordered the task force to cease fire.

The Filipino girl's brother volunteered to take a message to the

Japanese commander. He took off on a scrawny horse with a white flag and a message that stated that at 1200 that day all American fire would be halted for half an hour and that any of the defenders who wished to surrender should walk out with their hands over their heads and move toward the American lines.

What happened next is open to some controversy. One version of the story holds that the artillery started to fire on some Japanese who might have been surrendering. The other side of the story holds that the Japanese Abe Battalion commander rejected the offer out of hand, had his men kill the Filipino's horse, and sent the messenger scurrying back to the task-force lines.

Colonel Pearson resumed the attack at 1230 with a series of air strikes, artillery concentrations, and tank and tank-destroyer direct fire on the position. C Company of the 187th led the assault. The Japanese attempted to repulse the attack, but finally, the infantrymen who were advancing along the arc of the attack assaulted the position with rifles, grenades, flamethrowers and fixed bayonets.

That night, all fifteen surviving officers of the Abe Battalion marched, on the commander's order, to Mabato Point and committed hara-kiri. Later that night, a group of the enemy tried to escape down the road to the south, unaware that the 511th and a group of guerrillas had set up ambushes along the road. The result was a slaughter of enemy troops.

Eli Bernheim wrote that "on the twenty-first, we moved without opposition all the way to Mabato Point and found one of the dreaded mortars that had caused us such trouble. The action cost us sixteen dead and forty-eight wounded out of our present-for-duty strength, on 14 February, of 310 men."

By 21 February all organized resistance in the area of Mabato Point, Nichols Field, and Fort McKinley had ceased. By the 25th, both battalions of the 187th had moved by truck to Tagaytay Ridge for a brief respite from battle. The troopers of the 187th found the "ridge ideal with plenty of water available, the area secure, and the sleeping excellent, for the altitude insured cool nights. The scenery was lush and beautiful and the natives were eager to sell us fresh tomatoes to augment our ten-in-one rations." But the tranquillity would be short lived. There were more battles to come and more body bags to fill. The Japanese were far from defeated in the Philippines.

## Southern Luzon

On 10 February, the 11th Airborne Division had passed from Eight Army control to Sixth Army and, in turn, to Gen. Oscar Griswold and XIV Corps. On 23 February, General Griswold gave General Swing a new, broadly defined mission: Destroy all the Japanese forces in Luzon south of Manila. More specifically, this meant the reduction of the Japanese defenses at Macolod, the seizure of Lipa, and the clearance of Route 19, the main road through the Lipa Corridor, for five miles north of Lipa.

Through the guerrilla forces attached to the division and Sixth Army intelligence sources, it was clear to General Swing, and his G2, Lt. Col. Butch Muller, that the Japanese were far from defeated in the area. One enemy force formed a well-dug-in line from Laguna de Bay to Lake Taal along the line Mount Bijiang–Mount Maquiling–Hill 580–Hill 600–Mount Sungay. Another force occupied the Ternate–Pico de Loro sector, driven there during the division's initial drive from Nasugbu. The Japanese also manned a strong defensive position along the Mount Macolod–Lipa Hill–Mount Malepunyo hill masses. A large number of Japanese troops were holed up on the Bicol Peninsula north of Legaspi.

To assist the lightweight 11th Airborne Division, lighter still in that it had received few replacements since its arrival on Luzon, General Griswold assigned to the division the 158th Regimental Combat Team. He told General Swing to open the Manila–Santo Tomas–Lipa–Batangas highway so that the port of Batangas on the southern shore of Luzon could be used to mount further amphibious operations. The Manila-Batangas highway ran in a north-south line along the western shore of Laguna de Bay and then to the east of Lake Taal. In addition to that mission, General Griswold also told General Swing to open Manila Harbor by wiping out the Japanese forces in Ternate, on the southern shore of Manila Bay, southeast of Corregidor.

General Swing knew that his new missions would require total commitment of his seven-infantry-battalion division. At no time in combat did he ever have the luxury of units in reserve. Some of the battalions, by virtue of combat losses, were at an effective present-for-duty strength of just over two hundred fighting soldiers. But General Swing was not a commander to whine or plead his problems to his higher commanders. He knew his division and his subordinate commanders, their skills and esprit, and knew how to employ them most effectively.

The 187th had not yet operated as a regiment on Luzon; its two battalions were habitually attached to one of the other regiments, proving once again the need for a triangular regimental organization, a fact that seems to have been lost on the post–World War II Army reorganizers. But, finally, in early March, the 187th came together to fight as a regiment.

General Swing planned his attack this way: he ordered the 511th and the 187th to attack abreast, 187th on the right, eastward through the narrow neck of land between Lake Taal and Laguna de Bay, an area that was known to be heavily defended; he sent the 158th RCT along two routes, Balayan-Lemery-Bauan-Cuenca and Batangas-Lipa, the two prongs to join at Lipa; he assigned the 1st of the 188th to attack forces entrenched in Ternate and the Pico de Loro Hills on the southern shores of Manila Bay.

Mount Sungay was a large hill mass a few thousand yards above the north shore of Lake Taal. In late February and early March, the 187th was in a bivouac area just to the west of Mount Sungay. The regiment sent out daily patrols to find and plot the enemy positions to its east. Using intelligence data from division G2, 187th patrols, and guerrilla reports, the regimental S2 put together a picture of the enemy locations. He knew that the Japanese Fuji Force had dug into Mount Sungay and continued to prepare its defensive positions.

The 675th Glider Field Artillery Battalion, attached to the 187th, set up firing positions in the vicinity of an old golf course behind the 187th. Lieutenant Ernest L. Massad and his cannoneers harassed the Japanese covering force on Mount Sungay with constant barrages.

While the 11th's infantrymen and cannoneers were fighting the ground battles, the engineers were far from idle. Their main task was carving out roads along the cliffs and defiles in the rugged mountainous terrain around Lake Taal with their small airborne bulldozers, so small that they could fit into a CG-4A glider. One of the roads that they had hacked out was along a steep, sheer cliff on the north side of Lake Taal. The cliff was almost vertical except for razor-like noses that corrugated its surface. The top of the ridge was 2,400 feet above sea level. General Swing reasoned that if the 187th moved down this cliff and took up a position on the right flank of the 511th, it would gain much terrain for which the regiment would otherwise have had to fight by moving overland above it.

About three hundred yards west of Hill 600, the lead elements of the 187th came under extremely heavy mortar and automatic-weapons fire from the Fuji Force defenses, two miles west of Tanauan. The 187th, with the 1st Battalion on the left and the 2d on the right, deployed to double-envelop the Hill. It took three days of heavy fighting through bamboo groves on the north side of the hill for the regiment to overrun the key defensive position, a fortress of pillboxes surrounding a concrete water tank. On top of the hill, the 187th routed the enemy out of an underground garrison of large, interconnected caves. In the ensuing battle, many of the enemy were sealed in the caves where the 187th lead elements heard them screaming and beating against the dirt-filled exits.

On the fifteenth of March, the command of the 187th changed hands: Colonel Hildebrand left the division, and Col. George O. Pearson, formerly the regimental XO, assumed command. Lt. Col. Harry Wilson, USMA 1937, became the executive officer.

After subduing the enemy on Hill 600, the 187th moved east to the town of Tanauan. On 22 March, the regiment was relieved by the 1st Cavalry Division and moved by truck from Tanauan over Tagaytay Ridge south to Lemery, then north to Cuenca.

While the 158th RCT was still attached to the 11th Airborne Division, General Swing had ordered its commander, Brig. Gen. Hanford MacNider, to capture Mount Macolod. The 158th moved to the northeast and attacked and seized two small satellites of Mount Macolod—San Jose and Santa Rosa hills. An element of the RCT also made a frontal attack and overran the town of Cuenca. But before the 158th could take on the far more formidable task of reducing Macolod, General Krueger ordered the 158th out of General Swing's command to prepare for the Bicol Peninsula landing at Legaspi.

Colonel Pearson was assuming command of the 187th just as it was about to fight the bloodiest and, unfortunately, deadliest battle in its history—the reduction of Mount Macolod.

# 3: Mount Macolod

Mount Macolod was more than a speed bump in the road, more than a minor diversion to slow the 11th's and the 187th's fighting trek across southern Luzon. Macolod, some sixty miles south of Manila, was a mountain that rose some 3,107 feet on the southeastern corner of Lake Taal, the magnificent body of water carved out of the terrain by a volcano, centuries ago. The north and west slopes of Mount Macolod rise nearly vertically from the water of the lake. On the east and south sides, the drop is also vertical from about 1,200 feet; then three ridges descend gradually to the bottom of the mountain. Two of these ridges are bare noses leading into the highway that runs through Cuenca and Dita.

The north-south nose was known as Brownie Ridge and the one on the east as Bashore, after the commanders whose companies assaulted them. Brownie Ridge was the strongest position on the mountain and was honeycombed with tunnels and caves. The third ridge was heavily wooded and was actually a saddle connecting Mount Macolod with Bukel Hill, a lesser eminence some five hundred yards due east of Macolod. From the village of Cuenca on the south slope of the mountain a paved highway leads around the east face into the barrio of Dita, then turns sharply toward Lipa.

In the saddle between Macolod and Bukel Hill, on the northeast side of Macolod, the Japanese had constructed another of their diabolically conceived defensive positions. The Japanese had used Filipino laborers to construct the underground tunnels and then had slain the Filipinos when the work was finished to insure the secrecy of the position. From the air, only dummy positions were visible. But beneath the camouflage and the foliage, the mountain bristled with artillery and automatic weapons carefully aimed and emplaced to cover all approaches with an interlocking field of fire. By now, the intelligence team had identified the enemy as elements of the 17th Infantry Regiment reinforced by the 115th Fishing Battalion (Suicide Boat Unit), both units of the Fuji Force, a composite unit under the command of Col. Masatoshi Fujishige. The Fuji Force was responsible for the defense of the region south of Manila.

By the 22d of March, the 187th had completed its truck move from Tanauan to Cuenca and had immediately occupied the positions dug by the departing 158th. For its attack of Macolod, General Swing assigned to the 187th the 760th and 756th Field Artillery Battalions (155mm howitzers); the 472d (105mm howitzers); and the 675th Glider Field Artillery Battalion (sawed-off 105mm howitzers); a company of chemical mortars; a platoon of Sherman tanks from the 44th Tank Battalion; and Company B of the 127th Airborne Engineer Battalion.

When Colonel Pearson assumed command of the regiment, Lt. Col. Harry Wilson left the 1st of the 187th to become the regimental executive officer; Maj. Davy Carnahan replaced Wilson. When Colonel Tipton left the 2d of the 187th to command the 188th, Maj. "Jungle Jim" Loewus, recently arrived from the States, replaced Tipton.

On the night of 23 March, a guerrilla patrol had probed east of Dita and lost six men in a firefight even though the artillery forward observer with the patrol had been able to call in artillery fire on the enemy position. The next morning, Colonel Pearson sent G and F Companies to clear out the area. In the attack, tanks with the infantry battered down houses in the area, and the engineers deactivated land mines as the two companies moved through the outskirts of Dita. But the enemy was far from beaten. Northwest of the village, the Japanese, hidden in concealed caves, stopped the attack with heavy ground-grazing fire. Seven 187th troopers were wounded, including Captain Merritt, G Company's commander. Private First Class Arnold L. Baier was killed. At dark that night, the two companies withdrew to a perimeter two hundred yards south of Dita and the Japanese moved back into the village.

Colonel Pearson realized that constant infantry patrolling was not going to get the job done. He knew from the Japanese raids and the volume of their fire that he was opposing a strong force, well concealed and well armed. He knew that he needed air strikes and massive artillery fire to pound the positions before he sent his infantrymen in again.

On 24 March, beginning at 0900, the four battalions of artillery supporting the 187th concentrated on the area and the four fingers of Bukel Hill. A squadron of P-47s made a number of bombing runs and then strafed the village and the area around it. F and G Companies again tried to drive the enemy out of Dita with house-to-house fighting, somewhat of a rarity to the 187th soldiers, schooled as they were in the mud of Leyte and the open fields east of Manila. The intensity of the Japanese defensive machine-gun fire again halted the attack. Lieutenant William S. Massey, SSgt. Edwin A. Echols, and Privates Andrew Zrenchak and Gustav W. Lundt were killed, and a number of other 187th soldiers were wounded. The regiment estimated that thirty of the enemy were killed in the action. But it was also becoming apparent that the Japanese were stashed safely away deep in their underground tunnels during the bombing and strafing runs.

On 27 March, following a 4.2-inch mortar barrage by the 85th Chemical Battalion and air strikes using napalm, the 1st of the 187th swept around the village to positions north of Dita. The 1st Battalion continued its attack and, after more air strikes and artillery barrages, seized and dug in on Bukel Hill; the 2d Battalion held the key position near Dita.

For an attack on 28 March, Colonel Pearson sent both of his battalions in a frontal assault between ridges into the Macolod area. G Company, under its new commander, Capt. William M. "Buzz" Miley Jr., from the 511th, attacked with flamethrowers and burned out three enemy bunkers. But shortly the company came under heavy machine-gun fire that slowed its pace. E Company fanned out to the west of G Company. Both companies managed to fight to the top of a crest, although E Company was pinned down by heavy machine-gun fire from ravines to the west.

Earl Urish, who eventually became the first sergeant of E Company, 187th, was a private when he arrived in the Philippines in March with a number of replacements. Thirty-three of them were assigned to E Company. His first action was in the attack on Macolod.

"This was our baptism into combat," he wrote years later. "As we moved up the trail, Loewus (the 2d Battalion, 187th, commander) moved forward through our squad. I remember being surprised that he was wearing his insignia of rank. In a short time, we heard sniper fire ahead, then heavier Ml fire as our riflemen cleared out the snipers. Shortly, Loewus came back down the trail, a large bloodstained bandage covering his chest, two men supporting and carrying him.

"Loewus had been hit in the shoulder. About a hundred yards down the trail, the men carrying him put him down. He looked up and saw

Lt. Eli Bernheim, his S4. Loewus said, 'Boy, what I wouldn't give for a shot of Scotch.' The ever resourceful Bernheim reached into his musket bag and pulled out two small bottles of Black and White. He gave one to the major lying on the ground and drank one himself. Major Loewus was evacuated and replaced by Maj. Nat 'Bud' Ewing.

"With the snipers cleared out, we continued the advance," wrote Urish. "We had moved forward another hundred yards when Nambu machine guns opened up on both flanks and then to our front. Scrambling for cover, dragging the wounded along, we were completely pinned down by interlocking fields of fire. Predictably, the [Japanese] immediately started dropping knee mortars in on us. . . .In an orderly fighting withdrawal, [Ewing] saved his command to fight another day. E Company brought back its eleven wounded as we came off the mountain, thankful there no KIAs."

Both battalions of the 187th were forced to withdraw from the crest of the hill. Their new positions encircled the landward sides of Mount Macolod. But they were by no means out of enemy range. G Company was in a perimeter south of the Dita schoolhouse. At midnight, the company repulsed yet another Japanese banzai attack on its position. At 0500 the next morning, fifty Japanese swept F Company's and its attached guerrillas' perimeter with mortars and heavy machine guns. Result: eleven guerrillas were killed, ten wounded; Pfc. Francis T. McCoy killed; several F Company men, including Lt. James W. Roberts, wounded.

During the period 29 March–1 April, the 2d Battalion held a position near Dita. Heavy air strikes paved the way for the 1st Battalion to seize and dig in on Bukel Hill. But the Japanese continued early-morning banzai attacks, costly in men for both battalions. Sergeant Dowal D. Coplen, G Company, Sgt. Frank J. Lasala, C Company, and Pfc. Warren T. Miller, E Company, were killed in action.

On the night of 1–2 April, Staff Sergeant Ellis of C Company was in an outpost on Bukel Hill with his platoon. At about 0115, Ellis decided that he had to relieve himself outside his slit trench. He took the required three steps away and, in the kunai grass around the trench, found himself face to face with a Japanese officer about to attack him with his samurai saber. Ellis beat him to the draw and killed the officer with his .45-caliber pistol. "Deprived of their leader, the other [Japanese] turned tail and did not reappear that night," wrote Eli Bernheim later.

"On 2 April, the battalions attacked with all companies on line, and this time they were able to clear the area, as far as the base of the mountains, although they were unable to gain and keep a hold on the ridges, and one pocket of resistance remained between the two southern finger ridges," wrote the 187th historian.

On about 3 April, Capt. Cletus N. Schommer, the battalion S2; the motor officer; and a sergeant were ambushed by a Japanese patrol along the highway near Talisay. The three men were killed. In the face of heavy machine-gun and mortar fire, a foot patrol led by Lieutenant Bernheim went into the area and recovered the bodies.

It was obvious to Colonel Pearson that the Japanese held Talisay with a sizable force. He decided to attack. At 0700 on the fifth, F and G Companies started to move cross-country toward Talisay. At about the same time, Japanese 155mm artillery shells landed in Colonel Pearson's command post in a coconut grove near Guenting, where he was forming up the task force. Fortunately, the CP group was able to jump into foxholes previously dug by the 511th when it was in the area. About 1,500 yards from the barrio, F and G were hit by the same 155mm guns that had hit the 187th command post. The companies did not have a chance to dig in, and the men slid into nearby ravines. Tank destroyers moved to the Lipa highway under the artillery fire. The 674th Glider Field Artillery Battalion, commanded by Lt. Col. Robert L. Johnson, supporting the 187th, was caught on the move by the enemy artillery fire. Colonel Johnson had his battalion "execute a quick column left and move into positions along the highway to open counterbattery fire," wrote the 187th historian. "This sharp artillery action silenced the guns to the east before they could completely decimate the 2d Battalion."

On 6 April, G Company patrolling near Lumbang ran into a Japanese force of some seventy men. The company killed thirty of them. Other patrols probed the area and found piles of enemy equipment and munitions, some of it booby-trapped with airplane bombs. After an air strike and the concentrated fire of three artillery battalions, the 2d Battalion moved through the town of Sulac. Near the town, the men found "the gruesome remains of one hundred Filipinos who had been massacred by the [enemy] and thrown into a ravine," wrote the 187th historian.

During the period 3 to 17 April, the 187th probed the area of Macolod but did not launch an all-out attack to throw the enemy off the mountain. The 1st Battalion probed the ravines and gullies that wrinkled the surface of the mountain. On the seventh of April, the 1st mounted an attack, preceded by heavy artillery fire. A Company, led by Captain Carter, attacked along a forefinger of the hill, now known as Brownie Ridge. C Company moved up the north side of Cuenca Ravine; B Company was to the right of C. Major Carnahan's plan of attack had the companies converge at the head of the ravine. During the move up the hill, there was little enemy opposition. But when the companies met, the Japanese assaulted them with machine-gun, sniper, and mortar fire from camouflaged spider holes. Killed in the hail of fire were Capt. Paul G. Bashore, B Company's commander, noted for his aggressiveness ever since B Company's first combat action near Buri, on Leyte. Also killed were Pvt. Julian C. Palfrey, also of B Company, and SSgt. Travis B. Hawkins, of C Company. A number of 1st Battalion men were wounded.

While the Japanese artillery was pounding the 2d of the 187th near Sulac, an artillery air observer spotted a muzzle flash in a dense growth and poured in heavy artillery counterbattery fire. When the troops finally reached the area, they found that Colonel Fujishige, apparently unaware of the need to spread out his guns, had massed all of his artillery in one position. The counterbattery fire had effectively knocked out the bulk of the guns.

By this time, the 1st Battalion was a tired unit. Constant losses, a few each day, took their toll on the rank and file. And little progress had been made in reducing Macolod. "An estimated force of a few more than one hundred Japanese in an area of five hundred square yards had stopped us at every turn, this despite the concentrations of four battalions of artillery, a chemical mortar platoon, and continuous air strikes," wrote lst Lt. Eli Bernheim later.

"Yet we knew our riflemen were aggressive and bold and that our junior officer leadership was superb. In fact, the operation had, to date, cost us six fine officers, seven squad or platoon leaders, and a disquieting number of privates. One must realize that the regiment at the start of the affair consisted of two half-strength airborne battalions and a headquarters. And one must see the tangles, blind ravines, terraces, and saddles of that terrain to appreciate the problem confronting us."

On the night of 17 April, Private Harkink of F Company, "a bustling lad of twenty-two," had an eerie feeling. He had been in all of F Company's fights, but somehow he felt that his luck had run out. According to the historian, "Private Harkink and four of his pals from F Company returned from a well-deserved but unauthorized 'rest period' and cheerfully received, as a 'reward,' the precarious honor of acting as lead scouts for Company A, to which they had attached themselves. . . . Harkink solemnly inventoried his possessions and asked his pals to mail them and several sizable money orders to his sister. 'Tomorrow I am going to get it,' he predicted."

On the morning of 18 April, Harkink was killed near the head of A Company as it moved up a ravine to the right side of Bashore Ridge.

All during the night of 18–19 April, the enemy soldiers tried to infiltrate the perimeter to blow up the tanks and tank destroyers. Lieutenant William A. Clark, liaison officer to the guerrillas with the 1st Battalion, Pfc. Delbert R. McGrew, and nineteen of Colonel Moreno's band of guerrillas were killed. Colonel Moreno was badly wounded.

Colonel Pearson readied his task force for an all-out assault on Macolod. He placed some tank destroyers along the highway just west of Dita, where they could fire directly into the mouths of the caves in the side of the mountain. He moved some 155mm howitzers up to the front lines, where they could fire directly on the caves with armor-piercing shells. "At night," wrote the 11th Airborne historian, "howitzers and tanks were surrounded with perimeters and left as bait to encourage banzai attacks—long ago found to be the most profitable method of attacking the Japanese. For three days, a campaign of heckling was waged against the [enemy] in Macolod. Every second of the day and night some type of bullet landed among the Japanese positions—a burst of machine-gun fire, a mortar round, an artillery volley—no rest for the wicked, we thought, and with some it worked, for they stood up screaming, and were shot."

Colonel Pearson on the eighteenth of April launched his coordinated attack with his two battalions abreast, the 1st on the right, in a semicircle around the south and east slopes of the mountain. The 1st Battalion seized Bukel Hill and retained it as a point of departure. The troops found the going slow and rough, especially across the bare face of Brownie Ridge, where they had to run and crouch through machine-gun and mortar fire. The tank destroyers and the tanks fired directly into the cave targets. Captain Buzz Miley and his reinforced G Company moved out the afternoon of 19 April up the south side of the mountain with no opposition. He wrote of his attack down the mountain:

"We arrived at the top of Mount Macolod about 1500 and attacked down the west slope at daylight the next morning. The major concern was that we moved over shoulder to shoulder and expanded to cover the ridges and draws to the bottom. Caves and gun positions could not be bypassed and progress had to be slow since the personnel in the draws could not see those in the next draw. An excess of grenades were thrown down the slopes and into the caves. A large number of Japanese ran down the slope as soon as they realized we were above them and a large number ran out of the caves after a grenade was thrown in. Each cave was blown shut by the Engineers—536 radios were used to keep the platoons and squads abreast and to keep from allowing the Japanese to criss-cross to our rear."

In one episode in the fight down the hill, Sgt. Daniel R. Morris of G Company threw a grenade into a cave; it came back out. Sergeant Morris held the next grenade a little longer after he pulled the pin; this one exploded inside the cave. After the blast, Sergeant Morris could hear the Japanese moving around inside the cave on a boardwalk. In a few minutes, eighteen Japanese, wearing gas masks and with bayonets on their rifles, streamed out of the cave and skidded down the ravine. Harrison, a BAR man in G Company, killed them all. Lieutenant Anzerone with his platoon, now down to eleven men, picked off a number of snipers with his M1 before he was hit for a second time in the campaign. Private Campbell, the last of three brothers to be killed in combat in World War II, was killed coming down the ridge.

On 19 April, the 1st Battalion held its position and sealed all the caves in its area. C Company rolled drums of gasoline into the caves near Cuenca Ravine and then ignited them with grenades. The resulting fires killed a number of the enemy, cleared off the vegetation, and prevented the Japanese from infiltrating between C and B Companies.

By the twentieth of April, the battle for Macolod was over. That day, the regiment had lost a total of thirteen killed and eleven wounded. One of the wounded was Pfc. Archie Miller, whose Purple Heart on Macolod was the fifth he had earned on Luzon. To his fellow troopers of the 187th, he was known as the "Purple Heart Kid." His wounds kept him in the hospital for thirty-three days.

As the troops of the 187th trailed out of the ridges and ravines of Macolod, they turned over the mountain to guerrillas to prevent scattered, roving bands of Japanese from returning to their caves, rations, and ammunition caches.

When Buzz Miley and his troopers reached the bottom of the mountain, they saw an unusual sight: Sitting on the ground on a small rise near what had been the 1st Battalion's line of departure was Lt. Gen. Oscar Griswold, the commander of XIV Corps, with his chin cupped in his hands. He wanted to be in on the finale of the battle of Mount Macolod.

The battle for Macolod had been a bloody battle for the 187th. "In the months that we remained on Luzon," Urish wrote, "nothing would animate a group of 187th troopers so much as walking up and announcing that a Japanese force had moved back onto Macolod and the 187th had orders to dislodge them pronto. A sobering thought indeed. The kind that spawns bad dreams. And perhaps not entirely beyond the realm of possibility when you remember that Yamashita still had over fifty thousand soldiers in the Sierra Madre when the war ended."

General Fujishige was captured on Luzon at the end of the war. Colonel Ed Lahti, CO of the 511th, and Lt. Col. Henry J. Muller, the G2 of the 11th during combat, interviewed General Fujishige in Manila on 27 May 1946 in Luzon POW Camp No. 1.

One of the questions was this one: "How long had you worked preparing the positions on Macolod?"

His answer: "About one month. I personally made a seven-day reconnaissance of it and planned and organized the defense myself. My positions were so placed and camouflaged that they could not be seen by ground or air observation. This was the best position in southern Luzon. My subordinates prepared the other ones and they were not as good. Some of my best troops were on Mount Macolod. I actually cried when the commander was killed. This person who attacked this position did a good job and should be awarded the highest honor your army could give."

## The Mop Up

After the fall of Macolod, the one remaining Japanese stronghold in the 11th's area of operations in southern Luzon was Mount Malepunyo, a welter of conical hills covered with tangled rainforest and bamboo thickets, surrounded by precipitous slopes and interlaced with sharp ridges. The highest peak rose 3,160 feet above the plains of southern Luzon. There were no roads and only poorly kept jungle trails within the thirty-square-mile area of the mountain, requiring that the troops hand-carry small loads, Filipino bearers resupply and evacuate casualties, and two-seater, artillery observation Cub planes drop some emergency supplies.

General Griswold felt that Malepunyo was such a formidable Japanese bastion that he had originally planned to reduce Malepunyo with two divisions, the 1st Cavalry and the 11th Airborne. By this time, General Swing had set up his division CP in a schoolhouse in Lipa. There, late on the night of the twenty-second, he received a phone call from General Griswold, who told him that he still had the mission of reducing Malepunyo but that, instead of the whole 1st Cavalry Division, he would have attached for the operation only the 8th Cavalry Regiment from the 1st Cavalry.

General Swing's plan of attack deployed the 187th, shorthanded and weary after its fight for Macolod, to Tiaong to relieve the 188th and to prevent the retreat of the Japanese out of Malepunyo to the east. He moved the 188th, when relieved by the 187th, to Alaminos to attack due south. He held the 8th Cav in position at the mouth of what was known as the Grand Canyon, a gorge on the northeast slope of the mountain. Swing assigned the main effort to the 511th, which was on the right flank of the 8th Cav, to attack east along the Malaraya Hill canyon, and then move north to join the 188th and a special battalion-sized task force, TF Ciceri, named after its commander, Maj. John Ciceri of the 511th.

The division artillery commander, Brig. Gen. Frank Farrell, had gathered seven battalions of artillery, some organic and some attached, and spread them out around the foot of the mountain. B Company of the 637th Tank Destroyer Battalion, A Company of the 44th Medium Tank Battalion, and C Company of the 85th Chemical Mortar Battalion (4.2 in.) were also deployed for the attack. The artillerymen of D Battery, 457th Parachute Field Artillery Battalion (normally supposed to be an antitank outfit, but whose pack howitzers were admittedly grossly ineffective against tanks), broke down their pack 75s and lugged them up the side of the mountain to fire at the caves above the infantrymen instead of in front of them.

The 187th's area of responsibility was a large arc around the northern shore of Lake Taal. Colonel Pearson located his regimental CP and the 2d Battalion at Tanauan; the 1st Battalion, directly under division control, was at Tiaong, to cut off the Japanese retreating from Malepunyo.

At dawn on the twenty-seventh of April, General Swing launched his attack. The artillery fired some five thousand rounds of mixed-caliber howitzers in front of the infantry all around the base and sides of the mountain. Fighter-bombers pounded the enemy strongholds so close at times in front of the infantry that blood sprang from the noses and ears of the 511th troopers. The 511th paratroopers were so close because they noticed that the enemy went underground when they heard the planes and, immediately after the bombing, raced out of their caves to their fighting positions. By being so near, the 511th troopers killed many of the Japanese as they moved out of their caves and bunkers after the bomb runs.

By the thirtieth of April, after more close air strikes, hundreds of rounds of artillery, and after a bloody fight using rifles, hand grenades, mortars, and flamethrowers, the 511th was on the high ground of Malepunyo. Colonel Ed Lahti, the regimental commander, ordered all of his battalions to patrol the draws and slopes to flush out the last remnants of the Japanese Fuji Heiden. The patrols found large caves connected by wire communications and stocked with large stores of ammunition and supplies. Captured documents confirmed the contention of Lt. Col. Butch Muller, the 11th's G2, that the mountain fortress was the last stronghold of General (sometimes referred to as Colonel) Fujishige's Southern Luzon Defensive Force, the Fuji Heiden.

In General Fujishige's interrogation after the war, he indicated that his headquarters was in the Malepunyo area and that he "had about 1,200 men left [on Malepunyo] in the latter part of April." He also said that the strength near his headquarters was "three to four hundred, of which I took direct command during the attack by American forces." In answer to the question, "Did you ever visit your frontline units?" he said, "Yes, I went to the Mount Macolod–Cuenca area early in March and also had direct command of my troops in Malepunyo. My two horses had been killed and my car broke down, so I could not visit any other areas."

The 187th had deployed its two battalions along the likely escape routes of the Fuji Force. Major Davy Carnahan, the commander of the 1st of the 187th, remembers, "We laid ambushes up and down the river for a distance of some ten miles, endeavoring to cover every possible crossing. In those ambushes we accounted for some four hundred Japanese captured and killed. . . . About 2400 hours one night, movement across the bridges was noticed. The ambushers were alerted, and the [enemy] started across all three bridges simultaneously. In the uncertain light the men noticed some strange-looking objects among the columns of [Japanese], but couldn't identify them. . . . The surprise was complete and deadly, some one hundred [enemy] being killed and wounded, including quite a few high-ranking officers. One of our captives told us that we had just missed capturing General Fujishige, commander of all forces in southern Luzon, by a matter of seconds.

"The strange-looking objects that had so startled us and bewildered the men turned out to be sedan chairs, that all the ranking [Japanese] officers were being carried in."

During his interrogation, Fujishige was asked if he had left Malepunyo in a sedan chair carried by his men. He said, "I did not. I walked out personally leading about two hundred men."

During May, more replacements began to arrive. In May, the division had shifted to a new T O and E (Table of Organization and Equipment) that had, in effect, added a battalion to each of the former glider regiments, made the 188th Infantry and 674th Field Artillery parachute units, and added the 472d Field Artillery Battalion to Division Artillery. The 187th became a Para-Glider Infantry Regiment. The strength of the division increased from 8,600 to more than 12,000.

General Swing—indeed the entire Far East Command staff and command and the Joint Chiefs—expected that, in spite of Germany's unconditional surrender to the Allies on 7 May 1945, an invasion of Japan was a requirement for total victory. Thirty divisions from the ETO (European Theater of Operations) were on their way to the Far East. General MacArthur's headquarters had the plans ready: Operation Olympic, on 1 November 1945, an invasion of Kyushu with some 766,700 troops under General Walter Krueger, to secure airfields for the eventual invasion of Honshu; Operation Coronet, the invasion of Honshu, on 1 March 1946. General MacArthur had the men: in the summer of 1945, there were 1.4 million men in the Philippines ready to deploy; by December, there would be an additional 1 million. And the 11th Airborne had a part to play in both operations: in Olympic, a floating reserve; but in Coronet, the division would play a far more important role. According to the division G4, Maj. John Conable, "We were to be the lead division of XVIII Airborne Corps under General Ridgway. Our division and the 13th Airborne Division were to parachute onto the peninsula forming the east side of Tokyo Bay and establish a beachhead for a couple of armored divisions. . . . I can remember poring over aerial photographs of the area, trying to find some decent jump fields. We didn't find any."

General Swing wanted all of his men—especially the replacements—to be combat ready. He told his commanders to work the new men gradually into combat readiness by assigning them in small numbers to the patrols mopping up around the bivouac areas.

On 1 May, the division recon platoon reported contact with a Japanese company-sized unit in the vicinity of Aya and Calaway along Tagaytay Ridge. The contact was in the 187th's area of responsibility. Major Bud Ewing, CO of the 2d of the 187th, assigned F Company, reinforced with a section of 81mm mortars and a section of light machine guns (LMGs), to assault the enemy unit. F Company moved out of its bivouac area at dawn on the second. In short order, the company found the Japanese stronghold from which they poured out a heavy volume of automatic weapons and rifle fire. F Company spread out and attacked the position from three sides. One of the squads, which included a high percentage of new men, was led by Pfc. Joe R. Siedenberg, a veteran of Letye and Luzon.

Siedenberg deployed his men, led them in an assault on the Japanese position, overran the Japanese in his area, and killed twenty-seven of the enemy, with no loss to any of his men. The total kill for F Company that day was ninety-two enemy; that evening, the company had one man missing.

The next day, 3 May, Siedenberg was not so lucky. As his squad crept up a wooded draw late in the afternoon, it was pinned down by heavy automatic-weapons fire. One of his new men was wounded in the opening burst and fell to the ground, exposed to more Japanese fire. Siedenberg crawled across the open area to the wounded man. On the way, he was hit in the chest, but he crept on, gathered up the wounded soldier, and turned back to cover with rest of the squad. On the way back, he was hit twice more by Japanese small arms, but he continued to crawl and carry the wounded man to relative safety. Back with his squad, Siedenberg died of his wounds. Later he was awarded the Distinguished Service Cross for his gallantry. (After the war, and during the Occupation, the 11th Airborne's first post on Hokkaido was named Camp Siedenberg in his honor.)

In General Fujishige's interrogation in Manila, one question asked his opinion of American strategy and tactics. "I believe the strategy was good," he said, "but I do not know about American tactics as I did not personally observe small-unit actions." Another question: "Did you observe any faults in the American soldier?" "From the reports I received," he said, "the American soldier was courageous, but he needlessly exposed himself by advancing across open ground in the line of fire of our weapons. He stood up too much and fired too much but I suppose it was all right because he had plenty of ammunition."

By 10 May, the division had regrouped and had established a base camp on the outskirts of the devastated city of Lipa. The patrols and outposts continued apace. The men of the division who were not on patrols or outposts spent the first two weeks of May building camps in the coconut groves and around the airstrip near Lipa and in the area between Macolod and Malepunyo. Rows of neatly aligned pyramidal tents covered the open areas. The rainy season in May required the troops to floor the tents with bamboo or steel matting about a foot off the ground. Division Special Services built an amphitheater in a natural bowl near Mataasnakahoy for the traveling USO shows, division boxing matches, and movies.

On 8 May we heard over the radio that Germany had unconditionally surrendered to the Allies," wrote the 187th historian. "We were happy for all the men who had been fighting the battles of Europe, but we knew that there was still a large job to be done in the Pacific. Perhaps our days of fighting on a shoestring were almost over with."

Another milestone in the history of the 187th and the 11th Airborne was marked on 11 May. It was the first day since 31 January—a total of 101 consecutive days—that men of the division had not killed an enemy soldier. In the preceding days on Luzon, the division's troopers had killed an average of 93.8 Japanese per day. These were the ones who could have been counted; numberless others were dead in sealed caves and tunnels.

On the twenty-ninth of May, elements of the 187th took over the mission of garrisoning Manila from the 20th Infantry and came under the direct command of the Sixth Army provost marshal. Manila was in dire straits. Vast residential areas had been destroyed, industries were almost nonexistent, utilities were only marginally effective, and thousands of Manila's citizens had been murdered by the retreating Japanese. Among other tasks, the 187th rooted out surviving enemy soldiers, directed traffic, and placed twenty-four-hour guards on all business, residential, and port areas, to include the dance halls springing up throughout the city. In general, the 187th helped control a city whose police force had not yet been reestablished.

When the regiment returned to its base camp near Lipa, it spent two weeks finishing up its housing area and reorganized under its new T O and E. The 1st and 2d Battalions furnished officers and NCO cadres for the new 3d Battalion. In the old companies, the plan moved one third of the original veterans to the new companies and filled the ranks throughout the regiment with new men. Each company ended up with one-half to one-third veterans.

With the new T O and E, all the men of the division could now become parachute qualified. General Swing established the division's third parachute school on the south side of the Lipa airstrip. He also set up a glider school. The Lipa strip had been built by the Japanese and had been used to launch the parachute force that attacked the 11th Airborne Division command post near San Pablo, Leyte. The division engineers converted the old Japanese control tower into a forty-foot jump tower complete with slanting cables and instructors shouting, "Don't look at the ground—hold your heads up." The engineers also built tumbling pits, suspended harness frames, and a right- and left-hand mock plane-door. In about two months, the parachute school turned out over a thousand newly qualified paratroopers, including most of the former glider-riders from the 187th. The parachute course was brief: six half days of ground training and then five jumps from C-46s and C-47s the next week.

The glider school concentrated on equipment loading and "snatch pickups," a system whereby a CG-4A glider is at rest on the ground with its towrope attached in a loop to a vertical frame off to the side. For the pickup, a C-47, with a large hook dangling outside the plane, attached to a rope on a drum inside, roars by the glider at about fifteen feet altitude, hooks the noose of the glider towrope, and hauls the glider from a dead stop to some 120 miles an hour in a few seconds. Obviously, the "snatch pickup" was used infrequently.

By mid-June, the Japanese forces had been pushed back into the northwest corner of Luzon. The 37th Division was pushing north up the Cagayan River Valley along Highway 5. Guerrillas controlled the west bank of the Cagayan Valley. At the northern end of Luzon was a port named Aparri. In order to seal off that port, General Krueger decided to send an airborne task force to seal off Aparri. General Swing formed the Gypsy Task Force, some 1,030 men from the 511th, the 457th Parachute Field Artillery Battalion, a platoon from the 127th Engineers, and two platoons from B Company, 187th Infantry. Lt. Col. Henry Burgess, CO of the 1st of the 511th, was the commander. For the first time in the history of the Pacific Theater, gliders were used in combat. Somehow, the air corps had assembled six CG-4A's and one CG-13. For the parachute units, Col. John Lackey, CO of the 317th Troop Carrier Group, had assembled fifty-four C-47s and thirteen C-46s. The task force began loading at 0430 on the twenty-third of June.

The first plane off the Lipa strip was a C-47 piloted by Colonel Lackey. The rest of the planes followed and formed a V of V's, with the seven gliders bringing up the rear of the column. Fighter aircraft circled overhead. At 0900, Colonel Lackey spotted the 11th Airborne's Pathfinders' colored smoke on the drop zone at Camalaniugan Airfield, a few miles south of Aparri. The jumpers landed in the proper drop zone but the casualties were high: two men were killed with parachute malfunctions and seventy were injured—a high casualty rate of about 7 percent. Part of the problem was the high winds of twenty to twenty-five miles an hour and the rough terrain on the DZ, much of which was flooded rice paddies, carabao wallows, and bomb craters hidden by tall and thick kunai grass.

Burgess assembled his force and headed south to meet the 37th Division moving north. He met Gen. Robert Beightler on 23 June near the

Paret River, thirty-five miles south of Camalaniugan. For Sixth Army, the meeting of elements of the 11th and the 37th Division marked the strategic end of the campaign in northern Luzon.

During June and July, the 11th was totally involved in retraining, R and R, and reorganization. In late June, Col. Ducat McEntee arrived in the Philippines with his 541st Parachute Infantry Regiment aboard the USS *Johnson*. Colonel McEntee had organized the 541st from scratch in 1943 but had seen it depleted time after time to provide replacements for the European Theater airborne divisions. This time, he thought that the regiment would remain intact and be assigned as a unit to the 11th. But that was not to be. As soon as he debarked in Manila, Colonel McEntee was ordered to deactivate his regiment and assign his men to the 11th Airborne as replacements.

The 187th troopers, of course, had no idea of what was going to happen in the war or to them, in particular. "By the beginning of August," wrote the 187th historian, "there were all kinds of rumors making the rounds. It was said that we were supposed to jump ahead of the forces making the landings on Japan; at other times, we were scheduled to land in China, and for a while, Formosa was the favored DZ. The air corps was reportedly betting large sums, giving ten-to-one odds, that the war would be over by September 1st. Members of the 187th, always ready to pick up a little extra money, searched feverishly, but unsuccessfully, for those bettors. History has shown that we saved by not finding the betting air corps."

In August, the war in the Pacific took dramatic turns: on 6 August, the *Enola Gay* dropped an atomic bomb over Hiroshima; on 9 August, *Bock's Car* dropped a second atomic bomb on Nagasaki; on 10 August, Japan decided to surrender; on 14 August, Emperor Hirohito took the unprecedented step of addressing the nation to inform his people that Japan had accepted the Allied surrender terms; on 15 August, President Truman announced the end of the war in the Pacific.

At 0430 on the morning of 11 August, the 11th Airborne duty officer awoke General Swing with a long top-secret message that alerted the division to be prepared to move all combat elements and equipment by air on forty-eight hours' notice to a staging area on Okinawa for the eventual occupation of Japan. In short, the message meant that General MacArthur, recently appointed the supreme commander for the Allied

Powers, had selected the 11th Airborne Division to lead the Allies in occupying Japan.

At that time, I was a major, the division G3 Air. I flew up to FEAF Headquarters at 0530 that Saturday morning, 11 August. When I first arrived in the headquarters, the FEAF (Far East Air Force) operations officer, Col. Francis C. Gideon, told me that the planes would start arriving in Lipa in forty-eight hours. A few minutes later, the situation changed dramatically: Colonel Gideon told me to fly back to the 11th's CP, "right now," because the planes were already on the way to Lipa and would be arriving that afternoon.

Thus began for the 11th Airborne and the 187th another chapter in a relatively short but action-packed history.

# 4: Occupation of Japan

### Initial Occupation

On the 11th of August, a Saturday, Col. George Pearson had a phone call from Col. Douglass P. Quandt, the division G3. "This is an alert," Quandt told him. "Have your regiment ready to move out by air forty-eight hours from now. My staff will tell you what fields to use and generally what kind of planes you'll have. We don't know for sure yet because the air corps is still rounding up all the transports and bombers they can find to move the division out of here."

Colonel Pearson had an immediate unit commanders meeting, gave the order, and told them to get ready—post haste. The unit commanders returned to their bivouac areas, assembled their company commanders, and put out the word. In the next few hours, the commanders called all of their men back from the rest camps and weekend passes and had them standing by in their company areas. The commanders sorted out which men and equipment would fly to Okinawa and which men and equipment would follow by LST. Then they inspected the men and their equipment to make certain that each man had the proper military and personal gear for the trip, an historic event from either the unit or the individual viewpoint.

On the eleventh of August, the lead elements of the 11th Airborne Division left Luzon. At 2300 on the twelfth, a G3 staffer phoned Colonel Pearson to tell him that, at 0630 the next morning, trucks would arrive in his area to move his regiment to Nichols and Nielson Fields for air movement to Okinawa. Once there, Colonel Pearson learned, he would set up a very temporary camp—that meant the troops would bivouac in pup tents—to await the final peace terms settlement and the details of the air move of the 11th to spearhead the occupation of Japan.

At 1053 on the thirteenth, planes of the 54th Troop Carrier Wing took off from Nichols Field carrying the lead elements of the 187th to Okinawa. They landed at 1645 that afternoon. The rest of the regiment took off as soon as the Air Corps Troop Carrier Command could fly in the aircraft. Eventually, C-46s, C-47s, and B-24s—absent their bomb loads and with troops crammed into the bomb bays—carried elements of the

126

187th to Naha, Kadena, and Yotan Fields on Okinawa. The regiment closed on the eighteenth. A rear echelon of eight-six men under the command of Maj. William S. Bowers, the regimental S3, stayed at Lipa long enough to bring forward the heavy regimental organizational equipment by ship.

One problem facing the unit commanders of the 187th was that some of the young Filipino lads who had attached themselves to various soldiers during the days of combat somehow ended up on Okinawa with their heroes. They were sent back to Luzon, very reluctantly, as soon as the unit commanders found them and return transportation was available.

By the fifteenth of August, the bulk of the 11th had closed on Okinawa. The 54th TC Wing had rounded up 99 B-24s, 351 C-46s, and 151 C-47s to airlift 11,100 men, 1,161,000 pounds of equipment, and 120 special-purpose jeeps for communications, command, and supply.

But for the next two weeks, the division and the 187th were stuck on Okinawa, waiting for the details of the final negotiations. The weather was a combination of New Guinea and Leyte—blindingly hot one day and soaking wet the next. The commanders had expected the division to remain on Okinawa for a week at the most, and all heavy equipment, including the kitchens, were moving up by water. Consequently, the men lived in pup tents and ate ten-in-one, C, or K rations, cooked on squad cookers, rations tiresome after even just one day.

The terrain of Okinawa was rugged. Cleared and smooth campsites had already been taken and were still occupied by the troops who had fought for the island. The 187th had to set up its campsite on the sides of hills, several of which were Ryukuan cemeteries dotted with small tombs. "The opening into the tombs, which had been dug into the hillside, was in the shape of a heart, each hill having dozens of these hearts," remembers Gen. Albert Pierson, the assistant division commander of the 11th. On the hillsides, the heavy rains formed rivulets through the lines of pup tents. "Strong, hot winds sprang up," said one frustrated trooper. "The pup tents blossomed out like parachutes and took off."

The troops listened to endless lectures and orientations on the Japanese people, their customs, and their country. The troops were warned that no one knew exactly how the Japanese would react to the occupation: for this reason, the 11th would arrive in Japan "combat-loaded." There was even talk that this move was one gigantic hoax, and that thousands of well-trained, die-hard Japanese soldiers were waiting to slaughter the troops as they unloaded at Atsugi.

For the final leg of the trip to Japan, the division staff had a great deal of work and planning to accomplish. Major General William O. Ryan, the commander of the Air Transport Command—Pacific, was running the Okinawa-to-Japan leg of the move. In mid-August, he still could not determine what type and what number of aircraft would be available for the final leg. Nor did he know such basic facts as the size of the runways and the facilities at Atsugi to handle a steady stream of C-54s.

Even at this late date, General Swing still thought that he might be given a mission of parachuting a major portion of his division into the environs of Tokyo. On the twenty-fourth of August, he wrote to General March: "As you know, we have been sitting here prepared to drop on Tokyo in five hours' notice since the twelfth." But that mission never came off even though, on Okinawa, jumpers from the 11th tried parachuting from a B-24 because the C-46 could not make the round trip from Okinawa to Japan and back. As it turned out, the B-24 was a most inappropriate paratrooper airplane.

The plane that did play a prominent role in the move from Okinawa to Japan was the C-54, gigantic by comparison to the C-46 and C-47. ATC—Pacific assembled them from all over the world and crammed the departure airfields on Okinawa with them.

Meanwhile, on the nineteenth of August, a team of sixteen Japanese headed by Gen. Torashiro Kawabe, the deputy army chief of staff, landed at Nichols Field, outside of Manila, in an American C-54 they had boarded on Io-Jima. The delegation was to work out the details of the surrender with an American team, headed by General Sutherland, General MacArthur's crusty and tough chief of staff. General MacArthur refused to see the Japanese until the moment of final surrender.

General Sutherland met the Japanese in a conference room on the second floor of Manila's City Hall. The Japanese had left their swords at the entrance. General Sutherland instructed the Japanese to have four hundred trucks and one hundred sedans at Atsugi Airfield ready for the U.S. forces who would start landing on the twenty-third of August. The Japanese were concerned about the decision to use Atsugi. They pointed out that Atsugi was the training base for kamikaze pilots and a large number who refused to surrender were still in the area. General MacArthur's staff was also opposed to landing at Atsugi. The staff also pointed out that there were twenty-two Japanese divisions of 300,000 well-trained fighting troops on the Kanto Plain of Tokyo. General MacArthur had the final word. "Years of overseas duty has schooled me in the lessons of the Orient and, what was probably more important, had taught the Far East that I was its friend." General Sutherland did agree, however, to delay the landing on Atsugi until the twenty-eighth of August. At the meeting in Manila, final plans were also made for the peace treaty signing in Tokyo Bay aboard the USS *Missouri*.

GHQ ordered General Swing to form an honor guard company for General MacArthur. Each 11th Airborne infantry regiment furnished a platoon of soldiers with the proviso that each man had to be taller than five feet eleven inches. Captain Glenn Carter, executive officer of the 1st Battalion, 187th, was the company commander. The honor guard company was attached to the 3d Battalion, 188th, whose commander was Maj. Tom Mesereau, six feet three inches tall, and a former All-American tackle at West Point, class of January, 1943.

By 28 August, General Ryan's command had assembled on Okinawa almost every C-54 from around the world, enough so that only C-54s made the flight from Okinawa to Japan. General Ryan had also brought in some planes from civilian airlines. "From the heights above Kadena Strip, the silver four-engine transports seemed to stretch endlessly in all directions," wrote one of the 11th's soldiers. The use of only C-54s made the division staff job simpler. The plan called for both cargo and personnel planes to depart Okinawa at the rate of fifteen planes per hour for eleven hours per day.

On 28 August, an advance detail of officers and men from General Ryan's headquarters and the 11th Airborne flew to Atsugi to set up equipment for the main landings. Among other gear, the detail brought in radio equipment to set up a control tower. The 11th Airborne men reconnoitered the area for a suitable command post and quarters for the troops arriving within forty-eight hours and checked with the Japanese at Atsugi to ensure that GHQ's orders were being carried out.

Another typhoon on Okinawa caused a forty-eight-hour delay. But at

0100 on 30 August, the first plane in the lead echelon of the 11th Airborne took off from Kadena. Aboard were General Swing, Col. Alex Williams, the chief of staff, and the principal staff officers of the division. General Swing also took two items with him: a large American flag that he had procured from the Okinawa Command and a ten-foot-high piece of white canvas on which was painted in large letters CP 11TH AIRBORNE DIVISION. On the second plane were General Pierson, the alternate division staff, and a detachment from the 511th Signal Company with communications gear capable of reaching back to Okinawa.

General Swing's plane touched down at 0600, followed by a steady stream of C-54s. The occupation of Japan was under way.

General Swing was the first man out of his plane. According to one 11th soldier, "He was greeted by a Japanese delegation of army officers headed by a lieutenant general. There was much bowing, scraping, and showing of teeth, but General Swing remained coldly military. Towering handsomely almost a foot over the heads of the Japanese, he refused their extended hands and got down to business. He ordered [their] officers first of all to take off their samurai swords. They hesitated, saying that their sabers were not arms but symbols of their authority. General Swing cut them short. He said that from now on he was the authority and to put their sabers in a pile on the ground without further delay. The Japanese had no more comments as they hastened to unbuckle their swords."

The C-54s arrived in a steady stream. Early in the lift were Tom Mesereau's 3d Battalion of the 188th, to which was attached the honor guard, and the division band to be on hand when General MacArthur arrived. Other 11th troops on landing immediately fanned out to strengthen the perimeter around Atsugi. Colonel Pearson and a planeload of 187th troopers landed early in the flight pattern. Colonel Pearson knew that his mission after landing was to remain in the Atsugi area and guard the airfield.

As soon as they were assembled, General Swing sent Mesereau, his battalion, and the honor guard to the New Grand Hotel in Yokohama, the site of General MacArthur's headquarters for the next few days.

General Eichelberger and part of his Eighth Army staff landed at about 1200. At 1400 the supreme allied commander, General of the

Army Douglas MacArthur, arrived in his aptly named C-54, *Bataan*. He paused at the top of the ramp dressed in his khakis with pleated trousers, with his corncob pipe in his mouth at a jaunty angle, and his gold-braided uniform hat firmly in place. As he stepped down the ramp of his plane, the division band played the ruffles and flourishes appropriate to a five-star general and then the "General's March." General Eichelberger strode forward to meet General MacArthur. They shook hands and General MacArthur said to General Eichelberger in a quiet voice: "Bob, from Melbourne to Tokyo is a long way, but this seems to be the end of the road. This is the payoff."

Behind the band, the Japanese had assembled a number of vehicles for General MacArthur and his staff to move to Yokohama. General Whitney, a member of the GHQ staff, wrote:

"MacArthur climbed into an American Lincoln of uncertain vintage. The other officers found their places in the ramshackle motorcade. A fire engine that resembled a Toonerville Trolley started with an explosion that made some of us jump; then it led the way as the procession headed for Yokohama. That was when I saw the first armed troops in Japan proper.

"All along the roadway the fifteen miles to Yokohama they stood in a long line on each side, their backs to MacArthur in a gesture of respect. They were guarding the American supreme commander in the exact fashion that they guarded their emperor."

The reason that the Japanese police and soldiers along the route to Yokohama turned their backs on the American convoys is not clear. Some of the Americans thought that the Japanese were scorning them; others felt that "they could not bear to look on their conquerors." Others, including General Whitney, felt that they were paying MacArthur the same respect that they would have paid the emperor. Captain Ralph E. Ermatinger was the commander of the 511th's portion of the honor guard. He had a different version:

"Fact: Each Japanese soldier turned away from the road because he was commanded to do so by a civilian interpreter standing in the lead truck of the convoy. The interpreter was ordered to do this by a U.S. Army captain who also stood in the lead truck.

"As commander of the 511th contingent of the honor guard for General MacArthur, I, too, stood in the lead truck and witnessed the shouted

commands to 'about face' and saw the look of uncertainty and confusion on the faces of the Japanese soldiers, who appeared to have been
given other orders."

General MacArthur and his staff arrived in the New Grand Hotel in
Yokohama late in the afternoon of 30 August. General Whitney called
it "a magnificent establishment that had survived World War II intact."
He added: "The manager and his staff all but prostrated themselves as
they greeted us and showed us to the suite selected for General
MacArthur. We were tired and hungry, and we lost no time in going to
the dining room, where, amid the other American officers and almost
surrounded by solicitous hotel officials, we were seated and served a
steak dinner.

"I found it difficult to resist the impulse to snatch MacArthur's plate
away from him that first night and make sure that his food had not been
poisoned. When I voiced my misgivings to him, he merely laughed and
said, 'no one can live forever.' "

By the end of the day on 30 August 1945, 123 C-54s had landed at Atsugi, bringing in 4,200 troopers of the division and other support units.
The first serials brought in no large vehicles or heavy equipment because
General Swing wanted the maximum number of men, lightly equipped,
to land initially, given the unknown enemy situation at and near Atsugi.
What equipment came in was essential: two jeeps and one water trailer
per regiment, a five-day supply of ten-in-one rations, and squad rolls. The
188th landed first with 1,096 men; then came the 187th with 1,257 men.
The 511th landed next with 1,165 troopers. Mixed in with the 11th's serials were GHQ personnel, Eighth Army staffers, air corps equipment,
and men to set up and operate the controls at Atsugi for the follow-on
echelons, and correspondents and photographers.

By the evening of the thirtieth, the 11th's regiments had fanned out
to accomplish their assigned missions: Col. Ed Lahti's 511th moved to
Yokohama and posted the Yokohama-Tokyo road for about eight miles
beyond Yokohama; Col. Norman E. Tipton's 188th fanned out from Atsugi toward Fujishawa; and Col. George Pearson's 187th remained in the
Atsugi area to form a perimeter around the field.

"The regimental troops quickly took over their zone of responsibility and motorized and foot patrols were maintained throughout the
area," wrote Eli Bernheim after the war. "All Japanese installations con-

taining arms and equipment were seized, with inventories made and submitted to higher headquarters. The Antitank Company was given the mission of caring for the Allied POWs who were streaming into Atsugi Airdrome for transportation out of Japan. The regimental band gave daily concerts for the POWs, some of whom had not heard music since the beginning of the war. The regimental command post was set up at the Japanese Naval School, and rumors were that we were moving shortly to northern Honshu."

American prisoners of war began to leave the Japanese POW camps as soon as the American troops began to land. Less than two hours after the arrival of General Swing's plane at Atsugi, two American POWs arrived at the 11th Airborne Division command post. They had been in a camp several hundred miles south of Tokyo and had heard of the scheduled arrival of American troops. They walked away from their camp after the guards had left them to themselves; then they rode a train north and reported to the division CP.

General Jonathan M. Wainwright and Lt. Gen. Sir Arthur Percival had been held in a POW camp in Mukden, Manchuria. Shortly after the surrender of Japan, they had been flown back to Manila. MacArthur directed that the two generals be flown to Tokyo for the surrender ceremonies aboard the *Missouri*. They arrived in Yokohama on 31 August.

The morning of 2 September 1945 (3 September in Japan) was a singular moment in the annals of the world's history. On that morning, the U.S. battleships *Missouri* and *South Dakota* and the British battleship *Duke of York*, plus hundreds of other warships, were at anchor in Tokyo Bay. The *Missouri* was the site of the surrender. At about 0800, Admiral Nimitz and General MacArthur were aboard the *Missouri*. At 0815, the Japanese delegation climbed up the gangway of the *Missouri* and took their places in two rows in front of a mess table covered with green felt. After all was in order, MacArthur appeared from inside the *Missouri* and took his place facing the Japanese delegation. Grandiloquently, MacArthur spoke to the delegation and then motioned for Mamoru Shigemitsu, the one-legged Japanese foreign minister, to come forward and sign the surrender document. He limped forward, took a seat at the table, took off his yellow gloves and silk top hat, and then signed the document. General Yoshijiro Umezu, the Japanese Army chief of staff, was next. He marched forward, refused to sit, signed the document almost with a slash, and strode, ramrod straight, back to his place. Next it was MacArthur's turn. He picked up three pens and signed his name a few letters at a time with each of the pens. One he gave to General Wainwright, the second to General Percival and the third, a bright red one, he pocketed for his wife and son. Admiral Nimitz then signed for the United States, and representatives of other Allied nations signed for their countries. When it was finished, MacArthur said: "Let us pray that peace be now restored to the world, and that God will preserve it always. These proceedings are closed."

After the signing of the surrender document on 2 September, troops and equipment continued to land steadily. The division G4 and the quartermaster established supply dumps in the hangars at Atsugi using, for the most part, Japanese labor to unload planes, drive their makeshift trucks, and work in the supply depots.

On 7 September, the 11th Airborne Division closed at Atsugi. In the previous nine days, the ATC—Far East, under the command of Maj. Gen. William O. Ryan, had moved 11,708 men, 640 tons of supplies, and more than 600 jeeps and trailers of the 11th. It was the longest (1,600 miles) and largest air-transported troop movement ever attempted and completed.

The 11th and the 187th were now ready to begin the final occupation of Japan.

### Occupation

In their zones of responsibility, the 11th and the other divisions of Eighth Army occupying Japan carried out, to some degree, the tasks outlined by General MacArthur. One of them was to assist in the demobilization of the Japanese armed forces. On 2 September, those forces numbered 6,983,000 troops in some 154 army divisions. On the home islands, there were 2,576,000 troops in 57 divisions, 14 brigades and 45 regiments. The rest of the Japanese armed forces were strung along a huge arc from Manchuria to the Solomons and on the islands in the Central and Southwest Pacific. The responsibility for the demobilization of this huge force fell to the Japanese army and navy ministers. According to General MacArthur, "Eighth Army and the U.S. Navy supervised and coordinated this complicated and top-priority operation, but it was the Japanese themselves who performed the task."

From the beginning of the occupation, the U.S. troops were impressed with the total surrender of the Japanese people, "a surrender amounting to subservience," one of the troopers wrote. There were no incidents of revolt against U.S. forces. Another trooper wrote after the war, "We were amazed to find that the government which had produced the cunning, wily, almost beastlike men we had fought, could, in a few short days, impress on its vast population the need for conducting itself as a beaten race. . . . It was apparent that the Japanese, from the highest officials in the land down to the lowest classes of workers and farmers, were prepared actually, and seemingly mentally, to do our bidding."

On 14 September, the America Division relieved the 11th of its zone of responsibility in the Tokyo-Yokohama area; on 15 September, the 11th began its move by truck and rail to previously assigned sectors in northern Honshu. With this new move, the 187th moved from Atsugi Airfield to Sendai, where the regiment was housed in a Japanese Army arsenal, an area that would later be named Camp Schimmelpfennig, after the 11th's chief of staff who was killed in action near Manila.

The movement of the troops by rail was a remarkable operation. The 11th's G4 ordered the Japanese to have trains at certain stations on a specific time schedule. Given the pounding that the railroads had taken during the war, it was almost a miracle of management and improvisation that the Japanese railroad system could meet the schedule. But they did. The cars were old and reminded one trooper of the pictures he had seen of the forty-and-eight cars from World War I. But by 17 September, the 187th had closed into its new area.

Once the 187th had gotten to its area, its first mission was to make the barracks and other buildings habitable. By the standards of the World War II type barracks at Camp Polk, the Japanese barracks buildings were primitive. The plumbing was medieval, and the sewage was deposited in reservoirs and then collected by carts to be used as fertilizer on the local farms and gardens. The division historian noted that of all the traffic accidents within the division area, no 11th Airborne trooper was ever guilty of hitting a "honey wagon."

The barracks heating system was also crude and consisted mostly of potbelly stoves, at the rate of one per barracks. Many barracks burned when the temperatures went down.

General Swing set up a new organization—the Miyagi Task Force, composed of the 187th and the 188th Regiments and commanded by the assistant division commander, Gen. Albert Pierson. He, in turn, assigned each regiment its own area of occupation responsibility, wherein the principal mission was, according to John Conable, the division G4, "to collect and destroy all arms, ammunition, and armament factories. We were also charged with seeing that General MacArthur's edicts were carried out." The 187th spent most of its time improving housing and patrolling its assigned sector.

By the early fall of 1945, many of the combat troops of the 187th had returned to the States and discharge, the dates based on the number of "points" they had accumulated in combat and overseas service. Replacements—officers and enlisted men alike—were arriving by the hundreds to the units scattered over northern Honshu. Many were not jump qualified. General Swing, therefore, for the fourth time in the history of the 11th, established yet another jump school—this one at the former Japanese Air Corps base near Yanome, about fifteen miles from Sendai. (The others were at Camp Polk, New Guinea, and Lipa, Luzon.) From March through June of 1946, 3,376 men were graduated from the school at Yanome, approximately 75 percent of those who started the two-week course. With over 18,066 jumps in the period, the injury rate was less than one percent.

The 187th was, by this time, almost completely filled with paratroopers, in keeping with General Swing's requirement in 1943 that soldiers in the 11th be qualified both as paratroopers and glider riders. In the summer of 1946, General Swing started a glider school at Yamoto Air Base, renamed Carolus Field in honor of Cpl. Charles H. Carolus, killed in a glider crash near Manila on 22 July 1945.

In addition, in October of 1945, the division initiated yet another unique program, a flying school outside Sendai at a former Japanese Air Corps training field. The instructors were the division's liaison pilots and the planes, the L-4 and L-5 "spotter planes" of division artillery. The course was six weeks long, and at the end, the student had accumulated fifteen hours of dual flying and fifteen hours of solo. By June of 1946, twenty-five officers and seventy-five enlisted men had completed the course.

In January of 1946, Colonel "Big George" Pearson, an architectural engineer, left the command of the 187th, returned to the States, transferred to the Engineer Corps, and returned to Manila in 1946 as area engineer to assist in the rehabilitation of Manila and the Luzon railroads. Lieutenant Colonel Arthur H. Wilson, Jr. (the son of Arthur H. Wilson, USMA 1904, who won the Medal of Honor in the Moro Expedition in 1909), assumed command. Harry Wilson had been with the 11th from its activation.

In the months after the Japanese surrender, the 11th moved its major elements a number of times. In February 1946, the War Department inactivated the 77th Division, and General Eichelberger, still in command of the Eighth Army, assigned the area of northern Honshu and the entire island of Hokkaido to the 11th. The Division Headquarters moved into a bank building in downtown Sapporo, a city never bombed during the war. In February, Sapporo rested under seven feet of snow, its normal winter supply. Sapporo was also the site of the 1933 Winter Olympics. The Sapporo Grand Hotel became the bachelor officer quarters and club. It was a city that had been partially laid out by American engineers in decades past. Wide streets, American-style buildings, and ivy-covered walls of the University of Hokkaido reflected the American influence. Headquarters of the 187th and the 2d Battalion set up in an old Japanese barracks outside Sapporo; the Antitank Company and the 1st Battalion of the 187th moved to the port city of Hakodate; the 3d Battalion went to Asahigawa. In March of 1946, the 3d Battalion moved to the northern city of Bihoro, Hokkaido.

In the spring of 1946, the occupation of Japan had settled into routines. The commanders sought to improve the lot of their troops with upgraded barracks, mess halls, and recreational facilities. In Sapporo, the 11th built ski runs and clubs near the site of the old Olympics runs. General Swing built a pentagonal headquarters at Camp Crawford outside Sapporo and surrounded it with platoon-sized barracks for the troops of the 187th who had been living in winterized pyramidal tents.

In the summer of 1946, wives and children of men interested in staying in Japan for a year or more began to arrive in ships that docked in Yokohama. The first group arrived on 24 June. In Sapporo, the division headquarters and 187th troops used, as temporary quarters, Japanese houses that were remodeled according to American standards and filled with furniture built by the Japanese under American guidance. Later, Japanese construction companies built modest homes on the various posts. In Sapporo a lot of these activities, especially furniture construction, were without the approval of higher headquarters, but during one of General Eichelberger's trips to Sapporo, General Swing persuaded him that he was on the right path. After inspecting the area, General Eichelberger told General Swing that he didn't know whether "to relieve or commend him."

In June 1947, Colonel Pearson returned from the Philippines and assumed command of the 187th once again. But there was work to be done and missions to be accomplished.

"Patrol jumps" became routine for the paratroopers of the 187th on Hokkaido. Corporal Coleman V. Joyce joined Headquarters Company of the 3d Battalion in August 1947. He described the patrol jumps this way: "About ten of us would load aboard a beat-up C-47 and drop into little Japanese towns throughout the island. Very few of these people had seen an American before and none of them had ever seen a paratrooper until he jumped in on top of them. Little brown legs would pump madly as the Japanese dashed out to our tiny drop zone. They, particularly the youngsters, would help us roll up our chutes and carry the silk and our gear to the local inn.

"There was no such thing as a regular drop zone. We would just fly around looking for a field, then out the door we'd go. Once on the ground, the NCO in charge would set up a variety of missions, such as checking bridges and generally making a show of strength. On some occasions the whole population would come out to the edge of town to meet us.

"We also gave ski instruction to other men of the regiment. More men were hospitalized because of ski training than injuries by parachute jumps. The same winter our platoon conducted a drop at Wakkanai on the northern tip of Hokkaido. After landing we scrambled aboard a Japanese boat which navigated the strait separating Japan from Russian-held Sakhalin. Checking a little Japanese island in the middle of the strait, we turned around and headed back again. This time we returned to camp via the Japanese National Railway."

In June of 1948, Colonel Pearson, well known, among other things, for his piano-playing ability at parties in the evenings around Sapporo, was due to leave the 187th once more. One member of the 187th remembers his departure this way: "Everyone knew that the 187th deputy commander was scheduled to become the new regimental commander on George Pearson's departure. On his last night of command, 'Big George' was at the Camp Sapporo officers' club wetting down his travel orders and saying good-bye to his officers. Over to one side of the club, the deputy commander, a little loud after having a few, was relating whose head was going to roll the next day after a change-of-command ceremony. 'Big George' had to be restrained.

"Next morning, Col. George O. Pearson stormed into the division headquarters past division chief of staff, Lt. Col. Harvey J. Jablonsky, and into Maj. Gen. William 'Bud' Miley's office. (General Miley, a legend in airborne lore, had assumed command of the 11th Airborne Division on 2 February 1948 when General Swing left his command of five years to move south and assume command of I Corps in Kyoto, Japan.) In no uncertain terms, 'Big George' informed the general he would not turn command of his beloved regiment over to his deputy, and he told him why. General Miley sat quietly for a moment, then he walked out of his office to where Lieutenant Colonel Jablonsky was shuffling papers. Without any warning, he said, 'Jabo, get down to the 187th and take command.' Jabo almost fell out of his chair in total surprise. He obeyed orders. Lieutenant Colonel Harvey J. Jablonsky, two-time All-American, St. Louis University and United States Military Academy, became commander of the 187th."

The 187th carried on its occupation duties with a myriad of tasks, training, and R and R. The heavy winter snows of Hokkaido required ski training and cross-country snowshoe patrols if the troops were to be mobile in the field. In the spring, Colonel Jablonsky had his troops back at the Shimamatsu maneuver area for company-sized maneuvers.

But for the 187th Para-Glider Infantry Regiment, the days of occupation of Japan were coming to a close. In January 1949, the 31st Infantry Regiment of the 7th Infantry Division arrived in Sapporo to take over the occupational duties of the 187th. The entire 11th Airborne Division was finishing its tour in Japan. On 19 January 1949, the first echelon of the 187th left Sapporo. It was a three-man group headed up by Maj. Richard J. Allen, the regimental S3. Destination: Camp Campbell, Kentucky, the new home of the 11th and the 187th.

The main body of 187th troops sailed aboard the U.S. Army transport *General Hershey* on 19 February. It docked in New Orleans on 17 March. The 187th moved by rail to Camp Campbell. The 187th CP opened at 0800, 24 March 1949, at Campbell. The remainder of the regiment left Japan on 23 April.

The 187th's stint at occupying Japan was over. The regiment, bloodied in the battles of Leyte and Luzon, particularly at Mount Macolod, was about to begin a new chapter in its history. Unlike so many regiments born of the huge World War II expansion of the U.S. Army, it was not about to fold its colors. It had many more battles to live and fight through heroically. In the future, it would make the original glider-riders of the regiment proud of the heritage they had established.

### Fort Campbell, Kentucky

Camp Campbell was born in World War II during the days of the rapid buildup and expansion of the U.S. Army. It is located between the state border towns of Clarksville, Tennessee, and Hopkinsville, Kentucky. Camp Campbell was named in honor of General William Bowen Campbell, the last Whig governor of Tennessee. It was selected for development on 16 July 1941. On 4 February 1942, Army contract engineers started building the camp on 101,700 acres; a year later, yet another rapidly built Army camp was ready to house and train, eventually, an armored corps headquarters, three armored divisions, an infantry division, and supporting troops.

In 1949, however, the 187th soldiers found Camp Campbell in a state of neglect and disrepair. Once again, the troops had to make their home base livable. Fortunately, Campbell's wooden two-story barracks were of a fairly solid construction, unlike the tar-paper-covered shacks of Camp Mackall. (Even today, more than fifty years after they were built, some of the World War II buildings are still in use at Fort Campbell by the air-assault soldiers of the 101st Airborne Division [Air Assault], including the 3d Brigade of the 187th Air Assault Regiment.)

A number of changes, some major, faced the 187th when it arrived and settled into life at Campbell. For one thing, the Pentagon had decided, wisely, that after a number of disastrous glider operations in World War II, the flimsy, crash-prone gliders were no longer feasible vehicles for transporting men and equipment onto battlefields; the Pentagon scratched them from the inventory and relegated them to museums at Bragg and Benning. The air force now had transport aircraft that could parachute into combat the same heavy loads that had formerly been landed in gliders.

On 25 June 1949, in a significant event in the history of the former 187th Glider Infantry Regiment and later 187th Para-Glider Infantry Regiment, the regiment was reorganized and redesignated officially as the 187th Airborne Infantry Regiment. The reorganization assigned to the regiment new support units and some that had formerly only been attached. A Company of the 127th Engineers (the Engineer Battalion organic to the 11th Airborne Division) became the Engineer Company of the 187th AIR; Antitank Company became the Support Company, 187th AIR; the 11th Airborne Medical Detachment became the Medical Company, 187th AIR.

Colonel Harvey J. Jablonsky, "Jabo" to his troops among themselves, was still in command when the 187th returned to Campbell. He was a West Point graduate, class of 1934, where he had been an outstanding football player and captain of the team, two-time All-American, and eventually a member of the Football Hall of Fame (1978). At Campbell, Colonel Jablonsky determined to make his regiment the best in the 11th. One member of the 187th remembers that, "Jabo as a physical-fitness buff is reported to have said, 'Two things are necessary to make a good paratrooper—guts and physical fitness. I can't give the men the first, but I can give them the second.'" He proceeded to set up a tough airborne physical-training program that left his regiment as physically fit as any in the Army. As one of his troopers said, "He put fire in the regiment."

One of the highlights of the 11th Airborne Division's tour at Campbell was Exercise Swarmer. During the fall of 1949, the division intensified its airborne and individual training in preparation for Swarmer, an exercise designed by the U.S. Air Force's Lt. Gen. Lauris Norstad, USMA 1930, to determine the feasibility of establishing an independent, strong base in enemy-held territory completely by air, including, eventually, all resupply by air-landed transports.

During the 11th's occupation of Japan, because of the wide dispersion of the division over northern Honshu and all of Hokkaido, it never had the opportunity to engineer a full-scale, division-sized airborne operation. Swarmer would provide the occasion. The planning headquarters set up a special headquarters in a run-down former hospital at Camp Mackall, the 187th's birthplace. There, the army and air force planners worked out the details of the largest peacetime airborne operation ever attempted. But, according to Russ Brown, who was on General Norstad's planning staff in the old World War II hospital, it was mostly an air force operation with the airborne forces almost pawns in the overall air chess game.

To start the exercise, early in April 1950, an aggressor force landed on the Carolina coast. A second force, operating out of Florida, attacked north. It would prove ironic that the 11th Airborne Division would fight the "aggressors" over the same terrain where it had fought the "Knoll-wood Maneuver" in the fall of 1943, an airborne operation that proved finally to some skeptical, top-ranking officers (including General Eisenhower) that airborne divisions were practical and feasible entities. "Knollwood" thus saved the lives of World War II airborne divisions.

On 18 April, the 187th left Campbell for Greenville, South Carolina, and prepared for the large-scale airborne operation. On D-Day, 28 April 1950, the 187th and the 11th parachuted onto the drop zones at Camp Mackall, the same DZs and LZs used by the division for parachute and glider training in 1943. That afternoon, the 82d Airborne Division from Fort Bragg dropped in to join the 11th. The drop zone had been secured by L Company, 187th, commanded by 1st Lt. William E. Weber. In all, sixty thousand paratroopers were involved in the operation. Overhead, fighters from the Tactical Air Command provided cover, and Air Force transports, landing at the rate of one every three minutes, brought in tons of supplies onto the airfields captured by the paratroopers. The battle lasted for ten days, with the airborne warriors advancing, defending, and attacking. It was a hard training ground for the newly reorganized 11th, including the revamped 187th AIR.

Colonel Jabo's tough and resolute training program and his demand for perfection in physical and tactical training paid off. One night during the operation, he asked Major Rye Mausert if he could maneuver his 3d of the 187th through a great, supposedly impassable swamp behind an enemy force, that had been relying on the swamp for protection from the rear. According to one observer, "It was a terrible march, but the regiment managed it with weapons and full combat gear. Their forced march through the swamp was outstanding, and the maneuver umpires called it for the 187th, who won the battle."

The umpires in Operation Swarmer awarded the 187th the highest ORT (Operational Readiness Test) score of any of the six airborne regiments in the maneuver. And, according to one member of the 187th, "the high scores and combat readiness of the regiment were central to the regiment's being selected for battle in a place called Korea two months later."

But all good personal assignments must come to an end. On 5 June 1950, Colonel Jabo was succeeded by Lt. Col. Harry Wilson, the man who commanded the 187th in Japan between Colonel Pearson's command tours. But Harry Wilson's tenure this time was short-lived. On 21 June 1950, Colonel Frank S. Bowen, who had been a brigadier general in World War II, took command.

On 21 June, Colonel Bowen could not know that he was about to lead the 187th into one of the most famous and notable chapters in its history; the North Koreans had not yet attacked across the 38th parallel. But he was undoubtedly aware of the fine reputation of the regiment as demonstrated on Swarmer.

In a very short time, the training at Campbell would be over; the troopers of the 187th would have said good-bye to wives and friends; the peaceful days and nights of Kentucky and Tennessee would shortly be things of a sometimes, but not always, fondly remembered past. The 187th Airborne Regimental Combat Team was about to go to war once more.

# THE KOREAN WAR

# 5: On to Korea

The five-year-old fragile peace in the "Land of the Morning Calm" was brutally shattered by the eruption of massive North Korean artillery and mortar concentrations along the rain-soaked 38th parallel in the pre-dawn darkness of Sunday, 25 June 1950. Following the heavy artillery and mortar barrage that began at about 0400, seven North Korean divisions—ninety thousand men and some 150 T-34 Russian-made tanks—swarmed south across the arbitrary line dividing the North and South. The main North Korean effort of two divisions, each led by forty tanks and other mechanized equipment, smashed down the Uijongbu Corridor, an ancient invasion route aimed directly at Seoul, the South Korean capital, about forty miles to the south. Supporting this major thrust, from Kaesong in the west to Chorwon in the east, an arc of forty miles, Gen. Chai Ung Jun, the NKPA (North Korean People's Army) commander, concentrated more than half his divisions and artillery and most of his tanks. The remainder of the attacking force, in three secondary moves well coordinated with the attack in the west, moved south in a wide front along the main roads down the center of the peninsula and along the east coast.

The North's initiation of war had not been declared or broadcast or hinted; it was a surprise to the world, totally without warning; the attack itself was North Korea's declaration of war.

The mobile and tank-heavy North Korean force that rumbled across the border after the massive artillery preparation was a formidable one. Between 15 and 24 June 1950, the North Koreans had, without detection by the South Koreans, infiltrated an additional 80,000 men and their equipment close behind the parallel. Then Chai carefully and methodically deployed his total force, some 175,000 troops, along routes to the south that his staff had studied in detail, from maps and agents, over the past few weeks.

The United States had pulled most of its 30,000-man occupation force out of South Korea in the fall of 1948; one remaining regimental combat team left in July 1949. The U.S. Army left behind for the Republic of Korea (ROK) forces 100,000 rifles, 50 million rounds of small-arms ammunition, and 2,000 rocket launchers. But the U.S. left no tanks, no war planes, and no heavy naval aircraft. The U.S. authorities had deliberately designed the ROK force to have only a limited defensive capability.

On 1 July 1949, to train the ROK Army, the U.S. set up the Korean Military Advisory Group (KMAG) of 472 officers and men commanded by Brig. Gen. W. L. Roberts, 59, USMA class of 1913. With this change, General MacArthur in Japan was no longer responsible for South Korea; the State Department, in the person of Ambassador John J. Muccio, was. The KMAG was under his opcon.

General Roberts had been a doughboy in World War I and a tanker in World War II. For some reason, perhaps to intimidate the North Koreans or simply to improve the morale of the ROK forces, he developed a campaign to convince the politicians in Washington that the ROK Army was superb, capable of taking on and defeating any North Korean incursion across the border. To exploit the sham, he invited VIPs from the U.S. to observe carefully orchestrated field maneuvers by hand-picked Republic of Korea troops.

The subterfuge climaxed with the 5 June 1950 issue of *Time* magazine that reported that the "Americanized" ROK Army was "hardworking" and "first rate" and that "most observers now rate the hundred-thousand-man South Korean Army as the best of its size in Asia." In June 1950, two days before the invasion, General Roberts retired from the U.S. Army and left Korea for home. One of his final comments to Frank Gibney, *Time*'s correspondent in the Far East, was that "the South Koreans have the best damn army outside the United States."

But even according to KMAG internal reports, this was far from the truth. In fact, only about 25 percent of the sixty-seven ROK battalions had completed battalion-level training. In addition, there was a shortage of ammunition, 35 percent of the vehicles were out of commission, netting only 2,100 usable trucks and jeeps. Some 15 percent of the weapons were not functioning. The ROK's eight divisions of some five thousand combat troops had no tanks, only five battalions of light 105mm artillery, no 4. 2-inch mortars, and no recoilless rifles. And they had not even one combat airplane.

General Roberts and the entire KMAG, in fact, were well aware of the pathetic plight of the ROK Army. In March 1949, Roberts wrote to Gen. Charles Bolte, a member of the JCS, about the true, sorry status of the

ROK Army. Lieutenant Colonel Thomas D. McDonald, a member of KMAG, wrote in a December 1949 report that the ROK Army "could have been the American army in 1775." A 15 June 1950 KMAG report to the Department of Defense warned that supplies available for the ROK forces were only at a "bare subsistence level" and that the ROK forces could defend themselves for no more than fifteen days.

But what was even more detrimental to the Rhee government in South Korea and to the ROK Army were statements by the highest U.S. officials that South Korea was outside the United States' sphere of national interest. On 5 January, President Truman said that the U.S. had adopted a hands-off Formosa policy, indirectly affecting South Korea. A week later, Dean Acheson clearly implied that South Korea was outside America's strategic defensive perimeter. And a week after that bombshell, Sen. Tom Connally, chairman of the Senate Committee on Foreign Policy, was asked if South Korea was an "essential" part of the U.S. defense strategy. He replied, "No . . . I don't think it is very greatly important." The stage was set for the North to invade the seemingly friendless and isolated South.

On the morning of the North Korean attack, Capt. Joseph R. Darrigo, aged thirty, was a U.S. advisor to the 12th Regiment of the ROK 1st Division, deployed along the parallel at Kaesong, the ancient capital of all Korea. He had been with the 12th Regiment for six months, by KMAG standards a long tour. He had become an expert on the ROK Army and North Korean maneuvers and border incidents. In May of 1950, his deep concern about a pending North Korean attack intensified. He had watched the withdrawal of North Korean civilians from along the parallel, he noticed that the previously intense guerrilla raids and border incidents had sharply decreased, and, in early June, he heard the North broadcasting propaganda aimed at a peaceful unification of the peninsula. He sensed that the uneasy and misleading calm of the parallel was about to blow apart.

On the night of 24 June 1950, Darrigo was the only American officer along the 38th parallel. At about 0330 the next morning, he was awakened in his stone house by the sound of artillery. At first he thought that it was ROK artillery. But then he became aware of the intensity of the fire. Shortly, he could hear small-arms fire and bullets pinging against the side of his house. He grabbed some clothes, ran down the stairs, and bumped into his houseboy coming to warn him. The two of them jumped into Darrigo's jeep and drove rapidly into the center of Kaesong. Darrigo was startled to see a North Korean train pulling into the Kaesong station loaded with a full regiment of North Korean soldiers. Under heavy small-arms fire, Darrigo and his houseboy turned around and sped south to alert the 1st ROK Division. When Darrigo arrived at the Command Post, he could not awaken the guards. He finally slammed his jeep against the guard gate, got into the Command Post, and found that both the division commander, Col. Paik Sun Yup, and his American advisor Lt. Col. L. H. Rockwell, were in Seoul for the weekend. Darrigo relayed the news of the invasion to them by phone. By dawn, Paik and Rockwell were back at the 1st Division CP.

On that rainy, foggy Sunday morning, the ROKs had four infantry divisions and one separate regiment deployed along the parallel. But many of the officers and some of the men, as well as many of the KMAG advisors, were in Seoul or other towns on weekend passes. (The North Korean planners were obviously aware of the weekend laxity along the southern side of the border.) Only one third of the ROK forces were in defensive positions. The remainder were in reserve ten to thirty miles below the Parallel. Once launched, in most cases the North Korean onslaught overran the thinly manned ROK defenses with surprise, speed, and ease.

Within three days, a North Korean tank-infantry force rolled into Seoul. The North Korean attacks down the center of the peninsula and down the east coast kept pace with the main attack. All along the crumbling front, after some isolated heroic stands, the ROK forces fell back in haste and disorder, abandoning most of their arms and equipment along the way.

On 29 June, General MacArthur, accompanied by part of his staff and some reporters, flew into Suwon, an airfield twenty miles south of Seoul, to assess the extent and caliber of the North Korean invasion. After lunch, MacArthur drove up the Seoul highway through thousands of retreating refugees and ROK soldiers. Looking closely at the soldiers, MacArthur said grimly to one of his staff: "I haven't seen a single wounded man yet."

On 30 June, President Truman put South Korea back into General MacArthur's sphere of authority and authorized him to use all U.S. forces available to stem the North Korean advance. In Japan, General

MacArthur's main U.S. combat forces were poorly trained, non–combat-ready soldiers of the 7th, 24th, and 25th Infantry Divisions and the 1st Cavalry Division. The troops were used to the "good life" of the occupation. Most were recruits who had never been in combat, had never heard artillery fire, and hardly knew how to clean their rifles. According to Maj. Gen. William F. Dean, commanding general of the 24th Division, the troops had become "flabby and accustomed to Japanese girlfriends, plenty of beer, and servants to shine their boots."

Nonetheless, in early July, General MacArthur sent the 24th Division to Korea piecemeal, beginning with the 1st Battalion of the 21st Infantry Regiment, commanded by Lt. Col. Charles B. "Brad" Smith, USMA 1939. Colonel Smith was an experienced combat officer who had commanded an infantry battalion on Guadalcanal. On 1 July, Colonel Smith and his 440 men flew in aging C-54s from the U.S. Air Force base outside Itazuke, Kyushu. The flight to Pusan was only one hour, but because of fog and rain at both ends of the flight, it took all day to get Task Force Smith into Pusan. Just before Smith left the air base, General Dean told him, "When you get to Pusan, head for Taejon." That was his mission. Thus began the U.S. involvement in the Korean War. In the early weeks of the war, it was a disaster. And TF Smith unwittingly became the symbol of the untrained, non–combat-ready U.S. Army of Occupation in Japan.

On the evening of the second, TF Smith, 540 men strong, boarded a train and by the next morning arrived in Taejon. By early morning of 5 July, TF Smith was dug in on the Seoul-Pusan highway just north of Osan, eighty miles north of Taejon. At 0730, Smith spotted a column of eight NKPA tanks moving south toward his position. In the battle and retreat that followed, TF Smith lost 185 men, killed, wounded, captured, or missing in action. It had heroically but vainly held up the North Korean attack for seven hours.

In the ensuing days, the rest of the 24th followed TF Smith into Korea and took up blocking positions north of Taejon. On 14 July, the 25th Division arrived and extended the 24th's lines to the east. On the 18th of July, General MacArthur deployed the 1st Cavalry Division. These units failed to halt the North Korean assault and retreated slowly into the narrow confines of the "Pusan Perimeter."

Lieutenant General Walton H. Walker, commander of Eighth Army in Japan, was short and barrel-chested, and often described as a "bulldog of a man, feisty and tenacious, built like a fireplug. . . ." General Patton, who was Walker's commander in Europe, described him as "my toughest son of a bitch." General MacArthur appointed him the commander of all UN ground forces in Korea.

On 13 July 1950, General Walker established his Eighth Army advanced post at Taegu, and, with the consent of President Syngman Rhee, assumed command of all ROK forces. By mid-August, the North Korean forces had pushed Eighth Army back into the 140-mile "Pusan Perimeter" where it dug in and defended stubbornly for a month and a half against General Chai's repeated heavy attacks with a North Korean force now swollen to thirteen infantry and one armored division. In the interim, the UN force within the perimeter built up its strength with the addition of the U.S. 2d Division, the 1st Marine Brigade, four battalions of medium tanks, and the 5th RCT from Hawaii. Great Britain added the 27th Brigade from Hong Kong. With the constant prodding, the U.S. advisors restored some semblance of order and combat-effectiveness to five ROK divisions. In the coming weeks, the UN force continued its buildup, and, as the North Korean forces extended their lines of communications, the UN Command strengthened itself into an offensive posture.

Even though his command had been beaten back into a tight defensive corner of the Korean Peninsula, General MacArthur was not pessimistic. He knew that the North Korean lines were overextended, and that, temporarily at Pusan, he had the advantage of interior lines. And based on his World War II tactics of island hopping and landing his forces amphibiously in the enemy's rear, it was a "given" that he would exploit an amphibious end run to extricate his Pusan-bound forces.

On the fifteenth and sixteenth of September, Maj. Gen. Edward M. Almond, now commanding X Corps, consisting of the 7th Division and the 1st Marine Division, brought his forces ashore at Inchon, more than two hundred air miles from Pusan. In two weeks, X Corps recaptured Seoul from the outflanked NKPA.

On the sixteenth of September, in coordination with the X Corps landing at Inchon, General Walker launched an attack out of the Pusan perimeter with two U.S. corps and the two ROK corps abreast. Walker's forces originally ran into heavy opposition, but when General Chai recognized that his forces could be squeezed and totally smashed between Eighth Army and X Corps, he ordered a retreat to the north. The retreat was, in fact, a rout. Unfortunately, a large portion of the NKPA escaped the trap. At 0826 on the twenty-seventh of September, Sgt. Edward C. Mancil of the 7th Cavalry met elements of H Company, 31st Infantry, 7th Division on a small bridge north of Osan. X Corps and Eighth Army had linked up.

By the first of October, most of the NKPA survivors had retreated above the 38th parallel or had escaped into the mountains of South Korea. "For all practical purposes," wrote Roy E. Appleman in *U.S. Army in the Korean War,* "the North Korean People's Army had been destroyed. That was the real measure of the success of the Inchon landing and Eighth Army's correlated attack—General MacArthur's strategy for winning the war."

The stage was thus set for the pursuit of the remnants of the North Korean Army above the parallel and for the possible use of an airborne force to parachute behind the retreating enemy forces, to cut off their escape, to capture high-ranking military and civilians fleeing north out of Pyongyang, and to rescue UN POWs presumably being evacuated to the north.

On 1 August 1950, in Theater Number Three at Fort Campbell, Kentucky, Col. Frank S. Bowen Jr. announced to his assembled 187th Airborne Infantry Regimental troopers that the 187th had been alerted for overseas movement. By the twenty-seventh of August, the 187th became officially the 187th Regimental Combat Team with the addition of the 674th Airborne Field Artillery Battalion, A Company of the 127th Airborne Engineer Battalion, Battery A of the 88th Airborne Antiaircraft Battalion, and detachments of MPs, quartermasters, parachute maintenance riggers, and medics.

In the month following the announcement of the alert, Colonel Bowen, according to Arch Roberts in *Rakkasan!,* "quickly became known as an ambitious commander—and a very exacting one. Every operation . . . was squeezed dry of training for the men and the field commanders—from squad leaders on up to the RCT commander himself. This brass-knuckled training was to pay dividends in a much more grim situation less than a month away. . . ."

The RCT left Campbell aboard fourteen trains. The first one, carrying Colonel Bowen and his advanced party, left at 0001, 1 September, headed for Fort Lawton, Washington. There they boarded aircraft and flew to Japan. The remaining thirteen trains moved the main body of troopers to Camp Stoneman, California, near San Francisco, where the troops boarded the USNS *Heintzelman* and USNS *Anderson* for the ocean voyage to Sasebo, Japan, departing on the sixth and seventh of September.

When the advance party arrived in Tokyo, Colonel Bowen and his staff reported to the Supreme Headquarters, Allied Powers, for a briefing where he learned that the 187th was scheduled for immediate deployment to the Korean battle zone. Meanwhile, the remainder of the advance party flew on to Ashiya and then to Camp Hakata, Kyushu, where it arranged for quarters for the RCT at Camp Wood and set up a temporary 187th CP, complete with sand tables, a war room, and an operations center, in the old 13th Field Artillery Battalion area. Camp Wood was sixty miles from Hakata, so Colonel Bowen requested that the ships carrying the main body dock at Moji, a short distance from Ashiya, instead of Sasebo. Ashiya USAF Base was the home of the USAF C-119 Troop Carriers and thus a departure base for the 187th's move to Korea.

The 187th Airborne RCT was about to start the Korean phase of its long and illustrious history.

### 187th to Combat in Korea

On 22 September, the first elements of the 187th RCT began airlanding at Kimpo Airfield, seven days after the Inchon landings, too late to be a part of General MacArthur's calculating, surprising, and eminently successful sweep around the peninsula and the resultant severing of the NKPA lines of communication to the deep south. The 187th had moved by truck from Moji Port to Ashiya Air Force Base in Japan and then almost immediately by air to Korea with the 314th and 21st Troop Carrier wings. The 3d Battalion, commanded by Lt. Col. Delbert E. Munson, was the first to land at Kimpo, the major airfield about ten miles to the west of Seoul, across the Han River.

When the battalion landed, Munson assumed responsibility for the airfield, although it had been mostly cleared by the Marines from Inchon. The 1st Battalion, commanded by Lt. Col. Harry Wilson, who had led the 2d of the 187th in the Leyte and Luzon battles of the 11th Airborne, and the regiment for a time both in Japan and at Campbell, followed the 3d. Then the 2d Battalion landed. By the twenty-sixth of September, the entire 187th RCT was in Korea except for a small rear detachment at Ashiya and the Parachute Maintenance Company and the Personnel Section at Camp Kashii, Japan.

After the 187th had landed at Kimpo, it had the mission of clearing the Kimpo Peninsula that ran between the Han River and the Yellow Sea. "The Rakkasans attacked up the peninsula with a vengeance," wrote Fred J. Waterhouse, the 187th historian. "This was their first combat operation, and they were ready. By the fifth or sixth day in Korea, most of the men were pretty well adjusted to combat. Company L was ordered to move on an estimated company of North Korea guerrillas who were racing north. Friendly armor in the lead had been stopped at a blown bridge. First Platoon, L Company, took point. At 1230 on the twenty-seventh, Company L was ambushed by an estimated enemy force of four hundred men. The enemy allowed the Rakkasan truck column to advance halfway through a small village before opening fire. The fight continued for four hours with the Rakkasans inflicting heavy losses on the enemy, during which Lt. William E. Weber was wounded and later awarded the Silver Star for action during this battle. Withdrawing in orderly fashion, L Company carried out their dead and wounded without losing a single piece of equipment. Sgt. First Class Bailey, Sgt. Kenneth E. Stevenson, and Pfc. Clark Bradford were among the first battle deaths suffered by the regiment.

"On the twenty-ninth, 1st Battalion attacked northwest, driving to the extremity of the peninsula on the thirtieth. There were ten casualties in this attack, including the loss of Pvt. Gordon O. Fengstadt, a four-year veteran of the Rakkasans. Three hundred, of an estimated three-thousand-man force, escaped in small boats to a coastal island to the west. The next morning, the 1st and 2d Battalions, accompanied by a battalion of ROK Marines, attacked toward the west of Tongjin and completed mopping-up operations, while elements of the 187th moved south to secure and protect Suwon Airfield."

The attack toward Tongjin was not without its battles. "Moving west on the road toward Tongjin we spread out on both sides of the road, keeping a watchful eye on the ditches for 'sleepers,' North Koreans playing dead," wrote Sergeant Alexander after the battle. "In the approach march to a small village we came under moderate small-arms, automatic, and mortar fire. Most of the Reds fled before our marching fire but a few stayed to the bitter end. Two jumped up directly in front of our advance and three of us walking together fired simultaneously to get both of the running men. Just as suddenly, a machine gun opened up from a house on our left flank and we hit the dirt. . . . Crawling to a fence surrounding the mud hut, I threw a grenade. Out stumbled a North Korean soldier, who was quickly followed by a second man carrying a rifle. Inside the hut we found a drum-fed Russian machine gun, which we promptly smashed. The prisoners were herded to the rear. We continued our sweep to the hills, radioed for naval gunfire, and watched the hill erupt in beautiful geysers of rock, dirt, and smoke. There were no enemy left when we climbed to the top."

By the 2d of October, the entire 187th RCT was reassembled at Kimpo Airfield. From the time it had come in-country, General MacArthur had kept the 187th in (GHQ) theater reserve, under his direct control, waiting for the opportunity to deploy the 187th in an airborne operation behind the retreating NKPA, presumably to capture a large segment of the North Korean government and to rescue hundreds of American and ROK POWs. While the 187th trained and reequipped at Kimpo, and made a training parachute jump on the sand flats of the nearby Han River, rumors abounded that a combat airborne operation was imminent. The rumors had some justification: General MacArthur was a believer in the airborne concept, and he knew how to use his parachute forces. In World War II, he had employed the 503d Regimental Combat Team at Nadzab, New Guinea (and had flown in a bomber over the drop zone to watch the jump), the 511th RCT at Tagaytay Ridge south of Manila, and the 503d again on Corregidor—all very successful airborne operations.

At 1700 on the afternoon of 7 October, reconnaissance patrols from the 1st Cavalry Division were the first U.S. ground troops to cross the 38th parallel. On the morning of 9 October, Eighth Army began its advance across the border in force. General MacArthur's plan called for a double envelopment across the narrow neck of the Korean peninsula with the Eighth Army moving north up the western coast to overrun the North Korean capital, Pyongyang, and X Corps, landing amphibiously at Wonsan on the east coast on 20 October, to attack north and then inland. The plan was designed to entrap most of the NKPA south of a line from Chongju on the west coast to Hungnam on the east. The line was some fifty to a hundred miles south of the Manchurian border. By the twentieth of October, the 5th Cavalry Regiment of the 1st Cavalry Division had entered Pyongyang, against light resistance. The NKPA defenders had, lamentably, fled to the north untrapped.

Eighth Army had beaten X Corps in a race to capture Pyongyang. X Corps had been scheduled to land at Wonsan on 20 October, but because the mines could not be cleared from the harbor on time, it was not until 26 October that Col. Lewis "Chesty" Puller was able to lead his 1st Marines ashore. The main body, thirty thousand men, followed. They had been waiting anxiously and impatiently almost three weeks aboard ship to make the landing.

With Eighth Army's rapid move toward the North Korean capital, General MacArthur had decided to drop the 187th at Sukchon-Sunchon, north of Pyongyang, on 21 October. But when the ROK 1st and 7th Divisions entered Pyongyang on 19 October, they found that Kim Il Sung and his government and most of the NKPA had fled to the north. To try to block these forces, General MacArthur advanced the time of the jump to dawn on 20 October. He foresaw the 187th in a classic airborne maneuver: Drop behind enemy lines, attack him from an unexpected direction, block his escape routes, and crush him between the paratroopers and the advancing ground forces.

General MacArthur's plan for the use of the 187th was simple: Parachute the RCT onto two drop zones astride two main highways and railroads running north from the North Korean capital to block the main NKPA routes of escape. One drop zone was at Sukchon, about twenty-five miles north of Pyongyang; the other was at Sunchon, about thirty miles to the northeast of Pyongyang and seventeen miles to the east of Sukchon. The plan for the drop: Colonel Bowen and his command group, the 1st and 3d Battalions, plus a part of the 674th Field Artillery Battalion (about 1,500 troopers) would jump at Sukchon to block the two highways and railroad leading north from Pyongyang; on the twenty-first, the Commonwealth Brigade, attached to the 24th Division, would link up with the Sukchon team. For the second part of the plan, the 2d of the 187th, commanded by Lt. Col. William J. Boyle, plus some artillery (a total of about 1,300 men) would jump on Sunchon to block another highway and railroad; the 70th Tank Battalion would attack north from Pyongyang and link up with the 2d Battalion the day after the jump.

A primary mission of the paratroopers, and one vital to General MacArthur, was to intercept American POWs forced to move along with the routed NKPA columns. (When MacArthur returned to the Philippines in 1944, one of his major priorities was the immediate freeing of interned civilians and soldiers.) MacArthur had to assume that, with the immediate fall of Pyongyang, the North Koreans would move the POWs to the north. In fact, MacArthur's Intelligence Division had informed Colonel Bowen that a trainload of officials and American POWs, traveling very slowly at night, was on its way north from Pyongyang. That information heightened the sense of mission of the 187th.

General Walker was not happy with the 187th's mission. Like many armor-bred senior officers he was not an airborne enthusiast—and seemed to resent the fact that MacArthur had kept the 187th under his wraps for a month, depriving him of a highly trained force that he could have used in capturing Pyongyang. He also felt that the Sukchon-Sunchon jump might be too late to block the escape routes of the NKPA and the Kim government. General Walker did not, however, relay his feelings to General MacArthur.

Morale was high in the 187th. "We all became excited about the first combat jump in Korea," remembered Spc. Edward R. Gasperini of L Company. "Naturally the old paratroopers of World War II, those who had made jumps with the 101st and the 82d, and some who had not, bragged about their exploits in the 'old' airborne. Each was careful to tell us that all combat jumps were made at low altitude to escape concentrated ack-ack fire. This, of course, made us younger jumpers feel just great. This one was going to be my seventh jump."

At Kimpo, the paratroopers went through the usual precombat jump preparations: well-guarded, top-secret briefings on hastily constructed sand tables and maps; packing of equipment bundles; drawing and fitting of personal chutes and three days of rations; oiling and cleaning weapons; and, finally, striking camps.

At 1900 on the eighteenth, pilots and jumpmasters went through a final, detailed briefing at Kimpo. A heavy drizzle, continuing throughout the day, dampened the spirits of the keyed-up paratroopers. One of the briefers announced that if the weather worsened, the jump would be delayed in three-hour increments. Colonel Bowen's staff remained on high alert. Even though weather reports were unfavorable for the twentieth, plans proceeded as if the sun were shining.

At 0230 on the twentieth, in a heavy rain and darkness, the 187th troopers fell out for reveille, ate the traditional prejump breakfast, and then trucked by stick loads to their assigned planes on the ramps at Kimpo. At 0400, the troops drew chutes and began to adjust them. The rains still came; the jump was postponed for three hours.

In late morning, the sky began to clear, and, at 1030, the order came down the line to "chute up." In a short time, the paratroopers, loaded down with M1 rifles or carbines and .45-caliber pistols, packs, water, rations, ammunition, radios, personal gear, and main and reserve parachutes, climbed awkwardly into their planes. The RCT loaded into seventy-three C-119s of the 314th Troop Carrier Wing from Ashiya Air Force Base on Kyushu and into forty C-47s of the 21st Troop Carrier Wing, from Brady Air Force Base, Kyushu. Once the troops were aboard, the planes were jammed with men and equipment. A typical C-119 load was forty-six men in two sticks, fifteen monorail bundles, and four door bundles, two for each of the jump doors. A C-47 carried one stick of about eighteen men and three or four door bundles. Some men carried an extra Griswold container filled with small arms or light mortar ammunition. The planes were so crowded that some men had to sit on the floors.

At noon, the first aircraft carrying Colonel Bowen, thirteen pathfinders, riflemen, unit guides, and part of the RCT staff was airborne, headed for DZ William southeast of Sukchon. "I was a visual-aids man carrying panels which were to be placed on the ground to guide in succeeding planes, including resupply aircraft," remembered Sfc. William Ignatz. "In addition, I carried a case of smoke grenades, an M1 rifle, a .45, and full field equipment. We rendezvoused in a nine-plane V of V's over the Han River, then proceeded north along the west coast of Korea in waves of fifteen and thirty planes spaced about fifteen minutes apart. Colonel Bowen was very cool standing in the door looking for landmarks.

"Our monorail doors opened at the twenty-minute warning. I noted that we were still over the ocean. The red four-minute light came on just as we crossed the beach, headed inland. There was no flack or enemy fighter activity in our immediate area.

"The colonel stood up and gave the jump commands just like a training operation. Sticks were checked in the same manner and we were
ready to go. I felt pretty good about jumping with Colonel Bowen. 'If it
was good enough for the colonel it was good enough for me.'"

DZ William was in an area of dried rice paddies, surrounded on three
sides by mountains. A road ran to the east. The 3d/187th's mission was
to block the road; the 2d/187th's mission was to take the town of Sunchon and capture the train carrying the officials and the POWs.

As the troop carriers approached DZ William, fighter planes rocketed
and strafed the DZ area. At 1400, the lead transport pilot flipped on the
green light. Colonel Bowen, standing in the door with the slipstream
wrinkling his face and tugging at his strapped-down steel helmet, leaned
back from the jump door and yelled, "Go!" He leaped out the door and
was gone in the "peculiar sucking swish of sound that accompanies a
paratrooper into the prop wash," wrote Arch Roberts. The two sticks in
the plane shuffled rapidly to the rear with the characteristic sideslip motion of combat-loaded paratroopers and jumped out the two doors.
There was an occasional yell of "Geronimo" from World War II combat
jump veterans. In seconds, the sky was filled with strings of the opened
chutes of the rest of the serial. Fortunately, there was no enemy antiaircraft fire and only occasional sniper fire from the ground.

The 187th's first combat jump in Korea was under way.

### The Sukchon-Sunchon Battle

Lieutenant Colonel George H. Gerhart, 18th executive officer, led in a
second serial of nineteen C-119s onto the rice paddies of DZ William.
His force included Lt. Col. Harry Wilson's 1st Battalion, Regimental
Headquarters, Support Company, A/127th Engineers, Medical Company, and Service Company. These first two serials dropped 1,470 men
and seventy-four tons of equipment. During the drop, one man was
killed in his parachute by enemy fire, and twenty-five were injured. Both
serials were dropped fairly accurately with only a few sticks of men landing about a mile and a half to the east. Shortly thereafter, Lt. Col. Delbert Munson's 3/187th jumped onto the same DZ.

After the troop jump on DZ William came the heavy-equipment drop,
including 105mm howitzers, jeeps, three-quarter-ton trucks, 90mm antitank guns, a mobile radio transmitter, equivalent in weight to a two-
and-a-half-ton truck. The 674th Airborne FA Battalion (minus B Bat-

tery), under the command of Lt. Col. Harry F. Lambert, who jumped from the first plane with Colonel Bowen, dropped seven 105mm howitzers and 1,125 rounds of ammunition. The 674th recovered six of the howitzers in usable condition. This heavy-equipment drop from C-119's initiated that combination for the first time in combat.

After landing and assembling in short order, the 3/187th headed south of Sukchon, and set up roadblocks across the highway and railroad in its area. By 1630, it had secured its objectives, killed five enemy soldiers, and captured forty-two with no losses. Munson was prepared to resume the attack south along the railroad and highway toward Pyongyang. He had spread out his battalion along the high ground three thousand yards south of Sukchon. Company I was on the left, and Company K, commanded by Capt. John E. Strever, was on the right and had set up a blocking position along the Sukchon-Pyongyang road.

The 1/187th had the mission of clearing Sukchon, securing the high ground to the north, and setting up a roadblock to block enemy withdrawal to the north. Colonel Wilson sent patrols to the river in the vicinity of Naeman-ni. General Bowen had also ordered him to be prepared to move south toward Pyongyang.

"The first platoon of the Engineers reached the town of Songnani-ni at 1530 hours, where they were delayed forty-five minutes by enemy fire," wrote Arch Roberts. "Fifteen prisoners were taken by Sfc. Marcuso and his squad, and these were impressed as porters to move the engineer equipment on handcarts." When the platoon reached Namil-ni, it captured an additional 16 POWs and killed five North Koreans.

General Bowen, who, incidentally, was notified of his reappointment to brigadier general after the jump, established his regimental headquarters along the dykes of the Choeryong River, and by 1600 it was dug in. He set up his command post at Chany-ni on Hill 97.

DZ Easy, the other drop zone for the 187th, was two miles southwest of Sunchon. At 1420, Lt. Col. William J. Boyle led his 2/187th reinforced with B Battery of the 674th, 2d Platoon, A/127th Engineers, 4.2 mortar platoon of Support Company, a Pathfinder Team, one section of 90mm AT guns, and a Forward Air Control Party, onto DZ Easy. Twenty paratroopers were injured on this drop.

By nightfall, the 2d battalion had secured its objectives against very light resistance. "As the Rakkasans marched into Sunchon in a column of twos," one trooper, Pfc. Kirksey of F Company, remembered, "the

Koreans tossed rifles and other weapons out onto the street. The din was terrific."

During the drops on the two DZs on the twentieth and succeeding days, the 187th RCT dropped a total of approximately four thousand troops and more than six hundred tons of equipment and supplies. Included were twelve 105mm howitzers, thirty-nine jeeps, thirty-eight quarter-ton trailers, four 90mm antiaircraft guns, four three-quarter-ton trucks, and 584 tons of ammunition, gasoline, water, rations, and other supplies. Clay Blair, in *The Forgotten War,* wrote that "compared with most World War II airborne operations, the jump was outstanding—indisputably the best combat jump the army had ever staged."

The airborne operation had, of course, not gone unnoticed by General MacArthur. In fact, he and Generals Stratemeyer, Wright, and Whitney had flown in from Japan to watch the airdrop from the air. After he saw the success of the landings, MacArthur flew into Pyongyang, where he told reporters that the airborne operation had apparently taken the enemy completely by surprise. He suggested that some thirty thousand enemy troops, about half those remaining in the north, were trapped between the 187th and the 1st Cavalry and the ROK 1st Division at Pyongyang to the south, and that he had every expectation that they would be trapped and captured or wiped out. He said that the airborne operation was an "expert performance" and that "this closes the trap on the enemy." The next day, back in Tokyo, General MacArthur, flushed with the success he had witnessed over the 187th DZs, predicted too optimistically, "The war is very definitely coming to an end." Unfortunately, the Chinese would deem otherwise.

A large portion of the surviving NKPA had moved north of Sukchon before the 187th drop. No important North Korean Army or government officials were cut off and killed or captured. Civilians in Pyongyang reported that the principal North Korean officials had left Pyongyang on 12 October for Manpojin on the Yalu River. And, unfortunately, most of the American and South Korean POWs had been successfully moved into a remote part of North Korea.

On the morning after the drop, 1/187th had seized dominant terrain directly north of Sukchon to set up a blocking position on the main highway running north. Strong enemy rearguard forces held the next line of hills northward. That afternoon, patrols from the 1st and 2d Battalions made contact at Sunchon.

The most significant combat action after the drop involved the 3d of the 187th on 21–22 October about eight miles south of Sukchon near Opari. At about 0900, Colonel Munson started his battalion, in two combat teams, south toward Pyongyang from its roadblock positions: I Company along the railroad and K Company along the highway, in some areas a separation of about three miles. His mission was to meet the advancing 27th Commonwealth Brigade.

At about 1300, I Company reached Opari and was hit by an estimated enemy battalion supported by 120mm mortars and 40mm guns. MSgt. Melvin Stawser was a platoon sergeant in I Company. He remembers the heavy enemy fire hitting his platoon, and he managed to pull back by squads. Then the NKPA caught I Company in an ambush. The enemy laid heavy grazing fire into the I Company position. For two-and-a-half hours, I Company held out in a heavy firefight. But then the NKPA overran two platoons and forced I Company, with ninety men missing, to move back to Hill 281 west of the railroad. Fortunately the NKPA did not take advantage of the situation and withdrew to their former defensive positions on the high ground around Opari.

Private First Class Richard G. Wilson was a medic attached to I Company. During the battle at Opari, Wilson moved among the wounded, doing his best to give them first aid. In so doing, he exposed himself constantly to the heavy enemy fire of the mortars, 40mm pompoms, and rifles. When Munson ordered what was left of I Company to pull back, Wilson helped the wounded to safety and made certain that none was left behind. Later, Wilson found out that one of the men, previously believed to be dead, had been seen moving and attempting to crawl to safety. In spite of his friends' protests, Wilson returned to the battlefield to search for the wounded man. Two days later, a patrol found Wilson lying beside the man he had returned to aid. Wilson had been shot several times while trying to shield and administer aid to the wounded trooper. Wilson was subsequently awarded the Medal of Honor for his self-sacrifice.

K Company, moving south along the highway, ran into an estimated enemy battalion, a mile north of Yongyu. After a heavy firefight, the NKPA force withdrew south and east of town to defensive positions on high ground. K Company kept moving into Yongyu and dug in on Hill 163, just north of the town. The night of 21–22 October would prove to be a major mark in the battle history of the 3/187th.

In the Yongyu area, the road and railway are separated by some three miles. A line of hills running southwest to northeast cuts across the railroad and highway at Yongyu and Opari. It was the best defensive ground between Pyongyang and the Chongchon River. Along this line of hills, the NK 239th Regiment, about 2,500 men, had dug in. The 239th was the last regiment to leave Pyongyang and had the mission of fighting a delaying action north from Pyongyang. Now it was attacked by two separate forces from the rear.

"A column of singing Koreans approached our position just before dawn," remembers Spc. Gasperini, L Company machine gunner. "They were marching cross-country toward the road which was directly under our guns. The 3d Platoon was dug in on the forward slope, facing the road, with rice paddies in front offering a fine sweep of fire. A line of trees fringed the raised road. Johnson, the gunner, and I were in a two-man foxhole. As the 1st Platoon and Headquarters people fired a few bursts, the Koreans yelled that they were ROK troops. One platoon held fire for about twenty minutes to give these people a chance to identify themselves. By that time the light became strong enough to dispel all doubt. We opened fire with all weapons. A 57mm recoilless rifle knocked out a Russian truck which headed a column coming up the road. Meanwhile the enemy had dispersed and sought defilade behind the raised road. The Reds brought up a Russian machine gun but we kept knocking out the gunners as fast as they brought them up. None made it back to the road. Sergeant Martin, on a heavy machine gun on the military crest, kept up a stream of fire over our heads. The enemy was momentarily stunned by the volume and severity of our fire and the casualties suffered because of it. It took them about an hour to reorganize and deliver any type of organized attack upon the positions held by L Company and the Headquarters Company."

Master Sergeant Willard W. Ryals manned a machine gun at the base of the slope after three gunners had been knocked out. "When Capt. Waldo W. Brooks, the company commander, gave the order to fire," Ryals recalled, "we opened up with everything we had, including fifty-caliber machine guns. We trained a 3.5 bazooka on a culvert through which the [enemy] tried to rush our position. When it filled with enough of them, we would give them a round from the 3.5 and blow them out the other end. This went on for some time. A little farther down the slope I saw one of our guns was having a bad time of it. Three gunners were hit in rapid succession. Though in an exposed position, this piece was placed just fine for killing Reds. When the last man went down, I ran down the slope with lead flying around my head and got behind the gun and began hosing the jackrabbit North Koreans." For his heroics in the action, Master Sergeant Ryals was awarded the Silver Star.

Meanwhile, U.S. I Corps was advancing north. On the day when Pyongyang was secured, I Corps was headed toward the MacArthur Line, a line roughly thirty-five miles south of the Yalu River. Leading the attack was the 24th U.S. Division and the 27th British Commonwealth Brigade. At noon on the twenty-first, the British Brigade was on the main highway out of Pyongyang headed toward Sukchon. That evening, approaching Yongyu, Brigadier Basil A. Coad, the brigade commander, called a halt a mile or two south of the 3/187th positions, from which he could hear the sound of the firefight.

At daylight on the twenty-second, two companies of the Argyll 1st Battalion moved into Yongyu. There the Australian 3d Battalion moved through the Argylls. Lieutenant Colonel Charles H. Greene was the CO of the Argylls. He deployed his battalion with two companies to seize the high ground to the right of the road. He sent a fourth company to the left of the road to follow C Company. The Australians attacked with rifles, grenades, and bayonets against the NKPA using mortars and automatic fire. Colonel Green set up his command post in the orchard, where it was attacked by a large NK force. His small CP detachment killed 34 enemy soldiers. Three men of his personal staff were wounded. In the hand-to-hand fighting, the NKPA lost about 270 men KIA and 200 captured. Amazingly, the Australians suffered only 7 wounded. The enemy fled to the west, and the Middlesex 1st Battalion passed through the Australians and linked up with the 187th at about 1100.

"During this action near Yongyu," wrote Fred J. Waterhouse, "Lieutenant J. B. Nyquist, artillery observer with K Company, called for fire on approximately three hundred North Koreans observed assembling in the town of Yongyu. However, the howitzers of C Battery had been returned to their original position and were not available to fire. The battalion CO (Lt. Col. Harry F. Lambert) immediately ordered Lieutenant Simkins to take two guns of C Battery south of Sukchon to provide support for the battalion. After fighting his way past machine guns and rifle fire, Lieutenant Simkins moved his platoon into the prescribed position. The two howitzers emplaced about fifteen yards apart, with the FDC in between, were ready to fire by 0415 hours. By 0550 hours, these two guns had fired 145 rounds. On one particular fire mission, fifty-four enemy were killed. When 3d Battalion was relieved by the 27th Commonwealth Brigade, C Battery had killed over two hundred of the enemy in this action."

While at Sunchon, Colonel Boyle's troops had heard rumors that the NKPA had massacred many American POWs nearby. Unfortunately, the rumors were accurate. On the twentieth, a trainload of American POWs were northbound when the 187th parachuted into the area. The train pulled into a tunnel to hide; there the NKPA murdered sixty-six POWs. Brigadier General Frank Allen, the 1st Cavalry ADC, had led a search mission for the POWs. His team found the sixty-six bodies as well as seven other Americans who had died of disease or starvation. In the area, his team also found twenty-three thin, emaciated American POW survivors, many badly wounded, two mortally. Of the estimated 2,500 American POWs in North Korean custody, these ninety-six were all that could be found.

On the twenty-third, troops of the 3d Battalion moved back into the Opari area to search for any men who might have survived the battle. En route to the area, they captured fifty NKPA wearing civilian clothes. Shortly, the troops found several wounded paratroopers. On the same day, a patrol captured fifteen NKPA soldiers. "These people," Gasperini said, "were wearing pile jackets and jump boots taken from the I Company dead. We stripped them, shooting two who tried to escape. One of them was found wearing the clothing of Pfc. Wilson, I Company's medic. He, too, was shot while trying to escape. Later we found fifty North Korean uniforms discarded by the Reds, who had donned American clothing."

"Prisoners of war proved a difficult problem for the 187th," wrote CWO John Hudson later. "After being cut off, the enemy troops would change into civilian clothes, stand in front of houses in Sukchon waving South Korean flags. Sometimes the evaders would hide in the homes while women and children of the town waved the flags. At night, the 187th had to dodge the bullets of these 'civilians.' The MPs had the job of mopping up and rounding up the North Koreans."

For their gallant stand and heroism in the battle on Yongyu, the 3d Battalion of the 187th, 3d Platoon A Company 127th Engineers, and the 2d Section of the Antitank Platoon received the Presidential Unit Citation. In the battle, the 3d Battalion Task Force had killed 805 enemy soldiers, captured 691, seized a Russian radar set, thirty cargo trucks, and numerous machine guns and rifles.

During the Sukchon-Sunchon operation, the 187th had fought almost 8,000 NKPA troops, killing an estimated 2,764. The RCT captured 3,818 of the enemy. The total RCT casualties were 48 killed in action, 80 wounded in action, and one soldier dead and 56 injured on the jump.

Late in the afternoon of the twenty-third, the 2d Battalion left Sunchon on foot on the way to Sukchon and were picked up by a truck convoy about six miles away. They moved toward Pyongyang and arrived there about 2400, followed by the 1st and 3d Battalions. All of the other RCT units had already closed in.

Shortly thereafter, the 187th reverted to theater reserve with the ancillary mission of guarding Pyongyang, Chinnampo, the Pyongyang airfield, and the main supply route. It also awaited its next airborne mission. It was not long in coming.

## Between Jumps

By the end of October, brief clashes with Chinese troops in the sectors of both the Eighth Army and X Corps that had landed, on 26 October, well behind schedule at Wonsan on the east coast of North Korea posed a new, ominous, but as yet unappreciated threat to the UN Forces. In fact, the senior UN commanders in Korea, from General MacArthur on down, believed that the war in Korea was virtually won. On 3 November, General MacArthur's veteran G2, Maj. Gen. Charles A. Willoughby, estimated the CCF (Chinese Communist Forces) in North Korea at between 16,500 and a maximum of 34,000. On 6 November, he upped his guess to 34,500 Chinese facing both the Eighth Army and X Corps. The UN strength on that date was some 250,000 men.

Optimism was running high in the UN ranks. Department of the Army and General MacArthur were making plans to redeploy Eighth Army units from Korea, with the 2d Division slated to go either to Europe or the U.S. In the 1st Cavalry Division, many troopers thought that on Thanksgiving they would be on parade in the Tokyo Plaza, proudly wearing their yellow cavalry scarves. The First Cav even started turning in equipment in preparation for its return to Japan. The *New York Times* said, editorially, "Except for unexpected developments along the frontiers of the peninsula, we can now be easy in our minds as to the military outcome."

General Willoughby's figures missed the mark widely. By early November, the total CCF force in North Korea had grown to thirty infantry divisions of over 300,000 men.

On the 1st of November, 20,000 Chinese struck from the north and northwest simultaneously against the 1st Cavalry Division's 1st and 2d Battalions of the 8th Cavalry Regiment pushing northeast from the Chongchon bridgehead and against the 15th Regiment of the ROK 6th Division on the First Cav's right flank near Unsan.

Under the massive Chinese attack, the ROK regiment broke within two hours. In the 1st Cavalry Division sector, the Chinese drove a wedge between the 1st and 2d Battalions of the 8th Cavalry. Both battalions fell back on Unsan. By 2000, both battalions were out of ammunition, more or less overrun, and cut off. The survivors took to the hills. In the 1st of the 8th, 265 men had been either killed or captured. On the 2d of November, the CCF, in a well-planned trap maneuver, hit the 3d of the 8th, boldly broadcasting the attack with bugles and horns blaring. The lightly armed but veteran CCF units surrounded the battalion, set up a roadblock to its rear, and then, in hand-to-hand combat, overran the battalion, including its command post. Only 10 officers and 200 men escaped the slaughter. The battalion commander, Lt. Col. Robert J. Ormond, was killed. In the two battles, the 8th Cavalry Regiment lost over 800 men. Along the Chongchon River, the 5th Cavalry also fought a bloody and costly battle.

In the east, the Chinese hit X Corps. Near the Kotori plateau, the 1st Marine Division suffered heavy losses. For several days the Chinese fought savagely but then, surprisingly, broke off the attack. The CCF faded into the surrounding mountains, perhaps because after five days of hard fighting, the Chinese needed to rearm, regroup, and replenish their supplies. It might also have been a subterfuge to draw the UN forces deeper into the north, lengthening their already extended lines of supply.

In spite of the 1st Cavalry's horrible beating by the CCF between 8 and 23 November, Eighth Army and X Corps consolidated their positions and advanced slowly against moderate resistance as far north as the Chongchon River in the west and the Yalu in the east. Eighth Army had two U.S. and one ROK Corps—a total of eight divisions and two brigades, some 118,000 men—deployed across a seventy-mile-wide front ready to launch a major offensive on 24 November. General Walker believed that he faced about 50,000 enemy troops, half CCF and half NKPA. By his estimate, he had a two-to-one superiority, about right for an attack. In fact, the numbers were almost reversed. Unfortunately, General Walker also did not appreciate the weakness of the ROK II Corps.

By now, the Chinese were ready to spring their own onslaught. General Lin Piao commanded the Thirteenth Army Group. He had eighteen divisions deployed, ready to attack directly into the ROK II Corps and then turn into the Eighth Army's right flank in an envelopment designed to encircle and trap the Eighth Army in North Korea. In the east on the X Corps front, the CCF Ninth Army Group of twelve divisions was deployed to envelop the 1st Marine Division at Yudam and then destroy the 3d Division and two ROK divisions, thus driving a wedge between Eighth Army and X Corps. Piao's attack was scheduled for the night of 25 November; the Ninth Army Group attack was slated for 27 November into the Chosin Reservoir area.

When the Eighth Army attacked on 24 November, the lead units met little or no resistance—simply a few enemy squads and platoons using small-arms fire. In the ROK II Corps zone, the opposition was also light. In most places, the UN was virtually unopposed. Displaying his usual flamboyance, General MacArthur had flown over from Japan the morning of the 24th to witness the start of the attack. In fifteen-degree weather, he and General Walker "jeeped" along the front for about four hours. They visited I Corps, IX Corps, and the 24th Division along the Chongchon River. In the visit to IX Corps, Maj. Gen. Frank W. Milburn, the commander, mentioned, somewhat grimly and forebodingly, that "his patrols had found the Unsan area heavily defended and that the projected IX Corps attack in that area would not progress easily." His comments, however, were not taken too seriously by the optimistic high command, who continued to reflect misguided enthusiasm about the ultimate success of the offensive.

Just after the jump at Sukchon, Colonel Bowen (USMA 1926) was restored to his World War II rank of brigadier general, a grade he had earned as the G3 of General Eichelberger's Eighth Army from 1944 to 1946; he retained command of the 187th Regimental Combat Team. Colonel George H. Gerhart (USMA 1934) became the commander of just the regiment; Lt. Col. Arthur H. "Harry" Wilson (USMA 1937) retained command of 1/187th; Lt. Col. William J. Boyle (USMA 1939), who had won the DSC in the Battle of the Bulge, had a clash with General Bowen after the Sukchon-Sunchon jump and was replaced by Lt. Col. John P. "Poopy" Connor (USMA 1937); later, Lt. Col. Delbert E. Munson (USMA 1940) recovered from his wounds and resumed command of 3/187th.

Meanwhile, on 25 November, the 187th RCT was ensconced in an area around Sinmace, near Pyongyang, with a zone of responsibility including the entire Eighth Army service area, with particular emphasis on securing Pyongyang, the North Korean capital; Chinnampo; the Pyongyang Airfield; and the main supply route past the city. By the twenty-first of November, General Bowen had under his operational control the 187th, the 10th Philippine Battalion Combat Team, the 29th British Infantry Brigade, and the 5th ROK Division. On the twenty-fifth, he also assumed opcon of the Thailand Expeditionary Force.

In its zone, the 187th continued to receive reports of sabotage and guerrilla activity. In one incident, an NKPA lieutenant burned a large building, housing eight thousand POWs. The number of refugees straggling into the city continued to increase. On the defensive lines around their zone, the 187th troopers reported little contact with CCF but did fight an occasional small battle with NKPA guerrillas. Far more was yet to come.

On the evening of the twenty-fifth of November, as scheduled, Gen. Lin Piao unleashed his hordes of Chinese along the Eighth Army front. On the twenty-sixth, the CCF struck again. In the west, the CCF hit the 2d, 24th, 25th, and 1st Cavalry Divisions with heavy, relentless attacks. Three CCF divisions hit the marines in the center of North Korea near the Chosin Reservoir. In the northeast, two CCF divisions attacked and encircled three regiments of the 7th Division. With these attacks and the complete rout of the ROK forces on Eighth Army's flank, General Walker's situation became desperate. He faced a monumental decision. The Chinese had encircled many of his units and had seized the high ground to their rear. By the 28th of November, the situation was clear: he was forced to order a general retreat from the north and fall back into a solid enclave around Pyongyang.

On the afternoon of the thirtieth of November, the 2d Division tried to move south from Kunu-ri to Sunchon in freezing cold and a blinding snowstorm but ran into thousands of Chinese blocking the route in a carefully planned CCF ambush. In the ensuing battles over two weeks, the 2d Division suffered some 4,940 casualties and lost most of its equipment in a monumental military disaster. But the major elements of Eighth Army, because of the speed of their withdrawal, over 120 miles in ten days, were able to escape the brunt of the CCF onslaught.

General Walker formed Eighth Army into an enclave around Pyongyang. The 187th, the Eighth Army reserve, moved north through Pyongyang to set up blocking positions in the Sukchon area and to keep the road through Pyongyang open. The 187th's zone of responsibility extended from Sukchon and Sunchon to Seoul. The 187th was on the right and the British brigade on the left. But because General Walker did not have the units he needed to defend the area around Pyongyang, on 28 November he made the controversial but, to him, obviously necessary decision to abandon Pyongyang and all of North Korea. His new order: Withdraw south of the 38th parallel to the Imjin River, fight a delaying action on the way; destroy all U.S. supplies (vehicles, tanks, weapons, ammunition, rations, winter clothing, gasoline) that had been accumulated in Pyongyang; blow all railroad and highway bridges and culverts behind the retreat.

On 10 December, the 187th closed out of Pyongyang and set up a new CP at Sohung. Like the rest of the retreating U.S. forces, the 187th blew up the supplies left behind. "We went on a real tear," remembered one of the five men left behind to destroy supplies, "setting fire to large stores of Russian supplies and equipment captured by the regiment. We set explosions all over the city, blowing up ammunition and other supplies. On the eighteenth, we confiscated a Korean jeep and headed south. Before leaving, we blew up the Russian embassy. We hit the bridge a few hours ahead of the advancing Chinese, who occupied Pyongyang at midnight of the day we left."

The 187th fought a series of battles to keep the withdrawal route open. After Eighth Army had moved successfully south of the 38th parallel during the week of 6 to 13 December, General Walker called

General Bowen and told him that the majority of his, Walker's, forces were now south of the parallel. General Bowen said, "Wonderful," and immediately hung up the phone without waiting for any additional missions that might jeopardize his plan. Then he called his commanders together and told them: "I'm sick and tired of running from a shadow enemy. Tomorrow morning the 187th will turn about and move north until we contact this enemy and give him a real bloody nose." Then he gave the order to move north, emphasizing speed and caution to clear the high ground to the sides of the road.

"For two days the march north continued without contact," remembered Lt. Col. Rye Mausert, acting commander of the 3d Battalion. "Later on the afternoon of the second day, the lead units uncovered a small village. General Bowen ordered that we hold for the night and patrol aggressively. The next morning, just as I was about to order the companies to assemble and continue north, there, before our unbelieving eyes, columns of Chinese were moving south on the road one mile away. In columns of fours, without any lead unit protecting, the Chinese moved toward us. The 674th Field Artillery forward observer immediately relayed target information to his Fire Direction Center. Guns swung into position for a field artilleryman's dream.

"The Chinese continued to move toward us, completely oblivious to their peril. The entire 3d Battalion was as quiet as church mice. The air force notified us they would be on site shortly. General Bowen moved to the 3d Battalion CP. The 674th assured us they were dead on target. All 3d Battalion heavy weapons were also on target ready to go. By now the lead Chinese columns were 500–600 yards away. At this point, I gave the order to open fire." Field artillery, all battalion heavy weapons, even regimental antitank guns got into the act. The range was a little too far for the individual rifleman, but a few could not resist shooting. Most of the riflemen just watched in awe as the Chinese were slaughtered. Without orders, the Chinese were at a loss as to what to do. As the lead enemy soldiers fell, those in the rear moved forward to take their positions. But never a change in formation. They just moved up, got shot down, and fell. There were piles of bodies on the road, but they just kept coming.

"After fifteen minutes of continuous firing by the 674th, I received a radio message from approaching Air Force planes. 'Is this a private fight or can anyone get in?' It was excellent timing. Our guns were starting to get hot. Flying in at the head of the Chinese columns, the planes bombed and napalmed along the entire line of march to the end of the columns. As the planes flew in for their second run, it was more than the living Chinese could stand. They broke ranks and ran every which way—not by command but by sheer terror. Meanwhile our troops just watched in awe and cheered.

"By now all planes had used up their major ordnance, but they weren't finished. They now started rabbit-hunting—chasing down and strafing small Chinese groups. The planes ran out of ammunition and radioed, 'Okay. It's all yours,' and returned to base. There were no targets left. Pile after pile of dead enemy lay strewn along the road. In this action, there was not one single Rakkasan casualty."

General Bowen was now satisfied. He ordered the 187th to turn about. Early on the morning of the twelfth, the 1st and 2d Battalions, followed by the 674th Field Artillery, headed south. The 3d Battalion remained astride the road and, later in the day, followed the rest of the RCT as the rear guard.

On that same day, General Bowen received Eighth Army's plan for yet another major withdrawal—from Seoul and the northern sectors. General Bowen's mission: move south of the Han River to secure the Han River crossings; hold the crossings at all costs; conduct operations in the Hoengsong, Chechon, Wonju areas; provide protection for the evacuation of Kimpo airfield and the Inchon Harbor area.

For the next few days, the 187th blocked CCF probing attacks north of Wonju. Holding the Tanyang–Punji Pass, General Bowen deployed the regiment with the 1st and 3d Battalions on line and the 2d Battalion in reserve. According to Bill Weber, "This was particularly severe duty, as the temperatures hovered in the twenty- to thirty-below range (with windchill) and we were without winter equipment. Weapons would not function and men would become almost lethargic from the cold. The CCF were only about a hundred yards from our positions but, except for intermittent firing, they were suffering just as much, if not worse, than we. This type operation (all battalions involved) continued through 19 January 1951, when we were relieved by the 38th Infantry and passed to corps reserve."

On December 9, General MacArthur ordered General Almond to withdraw X Corps through Hungnam and relocate it in South Korea, the American units—the 1st Marine Division and the 3d and 7th Infantry Divisions—close to Pusan, and the Korean I Corps at Samchok. In an epic battle, the marines fought their way out of a CCF encirclement at the Chosin Reservoir. The marines brought out all their equipment, vehicles, casualties, and their dead. A marine corps study, based on captured CCF documents and POWs, estimated that the marines alone had inflicted on the CCF some 37,500 casualties. Other studies estimate that the CCF suffered 30,000 nonbattle casualties, primarily from frostbite. In all, the studies show that the CCF's casualties were as high as 60 percent of their forces, "a disaster," one Marine study concluded. On Christmas Day, the marines and elements of the 7th Division, some 105,000 soldiers and marines, plus 17,500 vehicles and 91,000 Korean refugees, left from the Hungnam port bound for Pusan.

On the twenty-third of December, General Walker was following his usual routine: speeding along narrow roads in the manner of his mentor, General Patton. He had been to the 24th Division CP and was on his way to the Commonwealth Brigade, to present an ROK Presidential Citation. His driver, MSgt. George Belton, with siren blaring, sped up the icy northbound lane of a highway whose southbound lane was lined bumper to bumper with military traffic. An ROK weapons carrier pulled out of the line directly in front of General Walker's jeep. He, his aide, Lt. Col. Layton C. Tynor, the driver, and his bodyguard, Sgt. Francis S. Reenan, were all thrown into a ditch. They were taken to the 8055th MASH unit. General Walker was dead on arrival. The other three survived and were evacuated to Japan.

General MacArthur, notified within minutes of General Walker's death, immediately called Gen. J. Lawton Collins, the army chief of staff. The two men had already decided that if anything were to happen to General Walker, Lt. Gen. Matthew B. Ridgway would succeed him. At 1130 on 25 December, General Ridgway landed in Tokyo. On the 26th, he had a conference with General MacArthur. After a long discussion of the situation in Korea, General MacArthur finally said, "You will make mistakes, as, of course, we all do, but even if you do, I will assume responsibility. You have my complete confidence." When General Ridgway asked if General MacArthur would "have any objection to my attacking?" General MacArthur replied, "The Eighth Army is yours, Matt. Do what you think best."

Within this framework, General MacArthur gave General Ridgway more latitude and greater control than he had invested in General Walker. He gave Ridgway complete authority to plan and execute operations in Korea and, in addition, and most significant, he assigned X Corps to the Eighth Army so that for the first time since the war began, the Eighth Army commander commanded all the UN ground forces in Korea to include U.S., Great Britain, Australia, Canada, New Zealand, India, South Africa, France, Greece, the Netherlands, the Philippines, Thailand, Turkey, Belgium, and Sweden.

General Ridgway's command consisted of about 365,000 troops, the majority of whom were ROKs and not part of Eighth Army. The next largest was Eighth Army, to which certain U.S. Air Force, U.S. Marines, and several United Nations units, including the Koreans, were attached.

At times, General MacArthur would still interject himself into military operations in Korea, much to the annoyance of General Ridgway, but for the most part, Ridgway was in command.

At 1615 on the twenty-sixth, General Ridgway landed at Taegu. Ridgway now had the mission of reshaping the Eighth Army, not only with weapons and equipment but also with backbone. He was taking over a force with a defeatist attitude, a lack of aggressiveness, and many listless and irresolute senior commanders. He felt that, among other remedies, the Eighth Army high command needed a "housecleaning." In his book, *Soldier,* General Ridgway wrote: "I must say, in all frankness, that the spirit of the Eighth Army as I found it on my arrival there gave me deep concern. There was a definite air of nervousness, of gloomy foreboding, of uncertainty, a spirit of apprehension as to what the future held."

With Ridgway in command, the war in Korea took a new turn. He spent his early days in the field with groups of men and officers from all the U.S. units and in conferences with his senior commanders, emphasizing offensive spirit, forward deployment of commanders with their units (division commanders at the battalion level, for example), the maximum use of firepower of all kinds, night marching and fighting techniques, detailed reconnaissance and knowledge of the terrain over which they would fight, confidence in themselves and their units, at least two hot meals a day for the troops, and the full use of the logistics chain to equip the soldiers properly for winter weather and arm them with ample ammunition and weapons. He set about relieving weak commanders at the highest levels, including four division commanders. He sought to infuse Eighth Army with a fighting spirit and hold the line at Seoul.

The need to revitalize Eighth Army was apparent and demanded immediate attention to avert a major catastrophe. On New Year's Eve, 31 December 1950, the Chinese crossed the 38th parallel and invaded South Korea in mass. The Fourth Chinese Field Army made a coordinated attack toward the rail center at Wonju. The Chinese 120th Division, a special unit equipped with superior weapons and equipment, moved toward the 187th.

The war was in a new phase, and the 187th Airborne Regimental Combat Team would continue to play a vital role therein.

### Battle of Wonju

The Chinese launched a massive assault across the 38th parallel at daybreak on New Year's Day, 1951. The subsequent invasion of South Korea was prodigious, "like floodwater down a mountain," Fred Waterhouse described it. Hundreds of artillery and rolling mortar barrages thundered across the terrain, erupting in a steady drumfire of explosions. Then came tens of thousands of walking infantrymen, blowing bugles and horns and shooting off flares, striding relentlessly with rigid discipline through U.S. minefields and rows of coiled barbed wire. They attacked along the entire front but directed their major effort against U.S. I and IX Corps in the west and center. Seven CCF armies and two NK corps penetrated deeply toward Seoul and the rail and road center of Wonju in the central sector. On order, the U.S. forces contracted around Seoul into a crescent-shaped bridgehead that ran along the south bank of the frozen Han River to Yangp'yong, thence to the Sea of Japan through Hongchon and Chumunjin.

Coordinating their move with the ROKs who were falling back in the east, I and IX Corps pulled back to the Seoul bridgehead. The U.S. X Corps (the 2d and 7th Infantry Divisions), after their amphibious pullout from the north, reentered the battle zone on 2 January. On the third, X Corps tool control of three ROK divisions in a new corps zone in the central front between IX and ROK III Corps.

"Late in the afternoon of January 2, I made one last tour of the lines," wrote General Ridgway. "Traveling by open jeep, I found all the corps and division commanders in action there, and got their estimates. The pressure was building up. It was time to go. Reluctantly, the next morning, I gave the order to fall back south of the Han, to leave Korea's ancient capital, Seoul, once more in the hands of the enemy." General Ridgway knew that standing still would invite destruction.

But he also knew that the enemy's logistical capabilities did not match his tactical abilities and would eventually slow him down. The Chinese lacked even rudimentary motor transports, and used packhorses, ox-carts, and human backs to move their relatively meager logistic system. General Ridgway knew that the combat troops would eventually outrun their supplies. So he decided to "roll with the punch." He ordered another withdrawal south to a line in the vicinity of the 37th parallel. This line ran from Pyongtaek on the Seoul-Taejon highway east through Ansong, northeast to Wonju, then to the east coast town of Samchok. The I and IX Corps were first to move into intermediate positions in front of Suwon, sixteen miles south of Seoul. Movement began on 3 January; the resulting bumper-to-bumper traffic clogged the few roads.

On the third of January, General Bowen received orders to move south to Suwon airfield prepared to attack on thirty minutes' notice to either Inchon or Wonju. The 674th Airborne Field Artillery Battalion, an integral unit of the 187th RCT, was scattered over a wide area, with each firing battery in direct support of its infantry battalion. Near Wonju, B Battery of the 674th Airborne FA Battalion set up in an abandoned X Corps ammo dump, fortuitously crammed with stacks of boxed 105mm shells.

"The battery had begun to displace in successive moves to the rear shortly after Christmas," remembered Sfc. Antonio G. Maria. "There was heavy traffic of all kinds on the roads, making our moves very difficult. . . . Many military convoys were headed south. Near Wonju we set up the battery in a level area surrounded by hills as the Chinese Fourth Field Army moved in on the UN positions. We fired missions all day, firing as fast as we could open the ammunition cases. In one twenty-minute period, my gun fired eighty rounds of high explosives, burning the paint off the tube in the process. Our forward observer told us that our fire caught thousands of advancing Chinese in the open, killing hundreds and breaking up many attacks."

Sergeant Aaron D. Kirksey of the 187th spent New Year's on the line at Wonju. "Small-arms fire got me out of the sack at daylight," he recalled. "Hurriedly dressing, I saw thousands of CCF coming down the valley and down both ridges toward our position. Everything that we could throw at the enemy was brought to bear on the advancing Chinese. The 96th FA Battalion, nearby, fired its eight-inch howitzers at point-blank range.

"The savage concentration of fire momentarily stopped the advance, but there were just too many for us. Our explosives and automatic-weapons fire tore great gaps in the line, but the Reds just closed up and kept coming. Unable to continue in the face of such heavy losses, the enemy finally withdrew, but we knew it was just a respite. At nightfall, we started walking back to Wonju. Here we established defensive positions in the hills and, on the fourteenth, the 2d Battalion jumped off in a counterattack. Three or four miles north of Wonju we came under small arms and machine-gun fire with some light mortar rounds landing in the F Company area. I set up my mortar and was able to knock out one troublesome machine gun with one round of white phosphorous. Crossing a paddy field, we lost some men crowded up in a ditch when a mortar shell landed among them. Taking the left flank hill, we started toward the second when we came under attack by four South African planes. They made repeated passes at us, dropping napalm and firing rockets and 20mm cannon. Finally one of the tank gunners who was accompanying us on the mission fired his fifty-caliber at the planes and they went away."

The Allied withdrawal, which began in early January, became a mass exodus amid scenes of utter destruction. At Kimpo 500,000 gallons of fuel and 23,000 gallons of napalm blew up in a great holocaust. Barracks, hangars, and other military installations burned. As the enemy entered Seoul from the north, office buildings, hotels, and homes went up in flames. Smoke swirled through the streets as hordes of civilians made their way out of the capital. Looters followed in their wake.

All during the day on 4 January, columns of UN jeeps, trucks, staff cars, and soldiers poured over the two floating engineer bridges that spanned the Han. "In that bitter January cold the ice was four or five inches thick, frozen solid except in the water adjacent to the floating bridges," wrote General Ridgway. "There men in rubber boats, armed with pile poles, fought the grinding ice floes away from the pontoons, in scenes reminiscent of George Washington crossing the Delaware. On these light, floating bridges the fate of our army depended. Beyond the Han were nearly a hundred thousand fighting men. Beyond it were all the heavy guns and tanks that were in the combat zone. And all of these, men and guns, had to be brought back across these bridges, or remain to be destroyed. . . . The decision to evacuate Seoul . . . set off one of the greatest mass flights of a frightened people in all history. . . . Out of the narrow alleys and byways of that great metropolis, at least a million of them poured toward those two bridges across the Han."

The raggedly clad refugees carried only small bundles or dragged their few possessions in rude carts. Some had only the clothes on their backs. Many died of exposure or starvation. Families broke up, children got lost, crying babies were taken from the backs of dead mothers, old people sat along the roads waiting to die. Seoul changed hands for the third time in a little more than six months.

The weather was abominable. In areas along the front, the snow was six feet deep, and temperatures dropped to thirty below zero. A large mass of the enemy forces shifted to the east to drive through the rough, mountainous terrain along the Hongchon-Hoengsong-Wonju axis. If this attack succeeded, the Chinese would drive a wedge through and swing behind the U.S. I and IX Corps. The capture of Wonju would seriously limit UN movement in the center of Korea.

By the ninth of January, it was becoming clear to General Ridgway that the Chinese had determined to make a strong attack through Wonju. He decided to hold on the central or Wonju front and, on 25 January, counterattack in the west with I and IX Corps in Operation Thunderbolt. He directed the X Corps commander, Gen. Ned Almond, to deploy the bulk of the 2d Division south of Wonju and the 7th Division to block on an east-west line from Chechon to Yongwol. He moved the 187th to Tanyang, a road hub south of the 7th Division.

On 13 January, following successive moves to Inchon, Kyongan-ni, Chonsen, and Yoju to set up blocking positions, General Bowen moved his CP to Punji to defend the Tanyang-Punji pass. The 187th was now under X Corps. General Almond attached the 3d Battalion of the 8th Cavalry Regiment to General Bowen. Temperatures continued to drop until subzero weather and deep snow were constants.

To defend the Punji Pass, the 187th had to fight its way to the top of the ridges overlooking the pass. Colonel Munson moved his 3d Battalion up a winding road to a mountain with L Company on the right, K Company on the left, and I Company in reserve. Initially, there was little resistance, but at the CCF OPLR (Out of Post Line of Resistance), the troops ran into increasing fire, nevertheless driving the CCF off the line. The snow got deeper the higher they fought. The enemy troops in white camouflage uniforms were hard to spot. Colonel Munson called in artillery and air strikes. The subsequent bombing and napalm blasted the enemy and also cleared paths through the deep snow. At about 1400, the enemy retreated over the top of the mountain, and the 3d Battalion moved onto it and dug into the snow.

At about 2100, the Chinese began a massive attack on the top of the ridge. But the 3d Battalion was well dug in and had clear lines of fire. No enemy soldier came within twenty-five feet of the MLR. "In spite of the enemy being cut down like ripe wheat," wrote Rye Mausert, the 3d Battalion XO, "as those in the front fell, those in the rear, screaming and blowing their by now famous bugles, passed on through, only to fall and add to their ever increasing dead. Finally, the remainder, if there were any, totally withdrew. Within minutes every enemy body was completely frozen into grotesque, contorted positions.

"Amazingly, with the tremendous enemy casualties, a check of the Rakkasan battalion revealed no friendly casualties. Two Rakkasans, in their enthusiasm, had used their bare hands to swing a machine gun. As they pulled their hands away, their skin stayed with the gun.

"Next morning the Rakkasans inspected the battlefield. Wading through waist-deep snow, we found dead enemy soldiers scattered throughout the entire MLR front, often in piles of ten or more. Already enemy bodies were as solid as rock from the cold. Even the most calloused Rakkasan, on inspection of the bodies, couldn't but feel sorry for them. Many had no shoes at all. Others wore sneakers. Some of the enemy dead had satchel charges tied around their waists. Trenches were dug in the snow, and after removing the charges, the bodies were dumped in and covered with snow."

On the third and fourth of February, thousands of charging CCF hit Lt. Col. Harry Wilson's 1st Battalion's dug-in perimeter. On the night of the 3d, B Company, the hardest hit, had six men KIA; the battalion lost fifty men, KIA and WIA. But the 1st Battalion held its position, inflicting heavy casualties on the CCF. In the fight, among others, the 1st

Battalion lost three first lieutenants: Robert B. Coleman, USMA '47; David B. Spellman, USMA '46; and Robert M. Garvin, USMA '47; attached from a tank company of the 1st Cavalry Division.

In Operation Thunderbolt in the west, six of the seven columns met only scattered resistance. Only the Turkish brigade east of Osan encountered stiff opposition. By nightfall, elements of the 35th Infantry of the 25th Division were on the south edge of Suwon, and in the IX Corps area, a column reached Inchon. During the rest of the month, I and IX Corps advanced slowly, ridge by ridge, phase line by phase line, to clear out almost every enemy soldier. During the first days of Thunderbolt, the Chinese launched a few small, unsuccessful night counterattacks.

On the central front, Ridgway order X Corps and the ROK III Corps to initiate an attack similar to the one in the west. This attack, named Operation Roundup, called for the ROK 5th and 8th Divisions of X Corps to launch enveloping attacks on Hongchon to prevent the regrouping of North Korean forces south of the town. At the same time, other units of ROK III Corps would attack to protect the X Corps's right flank. Roundup began on 5 February.

During the first day of the attack, there was little opposition. But by the sixth, both ROK divisions were meeting increasingly heavy resistance northeast of Hoengsong. By 8 February, strong North Korean forces were attacking the right flank of X Corps. The enemy was initially on the defensive but shortly began launching strong counterattacks all along the line. In some cases the enemy seemed to entice the UN into attacking. Intelligence and air observers began to pick up large enemy forces between IX and X Corps and other units moving east and south above Hoengsong and indications that the enemy had shifted the bulk of his forces in the west to the west-central zone. The threat of a counteroffensive became more certain.

On 11–12 February, elements of the Chinese Fortieth and Sixty-sixth Armies and the North Korean V Corps launched a massive attack north of Hoengsong against the ROK 3d, 5th, and 8th Divisions in subzero weather. The attackers swarmed across the snow-covered, ice-glazed, frozen ridges with the usual bugles blaring, whistles screaming, and drums beating. The Chinese penetrated the ROK positions and forced them to pull back. The three ROK divisions tried unsuccessfully to set up a line north of Hoengsong, but only remnants of the 5th and 8th Divisions were left.

Captain James B. Cook and his G Company of the 187th had been detached from the 2d Battalion and was in a blocking position just south of Hoengsong. The CCF had seized the hills on both sides of a road running out of Hoengsong. Elements of the U.S. 2d Division were surrounded by the enemy. On the twelfth of February, Company G was attached to the 2d Division's 38th Infantry Regiment along with a platoon of tanks from Company C, 72d Tank Battalion. The task force moved up to a small village about fifteen miles north of Wonju and found that about four thousand men from the 38th Infantry and the 1st ROK Division were trapped in a snarled column of vehicles and equipment at the northern end of the valley. Some ROK forces held a small section on the eastern side but took off after G Company arrived. A French company was dug in a small town at the mouth of the valley, prepared to move south. A Dutch battalion was also in the area.

What Cook and his men found was nothing short of a catastrophe. "In ditches on each side of the road lay dead and wounded men of the 2d Infantry Division, who had attempted to run the gauntlet during the day," wrote Fred Waterhouse. "The Rakkasans of G Company moved along the ditches firing their individual and crew-served weapons at close-range targets. The entire company stretched out along the road and was heavily engaged in holding the road open for survival in this nightmarish operation." The task force reached the two battalions of the 38th Infantry at 1900 hours.

"Key to the effective relief action were three partly blown bridges held by roadblocking Chinese supported by 120mm mortars and automatic weapons," wrote Arch Roberts. "Sizing up the situation, G Company pushed off with the tanks leading and troops, in platoon formation, following. The first partly demolished bridge was negotiated successfully, and, under a rain of steel, the enemy holding two successive crossings were killed. Reaching the stalled column about midnight, G Company extricated the trapped regiment and ROK forces by leading the column back down that same terrible gauntlet of fire to safety. Acting as the rear guard, the paratroopers held open the escape route to Wonju until all United Nations elements had cleared the mouth of the valley."

What the paratroopers saw as the column passed was brutal. The men of the 1st and 3d Battalions of the 38th and the ROKs had placed their dead and wounded on any available vehicle, including draping them across their howitzers. One paratrooper saw a three-quarter-ton truck, with the tailgate down, pass by. Protruding were the stubs of two legs of an American soldier. As vehicles came by, paratroopers placed on them the dead and wounded from the ditches. Sfc. Haywood was particularly courageous in his attempts, under fire, to save the wounded.

After the column passed, G Company and the Dutch battalion brought up the rear of the column. Without the tanks, G Company took an increased barrage of enemy fire. In the operation, G Company had six men KIA and "many" WIA. Lieutenant J. N. Epps was the G Company weapons platoon leader. His platoon lost all of its crew-served weapons. His platoon sergeant, MSgt. Philip J. Wilkes, was killed in action and received the Distinguished Service Cross posthumously.

G Company covered the rear of the column in the twelve-mile march south to Wonju. The survivors recall this action as the "Nightmare Alley Operation." Newspapers referred to the operation as "Hell's Canyon" and "Massacre Valley." The losses to the 2d Division and the Dutch battalion, which had fought valiantly during the withdrawal, were disastrous: 1,769 casualties plus the loss of 19 howitzers (fifteen 105s and four 155s) and 120 trucks, many of which had been carrying wounded.

Three years after the war, at Fort Benning, Captain Epps met Lt. Col. W. P. Kelleher, who had been the CO of the 1st of the 38th at Hoengsong. Epps found out that the soldier whose two leg stubs stuck out of the three-quarter-ton truck had survived.

"The key to the defense of the central front was the decision by Ridgway to hold Wonju," wrote Bevin Alexander in *Korea: The First War We Lost.* "Wonju assumed great importance because it was the junction of five main roads as well as a railway from Seoul to Pusan. The force that controlled Wonju had gone a long way toward controlling central Korea."

In the Wonju area, preparing for the expected all-out Chinese offensive, General Ridgway ordered the battered 38th Regiment of the 2d Division with the attached Dutch battalion and the 187th to make "the strongest possible stand to blunt the CCF." The force included seven American, one Dutch, and three ROK infantry battalions—about eight thousand men. He also massed over a hundred artillery pieces, including thirty 155mm guns and the twelve 105mm howitzers of the 674th. If these forces could not hold, Ridgway planned to withdraw them southeast to Chechon to join with the U.S. 7th Division and attack the left flank of the CCF penetration.

As expected, on the night of 13 February, the CCF launched a major offensive astride the corridor centered on the Chipyong-ni–Wonju road and rail network. The CCF, as usual, attacked with whistles, horns, and bugles blowing and fired salvos of heavy mortars and artillery. The objective of the attack was to penetrate the UN lines and envelop the rear areas, splitting X Corps from Eighth Army. In the Chipyong-ni area, the CCF surrounded the 23d Infantry of the 2d Division and the attached French battalion and used the ridgelines to bypass and continue their attack toward Wonju.

A map of the 187th battle area shows a series of east-west ridgelines. The ridges were numbered successively from south to north—Hill 339, Hill 340, Hill 341 and Hill 342.

The 3d Battalion made the final assault on Hill 342. Lieutenant Colonel "Poopy" Connor and his 2d Battalion was ordered to seize and hold Hill 340 and Hill 255 about three miles northwest of Wonju. Lieutenant Colonel Harry Wilson's 1st Battalion was in reserve.

For his attack, Colonel Munson had K Company between E Company on the left and L Company on the right. In K Company for the attack, Weber had two platoons up and one back in reserve. His artillery forward observer had fired several concentrations in front of the company. X Corps artillery could also reach the area in front of K Company. On Hill 339, Weber's men made contact with CCF outposts in well-prepared positions supported by automatic weapons and mortars. On Hill 340, K Company hit dug in CCF forces who lobbed grenades from as close as thirty feet. The paratroopers charged into the enemy trenches and with rifles, grenades, bayonets, and hand-to-hand fighting cleared the crest of the hill.

"The fighting was intense and continuous and the terrain favored the defender," wrote Weber. "Twice, I had to commit my reserve platoon to envelop a CCF perimeter in order to prevent CCF reinforcements. . . . At around dusk, we had progressed to and secured Hill 341. Needed time to resupply and secure the area. I notified Battalion that

I would make final attack on Hill 342 just after dark as the CCF demonstrated strong positions and company-sized strength thereon. Battalion concurred. E and L Companies were still engaged in trying to secure their final objectives. Thus, the CCF on 342 had support to their left and right flanks.

"Around 2400, I was using the FO's radio to adjust fires (he had been wounded and was temporarily out of action). I was kneeling near the top of 342 when a CCF grenadier tossed two grenades toward where I was. One landed behind the radio. I reached to pick it up and throw it back when it detonated. Took my right arm off three inches below elbow. Extremely cold weather aided me as I did not suffer shock or major loss of blood. My first sergeant put a tourniquet and field bandage on my arm and I remained operational.

"CCF attacks were continuous with only minimal hesitations. I estimate (later review confirmed) that they eventually committed a full regiment to the action (piecemeal). At one time, they overran my 60mm mortar section, but we ejected them and recovered the mortars and ammunition and they were operational in less than a half hour.

"During the battle, we were receiving major artillery support. Without this, we would have been in dire straits. After I was wounded, my FO had recovered from shock and was functioning! As well, by then L and E Companies had secured their objectives and were assisting with flanking fire.

"At about 0200, I got hit by incoming CCF mortar or artillery fire and my right leg was almost completely severed below the knee. As you might expect, that put me down though I remained conscious and I was able to function by voice commands. To be realistic, I guess all I was able to do was to encourage my men to hold. By then, what needed to be done was obvious to all my troopers. We weren't going to maneuver or be reinforced. All we could do was hold!

"And they did! By daylight, it was all over except for CCF stragglers who were 'policed up' as POWs. I Company was brought into position behind K Company to prevent any CCF encirclement. My wounded and KIA were being evacuated, as was I, when we received incoming indirect fire. I got hit again near the collecting point and was wounded in the right hip and abdomen. By then, I was only semiconscious and really don't have good recall.

"My casualties, from jumpoff on the morning of the fourteenth to daylight on the fifteenth, totaled 48. That represented about twenty-eight percent of my total strength. CCF counted dead around Hill 342 exceeded 200. Of these, about fifty were inside our perimeter! CCF POWs (some WIA) were over thirty."

Louis M. Richards was rifleman in K Company and later a member of the Rhode Island House of Representatives. In a recent interview with Fred Waterhouse, he remembers the conditions on Hill 342 the night K Company assaulted and took it. About 2000 hours, they readied themselves for the inevitable counterattack. Richards and another trooper were on a "listening post" on the flank of the hill. He recalls "with a shiver, the sudden Chinese bugle calls out of nowhere. They echoed across the frozen hills. He thought to himself *Some outfit is going to be hit by the Chinese*. Around midnight, the Chinese hit in force. They swarmed up toward the hill, thousands of them yelling and firing as they came."

Richards insists that K Company could not have held the hill without the "heroic efforts of I Company. In that bloody protracted battle, I Company acted as ammo bearers. They created a 'daisy chain,' moving ammo, especially hand grenades, up to K Company Rakkasans, who threw them as fast as they could. The entire hill glowed from the residue of white phosphorous."

"At dawn, the positions were covered with hundreds of dead Chinese. On the forward slope, hundreds more Chinese soldiers lay dead." He will never forget, he said, "the sight of fallen Rakkasans, aligned side by side, killed while firing from exposed positions." He believes that of about 180 Rakkasans who attacked, 28 were able to walk back down after the battle."

While the 3d Battalion was fighting the battle of Hill 342, Lt. Col. "Poopy" Connor's 2d Battalion was fighting about three miles northwest of Wonju on Hills 240 and 255 to regain the territory lost by the 38th Infantry to overwhelming CCF forces. At about 1400 on the 14th, the 2d Battalion attacked with F Company on the left, E Company in the center and G Company in reserve.

Twice, swarms of Chinese repulsed E Company's attack. In the final attack, E Company, with the 3d and 1st platoons in the lead, fought a brutal battle up the crest of Hill 240 and then moved toward the center of Hill 255. Connor committed G Company; it moved to the right about five hundred yards and began its battle for the right flank of the hill. In the E Company area, the troopers fought the Chinese in hand-to-hand combat—with grenades, bayonets, pistols, and rifles—and drove them off the hill.

In the G Company sector, Capt. James D. Cook sent his 1st and 2d Platoons to attack the large mass of CCF just to the north of E Company. He ordered Lieutenant White's 3d Platoon and Lieutenant Epp's weapons platoon, which had lost its crew-served weapons in the Nightmare Alley rescue operation, to seize the knoll and ridgeline on the north side of the hill. To get there, they had to cross a rice paddy and then assault up the ridge. "As they moved across the paddy," wrote Fred Waterhouse, "they were hit by small-arms fire. Halfway up the slope, 3d platoon was stopped by enemy fire. Lieutenant White hastily conferred with Lieutenant Epps. Epps told White to lay down a base of fire on the enemy. Lieutenant Epps would take his weapons platoon and maneuver to the left, then assault the summit of the north knoll. Lieutenant Epps and his platoon commenced their assault. They were hit by scores of enemy hand grenades. Epps was wounded in the thigh but kept moving up."

Lieutenant Epps wrote about the heroism of Cpl. Harry Stewart in the attack. "Corporal Stewart, normally a 60mm mortar squad leader, volunteered to man the light machine gun with no pintle earlier that morning. He aggressively moved out to the front of the platoon with his LMG when he heard my decision to attack. I yelled that I wanted a rifleman in the lead. He swapped the LMG for an M1 rifle with an ammunition bearer and took the lead again. As we approached the first knoll, we received heavy automatic-weapons fire and many hand grenades from the reverse side of the hill at close range. Corporal Stewart fired a clip of ammunition from his M1 and threw a grenade. The resulting grenade duel was fierce.

"Corporal Stewart again took the lead, but this time was again carrying the LMG. Sergeant First Class Ira Taylor, the 57mm recoilless rifle section leader, was killed by burp-gun fire as he attempted to throw a grenade. Three men, including myself, were wounded by enemy grenades. An enemy machine gun was situated in an old emplacement which appeared to be an enemy command post. As we closed in on this position, Corporal Stewart greatly assisted in destroying the gun and crew. With the enemy still throwing grenades, our supply exhausted, Corporal Stewart walked boldly up the hill firing his LMG from the hip into the enemy, who were only a few feet away. . . . From this position, he outflanked the enemy .50-caliber machine-gun position.

"Corporal Stewart, still exposed to the devastating fire, turned and knocked the enemy gun out by firing the LMG, again from his hip, at the range of approximately thirty yards. . . . The remaining Chinese around the .50-caliber machine gun ran down the reverse slope to the left in disorder. I saw about five or six fall in a grotesque manner as he fired into them. The rest of the platoon . . . gained the crest of the hill and completed routing the enemy.

"The 3d platoon joined the weapons platoon after moving up to the summit and the 1st and 2d platoons joined up on the objective just at dusk. Four hundred and fifty-one enemy dead were littered about the entire hill mass after this attack and approximately twenty to twenty-five U.S. Thompson submachine guns were found strewn about the hill, thus indicating the number of automatic weapons used by the enemy against the 2d Battalion's attack.

"From the very onset of the attack, Corporal Stewart's aggressiveness and obvious determination in completing the mission as well as his utter disregard for his own safety was an inspiration to men of the platoon. [He] enabled the very last element available to the battalion commander to be successful in recapturing this vital hill, which now blocked the enemy from seizing the road and railroad between Seoul and Wonju." Through the efforts of Lieutenant Epps, Corporal Stewart's initial Bronze Star with a *V* for valor was upgraded to the Distinguished Service Cross. By that time, he was also a master sergeant.

On the eighteenth of February, G Company had one more battle to fight in the Wonju area. Its mission: attack and clear the enemy from a strong point at Sillin-ni on Hill 738, a three-pronged mass, shaped like the letter E. Two feet of snow covered the slopes that angled upward in some places at forty-five degrees. Captain Cook sent his 2d and 3d platoons up the ridge to the right and his 1st platoon and weapons platoon up the center. The company immediately ran into heavy defensive fire. In driving the Chinese off the first ridge, Captain Cook was wounded and evacuated. His executive officer, Lt. John R. D. Cleland, took over. Other men from the company were hit by the grazing fire, grenades, and mortars, including Lt. R. D. Hewitt, Sgt. "Jumpy" Valent, and Pfc. Olaf P. Pulver, who later died of his wounds. Sergeant L. F. Sperduto charged up the hill firing his LMG from the hip; he was killed in the assault. Privates First Class Pulver and Morrison, a BAR team, fired as they moved up the ridge, keeping the charge going forward. At the top of the ridge, Lieutenant Cleland formed his men into a perimeter defense when he saw that the 2d Platoon had not taken the ridge on the right. Cleland went back down the hill and found some men from the 3d Platoon, whose leader, Lt. S. J. White, had been killed earlier. Cleland took what men he could find in another assault up the hill. Almost at the top, Cleland took a round in one arm. He continued the advance with his men but was hit again in the other arm. With both arms broken, he still moved forward into heavy enemy fire. Cleland finally stopped and withdrew his few men down the hill about two hundred yards and set up a perimeter. Before he was evacuated, he turned the men over to Sfc. Haywood. With the assistance of E Company, the remnants of G Company took the hill the next day.

But by Sunday, the eighteenth of February, the Chinese high commander realized that he was fighting a losing battle. General Ridgway began to receive reports from his corps commanders that the enemy was pulling back. He cautioned them that "it might be a ruse," but he felt that it probably was not. Intelligence soon confirmed that the withdrawal was actual and almost total. Lin Piao, the CCF commander, had ordered his shattered force to pull back to the old NKPA defenses just north of the 38th parallel. Presumably, he planned to regroup, bring in supplies and replacements, and attack later.

Ridgway immediately decided to launch counterattacks at the retreating CCF. The operation was called Killer. It would launch to the north eight infantry divisions (five U.S. and three ROK), some hundred thousand men, in a general but cautious attack designed to reestablish a line across Korea east from Seoul, to keep the retreating enemy off balance without giving him a chance to pause and regroup, and to kill as many of the enemy as possible—hence the name of the operation. By 28 February, all enemy resistance south of the Han had collapsed.

On orders, now under the operational control of X Corps, General Bowen pulled his 187th RCT out of the line at Wonju. On 28 February, the entire RCT had closed in to their rear assembly area at Taegu.

Rumors were rampant that the RCT was getting ready for another combat jump. The rumors proved to be correct. Munsan-ni was to be another chapter in the story of the 187th RCT.

### Munsan-ni

Operation Killer, designed, as the title implies, to eliminate as many of the enemy as possible as opposed simply to regaining territory, had not reached General Ridgway's expectations. In wretched weather that had slowed the advance of the UN forces both by road and rail, the Chinese and the NKPA had managed to escape the UN offensive by falling back, without disintegrating, along a broad front. By the first of March the UN line, located about halfway between the 37th and 38th parallels, followed a concave arc from south of the Han River in the west through Yang-p'yong and Hoengsong, then curved northeast to Kangnung. This did not satisfy General Ridgway.

With General MacArthur's approval, he planned a new offensive, Operation Ripper, devised, once again, to trap and then eliminate the maximum number of the enemy, destroy his equipment, keep up relentless pressure, prevent a counterattack, and split the Chinese and North Korean forces, most of which were located on the eastern front. Operation Ripper envisioned a general attack northward in the central and eastern zones to capture Hongchon and Chunchon and seize a line, designated Idaho, just south of the 38th parallel. The U.S. IX and X Corps would advance in the center through successive phase lines to Idaho; the ROK forces in the east would guard the right flank with local attacks; I Corps in the west would stay south and east of Seoul. The attack up the center was designed to envelop Seoul from the east.

At 0545 on 7 March, Ripper began with one of the most devastating and concentrated artillery barrages of the war to date. In twenty minutes, 148 howitzers and guns fired over five thousand rounds at enemy positions on the north bank of the Han. In a few minutes, tanks, AA guns, mortars, and machine guns joined in the assault. At 0615, the artillery shifted to deeper targets, and three battalions of the U.S. 25th Division swarmed across the Han in assault boats and established a bridgehead on the other bank. Across a fifty-mile front, six U.S. and five ROK divisions, about 150,000 men, moved out on the offensive.

At the same time, the ROK 1st Division made a thrust northwest of Kimpo Airfield, and the U.S. 3d Division launched a diversionary attack south of Seoul to divert attention from the 25th's crossings. At first, the CCF defended the 25th's bridgehead area with some vigor, but, after three days, left in disorder. On 7 March, on the central and eastern fronts, the UN forces made substantial gains and then continued their forward thrust. In some areas the defense was stubborn, but by 11 March elements of IX Corps had reached the first phase line. On 14 March, attacks on the next phase line began.

In the west, on the night of 14–15 March, a patrol from the ROK 1st Division probed the outer defenses of Seoul and found to its surprise that the enemy had virtually deserted the city. UN troops moved in. Seoul thus changed hands for the fourth time since July 1950. Within a matter of hours, once again the ROK flag flew from the National Assembly Building. The UN troops found a city devastated by the enemy. No utilities were operational; the Bun Chon shopping district had been flattened; wires dangled loosely from telephone poles; the city's original population of 1.5 million had shrunk to 200,000 ragged and mostly homeless civilians.

In spite of some of the most rugged, mountainous terrain yet encountered, X Corps in the center of the peninsula moved forward slowly through quagmires formed by the early, unusually heavy spring rains. Roads and bridges had been washed out. Supplies had to be hand-carried after having been dropped by FEAF cargo planes. In spite of the difficulties, by 17 March, IX and X Corps neared their third phase line in the center; the marines advanced on Chunchon, a well-defended enemy supply and communications base. There the marines ran into stiff opposition, and their attack involved hand-to-hand fighting, often with bayonets.

Hoping to set a trap, Eighth Army headquarters alerted General Bowen to drop the 187th behind the enemy forces near Chunchon on 22 March. But by the nineteenth of March, when UN armored patrols from the 1st Cavalry Division entered the Chunchon Basin, it became clear that the enemy had withdrawn, and a massed parachute assault would be unprofitable. General Ridgway canceled the drop, but meanwhile, on 21 March, the eighty C-119s and fifty-five C-46s planned for the drop had arrived at Taegu from Brady and Ashiya airfields in Japan. The huge fleet, parked wingtip to wingtip, completely filled the dusty, graveled parking area and thus forced the fighter aircraft normally based there to fly to other strips.

Once Seoul had fallen, I Corps took up positions along a line from Yongdungpo through Seoul's northern suburbs, thence to the northeast. General Ridgway increased the scope of Operation Courageous (Killer and Ripper had been dropped as operational names because of opposition from sensitive staffers in Washington) to include an attack by I Corps westward to the Imjin River. Eighth Army was back on a line approximately where the war had started some nine months before. Above that line, the enemy had assembled troops and equipment for a resumption of their offensive.

General Ridgway now wanted to bring I Corps forward from the Seoul area to the Imjin River at Munsan. This plan included the following operations:

The 187th, with the attached 2d and 4th Ranger Companies, spearheading the I Corps attack, would jump at Munsan-ni (about twenty miles northwest of Seoul) in Operation Tomahawk behind the NKPA I Corps; Two large armored task forces, Growdon and Hawkins, would attack to the north through Uijongbu and Munsan-ni, the latter to link up with the 187th and trap the North Koreans between the two forces, The ROK 1st Division and the U.S. 3d Division would follow the armored task forces.

For almost the first half of March, the 187th had been in "administrative" bivouac in an apple orchard at K-2 Airstrip near Taegu. General Bowen, always alert to the need to jump-qualify his new replacements, set up an airborne school. To practice for Tomahawk and because most of his veterans had not jumped since the Sukchon-Sunchon drop, on the eighth and ninth of March General Bowen led 4,033 men of the RCT in a mass parachute training jump near Taegu; one man was killed on the jump.

On the afternoon of 21 March, Brig. Gen. John P. "Jock" Henebry, commanding officer of the 315th Air Division, Col. R. W. Henderson, CO of the 314th Troop Carrier Group, Col. John W. Roche, CO of the 437th Troop Carrier Wing, General Bowen, and key members of their respective staffs, made an aerial reconnaissance of the Munsan-ni area. On this low-level flight, they selected two small DZs near Munsan-ni.

At the command post at Taegu, the 187th staff and commanders reviewed maps and photos of the area, outlined the drop zones, drew up the battle plan, and briefed the troops down to the squad level. "At the briefing by our platoon leader," remembered Specialist Gasperini, "he told us that we were going to jump at Munsan-ni, the same area where we had dug in on 15 December in the retreat south. The forty-eight hour linkup plan sounded good to me." Sergeant First Class William Ignatz, injured in the Wonju action, reported back from the hospital on 19 March. "Our pathfinder team leader, Lieutenant Maloney, put me in the first wave," he recalled. "I had the same beat-up white panels and a supply of colored smoke grenades. This was Sukchon all over again."

The logistics team in the RCT had to procure needed equipment from all sources. "I went back to Fukuoka to secure heavy drop packing and equipment from the Parachute Maintenance Company," Sgt. W. W. Ryals said. "Some QM people had recovered my lost 75, and I was in business again."

During the planning, it became clear that the 1/187th, scheduled to drop on the south DZ, needed three additional radio jeeps. General Henebry sent a C-119 to Ashiya Air Base in Japan to pick up the jeeps and bring them to Taegu. There the air crews rigged them for heavy airdrop and loaded them onto C-119s.

For a brief time, General Ridgway had considered jumping in with the 187th RCT, but he said later that it would have been a "damned fool thing to do." To dissuade himself, he had visions of a broken leg or strained back requiring him to give up command of Eighth Army. He opted to have his veteran liaison plane pilot, twenty-three-year-old Capt. Mike Lynch, fly him into the DZ during the operation.

On the morning of the twenty-third, General MacArthur sent General Ridgway a message that startled him: MacArthur authorized Ridgway to cross the 38th parallel in force and attack northward to Ridgway's proposed new general line, Kansas. MacArthur had made the decision on his own; the Joint Chiefs of Staff had not given him authorization. General MacArthur was beginning to overstep his bounds and get into the political arena, much to the administration's annoyance.

At 0300 on the morning of Good Friday, 23 March, under a full moon, the paratroopers of the 187th rolled out of their sleeping bags and started the precombat jump rituals—breakfast, forming into planeloads, loading into their combat gear, moving to their assigned aircraft, and putting on the parachutes that they had checked the previous day and left at the planes. Each paratrooper carried a full load of battle equipment: combat pack, basic load of ammo, grenades, rifle, .45-caliber pistol, canteens, first aid packets, and two parachutes—main and reserve. The troopers carried their combat packs slung in front of their knees; some had A-frame packs, loaded with automatic weapons, ammunition, and rocket launchers, lashed below their combat packs.

The 187th RCT troopers and the Rangers from the 2d and 4th Ranger Companies climbed aboard eighty C-119s and fifty-five C-46s. Fortunately, the weather was paratrooper perfect—clear visibility and low breezes. By 0700, the planes were loaded with troopers crammed along the walls of the planes; monorail bundles were in place. The planes revved their engines, creating huge clouds of dust, the jumpmasters checked their troops, and the long line of planes began to taxi slowly in line to the airstrip, churning even thicker blankets of dust that soon obscured much of the flight strip area. At 0730 the first plane roared down the runway and took off. Thereafter, at ten-second intervals, the rest of the planes followed in dust so thick that the pilots flew blind until after liftoff.

The air force commander and General Bowen and his staff had selected two drop zones, one to the north of Munsan-ni and one to the south. Onto the northern DZ would jump the bulk of the combat team: General Bowen and his staff, Colonel Munson's 3/187th in the lead, Colonel Connor's 2/187th, the two Ranger companies, and Lt. Col. Harry F. Lambert's 674th Airborne FA Battalion. Lt. Col. Harry Wilson and his 1/187th would jump on the southern DZ to provide a early-on linkup with the armored force moving north. Colonel Munson, who had been wounded by a "stray round in the small of his back," came back to the 3/187th in December 1950 after a two-month hospital stay in Japan. Major Rye Mausert had been the CO of the 3/187th in his absence.

Ahead of the troop carriers flew a C-54 Skymaster, the command ship, piloted by General Henebry. The FEAF filled the skies between Seoul and Munsan-ni with fighter aircraft that bombed and strafed the road network. Sixteen F-51 Mustangs circled the troop carriers in broad sweeps, ready to attack ground fire or enemy aircraft. The troop carriers flew a flight path out over the Yellow Sea and then directly back east to Munsan-ni.

During the flight over the Yellow Sea, one troop carrier had engine trouble and crashed into the sea. Shortly thereafter, Colonel Wilson's plane, the first one in the 1/187th column, developed mechanical problems and was forced to abort the mission and return to Taegu. The deputy flight leader moved up to lead the serial. At Taegu, Wilson impatiently demanded another airplane. He got it, but he and his staff therefore lagged considerably behind the battalion, a situation that eventually caused a problem.

At about 0900, the lead serial, Colonel Munson and his 3/187th and the 4th Ranger Company, jumped onto the north DZ. Directly behind them came the second and third serials with Colonel Connor's 2/187th, the 2d Ranger Company, General Bowen and his regimental staff, engineers, medics, and others, including the Eighth Army assistant G3, Lt. Col. Hank Adams, who had overseen the planning for Tomahawk. None of the troopers was hit in the air, but on the ground the paratroopers drew some light NKPA machine-gun and mortar fire. As they floated down, the paratroopers could see buildings burning around the DZs.

In an effort to speed up, Col. Harry Wilson's deputy in the second plane in the 1/187th serial skipped a landmark and headed directly for the southern DZ. But because of a "navigational error," he missed the south DZ and led the 1/187th directly onto the north DZ. Munson, already on the ground, recalled, "All those unscheduled people dropped on top of us, on a DZ that was already badly congested. It was like a Chinese fire drill. But what was more serious was that we didn't have a force on the south DZ, which was the linkup point for the armored task force."

When Colonel Wilson arrived over the south DZ, he was startled to find no parachutes on the ground where his battalion had supposedly jumped. "There was nobody there," he recalled. "We thought that they must have picked up their chutes and moved on. So we jumped anyway." When they landed, Colonel Wilson and the twenty-nine men of his battalion staff were greeted with machine-gun fire from some nearby hills. Fortunately, the NKPA stayed in the hills, and later in the day, patrols from Wilson's own B Company rescued them.

"My serial was airborne at 1000 hours," Sergeant Ryals remembers. "One plane had engine trouble and crashed into the sea during the flight. Another was lost from the preceding serial. We flew out to sea for our rendezvous, then flew north in column. Crossing the coast, I could see Chinese Communist forces dug in trenches surrounding the DZ. The air force, prior to the jump, had reported the enemy, in groups of a thousand men, moving in on Munsan-ni valley. USAF pilots called Munsan-ni 'Holiday Valley,' because of the large number of targets. . . . The village of Munsan-ni was burning in the near distance. Farmhouses ringed the drop zone.

"In some amazement, I saw that the green light had flashed on.

"Flipping out my 75mm door bundle, I followed after. As the engine noises subsided, I could hear a considerable amount of small-arms fire below. Landing in soft ground, I cleared my parachute harness and headed for my assembly area on the southwestern section of the DZ. A few minutes after we had secured the high ground in our sector, the heavy drop arrived and, with it, the attached medical unit from India." The Indian unit was composed of twelve members of the 60th Parachute Field Ambulance Battalion including surgeons, anesthetists, and medical technicians, under the command of Lt. Col. A. G. Rangarai. Among the members was a surgeon, Capt. V. Rangaswami, now a retired major general.

William "Fuzzy" Moore was a ranger assigned to the 4th Ranger Company who jumped with the company on the northern DZ at Munsan-ni. He recalls that "loading the aircraft and jumping seems to be a blank. This was Munsan-ni via parachute. I remember seeing the Indian medics with red turbans and large black beards. I don't remember how many days later Paddy Purcell (an Irishman and a member of the 4th Ranger Company) related to us that on hitting the DZ he was knocked out and when he came to 'here was a large Indian medic cutting his harness off' and what Purcell related to us was 'sure and bejesus I knew I was going to meet my maker but I didn't think he would be black.' This jump was made on 23 March 1951. I remember thinking, *Good Friday—no better time to be in the sky close to God.*"

On the jump, of 3,447 paratroopers, 84 men were injured with broken ankles or legs or severe bruises. Half returned to duty. Eighteen were wounded and one man was killed on the ground. The eighty C-119s of the 314th Troop Carrier Group and the fifty-five C-46s of the 437th Troop Carrier Wing dropped a total of 220 tons of equipment and cargo, including twenty-seven jeeps and trailers, two weapons carriers, four 105mm howitzers, twelve 75mm pack howitzers, and fifteen load-bearing platforms each carrying six hundred pounds of supplies.

During the drop, General Ridgway had been circling overhead in his L-4 liaison plane. At 1000, he asked Lynch to land. We were right in the middle of everything," Lynch remembered. "The next battalion jumped almost on top of us. I had to land to get out of the way. I said, 'Hold on. We're going in.' I made a bouncy landing on a piece of raised straight road—like a dike—about a hundred yards long. Ridgway went to find Bowen; I turned the plane around by its tail. Then a group of about fifteen or twenty [enemy soldiers] began to rake the 'landing strip' with machine guns. I had to dive over the embankment. I led a charge of paratroopers to get [them]."

Colonel George H. Gerhart was the XO of the 187th. After he landed and moved to the CP area, he saw General Ridgway. "At first I thought he had jumped with us," he wrote later, "but apparently he was there checking on the drop."

At about midmorning, army and air force helicopters landed on the DZs to evacuate the wounded. This was the first combat use of Air Force H-19 helicopters for air evacuation of wounded. The helicopters ferried the wounded and injured men to airstrips near Seoul, where Kyushu Gypsy C-47s were waiting to move them to army hospitals farther south.

During the drop, several troop carriers were hit by bullets, but only one was shot down. After making the drop, the pilot of another C-119 reported that his engines were smoking badly and that he thought that his plane had been hit by ground fire. Shortly after his message, both engines burst into flames and he ordered the crew to bail out. Five crewmen parachuted safely, but then the C-119 blew up in midair, and both the pilot and copilot were killed.

Near the north DZ, some four hundred troops of the 3/36th, 19th North Korean Division were dug in and well armed with light and heavy machine guns. They had arrived from Kumchon on the twenty-third and had the mission of securing the main road to Kaesong. The enemy resistance directly on the DZ, however, was relatively moderate and consisted mostly of artillery and mortar fire. The 187th S2, Maj. George F. Gormlie, learned later that the CCF had withdrawn into the 187th sector in order to draw the UN forces to the north and then envelop them with a counterattack. The CCF forces had been in the area for two or three days prior to the drop.

"The Munsan-ni jump was a much more difficult operation, initially, than the one at Sukchon," remembered Sgt. W. B. Alexander of A Company. "On landing on the wrong DZ, we jumped into an area occupied by strong enemy forces and these people had us under fire from the moment we hit the dirt. . . . The 1st Battalion marched all night to reach the 2d Battalion, which was heavily engaged. We immediately went into the attack and took the critical terrain to establish blocking positions to cut off the retreating Chinese and North Korean forces."

Robert Schusteff was a young ranger assigned to the 4th Ranger Company. His first day of combat was the jump on Munsan-ni. "Our company objective was the topographic feature located at the northernmost tip of the drop zone, identified as Hill 205," he wrote in a letter. "4th Company hastily assembled on the DZ and moved out toward our objective with the normal amount of confusion and a slight delay. During the approach to our objective we marched through an area which contained the body of a jumper from the 187th, who had crashed into the ground at a slightly higher elevation than the DZ, due to an error in dropping one of the serials which flew over the DZ in the wrong direction, thereby dropping the latter part of their sticks in the foothills. This particular jumper had apparently had a malfunction of his main parachute, which was still intact; and had activated his reserve parachute, which still had two stows of suspension lines remaining, which had not deployed when he collided with the earth. I remember that he was a very good-looking young trooper, blond headed, bright blue eyes, which were wide open. This was my very first day in combat, and this was my very first dead American soldier. It is a sight which has remained with me since that day."

While the 187th was still landing on the DZ, the two armored task forces, Growdon and Hawkins, were rumbling forward from Line Lincoln toward Munsan-ni and Uijongbu, respectively. Growdon's march was not without difficulty. The road along its route of march as the "most extensively mined area yet encountered in Korea." Growdon's force lost four Patton tanks, two jeeps, and a scout car to the mines and two Pattons to NKPA artillery. Task Force Growdon took twelve hours to travel fifteen miles, but the lead element linked up with the 187th about 1830. TF Hawkins had an easier run and was in Uijongbu in about two hours.

The night of 23 March was reasonably quiet for the troops of the 187th. The units pulled in and set up perimeter defenses for the night. On the morning of the 24th, General Bowen received orders to move to the east and north of Uijongbu to carry out the second phase of the operation: attack across seventeen miles of broken and heavily defended terrain toward Uijongbu Valley to link up with the 3d Infantry Division moving north. The 3d had run into strong CCF defenses and was advancing very slowly, hampered by the enemy and the heavy rains. Tanks from TF Growdon arrived in mass about 0400 on the twenty-fourth and reinforced the 187th's attack to the east toward Uijongbu.

Because of the condition of the rain-soaked roads, lack of fuel for the tanks, and no logistics tail, the RCT depended totally on aerial resupply for the basics of combat: ammunition and food. In fifty-six air drops between 24 and 27 March, Air Force cargo planes dropped 264 tons of critical supplies to the 187th RCT.

The 187th's attack up the Uijongbu Valley to link up with the 3d Infantry Division was a series of battles along ridgelines and up and down hills with narrow crests and steep slopes. The paratroopers had to get out of the valley and attack the hills and crests because the enemy forces had had time to dig deep holes and trenches and build defenses along the crests of the hills. They knew the value of holding "the high ground." They had also zeroed in their artillery and mortars. The paratroopers also found that the CCF and NKPA were somehow supplied with an endless number of grenades.

In one attack up the valley, E Company came under a fierce counterattack by horn-blowing, flare-throwing Chinese. Crossing a stream on a makeshift footpath, Capt. Jack B. Shanahan, the E Company commander, was killed as he tried to cross the levee.

"The Chinese counterattacked one of airborne companies with bugles blaring and screams of 'Banzai' filling the air," wrote Captain Crawford. "Congressional Medal of Honor winner MSgt. Jake Lindsey of Barnstable, Massachusetts, rallied his platoon and they met the charge with a countercharge. Cutting into the Red attackers, the troopers were shouting, 'Airborne,' and burying bared steel bayonets in fleeing, shrieking Communist soldiers."

In its sector, in the midst of rain and sleet so heavy that weapons and machine guns jammed, G Company hit a strong defensive position. Just after Capt. Jack Miley committed his reserve platoon, MSgt. Ervin L.

Muldoon, the machine-gun platoon leader in H Company, arrived in the area. He had been in Japan and had missed the jump. Lieutenant Jones N. Epps, platoon leader in G Company, pointed out H Company's location. That was the last he would see his old friend from Benning days. Muldoon was killed that afternoon leading an attack with such personal bravery that he was later awarded the DSC posthumously.

G Company lost two platoon leaders in the battle, wounded and evacuated. Ten G Company men were killed in action, including Sfc. James A. Vandergast, whose wife became a war widow for the second time. Her first husband was killed in World War II.

On 26 March, as his 2/187th moved up toward Uijongbu, Colonel Connor sent F Company to occupy Hill 178, a low hill on the flank of the battalion. Once again, the enemy was well dug into defenses on the hill. F Company made a strong assault but needed G Company's 3d Platoon to help in a counterattack. F Company's commander, Capt. Thomas H. Agee, and Lieutenant Hammock were casualties. First Lieutenant Samuel Muse became the company CO. All platoons were now commanded by NCOs.

The 2/187th next attacked Hills 507 and 519, rising above the valley. "At 0600 28 March," wrote Lieutenant Epps, now the G Company XO, "the 1st and 3d Battalions attacked east. By 0830, the 3d Battalion had seized Hill 299, but the 1st Battalion, meeting greater resistance, was still heavily engaged fighting for Hill 322. At 1200 hours, the 2d Battalion attacked in column through the 3d Battalion on Hill 299. Company E, leading, met stiff resistance the entire way along the razorback ridge from Hill 299 to the junction of the higher hill mass 507–519. As the attack of Company E began, enemy mortar fire landed on the reverse slope of Hill 299. Captain Jack Miley, commanding G Company, was down, seriously wounded."

Lieutenant Epps took over command of the company and moved past the head of the column to Hill 299, where he met the battalion S3, Maj. Hugh Howard, who briefed him on the situation. "Company G was in battalion reserve," wrote Fred Waterhouse. "Lieutenant Epps called his 1st and 2d platoon leaders forward to Hill 299 to inform them of the situation. The three officers listened to the battle and stayed informed by monitoring the radio net and observing the progress of the attack. They discussed the probability of attacking the summit as the company moved by bounds immediately in rear of F Company.

"Company F, commanded by Lt. Sam Muse, passed through Company E at the junction of the razorback ridge and the higher hill mass. In addition to the difficult climb up an elevation of 160 meters, Company F encountered a stubborn enemy using bunker-type emplacements. It was apparent from the first that the enemy had countless hand grenades and the determination to use them.

"Company F, like Company E, sustained many casualties in the close fighting uphill, and the company's attack spent itself with the capture of the first knoll on the 507–519 ridgeline. The 1st Platoon, Company E, located partway up the hillside, was ordered to continue the attack to seize Hill 507 only a hundred yards away. As the platoon rushed from the knoll to assault the objective, it was literally shot down. First Lieutenant William J. Nolan, the platoon leader, and several men were instantly killed by heavy automatic-weapons fire."

Colonel Connor ordered G Company, halfway up the hill, to attack without delay through what was left of Company F and the 1st Platoon of E Company. He told Lieutenant Epps that he had to take the hill before dark. Connor gave Epps the 4.2 mortars of Support Company to assist him. Lieutenant Roberts, the only officer left in F Company, briefed Epps on the enemy situation directly to his front, pointing out three machine guns on Hill 507 and two on a finger of a ridge to the north.

Lieutenant Epps looked at his objective. The knoll was only twenty yards wide and had steep slopes. On the left, there was a small clump of trees, but the right had been cleared off for fire lanes by the enemy. For his attack, Epps used all of the direct fire he could muster. The 60mm mortars registered on Hill 507, two light machine guns from H Company stayed on the crest, and two LMGs and one 57mm recoilless rifle from G Company were dug in on the right. The objective was too close for indirect fire, so Epps used the 81mm and 4.2 mortars and artillery to cover the finger of Hill 519 with smoke and HE (high explosive).

The first two platoons of E Company moved into position for the attack just as a preplanned air strike hit the finger of Hill 519. Epps had the machine guns, 57mm recoilless rifles, and 60mm mortars begin prep fires. After two minutes, the 1st Platoon jumped off. As it went around the knoll, the lead squad was hit with devastating enemy fire. Almost the entire squad was either killed or wounded.

Epps then sent the 2d Platoon to clear Hill 507. "The platoon leader, 1st Lt. Earl K. Woolley, led his men in column around the right side of the knoll at a dead run," wrote Fred Waterhouse. "The ridge was so narrow that the attacking 2d Platoon immediately masked the fire of the supporting direct-fire weapons positioned on the knoll. In crossing the open terrain, the platoon received little enemy fire until it reached the base of Hill 507. Here the assaulting troops were stopped by a tremendous amount of enemy hand grenades. The 2d Platoon countered with their own grenades, but the enemy grenades were far more numerous. First Lieutenant Leo Seifert moved his depleted 1st Platoon alongside the 2d Platoon to join the grenade battle. Both platoons, approximately thirty men, were crowded in a line across the narrow crest.

"About fifty feet ahead of Lieutenant Epps, Cpl. Lawrence N. Gardner and other Rakkasans were engaged in a hand-grenade duel. They were managing to pick up and return Chinese grenades to the enemy lines. Corporal Gardner was in the act of returning a large 'potato masher' when it exploded. The explosion flipped him over backward and tore off his right arm at the shoulder. He died within seconds. Corporal Gardner was awarded the DSC posthumously for his valor. Lieutenant Woolley led a bayonet charge up the short distance as his right squad began to outflank the enemy position."

Lieutenant Epps realized that his men had almost taken Hill 507, so he committed his 3d Platoon, commanded by an aggressive MSgt. Richard V. Goltra, to take Hill 519. He led the platoon on a fight along the ridge. As Goltra's men skirted the hill, a lone USAF fighter, ignoring the forward air controller, fired rockets into the south side of the hill, wounding four of Goltra's men who were in the lead. The enemy opened fire and badly wounded two men on the forward slope. MSgt. Goltra was wounded as he dragged one man to safety and wounded again as he hauled another wounded trooper out of the enemy line of fire.

During the fight on Hill 507, Lieutenant Woolley was blinded in his right eye by a grenade. He continued to fight with the ten men he had left from his platoon. Epps told him to dig in on Hill 507 and protect the company's left flank. Epps ordered Seifert and his 1st Platoon to follow the 3d Platoon toward Hill 519. Seifert and his men attacked so quickly that they overran several strong points that the 3d Platoon had missed.

It was getting dark, and Epp's G Company had not yet taken the final finger and rock outcroppings, the pinnacle of Hill 519. Epps contacted

Lieutenant Woolley by radio and asked him if he could take the finger of the ridge. Woolley said he could. Epps attached the 60mm mortar section and two light machine guns from H Company to Woolley's decimated platoon, and Woolley launched his attack. The LMGs, set up between Hills 507 and 519, delivered flanking fire on the finger. But just after leaving Hill 507, one BAR gunner, two riflemen, and the platoon sergeant, Sfc.William L. Dion, were wounded. This was Dion's second wound, but he struggled to his feet and continued the attack. Even with his limited platoon strength, Woolley, still half blind, and his men wiped out the enemy machine guns and killed twenty-five Chinese in their second attack. Epps told Woolley to leave the hill. He left Corporal Vumbaco in command of the remaining five men of the 2d Platoon. For his extraordinary heroism in the fight, Lieutenant Woolley received the DSC.

As the night sky darkened, Colonel Connor told Epps to wait until daylight before launching his final attack on the pinnacle beyond Hill 519. But when he moved forward the next morning, Epps and his men found that the Chinese had evacuated the pinnacle just before dawn. They found fifty enemy soldiers dead on the crest of the ridge and hundreds of dead and wounded in the valley between the finger and Hill 519. Air strikes, artillery, and mortars blasted the retreating Chinese. Epps's company suffered eight KIA and twenty-two WIA. After the fight, Epps had a company of two officers and eighty men.

"The entire RCT attacked the final hill on the sixth day [29 March]," wrote Captain Crawford. "The mountain was a huge honeycomb of entrenchments. In some places the Chinese had dug right through the mountain so they could bring up supplies and replacements for the front slope without crossing the ridgeline.

"The attack pushed off after daybreak as three battalions of determined paratroopers started up the seventy-degree slopes. Tanks and artillery fired hundreds of shells into the hilltop above them. The heavy-weapons companies fired every weapon they could muster into the slopes teeming with entrenched Chinese troops. Shells, bullets, and rockets tore through the air, pounding into the hills and rocks. 'The fire was so heavy,' said Sfc. Leo Kropka, 'that anyone who exposed part of his body was hit.'

"Climbing the steep slopes, the paratroopers were hit by a rain of concussion hand grenades. . . . Probing through the rocks and caves, the troopers dug out the Chinese with grenades and bayonets. Pfc. Norman Fullerton leaped into a hole, tossed a grenade into the recesses, dug into the mountainside, and routed a half-dozen enemy grenadiers. . . . Some holes had Chinese soldiers with whole boxes of grenades, throwing them as fast as they could be uncrated.

"As the 187th neared the top, Chinese soldiers began to flee down the opposite side. A Company, who could see part of the north side, mowed them down as they fled. . . . A machine gun operated by Sgt. Charles Ferguson fired ten thousand rounds of ammunition in an hour. . . . At five in the afternoon some of the 187th were on the top. . . . But by sundown, the troopers held the entire top commanding the main supply route of what had been a Chinese field army.

"During the battle, a Chinese radio operator cut into the American radio network to say, 'We'll return tonight to retake the hill. You're crazy to fight us.' They never lived up to that boast."

The 187th medics and a field surgical operating team of twelve men from the 60th Indian Field Ambulance Unit worked around the clock. Their "bloodshot eyes and blood-caked clothes told their story at a glance," wrote Captain Crawford. "Helicopters cut through the rain with their flailing rotors spilling water in sheets across the gray sky. Five at a time they came into the isolated command post and carried out the wounded. There was no other way out."

In the fight for Hills 507–519, the 187th troopers had decimated the 234th CCF regiment and seized dominant terrain in the area. On 29 March, the 187th linked up with the 3d Division and cleared the last vital route north along the Uijongbu-Chapmon axis. In the operation, Tomahawk by name, the 187th suffered heavy casualties, some 782 KIA and WIA. After the linkup with the 3d Division, General Bowen moved the RCT back to Taegu to reorganize, reequip, reman, and retrain. General Ridgway had made it clear to his staff that he did not favor using the 187th Airborne Regimental Combat Team in a strictly ground role. He felt that the highly trained paratroopers should be used primarily in airborne missions—dropping deep behind the enemy and boxing him in while UN ground troops moved forward for the kill.

"By the last days of March, as Ripper came to a close, Ridgway's forces had fought their way through rain and mud generally to the 38th parallel," wrote an Army historian in *Korea, 1951–1953*. "In the east the ROK

III and I Corps had pushed patrols more than twelve miles north of the parallel, and by 31 March South Korean troops were in control of the roads leading west and south from Yangyang on the east coast. In the west, an American armored column probed over the line north of Uijongbu above Seoul. All UN forces were in position on Line Idaho, and all geographical objectives had been taken. But the main body of the enemy had slipped away and escaped destruction. Ripper was thus a qualified success."

By the end of the first week in April, the Eighth Army G2 had positively identified nine Chinese armies, tentatively ten more, and eighteen NKPA divisions and six brigades. The G2 also suspected that the enemy now had a minimum of 750 aircraft, and the North Koreans were building airfields and lengthening runways for jet planes.

In view of these threats, Ridgway followed Ripper with Operation Rugged, a new advance toward a new line dubbed Kansas, 115 miles long, running along rugged, commanding terrain north of the 38th parallel. By 9 April, U.S. I and IX Corps and the ROK I Corps on the east coast had fought through shifting enemy resistance to Line Kansas. I Corps and the left flank units of IX Corps had continued to attack toward Chorwon, along a bulge in Kansas Line named Utah.

But in early April, two dramatic events took place. On 11 April, President Truman relieved General MacArthur of all his commands and named General Ridgway to succeed him. He ordered Lt. Gen. James A. Van Fleet to move posthaste from Washington to Korea to succeed General Ridgway.

Truman had decided finally that General MacArthur had publicly criticized the administration once too often, that he had been insubordinate in his dealings with Washington, that he did not differentiate between military strategy and foreign policy, and that he had been publicly disloyal by attacking the administration through conservative papers and the opposition party. After another such indiscretion, President Truman wrote on his desk calendar that "General Mac, as usual, has been shooting off his mouth."

Later, on 10 April, Truman told his staff, "I fired MacArthur yesterday from all his jobs." Then he added, "I can show just how the so-and-so double-crossed us. I'm sure MacArthur wanted to be fired." General MacArthur found out about it the next day—according to some stories, by an aide's hearing it on the radio, telling Mrs. MacArthur, who in turn went into the dining room and told her husband, who was hosting a lunch at the embassy.

General Ridgway learned of his promotion on 11 April from a newspaperman who walked up to him and said, "Well, General, I guess congratulations are in order." Pressed, the newspaperman would not explain. Later, Ridgway, back at his command post, got the message over the official radio.

By 19 April, all U.S. I and IX Corps units were along Line Utah preparing to continue the advance to Line Wyoming, an eastward extension of Line Utah. For two days, the U.S. forces attacked toward the high ground overlooking Chorwon at the base of the Iron Triangle. But then came the second dramatic event of April. On the twenty-second, the enemy attacked along the entire front, and the UN offensive halted. The Chinese and the NKPA abandoned cover and concealment and moved out into the open. "The expected enemy spring offensive was at hand."

The battles in Korea—the seesawing up and down the peninsula—were far from over.

# 6: Bloody Inje—Wonton-ni

At 1230 on 14 April, Lt. Gen. James Alward Van Fleet arrived at Taegu. General Ridgway and his staff met the plane. After a formal change-of-command ceremony, the old and the new Eighth Army commanders met with the press for a conference. Many correspondents were impressed with General Van Fleet and his credentials. He had graduated from West Point in 1915 with the class that "the stars fell on." Among his classmates were Bradley, Eisenhower, Stratemeyer, and Joe Swing, who, at one time in 1951, had seemed to be the likely choice to succeed General Ridgeway. *Time* magazine described General Van Fleet as "a rugged combat soldier and crack commander" who was "bigboned and muscular (6 ft. 1 in., 190 lbs.), blue eyed, with graying, close-cropped hair." He was also a teetotaler and a nonsmoker. One officer said that "above everything else, he was a fighting field soldier." Another said that "he had a natural friendliness that instantly set his subordinates at ease. . . . His quiet self-assurance transmitted to us a feeling of confidence. . . . He looked younger and even more vigorous than when I first served under him in 1944."

After the press conference, Generals Ridgway and Van Fleet met privately. General Ridgway told him that he would keep a tight rein on Eighth Army. He continued, very positively, "To the extent that you feel the situation warrants, please inform me prior to advancing in force beyond Line Utah" and "no operations in force would be conducted beyond the Wyoming Line without my prior approval." He added that "the Chinese Reds were ready for the biggest attack of all. They were supremely confident. There was no secret at all about their intentions. In fact, they were bragging openly on the radio that they were going to drive us back and recapture Seoul." After this conversation, the Eighth Army staff principals then briefed General Van Fleet in detail on the enemy and UN situation.

On 16 April, though, in spite of its bombast, the CCF had continued its withdrawal, and the Eighth Army advanced "practically unopposed." By 19 April, the lead regiments of I Corps were on Line Utah ready to attack the Iron Triangle. Included was the 5th Regiment of the 24th

Division, now commanded by Col. Harry Wilson, just recently the commander of the 1st Battalion of the 187th RCT.

In order to bring up supplies and organize the rear echelons, General Van Fleet called a forty-eight hour halt before moving north to Line Wyoming. He ordered the attack, Operation Dauntless, to resume on the morning of 21 April with I Corps, on the left, moving from Utah to Wyoming at the Iron Triangle and IX Corps in the center from Line Kansas to Line Quantico, above the Hwachon Reservoir. He felt that Dauntless would provoke a major CCF counterattack for which he was fully prepared. He planned to fall back in order, in compliance with Ridgway's Plan Audacious, trading real estate for an opportunity to kill the CCF. But he was adamant about keeping Seoul. He even speculated that "later in the summer" it might be tactically sound to advance north to Wonsan, by amphibious operations. When General Ridgway learned of this plan, he was not happy. He likened it to "the same damn situation that MacArthur had blundered into when he separated the X Corps. . . . I would have none of it," he said.

On the morning of 22 April, the assault regiments in I and IX Corps were advancing slowly and carefully in clear and crisp weather. But the capture of a Chinese officer and several enlisted men threw new red lines, boxes, and arrows onto the planning maps of the Eighth Army staff. One Chinese officer told his captors that the CCF would launch a major offensive that very night. Other captured CCF soldiers repeated the same message. I Corps commander, Gen. Frank W. Milburn, received a message from Gen. Babe Bryan, CG of the 24th Division, that the CCF attack would begin at 2100. He missed it by one hour.

At 2200 on the clear, moonlit night of 22 April, three CCF armies attacked the UN forces along a forty-mile front after a four-hour artillery bombardment. The initial attack was actually a secondary attack through the Kwandok Mountains in the Yonchon-Hwachon area of central Korea. By dawn the next morning, the CCF was in motion across the entire peninsula. The main effort hit the U.S. I and IX Corps with a double envelopment against the west flank to isolate Seoul, coupled with the secondary attack through the Yonchon-Hwachon area and a move against the eastern part of the line near Inje. Radio Pyongyang boasted that the ultimate objective—destruction of the UN Command—would be easily accomplished. One of the CCF's major goals was the capture of Seoul in a "powerful, lightning stroke" and presentation of it to Mao Tse-tung on May Day.

The CCF had some seven hundred thousand troops in Korea and used half of them in the assault, making it the biggest battle of the Korean War. Surprisingly, the CCF used little artillery after the first salvos, few tanks, to the surprise of the UN Command, and no close air support. The tactics were the same used in previous offensives—"human waves" of massed infantry in coordinated night attacks with bugles blaring and flares flashing to infiltrate and overrun the UN lines. At dawn, the CCF broke contact, and hid in natural and man-made defenses to protect themselves against the expected UN artillery fire.

The UN lines held firm across the front except in the central sector manned by IX Corps. In that area, the ROK 6th Division was positioned between the U.S. 24th Division on the left and the 1st Marine Division on the right. The CCF smashed against the ROK 6th Division in the Namdae River Valley south of Kumhwa and drove it back. The collapse of the ROK 6th left a ten-mile-wide gap in the line between the 24th and the 1st Marine Division. The two divisions rapidly refused their exposed flanks and held on.

In the face of the enemy crack in his line, General Van Fleet ordered the I and IX Corps to fall back slowly to Line Kansas, thus giving up the ground gained in the recent UN offensive. On 26 April, the CCF launched a strong attack on Seoul; on the next day, the CCF outflanked Uijongbu. Van Fleet directed the buildup of a new transpeninsular line to halt the enemy in front of Seoul and north of the Han.

On 29 April, UN planes strafed and stopped some six thousand enemy soldiers when they tried to ferry across the Han and attack down the Kimpo Peninsula to outflank Seoul. To the east of Seoul, the 24th and 25th Divisions stopped another CCF attempt to outflank Seoul. On the east-central front, the North Koreans attacked the ROK forces in Yanggu-Inje area and captured Inje, but by 29 April, that drive had been halted. By the end of April, the UN forces, supported by massed, heavy artillery and some 7,420 air sorties during the last eight days of the attack, had halted the enemy short of Seoul and the Han and held a strong defensive position. In I Corps, for example, the four artillery battalions of the U.S. 25th Division fired some 21,000 rounds of 105s and 2,500 rounds of 155s during the first twenty-four hours of the CCF offensive.

During the first week of May, there was a lull in the enemy operations while the Chinese and the North Koreans regrouped and brought supplies forward. General Van Fleet seized the initiative. He established regimental patrol bases eight miles in front of the defensive positions and sent armored patrols ten to twelve miles into enemy territory. Van Fleet planned a new offensive, but to the intelligence staffers the evidence that the enemy was preparing to resume the offensive was clear: the increased resistance to local attacks; the building of additional air bases; the movement of supplies south.

Because of these activities, during the first ten days of May, General Van Fleet strengthened his line with particular emphasis in the west. "The daylight hours of 15 May saw all the usual signs of impending enemy attack," wrote an army historian, "including an increased number of enemy agents trying to slip through the lines. Air patrols reported more bridge construction, and enemy probing attacks grew more numerous. Van Fleet's command made ready to stand firm.

"By 14 May [Van Fleet's] No Name Line had been considerably strengthened. The UN forces laid mines, registered artillery, established bands of interlocking machine-gun fire, and strung over five hundred miles of barbed wire. Interspersed among the minefields and triple-thick barbed-wire networks were fifty-five gallon drums of gasoline and napalm, ready to be detonated electrically. General Van Fleet resolved not to yield ground, but to hold his line with all the weapons and power at his disposal. As he phrased it, 'We must expend steel and fire, not men. . . . I want so many artillery holes that a man can step from one to the other.'"

The renewed attack came during the early evening of 16 May, when some twenty-one Chinese divisions, flanked by three North Korean divisions in the west and six in the east, smashed down the center of the peninsula against the X Corps and the ROK III Corps, "blowing the familiar bugles and horns and firing flares." Some 175,000 men attacked. Van Fleet's G2 had been expecting the major thrust to be in the west against Seoul. Consequently, Van Fleet had beefed up that part of the line. The X Corps held a thirty-seven mile sector of the front from Hongchon to Inje. On the right was the U.S. 2d Division with the ROK 5th and 7th Divisions on its right. The attack brought down massive artillery concentrations on the enemy. On 16 May, the howitzers of X Corps fired some 17,000 rounds; on 17 May, they fired twice that number or about 250 rounds per weapon. The twenty-four-hour-a-day barrages against the closely packed CCF forces killed, stunned, and wounded thousands of the CCF.

But in another sector to the east of the U.S. 2d Division, the Chinese crossed the Pukhan River and struck hard against the ROK 5th and 7th Divisions. By 1930 on the sixteenth, the two ROK divisions were heavily engaged along a twenty-mile front. They held for a time but then fell back, "disorganized and broken," abandoning artillery and crew-served weapons and even their rifles. "The ROK bugout, involving about forty thousand men, was the largest and most disgraceful of the Korean War," wrote Clay Blair.

The U.S. 2d Division held off the enemy until 18 May and then, with the 1st Marine Division, moved to the east to fill the gap left by the ROKs. IX Corps moved units to the east to cover the area left open by the 2d Division, and the marines. In its new locations, the 2d Division held firm and blasted the enemy with artillery. The 38th FA Battalion, for example, fired over 12,000 105mm rounds in twenty-four hours. To kill the enemy, all artillery units fired the "the Van Fleet load," five times larger than previous ammunition allowances. During the battle, the 2d Division lost some 900 men KIA and WIA and killed an estimated 35,000 of the enemy.

In the western sector, on the night of 17 May, an enemy force of some 25,000 soldiers struck toward the Han, but the 25th U.S. Division and the ROK 6th halted the drive in three days of heavy battle. By 20 May, the enemy attack was at a standstill. Van Fleet's troops stabilized their front. He decided that the time was propitious for a new offensive.

On 19 May, General Ridgway had arrived in Korea and conferred with General Van Fleet. Later, he flew in a Cub liaison plane over the 2d Division's area. When he returned, he, General Van Fleet, and General Almond, the X Corps commander, discussed the possibilities of an offensive. Almond believed that the time was ripe for a strong attack northeasterly up the Kansong road to Inje and beyond, to cut off tens of thousands of CCF and NKPA in the ROK sector on the right. But Almond said that he needed fresh troops and he reasoned the 187th RCT, which was in X Corps reserve and had been out of combat for some time, was the unit he wanted. Almond said that he would give it vehicles, tanks, artillery, and then, when the CCF had driven even deeper, strike with the 187th.

Ridgway, the experienced paratrooper commander from World War II, had forbidden the use of the 187th in a ground role. He reasoned that the 187th near an airstrip from which it could launch on short notice would be a constant threat and cause the Chinese high command to deploy thousands of troops in the rear areas to repulse potential airborne attacks. Another reason was that Ridgway considered the 187th "expensive, elite" troopers and did not want to use them as ordinary foot soldiers. Van Fleet recognized the possibilities in Almond's plan. He and General Ridgway had a five-minute private discussion in which they decided to give the 187th to Almond. "We will give you the 187th tonight," Van Fleet said to Almond. "It will go to Hoengsong."

The plan of attack, as developed by Ridgway and Van Fleet, would have X Corps hold the CCF for a few more days and prepare to counterattack on 23 May. IX Corps would attack on 20 May. In X Corps, the 2d Division, spearheaded by Task Force Baker, the 187th reinforced with tanks and corps artillery, would attack to the right of the Hwachon Reservoir from Hangye toward Inje, then northeasterly to Kansong to encircle and trap the retreating CCF and NKPA troops and retake the ground lost by the ROKs a few weeks earlier. I Corps would attack simultaneously to protect the left flank of IX Corps. The new Eighth Army offensive was named "Detonate." General Van Fleet hoped that the attack would forestall the enemy's possible counterstroke, threaten his supply lines, and eventually capture the Iron Triangle.

By 20 May, the enemy's offensive was at a standstill, and the X Corps front was stabilized. The 1st Marine Division held its portion of the No Name Line and the U.S. 2d Division prepared to retake the territory it had lost. On 20 May, the X Corps Artillery fired 49,704 rounds, and FEAF bombed, strafed, and napalmed the enemy positions in 154 close support missions.

At 0800 on 23 May, the X Corps launched its counterattack. The 1st Marine Division attacked north toward the east side of the Hwachon Reservoir at Yanggu. The 187th attacked up the Hangye-Inje road through the 23d Regiment of the 2d Division, which remained in its position. The 187th CP was located initially at Hangye along the banks of the Hongchon River, through which ran the road to Inje that snaked north-northeast about forty miles from Hangye to Puchaetul to Koritwi to Oron-ni to the town of Inje. The hills to the sides of the river were high and steep. Near Oron-ni there was a bridge across the river. About six miles north of Oron-ni and eight miles south of Inje, the Soyang River cut across the road. These were to become important markers in the 187th's bloody ground and tank attack toward Inje. By dark of the twenty-third, the 187th, supported by one company of Lt. Col. Eldridge Brubaker's 72d Tank Battalion, had moved about four miles up the road against light resistance to Puchaetul. The remainder of the 72d plus a company from the 64th Tank Battalion were scheduled to join Task Force Baker, but on the morning of the twenty-fourth, they were hours away from the 187's location.

In its attack up a ridge along the road near Chogut-An, A Company of the 187th found Cpl. Robert L. Hanson, C Company, 38th Infantry of the 2d Division, lying in a ditch. He had been wounded in both legs and had been abandoned by the CCF when they left the area in some haste.

General Almond arrived at the 187th CP by helicopter at 0940 on the 24th. In his usual raging, demanding style, he told General Bowen that it was absolutely critical that the 187th move out for the Inje at flank speed. He ordered General Bowen to form a task force of one infantry battalion, plus at least two tank companies and support elements, to move out at noon, to race to the Soyang River and establish a bridgehead. Then the rest of the 187th was to follow as fast as possible in trucks. General Bowen told his XO, Col. George Gerhart, to form up the task force as rapidly as possible and to command it. The mission was difficult, if not impossible, to launch at noon. The Soyang River was fifteen miles from the CP and the X Corps front lines. The 187th staff felt that the area was still infested with at least four Chinese divisions.

Lt. Colonel "Poopy" Connor's 2d Battalion was the infantry battalion in the Gerhart Task Force. Brubaker ordered his other two tank companies and B Company of the 64th to move as rapidly as possible to the 187th's position. To speed things up, Colonel Gerhart organized a small point force on the spot: four tanks, a recon squad from the 187th I and R platoon in three jeeps, and an engineer platoon in two trucks. The rest of B Company's tanks (eight), plus twelve tanks from the 64th would form up with the truck-mounted 2d Battalion as soon as they arrived. The rest of the 187th would follow later in the day.

The small point task force moved down the road and met troopers from the 187's I and R platoon and engineers two miles out of Puchaetul. The point reformed and moved out with two tanks in the lead, followed by a jeep, followed by two tanks, another jeep, and two trucks. The column got to the outpost at Koritwi-ri and halted. General Almond arrived there by helicopter and gruffly ordered them "to get those tanks on the road and keep going until you hit a mine. I want you to keep going at twenty miles an hour." The small point column fought its way along the road, reached the south bank of the Soyang River at 1630, and set up a perimeter.

In the meantime, Colonel Gerhart had formed up his task force and got it on the road to the north. Tanks were intermingled with two-and-a-half-ton trucks, quad .50 vehicles, and jeeps. By late afternoon, the column had fought its way thirteen miles through enemy defenses along the road ridges to Morumegi, located about two miles south of the Soyang, and joined up in the perimeter with the point force. The 2d Battalion remained there in an airhead type of defense until 26 May.

Lieutenant Colonel Rye Mausert was now the CO of the 3d Battalion, replacing Lieutenant Colonel Munson, who had rotated home early in May. Mausert described his part in the follow-on operation this way: "General Bowen issued his attack order. The 187th would attack in columns with the 3d Battalion leading. He ordered us to move as quickly as possible up the road to Inje. 'If a vehicle stops for any reason, push it off the road. If any of your attached tanks are stopped, push them off the road with another tank, your jeeps, or by hand, if necessary. Our other units will clear the high ground left and right. But if they are not along in time to do it, just clear a corridor yourself but keep going.' On the morning of the twenty-fifth, we moved out riding every available vehicle. There was no enemy action for the first few miles outside Hangye. We couldn't help but think *if it continues like this, we will be in Inje in a few hours,* but down deep in our gut we knew better. *Anytime now the stuff will hit the fan.* And it did."

William Ignatz was a rifleman in I Company. "The roads were a morass of mud and the fields were worse," he remembered. "Throughout the five-day advance we encountered groups of retreating Chinese. In some places we smashed through their defense positions. Nothing stopped us. When the Communist resistance stiffened, we would dig in for a few hours, plaster them with mortar and tank fire, then rush the strong points with rifle and bayonets."

All along the route of advance, the CCF were dug in primarily on the left or northern flank of the road. As the lead elements of the column passed, the Chinese in holes would push up their camouflage covers, throw some grenades, and then slide back. Their efforts knocked out jeeps and tanks that then cluttered the road. "To keep moving, there was only one solution," Mausert remembered. "In spite of orders, we had to clear the flank of the road at least two hundred yards deep. I ordered K Company to deploy two platoons to clear the flank. The remainder of the company remained with the lead tanks as infantry support.

"Initially, for the first few hundred yards, our troops were being fooled by the camouflaged foxholes, but it didn't take them long to learn, after a few casualties. Bayonets were fixed. If in any doubt, the ground was bayonet tested. Hundreds of Chinese died in their holes. Now the column could move forward, the major hazard close to the road being removed. Progress was slow but moved along about one to two miles an hour."

Short of Inje, the terrain flattened out, and the area had to be cleared on both sides of the road. Mausert ordered I Company to use two platoons to clear the area between the road and the river. The CCF defenses increased, and the enemy fought more strongly to hold his supply base at Inje. The 187th troops began to receive heavy mortar, artillery, and machine-gun fire, and their casualties increased—but not at the rate of the CCF's. They knocked out a couple of tanks on the road, but the tankers pushed them aside, and the attack moved forward. By late evening of the twenty-fifth, the 187th had seized Inje, and General Bowen had moved his CP to the outskirts of the town.

On the evening of the twenty-fifth, General Bowen called Mausert back to the 187th CP and told him to move out at dawn the next morning to clear the road to Inje that was now only one lane wide running along the river that cut through the hills. There were many sheer cliffs on the right and left of the narrow road. "Our tanks will be like fish in a barrel," Bowen told Mausert. "You will have to clear the ground on your left as you move forward. If vehicles get knocked out, push them over the cliff and move on."

Later that night, the CCF ambushed a convoy of Service Company's supply and ammo two-and-a-half-ton trucks behind the infantry column.

The CCF hit the convoy from both sides, killed two men, wounded many, and captured one man, Edward Hyatt. He died in an enemy POW camp far to the north months later.

Early on the morning of the twenty-sixth, Mausert and his battalion moved out. K Company deployed to take out the Chinese in their holes along the high ground but could not wipe them all out. The remainder fired at the column on the road with grenades and rifles. As the 3d Battalion's column moved slowly along the narrow road, Mausert's point men ran into a sizable CCF unit that was blocking the road to Inje. Mausert's men attacked and many of the Chinese either were killed, captured, or jumped off the cliffs along the road. The 3d Battalion moved forward a few miles and ran into another strong defensive position. K Company took heavy casualties. Mausert and I Company commander, Capt. Robert B. Tulley, moved up toward the K Company position through flat ground covered with rice paddies. In the middle of the field, enemy mortar fire blasted them, but the wet, mushy fields absorbed the blasts and covered them with mud, not shrapnel.

Mausert ordered Tulley to move I Company through K Company and take the CCF on the ridge holding up K Company. I Company, supported by heavy weapons from both companies and M Company's support fire, made a bayonet assault through the paddies and up the ridge.

"On 25–26 May 1951, 1st Platoon of I Company was riding tanks on the road to Inje," remembered MSgt. Al Ross. "There was heavy mortar fire and long-range enemy machine-gun fire. 1st Platoon managed to reach the outskirts of Inje just before dark. It had taken them over ten hours to fight through ten miles of road, and there were heavy casualties. The platoon rested on both sides of the road with the tanks in the middle of the road near a bend in the river.

"Next morning, the Chinese attacked in the high ground above the road. With I Company in reserve, K Company was ordered to clear and hold the high ground. That morning K Company took the high ground and repelled three Chinese attacks, but at the end only the peak of the hill—a long ridge to the front—had to be cleared and held.

"I Company was ordered to continue the attack. 1st Lt. Edward J. Maloney moved up with his 1st Platoon. An I Company machine gunner was killed by enemy automatic-weapons fire. A Chinese soldier suddenly opened up with a burp gun. Lt. Maloney took three rounds in the back, just below the shoulder, and died instantly."

Meanwhile, Lt. Epps's G Company rode tanks down the road as far as Puchoyon and then were forced by intense enemy fire to dismount and fight on foot. To the left of the road were hills and about a hundred yards to the right was the Soyang River. Under fire, the company neared a ford just past the village of Kwandae-ri. On Colonel Connor's order, the company started across with the 2d Platoon in the lead. Private First Class Saunier, carrying his BAR, was hit in the chest while in the stream but managed to keep moving. He lived to show off his ID tag with a bullet hole in it. The troopers were loaded with ammunition and weapons and crossing the stream under fire was a difficult task.

Epps ordered the 2d Platoon to take the high ground on the riverbank. As the other platoons waded ashore, Epps told them to keep moving to the north. Finally, the tanks were across and the attack moved ahead. But without the protection of the hills, the company began to take heavy casualties. Private First Class Piscione, Epps's runner, was hit but continued to move up and down the line relaying Epps's orders. Later Piscione received a Silver Star for his gallantry at the Battle of Inje.

Because of G Company's casualties, six KIAs and a number WIA, Connor ordered F Company to continue the attack through G Company to clear the hills to the front. F Company deployed in a line and swept forward. Connor moved his battalion forward about two thousand yards north of the ford into the low hills east of the Soyang River and set up a defensive position in thick foliage. The next morning at sunup, Rye Mausert's 3d Battalion, supported by Capt. Blaine E. Young and the quad .50 halftracks of his A Battery 88th Airborne AAA Battalion, continued the attack up the western side of the river.

"While the 3d Battalion cleared the western side of the river along the primary road," wrote Fred Waterhouse, "2d Battalion recrossed the river to the west side on a man-made footway of rocks. As the Rakkasans crossed the river, scores of enemy bodies floated past. Some bodies were hung up on the footway rocks. After reaching the road to the west side of the river, the 2d Battalion turned north following the 3d Battalion Task Force. . . .

"En route to Inje, the 2d's troopers saw hundreds of enemy dead in the draws on both sides. Along the road, there were also American dead which had been lying there for a long time. The next day, 28 May 1951, the 2d Battalion assumed the point of the advance."

On the twenty-ninth of May, G Company, with Lt. Charles L. William's 3d Platoon in the lead, attacked Hill 420 at Wonton-ni. About a thousand yards behind the hill was the enemy's artillery that had been shelling G Company since dawn. The 3d Platoon made it to the summit of the hill with little difficulty and knocked out the enemy position on the reverse slope, but began to be hit by heavy fire from another knoll. Then the CCF hit the 3d Platoon with a strong counterattack and caught the platoon in the open. Sergeant First Class Robert E. Miller, the platoon sergeant, and Sfc. Robert L. Jones, a squad leader, organized their troops in the face of the enemy fire. The troops came under heavy fire but managed to hold. Sergeant First Class Miller, in a heroic stand, fighting valiantly, was killed. Later he received the DSC. G Company would be forced to hold the hill for four days.

Just before midnight on the twenty-ninth, the 3d Platoon was again hit by a strong CCF attack and by two more before daylight. With machine guns, grenades, and rifles, the 3d Platoon held its position on the knoll. Privates First Class Lemone Wilson and Arellano, in exposed holes, fired throughout the night at the attacking CCF. During the night of 30–31 May, the CCF repeatedly attacked G Company on Hill 420— so often that the 3d Platoon was running short of ammo. Resupply came forward from the 2d Platoon just in time to meet another assault.

At 0200, the enemy stormed the 3d Platoon in the front and the 1st Platoon on the left flank of Hill 420. Grenades landed in the company CP area just behind the 1st Platoon.

Private First Class Carl M. Hamrick occupied a foxhole with Cpl. Rudy Hernandez on the forward slope held by the 3d Platoon. "The enemy attacked with artillery, mortars, and automatic weapons," Hamrick wrote later. "A heavy machine gun fired from a knoll to the north. The enemy's attack was directed mainly at the sector where Corporal Hernandez and I occupied a hole together. The enemy was massed just beyond the drop in the slope and twenty-five yards from our position. As the enemy charged at us, we 'opened up' with machine-gun and rifle fire. We had a fierce grenade battle in which both Cpl. Hernandez and I were wounded.

"Immediately after this, our platoon machine gun went out of action on our left. About four or five men on both sides of us began to withdraw. The enemy fire grew heavier. Corporal Hernandez and I continued to fire our rifles until his weapon had a ruptured cartridge. Without saying a word, he jumped out of our hole and charged the enemy with his inoperable rifle, bayonet fixed. As he threw grenades, I saw him run forward about ten yards and disappear in the darkness. I then moved from our position to another hole about fifteen yards to the left because the North Koreans were rushing me.

"I did not actually see Cpl. Hernandez use his bayonet on the enemy, but I saw the result of his fight when Cpl. Frogner, Sgt. Stanchuk, Pfc. Billingsley, and I found him at daybreak. With Lt. Williams leading, we moved forward and found Cpl. Hernandez about twenty-five yards in front of our position. He was lying head to head with a dead enemy soldier. There was another body five yards behind him, and three more just to his left front. All of the dead enemy soldiers had deep bayonet wounds on their upper bodies. Corporal Hernandez was badly wounded and unconscious. We evacuated him to the rear. During the action, the enemy had penetrated the defense perimeter but was stopped inside the perimeter primarily by Pfc. Billy B. Yates and Pfc. B. H. Borg. They had been positioned higher up the ridge. Lieutenant Williams led a short counterattack and restored the original defensive positions."

At daybreak, the patrol carried Hernandez through the company command post. When Lt. Epps saw Hernandez on the stretcher, he was certain that he would not survive the day. But he did survive and was later awarded the Medal of Honor. Lieutenant Williams received a Silver Star.

Along the route to Inje, the 1st Battalion, now under the command of Maj. C. M. "Mike" Holland, fought along the ridgelines against the same determined enemy that faced the 2d and 3d Battalions. Their casualties were heavy: 11 KIA and over 40 WIA. On the first of June, Pfc. Howard L. Dreyer, B Company, was awarded the Distinguished Service Cross posthumously for his gallantry.

The battle in the area was almost over. General Ridgway arrived in Korea on 28 May. He met with General Van Fleet and reviewed in detail Eighth Army's situation and plans. He noted among other things the unusually large number of POWs and the large stock of enemy weapons and other gear in UN stockpiles. "All three U.S. corps commanders," he wrote, "have reported a noticeable deterioration in the fighting spirit of CCF forces. In many cases, CCF POWs reported that their units were so desperately short of rations that the men had to eat grass and roots."

Captain (retired brigadier general) Bertram K. "Igor" Gorwitz had commanded B Battery of the 674th for a year and a half in the States and for nine months in Korea. On 7 May, Gorwitz turned his battery over to his XO and became an aerial forward observer for the 187th. He flew most often with Lt. Carl Schmidt, USMA '46. "During the period 14–19 May," Gorwitz wrote, "we flew constantly from daylight to dusk, adjusting artillery fire and advising the ground-based air force forward controller on the best air corridors for close air support aircraft least likely to shut down our own artillery or endanger his aircraft.

"On the twenty-first and twenty-second of May, the 187th conducted a three-pronged attack on the Hoengsong-Honchon area some forty miles to the east of Okchon. Again, as I recall, we had a productive period, long hours, and plenty of excitement. The enemy at that time was attempting to protect and keep open the routes north for several hundred thousand Chinese who had penetrated deeply to the south along the east coast of Korea. The North Korean and the Chinese held on to their positions tenaciously and there were few prisoners on either side.

"On or about the twenty-fourth or twenty-fifth of May, the RCT received an order from Lieutenant General Almond, CG of X Corps, to move with all haste to the area of Inje, near the east coast, to cut the routes of escape required by the Chinese forces moving northward in their long march up the coast. Carl and I flew to Inje and then south to spot the Chinese and pinpoint their furthermost advance to the north. We found the Chinese, thousands upon thousands, walking north, heads down and weary, many without weapons, no food in the rice bags, and apparently little or no ammunition—both a frightening and exhilarating experience seeing these masses who had beaten our forces up north now attempting to escape from our forces. I was also concerned that at any moment a thousand rifles could be pointed in our direction. Mile after mile, as we flew over them, they took no notice of us. None looked up and none caring that we were there and no one taking evasive action. We flew over the tops of their heads, turned over and dropped a few grenades, but I do not recall seeing a single upturned face or weapon. These Chinese columns were, of course, well beyond the range of our own artillery."

With the almost spectacular success of a now revitalized Eighth Army in May of 1951, the war began to take on all of the attributes of a stalemate. General Ridgway directed that X Corps go on the defensive, much to General Van Fleet's disappointment. "We had the Chinese whipped," General Van Fleet told one historian. "They were definitely gone. They were in awful shape."

But the Eighth Army did go on the offensive in Operation Piledriver to inflict "maximum casualties on a defeated and retiring enemy." The main weight of Eighth Army was in I Corps, which was attacking toward Chorwon-Kumhwa, two corners of the Iron Triangle. In fact, the Korean War Stalemate was about to begin.

Operation Piledriver was far more difficult and hazardous than General Van Fleet had anticipated. The resistance was strong, and massive CCF counterattacks possible. On 9 June General Van Fleet radioed General Ridgway recommending a "general halt . . . limiting further Eighth Army action to hit-and-run raids designed to throw a possible CCF counterattack off balance." On 14 June, General Ridgway concurred. By this time, the Eighth Army had occupied and dug resolutely into a wavy defensive line from Kansong in the east across North Korea above the 38th parallel and then dipping below the 38th in the west near Munsan and then along the Imjin River. The line included Chorwon and Kumhwa but not the northern point of the Iron Triangle, Pyongyang.

By June of 1951, several new conditions served to limit the aggressiveness of Eighth Army. Among them were these: a new rotation policy that would permit officers and soldiers with the longest service in the combat units to return to the States when replacements became available; rumors of a cease-fire along the 38th parallel; the rainy season in Korea with monsoon-like rains; strong CCF resistance; and troop fatigue.

In the last offensive, the 187th had suffered severe casualties—286 men killed or wounded. General Almond pulled the 187th out of its hard-won positions near Inje and sent the marines to relieve the 187th in place. Shortly after the 187th pulled out of Inje and moved to a rear area near Wonju, the engineers carved out a runway at Inje, and air force evac planes used the strip to evacuate thousands of wounded to hospitals in Japan during the next two years of the war.

"As the first year of the Korean conflict came to an end," reported an army historian in *Korea 1951–53*, "the United Nations could look back on their accomplishments with considerable satisfaction. South Korea had been cleared of the invading enemy, and the UN forces, after receiving and delivering severe batterings, had pushed north of the 38th parallel and successfully executed the missions that were within their power to accomplish. Thus, when on Sunday evening, 23 June, in New York City, Jacob Malik, deputy foreign commissar of the Union of Soviet Socialist Republics and his country's delegate to the United Nations, proposed cease-fire discussions between the participants in the Korean conflict, his proposal, while it may have been made for the convenience of the Chinese, came at a fortunate time for the Eighth Army."

The Korean War Stalemate was about to begin. By early June, General Bowen received orders to move the 187th RCT from Korea to bases in Japan, where, in proximity to air force bases and cargo aircraft, the RCT would remain in Eighth Army reserve ready to mount an airborne operation in short order to reinforce the troops in Korea. A new phase of the military history of the 187th was about to begin.

And with this new phase, came a new commander. On 27 July 1951, Col. Thomas J. H. Trapnell, forty-nine, USMA 1927, replaced General Bowen as the commander of the Rakkasans. At West Point, Colonel Trapnell had been an outstanding football player and had been nominated for "All American" honors. In later years, Colonel Trapnell became a survivor. In 1942, he was in the 26th Cavalry Regiment in the Phillippines. In one of the early battles, "There was Trap," wrote R. Ernest Dupuy in *Men of West Point*, "Maj. Thomas J. H. Trapnell, Class of 1927, from New York. When the Jap light tanks first came grinding at the 26th near Rosario, 'Trap' took a truck, drove back into the ruck, and fired a vital bridge, holding up the tanks." Major Trapnell was a POW from 1942 to 1945. Among his awards for combat in the Philippines were the DSC, two Silver Stars, and the Purple Heart. He survived the Bataan Death March and two POW ship sinkings. On the 5th of October 1951, Colonel Trapnell became Brigadier General Trapnell, receiving the first of his eventual three stars.

### Life in Japan
The 187th Airborne Regimental Combat Team had been severely bloodied in the first year of the Korean War—two combat jumps followed by weeks of savage, close-in, body-to-body combat in bitter cold and monsoon rains over steep, rocky ridges against an enemy with a seemingly endless tidal flood of replacements. The battle-tough but somewhat

weary troopers of the 187th gladly welcomed the order to leave Korea, move to Japan, set up camp, train replacements, prepare to return to battle by parachute with only a minimum alert, and remain Eighth Army's reserve.

Jacob Malik made his proposal for cease-fire discussions, and shortly after, the Beijing radio announced that China favored a truce. President Truman authorized General Ridgway to conduct negotiations with CCF generals. After some preliminary liaison work, both sides agreed to meet at Kaesong, a town on the west coast about three miles south of the 38th parallel and between the battle lines. Negotiations opened on 10 July with VAdm. C. Turner Joy, the Far East naval commander, acting as chief delegate for the United Nations. Lieutenant General Nam Il led the CCF delegation. Both sides agreed that combat would continue until a truce was signed, but neither side was ready to start large-scale operations.

All along the front that now extended 155 miles from the Imjin River to Chorwon, along the base of the Iron Triangle, and then north and east to the Sea of Japan above Kansong—combat had slowed down. All along the line U.S. I, IX, and X Corps and the ROK I Corps dug in, patrolled regularly, fired rolling barrages of artillery, seized more favorable defensive terrain, and captured prisoners. The U.S. Air Force interdicted the enemy front-line and rear-area installations, bridges, railroads, and traffic with air strikes. U.S. Navy ships offshore, including the USS *New Jersey*, with nine sixteen-inch guns, pounded the enemy lines. Naval units of nine nations blockaded the coastline of North Korea and bombed harbors, port cities, and supply points.

The enemy appeared to be following the same general tactics (without air force and naval assistance): hold the main line of resistance with screening forces in front. In August, Van Fleet's force totaled 586,769 troops, including 229,339 in Eighth Army and 357,430 from South Korea, the U.S. Marines, and the Fifth Air Force.

Battles flared along the line at Bloody and Heartbreak Ridges. "It was 22 October before the liaison officers met again," wrote an army historian, "and three days later the plenipotentiaries once more resumed the negotiations that were to continue for many weary months. Meanwhile, for the soldier at the front, the war went on."

And for the troopers of the 187th, life in Japan carried on with training, jumpmaster schools, parachute jumps at various camps, and nightlife in town. Fred Waterhouse reports that at the jumpmaster school "all jumps were made on the Camp Hakata golf course, and more than one group of golfers had to wait while two jumpers and their door bundles hit the DZ, sometimes on the third tee. This small jumpmaster course was only a beginning—the school would shortly be giving basic parachute training to officers of the Japanese Army Self-Defense Force."

Life in Japan for the 187th was about to take on more significance. The Koje-do riots would grab their attention.

### Koje-do

General Mark Clark called it "the biggest flap of the war." General Ridgway said that it "was hardly the ground a sane man would have chosen to erect campsites." They were both speaking about the United Nations Prisoner of War Camp No. 1, on Koje-do, a rocky, hilly, 150-square-mile island in the Korean Strait thirty miles southeast of Pusan. From its beginning in 1951, the POW camp produced nothing but a series of problems for the UN Command. Eventually, it became a prison run by the inmates.

For one thing, it was grossly overcrowded; by May of 1952, the camp held some 150,000 North Korean and Chinese POWs and civilian internees in a compound originally designed for 38,400. Another problem was the fact that the ROK and U.S. forces guarding the camp were, according to one report, of "extremely low caliber." A third difficulty was the constant clashes in the compound between pro- and anticommunist prisoners and civilian internees. And a fourth embarrassment was that General Nam Il, the chief of staff of the North Korean People's Army (NKPA), had infiltrated handpicked NKPA officers into the compound to stir up riots, demonstrations, and murder anticommunist POWs and civilians.

The camp consisted of four barbed-wire enclosures, about as "big as baseball stadiums," each divided into eight compounds, each jammed with six thousand prisoners. "High barbed-wire fences surrounded these compounds with sentry towers on all four corners," wrote Fred Waterhouse. "As many as seven thousand prisoners existed in one enclosure, living in squad tents, some Quonset huts, and great, flat one-story huts with corrugated sheet metal roofs. As UN sentries walked post outside the enclosures, communist sentries kept pace, walking post inside. They also built their own sentry huts adjacent to the UN towers on the corners."

As early as June 1951, violence became the norm at Koje-do when the POWs attacked a UNC work detail, leaving three dead and eight wounded. In August, the POWs demonstrated and left eight dead and twenty-one wounded. In September, a "people's court" ordered fifteen of their own prisoners murdered. Soon thereafter, the POWs killed three more during mass riots in Compound 78, requiring the UN commander to rush in troops to save some two hundred POWs whose lives were in danger.

The camp administration, run by the 2d Logistical Command that was in charge of all United Nations Command POW camps, carefully carried out the principles of the Geneva Convention of 1949 regarding prisoners of war. And the International Red Cross inspected the camp frequently. But on 18 December, a large and savage rock fight broke out between compounds, followed by riots and demonstrations that left fourteen dead and twenty-four injured. Koje-do was getting out of UN hand.

But amazingly enough, the UNC had permitted each compound its own metalworking shop, issued the POWs gasoline to start fires, left the gates and sally ports unlocked so that work details could enter and leave more easily, and kept guards out of the grossly dangerous compounds at night, when beatings, "kangaroo courts," and murders of uncooperative POWs went on unpunished.

In the face of the increasing turmoil in the camp, in October 1951, General Van Fleet activated the 8137th Military Police Group, with three assigned battalions and four escort guard companies, to assist in policing the camp. In November, a battalion of the 23d Infantry Regiment joined the UN Koje-do force. By December, more than 9,000 U.S. and South Korean troops were guarding the camp.

In November, the UN command started screening the POWs to extricate and release the innocent South Koreans who had been swept up with North Koreans. One estimate held that there were some 38,000 "civilian internees" on the island.

On 18 February 1952, some thousand-plus inmates of Compound 62 fought the 3d Battalion of the 2d Infantry's 27th Regiment that was providing security for the screening teams. Fifty-five POWs were killed, twenty-two died later, and 140 were wounded. One American was killed and thirty-eight wounded.

On 23 February, the North Korean and Chinese delegation at Panmunjom protested vigorously against the "sanguinary incident of barbarously massacring large numbers of our personnel." The Reds managed the news to the extent that "thereafter, the POWs were virtually masters of their compounds," wrote George Forty in *At War in Korea*, "while the guards could do no more than stay outside the wire, under orders not to use force."

On 8 April, the UNC began an additional screening of the POWs to determine those who did not wish to return to North Korea or China. Because of the screening, the violence, carefully planned by the POW leaders, began to increase even more savagely. On 10 April, when U.S. medics went into Compound 95 to pick up a wounded man, a wave of screaming prisoners surrounded them and took them prisoner. Brigadier General Francis T. Dodd, the U.S. commander of Koje-do, rescued them by sending in a hundred unarmed ROKs. The POWs continued to resist forcibly with riots and mass demonstrations. On 13 April, Van Fleet told General Ridgway that screening could continue only by "forced entry." To beef up his forces further, Van Fleet sent the 3d of the 9th Infantry to Koje-do.

Throughout the compounds, "the North Korean leaders were brutal to their own men," Fred Waterhouse wrote. "Discipline was harsh. The prisoners arrogantly practiced their own riot-control drill with tent poles and sticks. They swaggered in the compounds, goose-stepping, and performing bayonet drill with wooden sticks. Against standing orders, they erected large outdoor stages, painted pictures of communist leaders, played military marches over the loudspeaker, and flew homemade North Korean flags. The POWs threw rocks, sticks, and human excrement at UN guards."

The lack of discipline and the anarchy in the camp reached a climax on 7 May when General Dodd, after talking at some length to a mob of prisoners through the wire at Compound 76, was grabbed by a group of prisoners who had run out an open gate, reportedly at the sound of a whistle, and dragged him into the compound.

When Van Fleet heard of the debacle, he added the 2d Division's 38th

Regiment, and B Company of the 64th Medium Tank Battalion to Koje-do. He also sent Brig. Gen. Charles F. Colson, I Corps chief of staff, to take command of Koje-do.

The prisoners held Dodd for four days while General Colson negotiated with them. Dodd was finally freed at 2130 on 10 May (even though Colson had demanded a 1000 hour release) only after Colson had said in writing that there would be "no more forcible screening or any rearming of POW in this camp, nor will any attempt be made at nominal screening" and admitted that "there has [sic] been instances of bloodshed where many POW have been killed and wounded by UN forces." This was the admission that the Communists had been striving for. They exploited it worldwide.

On 12 May, two days after Dodd's release, Gen. Mark Clark succeeded General Ridgway as commander of the Far East Command, and General Ridgway succeeded General Eisenhower as the NATO commander. General Van Fleet remained the UN commander in Korea.

The time had finally arrived for the UNC to put down the revolt in the compounds, especially the notorious Compound 76. On Dodd's release, Brig. Gen. Haydon L. Boatner had taken over command of the camp.

In the early hours of 17 May 1952 at his command post in Camp Chickamauga, Gen. Thomas J. H. Trapnell received orders to move the 187th RCT to Koje-do. At the same time, Maj. Gen. Chester F. McCarty was notified that the 315th Air Division would airlift the entire 187th to Pusan, Korea, beginning that afternoon. McCarty and his staff immediately left Tachikawa for Ashiya by C-54, three flying hours away. General Trapnell and key members of his staff flew to Ashiya in Cub liaison planes. Together, the commanders and staffs and Colonel Maurice F. Casey Jr., CO of the 403d Wing, set up a joint command post at Ashiya. Colonel Casey was already drawing up plans for the move.

The 187th troopers had moved out of training areas and barracks at Chickamauga and Wood in some haste. "I was a squad leader in L Company at the time," recalls Anthony S. Fiore. "I remember that on the fifteenth, our platoon sergeants had a sudden emergency huddle in the old man's office. Minutes later, they called the men together to tell us we had four hours to get ready to move back to Korea. I assumed we were going to make a combat jump. Koje-do was the last thing on my mind.

At Ashiya, we were issued jump scarves (camouflage-colored neck pieces, normally the signal for a combat jump) and boarded C-119s, combat-loaded. We were all chagrined when, at Pusan, we were issued a basic ammunition load and shoved aboard LSTs. On the overnight water movement, we learned that our target was the compounds."

The paratroopers of the 187th were amazed, disgusted, and shocked at the filth, dirt, and anarchy that they found in the Koje-do prison camp. Ron Simmons was in Support Company of the 187th. "We arrived at a dock in Koje-do and unloaded from the LSTs," he wrote later. "Then we drove through a series of dirt streets that were surrounded by POW compounds. . . . Some of the POW compounds had dead bodies laid out near the fences. These bodies were covered with blankets. Lime was spread on top of the blankets. It was a tense situation.

"Support Company settled into a series of platoon-sized tents that were located slightly above the base of a hill. We could look down onto the prison compounds. They were an ugly sight. Mean and hostile. The prisoners did as they chose within the compounds. We were told that there were around a hundred thousand of the bastards inside the compounds. We hated them and we did not trust them. . . . We stacked our boxes of mortar rounds on pallets outside the tents in the company area and covered them with tarps. These were within sight of the POWs. . . . The POWs postured. They marched, sang Communist songs, and practiced their own form of bayonet drill. . . . It rained and got muddy. We spent much of our time in our tents, listening to the singing and chanting from the POWs below us, until it got on our nerves. Our hatred for them grew stronger."

David H. Carter was a rifleman in A. Company of the 187th. "My first impression of Koje-do was one of indignation," he wrote later. "All compounds were flying North Korean, Chinese Republic, and Russian flags. The barbed wire fences were strung with imprecations in English, and in each compound, the Reds had constructed a reviewing stand plastered with prominent Red Stars."

During the next month, the 187th established itself on Koje-do in battalion areas some distance from the compounds. The 1st Battalion, now under the command of Lt. Col. Russell E. Whetstone, occupied a large area as big as a football field. With the usual "by the numbers" technique, the NCOs laid out the company streets and the men set up their pup tents. In short order, squad tents replaced the pup tents and became company and battalion CPs. . . .The POWs used fifty-five gallon drums cut in half for latrines. Each day the drums had to be emptied into the ocean. The 187th ran "honey-bucket" details, guarding the fifty POWs who carried the drums on poles through wire handles attached to their tops. This was a daily, dawn-to-dusk operation. And by Geneva Convention rules, the POWs were allowed a ten-minute break each hour. "Then," remembered one of the men who guarded the POWs, "the prisoners would drop their poles and honey buckets, squat, smoke, and make demands."

But then the troopers got into the construction business. "Relieving the 38th Infantry," Fiore wrote, "we assumed the mission of breaking up the massive four-thousand- to six-thousand-man compounds into smaller controllable units. To accomplish this, we first had to build two thousand-man compounds divided into four sections holding not more than five hundred prisoners each. The sections that came under our control were compounds 76, 77, 78, 80, and a female compound, totaling about twenty thousand North Korean and Chinese prisoners."

"Compound 76 was the headquarters of the island. Tunnels linked all surrounding compounds, and messages were impertinently sent between camps by wigwag signals. The POWs were completely out of hand."

In order to block the view inside the compounds, the POWs began to hang their blankets on the barbed wire. Previously, the UN commander would negotiate. Now the troopers of the 187th used flamethrowers to burn the blankets. Colonel Lee Hak Ku, the POW leader, complained, of course, to the Red Cross. However, no more blankets were issued.

The 187th troopers broke up intermittent rioting in the various compounds. "The paratroopers would move to the site and quell the disturbance with tear-gas grenades, the old beer-can type, with a long, burning fuse," wrote Fred Waterhouse. "The POWs had time, and tossed the grenade back at the Rakkasans. The POWs got the surprise of their lives one morning when the Rakkasans received shipments of the new fast-burning baseball grenades. The Rakkasans tossed these tear gas grenades and as usual the POWs grabbed them. The grenades went off in their hands. . . . Meanwhile at all battalion headquarters, sand tables were being built with replicas of the compounds. Briefings began; the paratroopers were getting ready to move."

During the weeks that the 187th had been on Koje-do, the intelligence officers had been gathering information about the actual conditions of the POWs and their armaments inside the compounds. "We knew that the POWs had been saving their fuel oil and storing it inside the buildings," wrote Ron Simmons. "We also knew that they had fashioned Molotov cocktails to use against us. It was rumored that they had a few guns. We knew that they had knives and spears. We also knew that they had dug a network of trenches. These were both inside and outside the tents and buildings. The POWs were prepared to resist our takeover."

By 9 June, the troops were ready to move the rebellious POWs from Compound 76 to the newly constructed, smaller areas. General Trapnell's plan had the 3d Battalion facing the entrance to the compounds, with special attention to Compound 76; the 2d Battalion would support from the rear; and the 1st Battalion would enter by force, if necessary, to move the 6,400 POWs to the new area. Everything had been planned down to the most minute and specific detail. Phase lines had been set up within the compound, and the troopers would cross the phase lines on a schedule. Phase Line A covered one-eighth of the compound; Phase Line B was down the center of the compound.

On the afternoon of the 9th, General Boatner notified Colonel Lee that the transfer would take place the next day and that he should form the POWs into groups of fifty for the transfer.

At 0600, the 187th moved to its planned positions around Compound 76. General Boatner summoned Colonel Lee to the main gate and ordered him to prepare his POWs for the move to the new compound. He refused and demanded negotiations. Boatner gave him a thirty-minute ultimatum to move out. In addition, over the loudspeaker system came the notice to all the POWs in the compound to put down their weapons, assemble in the open, and sit on the ground with their hands on their heads. Long after the thirty-minute ultimatum had passed, Lee and his men had stubbornly refused to comply. Generals Boatner and Trapnell stood on a low hill outside Compound 76 and waited. The 187th moved into its attack mode.

Master Sergeant Raymond W. Patrick was a rifle squad leader in the 2d Platoon of C Company. At the beginning of the effort to reduce Compound 76 in his sector, he recalls that his CO went to the gate and asked to see the "officer in charge of the camp without delay. I could see his crew-cut hair bristling with anger that made his field cap rise up and down.

"Well, the. . . CO of the camp had arrived standing approximately two feet from our CO's face. Indignation and arrogance showed on his face. I was standing about three feet from our officer in charge. . . .

"Our officer in charge finally said to the prisoner, and I think I can still quote his words, 'I am giving you bastards just thirty minutes to form up at this gate and prepare to march to the preselected areas we have prepared for you.'

"At that time the [prisoner] looked up into our CO's face, not saying a word, and spat right into his face. The prisoner hurriedly did an about-face and ran back into the compound, pulling the gate closed behind him. Our CO took off his cap, slamming it to the ground, saying, 'You SOBs asked for it,' and within fifteen minutes all hell broke loose. I don't know the companies that were preselected to go in, but they were prepared with fixed bayonets, etc., and they went in battering the gate open."

On the far side of the compound, Support Company was deployed along a small hill overlooking the compound. On order, Capt. Harry Sanders directed his men to lob tear gas and concussion grenades over the remnants of the barbed wire. The 187th Engineers had cut a hole in the wire in front of Support Company. "A Company moved forward, as elements of the 1st Battalion made the initial breakthrough of Compound 76," wrote Carter. I had twenty-nine men armed with rifles, and two flamethrower men. When the paratroopers actually moved in through the wire fence, the surprised North Koreans jumped into their first line of trenches running parallel with the fence. Others fled to dug-in tents and barracks to make a fight of it. All were wearing uniforms, carrying spears made from tent poles with metal knives strapped to their belts. I saw that they had contrived homemade gas masks. These masks had eyepieces made from cigarette packages. Air was filtered through tin cans filled with sugar and charcoal. The spears were four to six feet long with blades up to fifteen inches. Others carried flails made from barbed wire."

Lieutenant Colonel Whetstone, Capt. O. G. Garrett, S3 of the 1st Battalion, and MSgt. James Bowie, the battalion operations sergeant, went through the breach in the wire with A Company. The POWs were reacting frantically. They threw sheet-metal spears, Molotov cocktails, rocks, and sticks at the advancing troopers. They ignited the hidden caches of gasoline stored in the tents and buildings, setting the compound on fire. A Company pushed through the first line of POW skirmishers to the first trench line about ten feet inside the wire. Captain Garrett spotted a group of POWs running into a tent. He yelled to Cpl. John F. Sadler, a flamethrower, "Son, burn that tent down." "At this point, a North Korean speared one of my flamethrower men (Cpl. John F. Sadler) in the groin," wrote Carter. He fell against Captain Garrett and died minutes later, before he could be evacuated from the compound. "One of the riflemen seized the flamethrower and we moved to the first tent and quarters," continued Carter. "These tents were well dug in and behind them extended long, corrugated metal-roofed, sunken burrows with mud and stone walls about three feet high. These proved to be the strong points from which the POWs made their most determined stand.

"Confusion grew as we attacked the tent to collapse it. The North Koreans were thick in the building and trench surrounding it. As we approached, the prisoners stabbed at our people with their long spears and threw Molotov cocktails into the midst of the moving squads. Retaliating with thermite grenades and flamethrowers, the building was soon ablaze. Our people risked their lives diving into these burrows to rescue screaming, slashing, fighting Koreans. We pulled out about two hundred men from the first building. As quickly as the Reds were subdued, they were hustled to the rear and immediately moved into the new enclosures. This same thing was occurring all through the camp."

The 2d Battalion had pushed into the compound from the rear and had forced thousands of the POWs into a huge, tightly massed, unruly mob of shouting, screaming prisoners. Within about ten minutes, the troopers halted their advance on Phase Line Baker, and tanks moved in to the rear of the infantry line. Tear gas wafted in thick clouds throughout the compound. The tanks showered the area with their flamethrowers. The Rakkasans could see POWs who tried to surrender being murdered with knives and spears by the camp leaders near the center of the compound. Finally, in about two hours, the 187th had gained control of Compound 76. The POWs had decided that their situation was hopeless, threw down their arms, and walked toward the gates to be moved to the new areas.

"Then the POWs began to surrender," wrote Ron Simmons. "They were herded out of Compound 76. They were stripped naked, and were stuffed into open semitrailers with wire mesh stretched over the tops. Off they went, naked and smelling of tear gas." At the new compound, they were issued a set of fatigues and a rice bowl. Major Peter L. "Spider" Kelley, the XO of 1st Battalion, was at the gate working with the medics, checking on all the proceedings.

In the so-called battle of Koje-do, the POWs had 43 men killed and some 139 wounded—half by their officers. The 187th lost one man, Cpl. Sadler, and suffered 13 casualties. After the compound was cleared, the 187th intelligence units combed the burned-out, filthy area and found 1,000 Molotov cocktails, 3,000 metal-tipped spears, 4,500 knives, thousands of dollars of currency, a working telegraph set, and mockups of the M1 rifle and .30-caliber machine guns. In one of the tunnels, they found a woman and a child. In another isolated part of the camp, the intelligence men found the bodies of more than 50 anticommunist prisoners who had been executed and thrown down wells. They found another 100 bodies in unmarked shallow graves. And most revealing, they found an operations plan for the breakout of the POWs and the seizure of the island, set for 20 June 1952.

The next morning, the 187th deployed across the road to Compound 78, ready and armed to evacuate that compound, as it had Compound 76, with force, if necessary. But the 78ers had witnessed yesterday's onslaught and decided that docile surrender was the better course of action. General Trapnell gave the 6,000 POWs thirty minutes to form up and move out. After going back to their tents to gather personal belongings, the POWs complied peacefully, right on time.

The intelligence section moved into that compound and began its search. In one headquarters hut and in a consolidated POW mess, the unit found that every desk drawer, file cabinet, and POW cargo pack, and scores of pots and pans on the still hot stoves were loaded with human excrement. The irony of the gesture was not lost on the enraged troopers of the 187th.

A final and concluding epitaph to the Koje-do experience was a cover of *Life* magazine a couple of weeks after the burndown and reestablishment of UN control over the Koje-do prison: the cover pictured Major David Korn, the 187th Regimental S2, holding Colonel Lee by the hair of his head amid the carnage of Compound 76. The troops had found Colonel Lee cowering in a ditch. He had tried to pass himself off as a female before capture. In actuality, and finally, Colonel Lee, who had expected to be killed, was put in solitary confinement for the rest of his stay on Koje-do and was no longer a problem.

The Koje-do was "mission accomplished" for the 187th Airborne RCT. But it was not back to the "heaven" of Beppu and Kumamoto for the Rakkasans. For the 187th, it was back to Korea and the defensive line near the Iron Triangle sector, with a new commander.

### Kumhwa Valley—1952

The "talking war" had been going on in Korea ever since both sides' senior delegates had met for the first time at Kaesong on 10 July 1951. During the year after the initiation of the long drawn-out negotiations, the battlefield took on an entirely different look. The two sides were drawn up roughly along the 38th parallel in ever increasingly sturdier, deeper, and more elaborate defensive positions. In the rear areas, some positions took on the guise of underground barracks and offices. On 29 July 1952, Colonel Westmoreland, thirty-eight, replaced General Trapnell, who left the 187th to lead the MAAG in Indochina. From the beginning of his military career, William Childs Westmoreland had been destined, inevitably, for high rank and extraordinary commands. At West Point, he had been the first captain of his USMA class of 1936. In combat in World War II, he was an artillery battalion commander and a lieutenant colonel at age twenty-eight, and as the 9th Division Artillery executive officer and, later, as the 9th Division chief of staff, a full colonel at age thirty. After the war, he reverted to lieutenant colonel rank but, in the spring of 1950, regained his full colonelcy. When he was notified that he was to command the 187th, his initial reaction was that the RCT commander's rank had been downgraded to colonel.

After its successful mission on Koje-do, the RCT returned to Korea and set up a base camp in a crab apple orchard near the airstrip at Taegu, where the troopers could hear the F-84 Thunderjets blasting off for strikes along the relatively static Chinese and NKPA lines. But because they were near the Taegu airstrip, many of the 187th troopers thought they were getting primed for another combat jump.

On 29 July, Colonel Westmoreland flew into the Taegu strip and was greeted by the interim acting RCT commander, Col. Joseph R. Russ, a West Pointer from the class of 1935. On Colonel Westmoreland's assumption of command, Colonel Russ became the deputy commander. Later, Colonel Russ told Colonel Westmoreland that he had no difficulty with the command arrangement. Colonel Westmoreland was definitely in command. By this time, the 1st Battalion was commanded by Lt. Col. Russell E. Whetstone; the 2d Battalion by Maj. Charles M. Holland; the 3d Battalion by Lt. Col. Dow S. Grones; and the 674th Artillery Battalion by Lt. Col. Stuart M. Seaton.

"Although the unit [187th] had seen action earlier in the war," wrote General Westmoreland in *A Soldier Reports*, "the men had for long been in reserve in Japan and needed refresher training. An event the morning after my arrival pointed up how much still remained to be done.

"To observe an exercise that was to involve live firing, I stood on a hilltop with the battalion commander. When he called for preplanned defensive fire, mortar rounds began to land all over the hill. A lieutenant standing at my side was severely wounded, along with a machine gunner and several other men. I quickly ordered a cease-fire.

"An investigation revealed that the errant rounds were from a 4.2-inch mortar. Checking with the warrant officer in charge, I found that he was unqualified to command a mortar platoon. The incident enabled me to cadge ten more days of intensive training before the combat team went into action." The proud but chagrined officers in the 187th must have wondered what kind of an impression this accident made on Colonel Westmoreland's initial assessment of his new command.

When he joined the RCT, Colonel Westmoreland had more than fifty jumps (he had commanded the 504th Parachute Infantry Regiment of the 82d Airborne Division in 1946 and 1947, and thereafter had been the division chief of staff, but had not jumped in over a year). On the morning of the thirtieth, he jumped with one of the battalions making a training jump. Thereafter, he made it a point to jump with each of the battalions. His second jump was almost a calamity. "I made a poor exit from the aircraft," he said later, "and my parachute failed to open. Not until I was about three hundred feet above the ground did I finally succeed in shaking it loose. It blossomed just in time. I should have pulled my reserve chute; I had flirted needlessly with death."

On 4 August, the Rakkasans boarded trains and trucks and moved north to Chipo-ri, a marshaling area where the RCT prepared to move up on the line. At Chipo-ri, Colonel Westmoreland began to put the RCT back into top-notch physical condition with runs up and down nearby mountains. On 8 August, Colonel Westmoreland, his staff, and battalion commanders were briefed on the 187th's new mission at the CP of the 17th Infantry of the 7th Division. The op plan called for the 187th to relieve the 17th Infantry secretly in its positions above Changnim-ni in the Iron Triangle, the bottleneck through which the invasion had started initially. In keeping with the overall plan to prevent the enemy from knowing that the 187th was "on line" and, therefore, not an operational airborne threat to their rear areas, the 187th removed all patches and traces of its unit designation from uniforms, vehicles and equipment. For the move, a company of the 17th Infantry screened the area during which Westmoreland went up to select deployment areas for the RCT. Thereafter, the RCT came on line in the vicinity of the Hanton-Chon–Namdae River Valley on the central front. For the next two months, the RCT settled into its defensive positions. It was now known as the "Blackjack" RCT.

"The war of maneuver in Korea was over, . . ." wrote Ernest B. Furgurson in *Westmoreland, The Inevitable General.* "Neither the 187th nor any other UN command was allowed to conduct more than limited offensives, local thrusts and parries to take control of dominating terrain, to deny the enemy an observation post, to capture prisoners, to keep the other side guessing. This did not mean a unit had to carry on a passive war, however, and the lines across that section of the triangle became active on the arrival of the 187th. Many of the positions it inherited were poorly sited, considered by Westmoreland indefensible. He promptly started adjustment of his lines, straightening bulges, covering avenues of approach, pushing out five hundred yards here, a thousand there. He also ordered quickened patrolling and raiding, sending out platoon-sized combat patrols to strike enemy positions across the valley."

A couple of thousand yards behind the main line, the 674th Airborne FA Battalion was deployed in a firing position and in direct support of the 187th infantry battalions. This meant that every company on line had a 674th artillery forward observer (FO) team at an observation post in a forward position from which the FO could see the area in front of the infantry and the enemy lines across the valley. The FO had a battery commander's scope (BC scope) and a forty-power spotting scope through which he could look at the enemy positions in detail. The FOs were in direct radio contact with the fire direction center (FDC) of the 674th and with each other. Lieutenant Walter Klepeis, A Battery, 674th, Sergeant Edwards, the FO sergeant, and Corporal Bondie were at OP #5, with C Company, 187th, on the morning of 14 August.

Early that morning, Sergeant Edwards was on duty in the FO team bunker observing the valley to his front through the BC scope that rested on the edge of the hole. Suddenly, Sergeant Edwards woke up Lieutenant Klepeis, and said, "Lieutenant, you better wake up—there's a patrol out there that looks like our men walking near the enemy line." Klepeis looked through the BC scope that Edwards had oriented on the patrol but could not see anyone because of the fog. He did note, though, that it was near a preplanned artillery concentration. Edwards called the company commander, Capt. William C. Kouts, and told him about the patrol. Klepeis called the FDC and gave it the concentration number. Sergeant Edwards reoriented the BC scope, looked through it, and said, "They are walking back toward us. They must have been lost." But in almost his next breath, he said, "My God, Lieutenant, there are hundreds of Chinese running to cut them off. Oh, God, they are trapped." Klepeis, even though he could still not see the patrol or the Chinese, ordered the FDC to fire "Battalion in Effect" on the concentration he had given them. Captain John H. Fye III, the 674th Assistant S3 operating the FDC, told Klepeis to get a bracket on the area first. Klepeis hurriedly adjusted one battery, whose rounds landed amid the running Chinese. The enemy soldiers stopped in place. Edwards, following the action through the BC scope, told Klepeis to adjust to the left. Klepeis gave the adjustment to the FDC and said, "For God's sake, fire the Battalion in Effect." He got it. The rounds landed squarely on the enemy troops. This gave time for the 187th patrol from A Company to start running to the left, toward the 187th lines. But this would have put them squarely into another group of Chinese trying to trap them.

"At this point I observed through the BC scope a strange thing happening to a group of Chinese soldiers just out of the impact area," wrote Kelpeis after the action. "What I presumed to be a Chinese NCO or officer was running among his men, kicking, shoving, and pushing them to get going toward or directly into the artillery impact area. Needless to say, he wasn't having much success with this endeavor.

"Now smoke and debris from exploding shells obscured our view from OP #5 and we couldn't see the enemy or our patrol. Our first volley, from the three batteries, had landed on the majority of the attacking Chinese—I couldn't have gotten a better spread or accuracy. But now, without visibility and not seeing the enemy, I was about to give the cease fire order when a voice (later identified as Cpl. Lester Hammond, the patrol's radio operator) came over the infantry radio in our bunker. In a rapid fire voice, he told us to 'keep firing—your shells are landing right on them. I can see Chinese all over. There are many dead. You killed a lot. Keep firing.' I told the FDC to keep shooting, and I had radio contact with the patrol and they requested we keep shooting and that the fire was effective. . . .

"Corporal Hammond, with the patrol, now made several adjustments which I passed on to our FDC. The shells were cracking over our OP in super quick time. Now Corporal Hammond said, 'I'm hit,' and I'm pretty sure he said, 'They shot me in the leg,' but he continued to adjust fire. In 10–15 minutes the radio went silent. Corporal Hammond wasn't talking, and he wasn't answering my calls. I thought perhaps the Chinese were too close, and he didn't want to reveal his position by talking, or he was KIA.

"Now, other groups of Chinese were running toward the scene of battle so I started firing at them, splitting our battalion into separate batteries. But I was very worried about the patrol, and the awful silence from Corporal Hammond. Lt. Thomas V. Parkinson, the FO on my right flank, requested a battery to shoot at some Chinese in front of him that were running toward our little war. Not hearing from Corporal Hammond, I gave it to him. I was about to request cease fire in Corporal Hammond's area when his voice came over the infantry radio, very weakly, saying 'Keep shooting . . . the Chinese are all over . . . I can see hundreds dead,' and then he faded out again. I could hear the artillery shells exploding very close to him when he had the mike button down. We continued to shoot knowing Corporal Hammond was hurt. Then, I again heard his weak voice. He asked for an adjustment that my gut feeling said would result in the shells falling on him and I told him so. His next words were to the effect, 'Don't argue with me, Lieutenant. Shift fire.' Also he said, 'The Chinese will kill me anyway.' I asked him if the rest of the patrol was near him. I could barely hear him say he was by himself and no other patrol members were near him. His last words were, 'For God's sake, Lieutenant, keep firing.' I had now one of the toughest decisions to make, i.e., shift the fire onto Corporal Hammond and probably kill him, but hopefully save the lives of the others, or not shift and maybe save Corporal Hammond, but maybe lose the rest of the patrol. I prayed to God to help me make the right decision. I shifted the fire as he requested. The artillery shells killed this very brave man. There was no response from Corporal Hammond after I shifted directly onto his position. Cpl. Lester Hammond gave the ultimate sacrifice."

While Klepeis was still adjusting fire in the valley, Lieutenant Colonel Whetstone and Captain Kouts arrived at the OP. Whetstone immediately set up a relief force to find the patrol and bring it back. Shortly thereafter, Colonel Westmoreland appeared. Meanwhile, Kouts organized a relief force from C Company, including Lt. Henry S. Sachers and MSgt. Philander Henderson, and sent it out into the valley.

From the OP, Klepeis spotted more and more of the Chinese along the valley floor. Colonel Westmoreland and Whetstone also found targets. Klepeis shot at them adjusting the batteries as the targets came into view. From the valley, Sachers reported that there were many Chinese dead and some "seemingly disorganized and disoriented. Some appeared dazed, walking around as zombies." At one point, Sachers radioed that he and his men were under machine-gun fire from a hill. Klepeis looked at his map, saw a finger from the hill that looked suspicious, and fired a concentration on it. With great good luck and precise shooting, the adjusting rounds knocked out the machine gun. "My God, you killed them all . . . it's unbelievable," Sachers yelled into his radio mike.

Later that day, in temperatures up to 102 degrees, Sachers and his team moved carefully along the valley, finally made contact with the lost patrol, and recovered Hammond's body. As Sachers and his men were withdrawing, the Chinese attacked. Klepeis and Lt. Thomas V.

Parkinson were firing six missions at six different targets with the three batteries of the 674th, the 4.2 mortars of Support Company, 155s from Corps Artillery, and 81mm mortars of the 1st Battalion. Not to be outdone, the Chinese artillery fire whistled over the OPs and landed in the rear. Parkinson, on Klepeis's right flank, was wounded, but continued to function.

Throughout the broiling heat of the afternoon, the battle raged on. At one point, Parkinson called to Klepeis and said, "I see hundreds, maybe a thousand Chinese . . . they are forming up or gathering and running toward you . . . give me at least a battery." Klepeis still had targets in front of him because the Chinese were trying to block the escape of Sachers and his men. But Klepeis passed a battery to Parkinson and told Colonel Westmoreland and Whetstone about the Chinese movements in front of Parkinson's OP. Klepeis then asked the 4.2 mortar FO to zero in on a long hill to his front. Unfortunately, the 4.2s were out of high explosive (HE) ammo. Klepeis told the mortar FO to fire whatever he had—"smoke, flares, or anything you got."

Klepeis checked the area through his BC scope and saw hundreds of Chinese swarming over the hill. But when the 4.2 mortar smoke landed, Chinese near the smoke stopped because they knew from past experience that smoke was the usual precursor for an air strike. But Klepeis knew that no air strike had been planned. Parkinson was still firing to the right, and with what Klepeis could see in front of him, he feared that "it was doubtful we could stop them with the available artillery support. As I looked through the BC scope, I suddenly saw hundreds of additional Chinese still running around the white smoke over the hill. Then a miracle occurred. I saw all the enemy stop and squat, kneel, or lie prone. Out of the corner of my eye I saw a P-51 in a dive-bomb position. I noted its circle insignia indicating it was probably of the South African Air Force. It released a bomb which landed in the white smoke area on the enemy. The blast shook our bunker severely. Much to my amazement, the Chinese turned and ran back toward their own caves. They were in complete panic! Our savior P-51 made another run and dropped another bomb on the white smoke on the hill. I asked FDC if they ordered the air support. Captain Fye and Major Felix didn't know anything about the strike. We were helped seemingly from heaven. Lieutenant Parkinson kept shooting his battery as the Chinese ran back to their caves."

Late that afternoon, Lt. Henry Sachers and his men plus the patrol of which Hammond had been a part came back safely to the forward line, carrying Corporal Hammond's body. The others in Hammond's patrol were Sgt. Samuel Payne, Cpl. William Liell, Cpl. Clyde Rich, Cpl. Joseph D'Amato, and Pvt. Mason F. Bowen. Sachers was so grateful to the artillerymen that he and some of his team came to Klepeis's bunker OP that evening to thank him for the artillery support—especially the two adjusting rounds that knocked out the machine gun firing at Sachers and his men.

Klepeis finally found out, two days later, that the Corps Artillery had planned an air strike deep in the Kumhwa Valley, with the target identified by white smoke from a Corps 155 howitzer. But the pilot missed the 155 white smoke, dropped on the 4.2 mortar smoke, and saved the day for Sachers and his men. After the air strike, the Chinese stayed holed up.

All of the members of Corporal Hammond's patrol earned Purple Hearts. Sergeant Payne received a Silver Star. Corporal Lester Hammond Jr. was awarded the Medal of Honor.

Through this stage of the "static war," Eighth Army put pressure on all of the units along the line to capture Chinese soldiers for their intelligence value. Captain O. G. Garrett, the RCT S3, and Lt. James E. Hamlin, the RCT Asst S3, came up with a plan. What we'll do, they said, is send a liaison plane over the Chinese lines, have it develop an engine problem, have the pilot parachute out, then have the plane fly over a hill spewing smoke and explode in a crash on the other side, out of sight of the Chinese lines. The Chinese will certainly come out of their caves to recover the pilot. They talked the plan over with Capt. Eldon O. Basham, the RCT aviation officer, who thought that idea had possibilities. They took it to Colonel Westmoreland, who approved it enthusiastically.

It fell to the aviation section and the 187th I and R Platoon to implement the scam. First, they built a dummy, named "Johnny Mack Jr." after the platoon's call sign. Private First Class Jesse C. Gutierrez volunteered his fatigues for the dummy. He and Cpl. Robert A. Disney of the Aviation Section had cannibalized an abandoned F4U marine plane from the 7th Division strip and, with Capt. Jim Wade, the RCT motor officer, had put together the smoke screen.

At midnight on 28 September, the I and R Platoon squads, five minutes apart, slipped stealthily past friendly lines and followed an abandoned aqueduct that ran along the base of OP Zebra toward Hill 205, occupied by the Chinese. Finally the platoon came to a small grove of trees that ran less than two hundred yards from the base of Hill 250. The men hid in the foliage and took up positions of two men each, so that one could doze while the other watched. "In the darkness and the damp, clinging chill," wrote Sgt. Mike Ward, "men could be heard making a futile attempt to wrap themselves in ponchos or whispering to a friend through chattering teeth." The platoon could also see the dome of Hill 404, where the Chinese were also entrenched. They stayed under cover throughout the day, listening to the artillery whistle overhead and burst into the Chinese bunkers.

At about 1700, the platoon heard the motor of a liaison plane in the distance. The Chinese took it under fire as it flew near Hill 404. Captain Basham was the pilot and Sfc. Joseph McGonagle was riding in the backseat of the plane holding the dummy in his lap. Suddenly the plane belched clouds of white smoke, spun earthward, then leveled off at about six hundred feet and glided over the platoon's position. McGonagle threw out the dummy, its chute popped open, and came to rest about six hundred yards south of the platoon position. The plane wobbled out of sight behind a hill and, in the vicinity, the RCT engineers set off a huge explosion of gas, a fifty-five gallon drum filled with napalm.

"The I and R Platoon waited in hiding," wrote Fred Waterhouse. "Would the Chinese fall for the trick? Captain Harry Sanders, assistant RCT S3 and an observer of the operation, looked over at Lt. Francis Brown, the I and R Platoon leader. 'Get down,' Brown whispered. About two squads of Chinese soldiers came walking down a trail. The Reds in their mustard-colored uniforms could be heard talking. Sergeant Robert E. Jarrell watched one Chinese come within twenty yards of him. Corporal Charles E. Foster, assistant BAR man, was afraid the Chinese could hear his heart beating. Lieutenant Brown held his fire until the last minute. Then he opened up and the entire platoon blasted away. It was over in seconds."

Lieutenant Brown gave the order to cease fire. They had captured one wounded Chinese soldier and immediately set out for their own lines. Lieutenant Andrew P. Rutherford had a support platoon from E

Company awaiting them at outpost Zebra and was laying down covering fire as the platoon came across the valley. Enemy artillery fire exploded near the platoon, but it moved rapidly to the 187th ridgeline. Unfortunately, the Chinese prisoner died on the way.

Colonel Westmoreland met the I and R Platoon behind the forward line and congratulated them on the brilliant ruse that was almost successful. A few days later, Lt. Gen. Reuben E. Jenkins, CG IX Corps, awarded Lieutenant Brown the Silver Star and each man in the I and R Platoon a Bronze Star. He told them, "You have exhibited the true airborne spirit . . . full of dash, fire, and vinegar . . . you were battle smart. I have seen quite a few small units in action, but for my money, this I and R Platoon is number one, truly first class."

For the next few weeks, Colonel Westmoreland and the 187th were far from idle. The 187th worked at constructing bunkers and outposts along the new defensive line Missouri, along the Hanton-Chon–Namdae River Valley on the central front. Colonel Westmoreland sent patrols into the valley, supported by loudspeakers blaring at the Chinese on Sugar Loaf Hill, in an attempt to capture prisoners; he integrated the RCT's mortars into the artillery FDC; he used the quadruple-mounted .50-caliber machine guns of the AAA Battery for overhead supporting and interdictory fire; and he increased the training and use of the countermortar radars.

In the middle of September, the 187th was pulled off the line, moved to an airfield north of Seoul, and reverted to its traditional role as an "airborne" outfit with a return of patches, jump wings, and unit insignia. General Jenkins wired the 187th that "I hate to lose you. . . . I like the spirit and the guts exhibited by the 187th. Wherever you go, I want you to know that I will remember especially the action of your I and R Platoon."

The 187th's last mission on its second tour in Korea involved a part in Operation Feint, an Eighth Army stratagem designed to lure the enemy forces into the open, making them easier targets for air strikes, naval gunfire, and massive artillery bombardments. According to the FECOM plan, Eighth Army would "go through the motions" of preparing for a major offensive to link up with an amphibious operation over the beaches at Kojo on the east coast. In the plan, the 187th would theoretically make a combat jump somewhere in the vicinity of the landing at Kojo.

To prepare for the operation, each battalion made practice jumps from the 315th Wing's C-46s and the 483d Wing's C-119s, including heavy drop of jeeps, a weapons carrier, artillery howitzers, and heavy platforms. The first battalion hit the familiar DZ near Taegu in good order, took a nearby village, marched five miles, and then boarded trucks for the ride to the airfield. The second day, high winds canceled the jump. On the third day, the jump went as scheduled except for a weapons carrier that made the drop without the restraint of parachutes. For the next two days, the men of the 187th were tightly sealed in barbed wire enclosures around their tent city in the orchard near Taegu, with no visitors or Korean laborers allowed in the tent camp.

The 187th troopers and the airmen of the Troop Carrier Wings were positive that they were going to make another combat jump. On the fourth day of the 187th's isolation, navy and air force planes attacked the beachhead near Kojo, north of the MLR. On the fifteenth of October, the Navy launched mock amphibious landings along the east coast. C-46s and C-119s in V of V's, but with only flight crews aboard, flew over the mock amphibious landing areas and then headed out to sea. Shortly thereafter, waves of fighter bombers hit the area. But the enemy reaction was almost negligible. Eighth Army called off the land operations and "Operation Feint" lived up to its designation.

That night, C-124s began lifting the 187th back to its home bases on Kyushu, ending its second tour in the Korean War. There was one casualty: Cpl. Leslie Step, ex-ranger, broke his leg when he fell from the top of the main gate at Camp Wood while he attempted to hang a Welcome Home banner. The rest of the RCT made it without much difficulty.

# 7: Japan—and Korea—Third Time

By the fall of 1952, Kyushu, its permanent location, had become a home base to the 187th RCT. When the troops returned from Korea to Camps Chickamauga, Wood, and Kashi, they found their noncombat gear about as they had left it in their barracks and foot lockers. Married officers and NCOs, whose wives and children were in Japan, either in quarters on the small posts or in housing in town, were welcomed with the proverbial open arms. The single troops remembered well the streets and clubs of Beppu and Kumamoto and returned to familiar haunts in droves. But the mission of the 187th, theater reserve, required that the RCT remain in the highest state of readiness for quick deployment to combat in Korea by parachute or other means.

"This mission neatly complemented Westmoreland's diagnosis of what the RCT needed," wrote Ernest B. Furgurson. "That was more work and less cohabitation with the friendly population. Westmoreland began a training schedule intended not only to keep the RCT sharp in individual and unit combat skills, but also to wear the paratroopers down so that by evening they had little energy left to fuel a search for off-post diversion. He also ordered a halt to overnight passes, a regulation that caused a temporary wave of grumbling. . . . But the morale in the 187th reflected Westmoreland's concern for his troops, and their realization that his regulations did not mean he was antagonistic toward them. He encouraged their organization of an enlisted men's beer club, called the Rakkasan Club. . . ."

The winter and spring of 1952–1953 was a period in which General Westmoreland, promoted to brigadier general on 7 November 1952, honed the 187th to a fine edge of military perfection and combat readiness. In the past, the men of the 187th had been proud, tough, and well trained—paratroopers who believed that "legs" were definitely in a caste below them on the military scale. But in the period under General Westmoreland, he glazed the 187th with a new patina of the martial way of life. At the home bases, the troopers were inspected in ranks at morning formations, had their barracks and lockers checked on a daily basis, paraded sometimes once a week with the 187th Drum and Bugle Corps providing the music, and, on frequent occasions, stood full field inspections with their personal gear laid out in precise symmetry in front of their carefully aligned pup tents. "Spit shine" and Brasso took on new meanings.

But there was more to it than what seemed almost like a return to pre–World War II soldiering. This was an elite airborne unit with two combat jumps in its record, the only airborne unit in the theater. And General Westmoreland saw to it that its parachuting expertise, physical fitness, and combined arms proficiency were as sharp as its soldiering skills. "Every man a tiger" became the slogan of the 187th. The "tigerization" program called for accelerated physical training (PT and four-mile runs before breakfast), increased training in hand-to-hand combat, and stepped-up small-unit training problems, to perfect the NCOs at their trade. He also made certain that his officers and NCOs applied the proper leadership techniques. Frequently, he sent out letters to his officers at battalion and company level emphasizing certain leadership techniques, and distributed pocket-sized cards containing abbreviated military aphorisms and reminders. One, for example, outlined a step-by-step sequence for issuing combat orders.

The troops at Beppu used Mori as their training area; the artillery battalion and the infantry battalion at Camp Wood, ninety miles across the island from Beppu, used Oyanahara to practice their infantry maneuvers and artillery firing. Some of the maneuvers lasted for over ten days in both the heat of the summer and the cold and deep snow of winter on the island of Kyushu. One exercise involved a night compass course in a raging blizzard. Again and again, infantry companies deployed in the attack, made night advances and withdrawals, dug in for the defense, and then moved out on the offensive, with all supporting weapons zeroed in on the hypothetical enemy. The 674th spent at least a week per month at Oyanahara firing battery and battalion tests and supporting the infantry. And in the 674th, the Red Legs who were on battery punishment made the twenty-six-mile march to the range on foot.

Initially, training jumps were limited in size, some using single aircraft and some just three. At Camp Wood, an open, grassy field adjacent to the built-up area served both as an airfield and a DZ. Frequently for "pay jumps," a C-47 would arrive, load up with men already at the field, take off from the grass strip, make a pass, drop nineteen or so troopers, land, pick up another planeload, and repeat the process. The only hazard was high tension lines that ran along one boundary of the DZ/runway. Later, the jumps initiated at Ashiya expanded into tactical maneuvers of battalion and larger size.

One such jump was near Mount Fuji, an airborne maneuver in coordination with XVI Army Corps in the spring of 1953. Thirteen C-119s in a V's-in-trail formation delivered a reinforced infantry company in a three-hour, nonstop flight from Ashiya and dropped the troopers on the slopes of snow-covered, 13,090-foot Mount Fuji, an operation designed "to stop an enemy force attacking through a pass from the south." "The flight from Ashiya," wrote Fred Waterhouse, "arrived at Fuji on schedule, at a time when the sun and cherry blossoms made snowcapped Mount Fuji seem particularly beautiful. The troopers jumped in good form, hit the volcanic ash drop zone without difficulty, and went right into a twenty-four fighting maneuver in conjunction with defending XVI Corps troops. It was the first time paratroopers of any nation had ever jumped on the slopes of this sacred mountain."

In the spring of 1953, the war in Korea continued to fluctuate back and forth along the front. In May, the truce talks resumed at Panmunjom after a hiatus of six months, with most of the interminable debates centered on petty points and exchange of prisoners. U.S. hopes for an armistice faded. On 28 May, the CCF launched along the entire truce line a powerful offensive that forced the U.S. 25th Division and the attached Turkish brigade to withdraw from five hilltop outposts east of Panmunjom. The main thrust of the CCF offensive, however, was shortly after dark on 10 June against the ROK positions in the central front near Kumsong. Several ROK divisions broke and ran, leaving large holes in the defensive line. General Maxwell D. Taylor, who took command of Eighth Army on 11 February 1953, shifted boundaries between II and IX Corps and filled the gap with reserve divisions. By 18 June, a slackening of CCF pressure enabled General Taylor to stabilize the front. Nonetheless, he wanted additional forces from theater reserve deployed along the line. This meant the 187th RCT and the 34th RCT from the 24th Division in Japan.

On 19 June 1953, at the three main 187th camps, the order went out: all men report back to base camps. Unit commanders assembled their men, took reports, issued orders, checked combat gear, and within hours, loaded their troops into trains for the ride to Brady and Ashiya

Air Force Bases. At the airfields, unit commanders issued their men the greenish, camouflage-colored silk scarves that were the 187th's personal trademark for combat. It signaled to the troops that they were headed back to the line in Korea. Some men thought that the scarves were indicative of a combat jump. No so, in this case.

In spite of the relative stability of the front, the artillery on both sides fired with almost reckless abandon. In June, for example, the UN artillery forces fired some 2,710,748 rounds and inflicted 36,346 casualties; the enemy fired 329,130 rounds and caused 23,161 casualties.

On the twenty-second of June, the 674th Airborne Field Artillery Battalion went onto the line to the east of the Chorwon Valley in direct support of the Capital ROK Division and under the control of the IX Corps Artillery. At one point, the commanding general of Corps Artillery, Brig. Gen. Andrew P. O'Meara, had decided to send the 674th to another area. But before he made the final decision, he decided that a 155mm battalion would be more appropriate. The 555th FA Battalion moved into the area. In its new location, the 674th sent out FOs to the forward lines and picked up the cadence of the artillery shoot going on between and over the lines. In some cases, Corps Artillery operations center called for maximum rates of the battalion's fire at preselected concentrations. In some cases, the firing was so continuous that the battalion's cooks, drivers, clerks, and spare officers broke out the ammunition to feed the red-hot 105mm howitzers. The 674th remained with the ROKs until 13 July.

Meanwhile, the 187th, less the 674th, had gone into theater reserve in the vicinity of Seoul and continued its training and jumping, including night jumps along the Han River banks. On the thirteenth of July, the Chinese attacked the IX Corps right flank with three divisions and soon broke through the ROK lines. The Capital ROK Division collapsed, fell back, and made matters worse for the ROK II Corps that was already in trouble. All along the line, the ROK 3d, 6th, and 8th Divisions retreated under heavy Chinese pressure. And the 555th FA Battalion, in the area to which the 674th had almost been sent, was overrun.

I was a lieutenant colonel and commanding officer of the 674th at the time. On 13 July, while the 187th was moving up on line, the 674th had to move across a wide valley to get into a position to support the 187th directly. We were forced to move across the valley knowing full well that the Chinese had the Kumhwa Valley under direct observation from the hills to the north. Fortunately, the morning of the move, the valley was enshrouded with fog, and I was able to send the battalion across one or two guns at a time without being picked up by the Chinese. With little difficulty, I had the battalion in position behind the 187th by afternoon.

The 187th moved into defensive positions around Kumhwa, on the right flank of the 2d Division, astride Route 3, the "bowling alley" toward Seoul. It was roughly the same area that the 187th had occupied during the fall of 1952. An ROK division was on the east. General Westmoreland, after an intensive reconnaissance of the area, and aware of the CCF forces to his front, decided to place the 1st Battalion on Hill 624, which covered the entire corps front. From the hill, the troops could see routes east and west along which the corps artillery was deployed. Their guns dominated one likely CCF invasion corridor through the valley. The other two battalions were deployed to the west.

At the same time, Maj. Frederick J. "Fritz" Kroesen (retired four-star general) was in command of 1/187th. He had arrived in Beppu in May of 1953 and joined the 2d Battalion as the executive officer to Lt. Col. George S. Beatty Jr. "With alert to go to Korea," Fritz wrote recently, "I was suddenly transferred to 1st Battalion as Gallagher's XO in early June. Got to Korea, within a week, Gallagher on emergency leave to U.S., and I became acting CO for about thirty-five days."

After General Westmoreland had gone over the front-line positions with his battalion commanders, he returned to the 187th command post, set up adjacent to the dug-in and sandbagged firing positions of the 674th howitzers. He reviewed the situation with his staff and the commanding officer of the 674th and then got ready to repel any attacks down the corridor that he knew his troops could defend. But the situation would not remain calm.

"When a Chinese Communist attack drove a salient into the lines of two adjacent units, it left my combat team holding a critical shoulder of the salient," wrote General Westmoreland in *A Soldier Reports*. "In the middle of a black, rain-sodden night, the 2d Division Commander, Maj. Gen. William L. Barriger, telephoned to direct me to withdraw one of my battalions from a hill that I considered a key to my entire defensive position.

"I objected. I had been to the hill (Hill 624) that afternoon, I informed General Barriger, and the troops were well dug in and fully capable of holding. Neither did I consider it advisable to move without reconnaissance into a new position in the middle of such a night, and the proposed move would expose my own headquarters, which would also have to be moved. Yet General Barriger was adamant. When I insisted that I deemed the move ill-advised, he became irate and issued what he called a 'direct order' to withdraw the troops immediately. It was such a grave mistake, I believed, that I again asked him to reconsider. When he threatened to relieve me, I had no choice but to obey, but I made clear that I followed the order only under protest.

"Under miserable conditions, Maj. Frederick J. Kroesen, later to serve as a general officer in Vietnam, executed a withdrawal that only experienced troops could have accomplished, and to assure the integrity of the combat team's position, I had quickly to organize a provisional battalion made up of cooks, clerks, and drivers to occupy a blocking position. Fortunately, American counterattacks eliminated the enemy salient before the Chinese could take advantage of the key terrain my men had been forced to abandon."

Even though the Chinese had launched their last major offensive of the war, the skirmishes and the artillery fires along the front did not cease. On the seventeenth of July, MSgt. Charles Hockman, the command sergeant major of the 1st Battalion, was killed by artillery fire. Small patrols from both sides raided across the line, firefights and sniper fire were routine, and infiltrators through the wire at night were common. On the night of 20 July, the Chinese launched an attack with heavy artillery preparation and seized an ROK-occupied hill near the 187th position.

In the trenches on the front line, the troops found excitement that they could have done without. "My hedgehog, a forward point on the MLR, was overrun by Chinese," wrote Anthony S. Fiore of L Company. "I ran back to the squad area to find two Chinese standing on my bunker. I shot one and Lt. Osborne, my platoon leader, got the other. Jumping into the trench, I saw my machine gunner lying dead over his gun and the BAR man dead in front of the CP, and two walking wounded were staggering up the hill to the rear. I had three men left in my squad, including myself. I threw five CCF bodies out of the trench and prepared to hold against further infiltrators. Chinese patrols hit our outpost positions repeatedly in the next few days but none got through."

"My squad was set up in an outpost position at the base of X-ray Hill," remembered Sgt. Richard E. Simpkins, an M Company machine-gun squad leader. "At night, the Chinese would infiltrate and cut our barbed wire. Occasionally, small groups would raid our trenches for prisoners. Skirmishes and firefights continued as the armistice looked more and more promising. . . . On the twenty-seventh, we were advised that the truce would become effective at 2200 hours. Orders were to clear our weapons at 1800 hours, so as to prevent any incident that might compromise the truce order."

But the 187th was doomed to lose one more soldier, the last of the Korean War. Just five hours before the cease-fire, Sgt. Carl A. Hammer, 22, a machine gunner, was killed in a skirmish along the line.

"We had heard truce negotiations so many times that I doubted the cease-fire was actually going into effect," remembered Anthony S. Fiore. "I remember a full moon, as we sweated out the hours until 2200. We could hear fire above Sniper Ridge until about 0300 in the morning. Artillery and 90mm fire continued throughout the night. The ROK soldiers were singing in their bunkers. The next morning, the line was strangely quiet."

"Then somehow, the war ended!" continued General Kroesen. "Lt. Col. Dan Gallagher (who had been on temporary duty to the states) returned and resumed command. He and Jack Belford designed our Blackjack Bastion position and I went back to inspecting messes and motor pools."

At the first light of dawn, Americans began the onerous job of policing up and getting their gear together to leave the area. "We picked up cigarette butts, old paper, cartridge cases, and other rubbish, and tossed it into the river separating the forces," Simpkins wrote. "The CCF looked like ants crawling all over Sniper Ridge. Two of my machine-gun squad crossed over the line with C rations to use as trading material for souvenirs. They got to the enemy trench line when two Mongolian types stood up and waved burp guns at our people. They came back crestfallen by this unfriendly treatment."

Then down the line to the troops came an order that they would just as well have skipped: Dismantle the bunkers and defenses of the old

MLR, move back a few thousand yards to the Nebraska Line, and there build a new and more elaborate position. For the next three days, the troops on the old MLR broke down or blew up bunkers, strong points, and outposts. By 1 August, the RCT had moved to the new line and started the construction of "Blackjack Bastion," a system of bunkers and trenches straddling the "bowling alley" into Seoul. And because Blackjack Bastion belonged to the 187th, it would be the best-built defensive bulwark along the line.

"Paratroopers are magnificent soldiers," wrote General Westmoreland, "but they are also a very lively lot and require firm discipline and regimented activity if they are to be held in check. Since building new defenses along an armistice line failed to sap all their energy, I began a demanding physical-conditioning program under the slogan 'every man a tiger.' Calisthenics, long runs before breakfast, athletic competitions in the evening."

On 1 October, General Westmoreland had received orders to move the 187th back to Japan. On the third of October, the 187th moved to Inchon and boarded the *General Pope* for the trip across the Yellow Sea to their home bases on Kyushu. On 5 October, the *General Pope* docked in the port at Moji, Japan, and the following day troops assigned to Camp Chickamauga moved to Beppu by train. "Met with a thunderous 'Welcome Home' reception given by the local merchants, political figures, and townspeople," wrote Arch Roberts, "the Rakkasans staged an impressive 'combat dress' parade up 'Broadway' to the camp. Camp Wood troops continued by water to Sasebo, arriving there on the seventh of October."

The arrival of the 187th in Japan marked the end of the combat team's third and final combat tour in Korea. It also marked the end of General Westmoreland's command of the RCT. He headed to Washington for one of his numerous tours in the Pentagon. On 19 October, Brig. Gen. Roy E. Lindquist assumed command of the 187th in a ceremony at Camp Chick.

When he assumed command, General Lindquist was forty-eight years old. He was a member of the USMA class of 1930 and had commanded the 508th Parachute Infantry Regiment in Europe in World War II. Among his other decorations were the Silver Star and the Purple Heart. In actuality, his World War II wound had been very serious, forcing him to limit his parachute jumps to water landings only. Presumably because of his jump limitation, he also insisted that his battalion commanders limit their jumps. He grounded me, the battalion commander of the 674th, for example, because I made three jumps one morning at the Camp Wood DZ and forbade me from jumping the following month with my battalion on a battalion airborne exercise.

For the next twenty-one months, the 187th went about its training and duties in Japan with its usual vigor, discipline, and unique paratrooper enthusiasm. Many changes of command had taken place at battalion and company level. New men arrived and were integrated into the units. "Point" accumulation sent many of the combat veterans Stateside.

But training went on, undiminished. The 187th conducted training exercises with the U.S. Marines and, in a unique international training effort, opened a jump school specifically for carefully selected officers of the Japanese Ground Self-Defense Force. In October, the jump school at Camp Hakata graduated the first Japanese paratroopers after their fifth jumps. The Japanese officers became the cadre for a Japanese parachute unit.

By October of 1954, rumors of a different sort floated through the 187th's camps. It was not back to Korea this time but back to the land of the "Big PX," the States, where some of the girls had blond, brown and red hair. The U.S. Army had instituted a scheme called "Gyroscope," whereby units in the States would replace their counterparts overseas, thus creating "rotation with stability." Unit rotation, thought the army planners, was a far more efficient scheme to maintain unit integrity than sending individual replacements month by month to fill out the vacancies left by rotating overseas officers and soldiers. Thus, it came to pass the 508th Airborne Regimental Combat Team from Fort Bragg, North Carolina, would replace the 187th in Japan on an equal basis. And the exchange would involve one of the largest airlifts in U.S. Air Force history.

In February 1955, an advance party of eight officers from the 508th arrived at Beppu to plan the major airborne swap. The air force planned to airlift the two RCTs in the Eighteenth Air Force's giant (at least by the standards of 1955) Globemasters for the 12,900 mile trip from Fort Bragg to Japan and the return to Fort Bragg. The 187th's return to the States would involve a number of stops: from Kysuhu, to Wake Island, to Hickam Field in Hawaii, to Travis Air Force Base in California, to the strip at Camp Mackall, North Carolina, the original home of the 187th and adjacent to Fort Bragg, the RCT's final destination.

To initiate the exchange, advance parties of each RCT arrived and departed Kyushu. Camp Hakata became the marshaling area and Itazuke Air Force Base the departure airfield. The first group of four hundred Rakkasans moved out on 27 May in commercial aircraft, while an equal group of 508th paratroopers arrived in Kyushu. On 30 May, the first plane of the 508th landed at Itazuke Air Base; the waiting advance elements of the 187th boarded the plane immediately. On 12 July, the first plane carrying the main body of troopers taxied down the runway and was airborne at 1000 hours. A few minutes past Wake Island, Col. Curtis J. Herrick, the former deputy commander of the 187th, assumed command from General Lindquist. Colonel Herrick's command tour would last only until August.

"From the land of Fujiyama with its snowcapped mountains and fragrance of cherry blossoms to the sun-kissed shores of California," wrote Capt. Arch Roberts, "across the Rocky Mountains and the turgid Mississippi, down to the shadowy pinehills of North Carolina, they came by the thousands; the return of the mighty and powerful Rakkasans, home at last, after five history-making years in the Far East, veterans of Korea, guardians of Japan, and the most mobile striking force in the Pacific; the 187th RCT with its proud paratroopers had returned from a job well done."

By 17 July, thousands of paratroopers and their dependents had made the fifty-two-hour flight and the biggest airlift in history was over. The assignment of the 187th to XVIII Airborne Corps at Fort Bragg marked the end of the RCT's five years in the Far East. But for now, the 187th was about to begin a series of confusing Stateside assignments.

# 8: Army Reorganizational Turmoil

**Army Reorganizational Turmoil**

Colonel Herrick's command of the 187th Airborne RCT was on an interim basis. In August of 1955, after about one month in command, he was replaced by Col. Joseph F. Ryneska.

At Fort Bragg, the 187th Airborne RCT was directly under the command of XVIII Airborne Corps. Many changes took place within the ranks of the 187th as the veterans of Korea and Japan left for other assignments or returned to civilian life—full of the disciplined airborne spirit, thankful for the experiences, but ready to move to other, undoubtedly less demanding, pursuits. For the next few months, the 187th's ranks filled with many new men who had to be trained in the Rakkasan spirit plus in the unique and rigorous military expertise that had become standard in the RCT.

"The Rakkasans looked airborne when you saw them," wrote Bob Domitrovits in the summer 1989 issue of the *Rakkasan Shimbun,* the "Voice of the Steel Berets." "Most wore tailored-down ODs. Tapered pants to their low bloused boots. Beppu pistol belts with big brass buckles. Most of all, they wore their awards, citations, ribbons they had earned in the Korean War. The Rakkasans were sharp." But the stay at Fort Bragg was to be relatively short-lived. In January of 1956, another transfer loomed.

In the post–Korean War period, the army was in the throes of a major reorganization. The Cold War was descending into glacial conditions, and the army prepared to meet its challenges. Gyroscoping units switched back and forth across the Atlantic and the Pacific. "Massive retaliation" became a policy and resulted in drastic cuts in the end-strength of the army during the Eisenhower years. The army attempted to cope with the new strategy with two major reorganizations of the army divisions that caused turmoil in the ranks and in the command structure of the Army. "First came the pentomic (or pentana) plan of 1957–1959, then the Reorganization Objective Army Divisions (ROAD) plan of 1962–1964," wrote Stubbs and Connor in *Armor-Cavalry,* in the Army Lineage Series. "Underlying these reorganizations were developments in nuclear weapons—without loss of massed firepower—

mandatory characteristics for military forces. Combat areas of future nuclear wars were viewed as much broader and deeper than battlefields of the past, requiring small, self-contained, fast-moving units. Speed was imperative, not only for the concentration of forces but also in dispersion for defense. On the other hand, the army had to retain its ability to fight limited or nonnuclear wars, where the requirements for mobility or dispersion were not as important." The 187th found itself in the midst of these substantial changes.

In the spring of 1949, the 11th Airborne Division had arrived at Fort Campbell, Kentucky, after combat in the Philippines in World War II and almost four years occupying Japan. Early in the spring of 1956, the 11th gyroscoped to Germany. Rumors among the troops had it that the 101st Airborne Division of European World War II fame was about to be reactivated and that the 187th would have a major part in forming the new division. They were right.

At Fort Bragg, in January of 1956, Colonel Ryneska got the order: Move the 187th to Fort Campbell. By bus and truck convoys in a move appropriately called "Operation Gypsy," the Rakkasans left Bragg on 19 January and then settled into Fort Campbell in the barracks only recently vacated by the 11th Airborne Division.

Some few of the arriving troops who were interested learned that Fort Campbell was named in honor of Gen. William Bowen Campbell, the last Whig governor of Tennessee. He was elected colonel of the First Tennessee Volunteers, the "Bloody First," and is remembered in history as he led the storming of Monterey in 1846 with the cry, "Boys, follow me." What all of the troops did learn almost immediately was that Fort Campbell is located on the Kentucky-Tennessee border between Hopkinsville, Kentucky and Clarksville, Tennessee. They also found out that Fort Campbell was substantial—some 101,700 acres—with large drop zones, wide maneuver areas, and deep firing ranges.

"Training continued for the Rakkasans," wrote Bob Domitrovits. "Green recruits were to be molded into new Rakkasans. Double timing, push-ups, sit-ups, were the name of the game. Jump school would have been tough enough, but taking Advanced Infantry Training by airborne cadre made the next eight weeks feel like eight weeks at jump school."

On the twenty-seventh of March, the 187th formed "Combat Test Group Neptune" and began a series of training exercises and tests in the army's new pentomic concept. There were four tests over a period of some four months, during which the 187th rarely left the field. The tests included a parachute assault and a linkup with an armored force; an air transportability test; a raid in which the troopers parachuted into a DZ, destroyed enemy installations, and then were extracted by air transports. The fourth was a final examination testing all aspects of ground combat.

On 19 June 1956, the 187th felt the changes brought on by the new pentomic mode—the 187th was deactivated as a regimental combat team and faded temporarily from the active army roster. On the same day, the three battalions of the 187th were assigned to cadre the 101st Airborne Division, reactivated on 21 September at a ceremony attended by the secretary of the army, Wilbur M. Brucker, and the army chief of staff, Gen. Maxwell D. Taylor. At the ceremony, General Taylor, commander of the 101st in the Normandy invasion and later in the fight across Europe, presented the colors of the 101st, the "Screaming Eagles," to its new commander, Maj. Gen. T. L. Sherburne. With its reactivation, the 101st became a pentomic division, a poorly conceived organization centered on a pentagon concept: to replace three infantry regiments, the pentomic division had five infantry battle groups of five companies (no battalions of infantry), plus separate battalions dedicated to command and control, communications, engineers, and artillery. It was a doomed organization almost from its start. On that same date, the 187th was redesignated the 187th Airborne Regimental Combat Group.

On 1 March 1957, the 1st Battalion of the 187th emerged from the obscurity of army records and was reactivated as the 1st Airborne Battle Group, 187th Infantry, under the command of Col. Norman G. Reynolds, and assigned to the 11th Airborne Division in Germany. It left Campbell in the spring of 1957 and remained overseas for the next fourteen months.

On 25 April 1957, the 2d Battalion of the 187th became the 2d Airborne Battle Group, 187th Infantry, under the command of Col. Melvin Zais, a renowned paratrooper in World War II and later the commander of the 101st in Vietnam. On this same date, the 3d Battalion, 187th was deactivated.

The 1st Airborne Battle Group, 187th Infantry, joined the 11th Airborne Division in Augsburg, Germany, and moved into Gablingen

Kaserne. For almost a year, the battle group trained with the division in the rugged and scenic hills of the Hohenfels training area in Germany. On 15 March 1958, at a formal parade at Gablingen Kaserne, Lt. Col. Thomas W. Sharkey took over command from Colonel Reynolds.

In the spring of 1958, U.S. interests in the Middle East were compromised when rebel uprisings, aided and sponsored by pro-Nasser and Soviet agents, threatened pro-Western governments. In May of 1958, troubles sprang up in Jordan, Iraq, Lebanon, and Syria. On the fourteenth of July, President Eisenhower, reacting to the overthrow of King Faisal's government in Iraq, alerted U.S. forces, including the 1st Airborne Battle Group, 187th Infantry, in Germany, for deployment. On 15 July, President Eisenhower sent the ninth Air Force, the tactical strike force, and air transport planes from Donaldson Air Force Base in South Carolina to Europe. The Sixth Fleet moved toward Middle East waters. Included was a naval task force of seventy-four ships, including three carriers and two cruisers, and 45,000 men, including 5,000 marines. The marines landed at and occupied the Beirut airport in Lebanon, a state torn with violence, "to help preserve that country's government in the wake of internal revolts and a coup in neighboring Iraq." The U.S. and the marines' mission: show support for President Camille Chaumon's government of Lebanon.

In Germany, on 1 July 1958, the 11th Airborne Division was deactivated and the 1st ABG, 187th, was assigned to the 24th Infantry Division (Pentomic). In the 24th Division there were now two airborne battle groups, the 1st ABG, 187th Inf. and the 2d ABG, 503d Inf. The 1st ABG, 187th, was now commanded by Col. Thomas W. Sharkey, USMA, 1941.

On 14 July, the 187th returned to Gablingen by airdrop after two weeks of rugged training at Hohenfels. On the fifteenth of July, Colonel Sharkey got orders to move the 1st ABG, 187th from Germany to Adana, Turkey. On the sixteenth, the 187th began a massive air movement from Furstenfeldbruck Airbase, near Munich, Germany, to a staging area in Adana, Turkey, and then to the Beirut International Airport. By the time the lift was over on 19 July, some 1,800 paratroopers and all of their combat equipment, including rifles, machine guns, jeeps, ammo, and artillery had flown to Beirut in some seventy-six C-119s, C-124s, and C-130s. By now there were 7,200 combat troops in Beirut, including three battalions of marines and the 1st ABG, 187th. The Rakkasans set up camp, named Camp Zeitune, in an olive grove near the airport and manned a perimeter defense around the airport. Along with the marines, the Rakkasans made show of force in and around the area.

The summer passed under a wilting Lebanese sun. As the political situation cleared a bit, the U.S. forces trained the Lebanese forces in the use of American arms and ran a combined land-sea-air training exercise on the shore adjacent to the historic ruins of Byblos. The Rakkasans continued to man the roadblocks, patrol the mountains, and jumped occasionally on a drop zone named the "Sahara."

Five members of the USMA Class of 1956 were lieutenants in the 1st Airborne Battle Group, 187th, in Lebanon. Before their careers were over, they had achieved substantial rank: John W. Nicholson and Arvid E. West became brigadier generals; Michael J. Conrad, a major general; Robert D. Hammond, a lieutenant general; and John W. Foss II, a four-star general.

By October, 1958, after three and a half months in Lebanon, the situation eased sufficiently enough to permit the return of the 1st ABG, 187th, to Augsburg, Germany. Later, on 20 November 1958, Colonel Sharkey turned over command of the Battle Group to Col. Donald C. Clayman at a change-of-command ceremony at Gablingen Kaserne. This was Colonel Clayman's second tour with the Rakkasans: in 1951 and 1952, he had served as the 187th deputy commander. Colonel Clayman graduated from Cornell in 1935 and served in World War II as a battalion commander in both the 47th and 60th Infantry Regiments. Among other decorations, he won the DSC, two Silver Stars, and two Bronze Stars.

Shortly after its return to Germany, it was the 1st ABG, 187th's turn to gyroscope. On 9 February 1959, the Battle Group arrived in New York harbor aboard the USNS *Buckner,* staged through the Brooklyn Navy Yard, and entrained for a trip to Fort Bragg, North Carolina. In March of 1959, the 1st ABG, 187th, reassembled at Fort Bragg and joined the 82d Airborne Division as part of the XVIIIth Airborne Strategic Army Corps (STRAC). Units of the 187th now had the distinction of being or having been part of the 11th, 82d, and 101st Airborne Divisions.

Another member of the USMA Class of 1956, Lt. H. Norman Schwarzkopf, had joined the 2d ABG, 187th Infantry, with the 101st at Fort Campbell. "When I reported for duty at the 101st Airborne Division at Fort Campbell, Kentucky, in early 1957," he wrote in his book *It Doesn't Take a Hero,* "I was the typical new West Point graduate—eager to serve my country, hungry for glory, filled with the wish to be a leader of men. . . .

"The army that I entered was suffering from the aftereffects of Korea; officers and noncommissioned officers were in short supply and budgets had been cut so severely that there weren't even enough funds for day-to-day operations. In the age of massive retaliation, the army believed itself in danger of being completely overshadowed by the air force. Despite this pessimistic outlook, my friends and I were not discouraged. . . . Who had ever seized and held territory with an airplane? Our job was to be ready when called upon."

In June of 1958, Maj. Gen. W. C. Westmoreland became the new commanding general of the 101st. He concentrated not only on combat readiness but also on improving the productivity of the post maintenance and administrative services. But during his stay with the 101st he became disillusioned with the "pentomic division." "Under the concept," he wrote in *A Soldier Reports,* "infantry and airborne divisions would have five battle groups of 1,400 men each, each one therefore larger than a battalion but smaller than a regiment, which could be employed in battle singly or in combination. Since the battle group replaced both the battalion and the regiment, one echelon of command was eliminated in the organization, which cut down on staff overhead. . . .

"As I prepared to relinquish command of the 101st Airborne in 1960, I recommended abolishing the pentomic division, primarily because I had found the control of the five separate battle groups by the division headquarters and five companies by a battle-group headquarters was difficult. I recommended reestablishing a regimental-level headquarters, additional artillery, and better communications as necessary to give the division staying power. That was what the army eventually adopted."

On 21 December 1960, Col. Arndt L. Mueller, a World War II combat veteran with the 6th Infantry Division in the Pacific, assumed command of the 2d Airborne Battle Group, 187th Infantry. For the next two years, the battle group trained, trained, and trained. In late 1962, to prove that its training was not in vain, it went on full combat alert as a reactionary strike force during the Cuban missile crisis.

The army was in the throes of initiating another major development in tactics and organization—the "air assault" theory. The various units of the 187th Infantry would play a part.

### Air Assault

In the early sixties, some forward-looking savants in the Pentagon were urging the army to explore new ways to fight wars whose battles might not always be fought with massive fleets of tanks, scores of artillery battalions, and hundreds of bombers and fighters. In the future, they reasoned, all wars might not be unlimited. Even President Kennedy, whose massive retaliation strategy was his answer to the immense and continued military buildup of the USSR, encouraged the army to search for a "new look."

In January 1960, the army chief of staff established the Army Aircraft Requirements Review Board, chaired by Lt. Gen. Gordon B. Rogers, deputy commanding general of the Continental Army Command. The board met at Fort Monroe from 29 February to 6 March. It reviewed the Army Aircraft Development Plan, discussed roles and missions of army aviation, projected army funding, assessed combat surveillance requirements, and examined procurement plans. "With historic hindsight," wrote Lt. Gen. John J. Tolson in *"Airmobility—1961–1971,* "it is apparent that the scope of the 1960 Rogers Board review was limited. It obviously did not constitute a major advance in tactical mobility for the army. But in comparison with the advances made during the 1950s, the board's objectives, if obtained, would have represented a substantial gain in mobility through the use of aviation."

But at least one part of the army was making some progress in imaginative and visionary use of army aviation. In 1960, Lt. Col. Russell P. Bonasso, the aviation officer of the 101st Airborne Division, persuaded the commanding general, General Westmoreland, to centralize control of all aviation assets in the division. As a result, General Westmoreland authorized the formation of the 101st Combat Aviation Battalion—the first such organization in the army.

The army continued to study and forward to DOD its aviation requirements. During January and February 1962, analysts in the secretary of defense's office reviewed the army's submissions. "Their review was extremely critical of the army's so-called caution," wrote General Tolson. On 19 April 1962, the secretary of defense, Robert S. McNamara, sent the army a strong, pointed, and "now famous" message in which he concluded that the army's current program was "dangerously conservative." He prodded the army to open its mind to innovation and break away from the tactics and equipment of the past. He directed the army to investigate enhanced "land warfare mobility" and that the examination be conducted in an "open and free atmosphere."

The result of the secretary's memo was DA's directive to Gen. Herbert B. Powell, commander of the Continental Army Command (CONARC), to establish the Tactical Mobility Requirements Board. He appointed as its president one of the army's most open-minded generals, Lt. Gen. Hamilton H. Howze, the commander of the XVIII Airborne Corps at Fort Bragg. The board's secretary was Col. John Norton, who had been the G3 of the 82d Airborne Division in World War II under Gen. "Slim Jim" Gavin. Both General Howze and Colonel Norton were Army aviators. There were six other officers and six top-level civilians named to the board. The board became known throughout the army as the Howze Board. General Powell, under guidance from the Department of the Army, directed General Howze to look to the future and determine the army's aircraft requirements and tactical organizations for the years 1963 to 1975. A shorter version of General Howze's mission was to determine if "ground vehicles could be replaced by air vehicles and, if so, to what extent?" The army did not know it at the time, but these would be the years of the buildup, combat, and withdrawal from Vietnam, the place where the army's air mobility and air support would be put to the ultimate test.

The Howze Board reached out to the army, air force, and industry for new ideas, equipment, organizations, and tactics. The board developed many recommendations that used army helicopters and fixed-wing aircraft in close support roles, as battlefield transportation, and as tank-killers. The board conducted a series of forty tests in basic flying techniques, small-unit deployment, and air support with helicopters. The board's recommendations were so extensive that the army decided to test them radically, unrelated to current organizations and tactics. DA organized an entirely new division to be the test bed. On 1 February 1963, the 11th Air Assault Division (Test) was activated at Fort Benning,

Georgia, under the command of Maj. Gen. Harry W. O. Kinnard, the veteran G3 of the 101st Airborne Division, made famous by its stand at Bastogne in the Battle of the Bulge at Christmastime, 1944. In theory, the 11th was to be a "light" division capable of air movement by air force and/or army aircraft. The planners scrubbed previous Tables of Organization and Equipment, made many innovative changes, and came up with plans for a "lean" division.

In December 1960, based on recommendations from General Westmoreland and other dissatisfied "pentomic" division commanders, Department of the Army directed Continental Army Command (CONARC) to reevaluate the pentomic concept. In April 1961, the Secretary of the Army approved the CONARC study, ROAD (Reorganization of Army Divisions), basically returning the Army divisions to the triangular concept, with three brigades or battle groups per division. In February 1962, the ROAD reorganization began. By June of 1964, all fifteen regular divisions had been reconfigured according to the ROAD plan.

On 1 February 1963, the 3d Airborne Battle Group, 187th, was resurrected from the army's dusty record books and, on 7 February, was activated as the 3d Battalion, 187th Infantry of the 11th Air Assault Division at Fort Benning, Georgia, as a relatively standard, nonpentomic infantry battalion. In the 11th, the 3/187th was joined by 3d Squadron, 17th Cavalry (minus B Troop), and the 10th Transportation Brigade, composed of several battalions of both fixed- and rotary-wing aircraft. At the initial manning, the 11th had only 3,023 men but was at full strength by 1964. In July 1963, the 1st Airborne Brigade of the 11th was fleshed out with the activation of the 1st Battalion of the 188th Airborne Infantry and the 1st Battalion of the 511th Airborne Infantry. With these additions, the 187th, 188th and 511th, the original glider and parachute regiments of the original 11th Airborne Division, formed in February of 1943, were once again on the rolls of the 11th—this time an "air assault division." In addition to the standard infantry, artillery, and support units, the division included an aviation group with enough aircraft to lift one-third of the division simultaneously.

In July of 1963, Lt. Gen. W. C. Westmoreland, former commander of the 187th Airborne Infantry Regimental Combat Team in Korea and Japan and of the 101st Airborne Division, assumed command of XVIII Airborne Corps.

For over two years, time and time again, General Kinnard and the 11th Air Assault Division developed, tested, refined, and retested the division's equipment, organization, and tactics. Test sites were in the low country and swamps of Florida, and the hills of Georgia and North Carolina. The 187th and other battalions of the 11th tested the helicopter in numerous combat roles, command and control, attack formations, scouting and screening, reconnaissance, aerial resupply, and air-assault tactics. During the trials, the air force and the army argued about whose role was "close support" on the battlefield and whose mission was tactical air mobility.

The 3d Battalion of the 187th stayed with the 11th as an air-mobility test-bed unit for a year. On the third of February 1964, it was relieved of assignment to the 11th AA Division and reassigned as an organic unit of the 3d Brigade of the 101st at Fort Campbell, where its airmobility expertise was put to good use training the rest of the division. From 1964 until 1971, the other two infantry battalions of the 3d Brigade, 101st, were the 1st and 2d Battalions of the 506th Infantry.

Following activation in 1964, the 3d Brigade took part in Exercise Desert Strike in the Mojave Desert. In 1965 exercise, the 3d Brigade participated in the 101's CPX Gold Fire and Eagle Jump. In May of 1966, the 3d Brigade took part in the division's exercise Eagle Prey I "designed to teach the troopers the methods of combating guerrilla warfare." During September of 1966, the 3d Battalion of the 187th flew to Norway, where it participated in NATO Operation Bar Frost.

On 1 February 1964, the 2d Airborne Battle Group, 187th Infantry, 101st Airborne Division, was deactivated. On 6 March 1964, the 1st Airborne Battle Group, 187th Infantry, that had served in Germany, Beirut, and Fort Bragg, was designated the 1st Battalion, 187th Infantry, relieved of assignment to the 82d at Bragg, and transferred to the 11th AA Division at Fort Benning for training and testing.

On the seventeenth of March 1964, the Second Brigade from the 2d Infantry Division at Fort Benning was added to the roster of the 11th Air Assault Division for additional air mobility tests. Additional changes in the division began with the additional units. In one major organizational change, three battalions of thirty-six helicopters each were added. The helicopters were armed with 3.5 inch rockets and constituted the division's aerial rocket artillery. Colonel (later Brigadier) General B. K.

Gorwitz, once with the 187th's 674th Airborne FA Battalion in Korea, was the 11th's division artillery commander. He wrote about the army's wisdom in keeping conventional artillery.

"We had three battalions of 105mm howitzers that had the capability to fire around the clock, in all weather, on station at all times, and a reload capability unattainable by helicopters. The air force did see the armed helicopters as an attempt to take over their close-in air support role."

Once more, the Pentagon brass decided that the 11th's colors should be cased. In June 1965, the colors of the 1st Cavalry Division in Korea were put on a plane and flown to Fort Benning. In a simple ceremony, the colors were presented to the 11th Air Assault Division (Test). On 30 June 1965, the 11th Air Assault Division (Test) and the 1st Battalions of the 187th, 188th, and 511th were inactivated. The next day, the 1st Cavalry Division (Air Mobile) was officially activated pursuant to GO 185, Headquarters 3d Army. The men for the new division came from the 11th AA Division and the 2d Infantry Division at Fort Benning. It was a formidable force, with 15,847 officers and men, six Mojawk fixed-wing aircraft, 287 Huey helicopters, and 48 CH-37 Mojaves.

In a recent letter to me in which he discussed his tour as commander of the 11th Air Assault Division, Lt. Gen. H. W. O. Kinnard wrote, "I focused from the outset, and until the very end, on recreating in the 11th Air Assault Division (and then in the 1st Cavalry Division) the spirit and esprit of the paratrooper. From the moment I received my marching orders from on high, I felt that an 'Airborne state of mind' was a sine qua non for realizing the maximum potential of the helicopter force. . . . At the end of our testing period—in my final report—I strongly recommended that all the combat arms of the division should be jump-qualified. This recommendation stood up pretty well as the report was staffed—on up through CONARC—but was regarded as a bit nutty by H. K. Johnson, then chief of staff. He did, however, discuss my recommendation with Buzz Wheeler (the chief of staff who had given me my marching orders, and who at the time was the chairman of the Joint Staff). Wheeler rather liked my idea and the result was a strange compromise in which one of our three brigades was designated as airborne. This was the structure which we transposed into the 1st Cav. Our 1st Brigade, under Elvy Roberts, was authorized to be parachute-qualified with a complement of other units in the division (one FA Bn and so on).

"My bias was evident, as well, in the key officers and NCOs which we assembled at Fort Benning. I won't go into the arguments here; in you I'd be preaching to the choir. Suffice it to say that nothing in our Testing Phase, or later in our combat experiences, changed my original thought that assault by air requires a special breed of cat, whether the mode is parachute, glider, or helicopter."

During the early and middle sixties, the army lived—sometimes struggled—through major changes in its tactics, organization, equipment—its very psyche. The 187th Infantry also felt the reverberations—at times quakelike. The battalions of the regiment became battle groups, then back to battalions, then to activations, then to transfers across the Atlantic and back, and then to inactivations. By 1965, the sole identity of the 187th Airborne Infantry Regiment rested with the 3d Battalion, 187th Infantry, one of three relatively standard infantry battalions (no longer forced into the aborted "pentomic concept") in the 3d Brigade of the 101st Airborne Division at Fort Campbell. Shortly, it would prove its fighting mettle once again—this time in Vietnam.

20 October 1950: Rakkasans first combat jump in Korea. 1st and 3d Battalions drop on railway junction at Sukchon while 2d Battalion parachutes onto Sunchon.

In Lipa, Luzon, the "Angels," just out of combat, stand tall in a full division review in honor of General Joseph W. "Vinegar Joe" Stilwell on 9 June 1945.

Martha Tilton, Larry Adler, Lanny Ross and World War II USO entertainers, ride with the Angels, on a training jump in New Guinea, 1 August 1944.

Mass training jump of Rakkasans near Taegu, South Korea, 15 March 1951.

Good Friday, 23 March 1951, Teagu Air Base. Rakkasans load for second combat jump in Korea at Munsan-ni.

Mass drop of Rakkasans beginning the Munsan-ni operation.

Rakkasans parachute into combat at Munsan-ni on 23 March, 1951.

Flying Boxcars (C-119s), dropping Rakkasan paratroopers on Munsan-ni on 23 March 1951.

Rakkasans' biggest parachutable artillery piece, 105-mm howitzer dropping on Munsan-ni on 23 March 1951.

Typical terrain found around Dong Ap Bia Mountain in the spring of 1969.

The battle scarred terrain of Dong Ap Bia Mountain, soon after the ferocious combat.

Army soldiers carry their wounded after the battle that became known as Hamburger Hill.

Assault helicopters backing up ground forces during covering force operation in northeast Saudi Arabia, November 1990.

The high-tech Apache AH-64 awaits action in northwest Saudi Arabia.

Brigadier General Hugh Shelton (right), 101st Assistant Division Commander, and Lt. Col. Dick "Commander" Cody, CO of 1/101st Aviation Brigade, who led eight Apache helicopters to fire the first shots of the war.

August 1990—The move to combat begins. Troops of 1/502d Infantry assemble with their gear in an aircraft hanger at their home base, Fort Campbell, Ky., waiting for a flight to Saudi Arabia.

In Fort Campbell, an Apache AH-64, right before being loaded into a C-5A for the flight to Saudi Arabia, August 1990.

August 1990, Ft. Campbell. Screaming Eagles of the 101st Airborne Division load up in C5-As for the long flight to Saudi Arabia from Ft. Campbell, August 1990.

Camp Eagle II (Camp Eagle I had been the base camp of the 101st in Vietnam), the 101st's home base at King Fahd International Airport in Saudi Arabia.

Camp Eagle II. Apache AH-64 helicopters lined up before their historic attack into Iraq.

Rakkasans in Desert Shield, November 1990, covering an area in northeast Saudi Arabia before the battle.

Rakkasan in AO (Area of Operations) Normandy, forward edge of 101st's in covering force, December 1990.

Forward Operating Base (FOB) Cobra, 95 miles deep into Iraq. FOB Cobra was the relay point for the Rakkasans' deep penetration to the Euphrates.

Late January 1991—Aircraft shuttling 101st troops across Saudi Arabia in the opening phase of Desert Storm.

Lieutenant Colonel Dick Cody's Apache loaded for the attack: 8 Hellfire missiles, 19 rockets, and an auxillary 230-gallon fuel tank.

Iraqi soldiers captured deep inside Iraq along Highway 8.

Tactical Assembly Area (TAA) Campbell. 101st's assembly area in northern Saudi Arabia prior to the launch into Iraq.

Major General J. H. B. (Binnie) Peay III leading his Desert Storm troops in the New York victory parade.

# THE VIETNAM WAR

# 9: On to Vietnam

The Rakkasans had fought through the jungles of Leyte; the cities, plains, villages, hills, and rice paddies of Luzon; they had twice parachuted into North Korea, fought the Chinese in fluid, raging battles, and, on a third tour to Korea, had fought a massive, sometimes mobile defensive battle from dug-in positions on the hills along the DMZ. Vietnam, however, was an entirely new experience, not only for the Rakkasans but for every U.S. soldier deployed to the area. There were no fixed battle lines, no plan to invade and attack the enemy on his own terrain. The U.S. national mission—the strategy—was complicated and difficult for anyone, let alone the ordinary trooper, to understand; his day-to-day tactical objectives were scattered and along no fixed lines.

The Rakkasans who would fight in Vietnam heard new terms: *counterinsurgency, pacification, search and destroy, firebases, hot landing zones, lerps.* They would have to adapt to the new tactics, to the constant danger of mines, booby traps, ambushes, satchel charges, and to the need to be able to distinguish just which Vietnamese was the enemy. They would have to become experts in helicopter assaults into hostile zones, requiring them, fully combat loaded, to jump out of hovering helicopters under fire, to find the elusive enemy in the thick tropical jungles, the sheer, rocky mountains, the vast swamps, the coastal plains and beaches, and in the cities and villages. It was a war primarily to eliminate the enemy—not to seize and hold terrain. Pacification, so went the theory, would take care of that problem. In some cases, combat was purely defensive—the establishment and maintenance of small outposts in rural areas. In others, it was purely offensive—surround the enemy, blast him with artillery, slash him with gunships' rockets and machine guns, carpet-bomb him with B-52 "arc lights," napalm the forests covering him, and then attack to destroy him with the infantryman's weapons—machine guns, rifles, grenades, mortars, even bayonets. It was a new ball game.

During the period 6 July to 29 July 1965, the 1st Brigade of the 101st Airborne Division, under the command of Brig. Gen. Willard Pearson, deployed from Fort Campbell, Kentucky, to Vietnam and established a base camp in the Cam Ranh Bay area. On 22 August, the brigade moved north by sea and air to sweep clear the An Khe area of Binh Dinh Province, securing the area for the arrival of the 1st Cavalry Division (Air Mobile). The 1st Brigade was the first element of the 101st to arrive in Vietnam.

It was not until eighteen months later that the rest of the division got orders to move to Vietnam. "The culmination of the division's preparations was Operation Eagle Thrust," wrote General Tolson. "This lift was keynoted by the departure on 8 December of the commanding general, Maj. Gen. Olinto M. Barsanti, in an aircraft piloted by Gen. Howell M. Estes Jr., commander of the Military Airlift Command. On 18 December 1967 the last airplane touched down in Vietnam, ending the largest and longest military airlift ever attempted into a combat zone. The move required 369 C-141 Starlifter aircraft missions, and 22 C-133 Cargomaster aircraft missions, ultimately lifting 10,024 troops and over 5,300 tons of the division's essential equipment."

The first paratroopers of the 3d Brigade to arrive were the troopers of the 3d Battalion, 187th Infantry, under the command of Lt. Col. John F. Forrest. Convoys of trucks took the Rakkasans from Bien Hoa Air Base to Phuoc Vinh, about thirty miles west of Saigon, to begin setting up and occupying a base camp. In short order, once established there, the Rakkasan squad and platoon leaders worked in the field with the seasoned NCOs and officers of the veteran 1st Infantry Division on small unit tactics. A new life for the Rakkasans, sometimes hazardous, sometimes boring, had begun.

In mid-March, Company D of the 187th, commanded by Capt. Paul W. Bucha, 25, a "star man" in the USMA Class of 1965, was on a reconnaissance in force mission near Phuoc Vinh in Binh Duong Province, part of the so-called "Iron Triangle." The company had been inserted by helicopter into the suspected enemy stronghold. It was no longer suspect when the enemy reacted with small arms and machine-gun fire. Captain Bucha "aggressively and courageously led his men in the destruction of enemy fortifications and base areas and eliminated scattered resistance impeding the advance of his company," read his citation.

On the eighteenth of March, D Company, preceded by the brigade's "Phantom Force," the long-range reconnaissance patrol (LLRP— "lerp"), was advancing through the heavy jungle growth and came unexpectedly upon an North Vietnamese Army base camp. The NVA were also surprised. Delta Company's lead elements came under fire from heavy automatic weapons, machine guns, rocket-propelled grenades, claymore mines, and small arms fire from an estimated enemy battalion. Bucha moved up to the area where troops had been hardest hit, organized the defense, and called up reinforcements from his company. One element was pinned down by heavy machine-gun fire from a concealed bunker some forty meters to the front of the positions. Bucha crawled alone through the fire and destroyed the bunker with hand grenades but was wounded by shrapnel fire.

The enemy continued to attack—now out of their bunkers. Bucha pulled the company back into a perimeter some thirty meters in diameter and established the defense. All night, he moved through the perimeter, distributing ammunition, checking the defenses, and, with smoke grenades, directing artillery and gunship fire to within hand-grenade range of the perimeter. Using flashlights in view of enemy snipers, he directed the medical evacuation of three helicopter-loads of his seriously wounded troops and the helicopter resupply of his company.

At daybreak, he led a rescue party to recover the dead and wounded who had been ambushed in the first encounter. Shortly thereafter, B Company joined D Company in an assault on the NVA base camp and, in two days, destroyed it. One hundred fifty-six NVA dead littered the area. "For his extraordinary heroism, inspirational example, outstanding leadership, and professional competence" during the intense combat, Captain Bucha was awarded the Medal of Honor. Unfortunately, Medic Sp5 Dennis Moore and 2d Lt. Jim L. Sherrill were two of the Rakkasans killed in the action.

In March of 1968, Maj. Stanley Shaneyfelt assumed command of the 3d of the 187th. For the next few months, the battalion, from its base camp near Dak To, made a number of small-unit helicopter-combat assaults near Dak Pek, to help secure a small Special Forces outpost. Until June 1968, contact with the NVA was minimal. A Company did, however, discover three bulldozers along a two-lane highway cut through the jungle and destroyed them with thermite grenades. Shaneyfelt targeted the road for B-52 strikes, to deny its use as a supply line from Cambodia.

The 3d of the 187th's mission now was to relieve all units of the 199th Light Infantry Brigade and assume the defense of the Phuoc Vinh compound. The Rakkasans settled in to maintain equipment and make local daylight sweeps and night ambushes.

On 13 June, Major Shaneyfelt deployed his battalion by C-130s to the 25th Division base camp at Cu Chi, where he would come under the opcon of the 25th Division. His mission: Conduct reconnaissance-in-force operations along the Song Vam and Dong Co Rivers to interdict lines of communications and supply from Cambodia and Laos into the Saigon area.

On 27 June 1968, the Rakkasans received a formal military order that would rankle their paratrooper hearts: the army chief of staff had redesignated the 101st as the 101st Air-Cavalry Division. The name change brought such protests from the veterans of the division that on 26 August the division became the 101st Airborne Division (Air Mobile).

At the beginning of August, the Rakkasans had three missions: defense of the Phouc Vinh base camp, training and maintenance, and reconstruction of the base camp perimeter. A and D Companies and the battalion headquarters were at Phouc Vinh, C Company was at the Song Bo bridge, and B Company was opcon to the 2/506th at Cu Chi. The battalion sent out a number of patrols but combat activity was very limited during the month.

At the beginning of September, the 3d of the 187th was based at Trung Lap. Lieutenant Colonel George M. Sheets was now the battalion commander. Sheets received an order to launch a helicopter assault to seal the large village of An Phua, south of Trang Bang, supposedly a base for the Viet Cong. At 0330 on the first of September, a large force of the 3d of the 187th, C and D Companies of the 506th, VN National Police, Regional and Popular Forces launched into the area. They found many bunkers and it was obvious that the VC were in the village; twenty civilians were evacuated immediately for questioning.

For the next four days, B and C Companies built Firebase Shafter near the Saigon River, east of the Trung Lap ARVN (South Vietnamese Army) Training Center. D Company and the recon platoon reconnoitered in force and set up night ambushes near Firebase Shafter. A Company came under the opcon of the 2d of the 506th that was cordoning a hamlet thought to hold a reinforced NVA Battalion. In the early-morning hours of the sixth, the Battalion Tactical Operations Center monitored a transmission reporting that a heavy NVA force had broken into the A Company's position. At first light, Sheets sent C Company by air to assist A Company.

The next day, 7 September, Sheets sent B and C Companies by Eagle flights to assist. Several insertions met with no contact until a platoon from C Company came under heavy fire near the village of Son Ho. Sheets sent additional troops from B and C Companies to help out. Sheets and Colonel J. B. Conmy, the 3d Brigade commander, moved their command groups to the battle site in order to control the action more closely. They used eighteen tactical air strikes and over 9,500 rounds of artillery to force the NVA to withdraw. The battle lasted for two and a half days. A sweep of the battle area found 141 enemy dead and 5 POWs along with many weapons and mortars. The troops nearest the battle estimated that the NVA had also carried out over 100 bodies. In the fight, A company lost 34 men KIA and 45 WIA. The 3d of the 187th was awarded a Presidential Unit Citation for its valor in the battle of Trang Bang.

On 14 September, the 3d of the 187th moved to an area six kilometers south of the Ho Bo Woods and spent two days building Firebase Pope. Per standard operating procedure, C and D Companies set up ambush sites around the base. At 2140 on the sixteenth, one of C Company's ambushes was hit by an NVA platoon. A few minutes later, D Company's 1st Platoon twenty-four-man ambush found an NVA group moving into their "kill zone." When the platoon counted over 300 enemy armed with 50-caliber machine guns, 82mm mortars, and RPGs (rocket-propelled grenades), Lieutenant Ballard, the platoon leader, decided not to trigger the ambush, and instead called in artillery that he adjusted to within twenty-five meters of his ambush site. He also notified the battalion command post at Firebase Pope of his situation. Ballard and his men held on.

On 20 September, Sheets closed Firebase Pope, moved the battalion to an area southwest of Trung Lap, and for the next five days set up Firebase Patton II. On the twenty-fifth, A and C Companies launched Eagle flights throughout the area, with limited results. In its night position on the twenty-fifth, A Company lost two men KIA and six WIA to incoming mortars. On the twenty-seventh, the command group and B Company moved to Bau Trai to work with the 25th Infantry Division. October opened with only minor fights. The Rakkasans helped keep open Highway 7A from Bao Dieu village to Trung Lap. "Almost every evening at 1730 hours during the commander's briefing," wrote one Rakkasan, "the firebase was mortared by the VC. . . . Casualties were minor, none requiring evacuation."

Since its arrival in Vietnam, the 3d of the 187th had moved independently throughout III Tactical Corps Zone so often that it became known as the "Nomad" Battalion of the 101st. In early October, Maj. Gen. Melvin Zais, the commander of the 101st, ordered Sheets to move his battalion back under his control. On 8 October Sheets closed out Firebase Patton, and, by 1500 that afternoon, C Battery of the 319th FA Battalion, then in support of the Rakkasans, had moved by Chinook helicopters to Phouc Vinh. While the infantry was waiting for trucks to move them to the airstrip at Cu Chi, the VC dropped twenty-five 82mm mortar rounds inside the perimeter, wounding some nineteen men. The convoy left Patton at 1830. At Bao Dieu, the VC hit one truck with an RPG round, killing six and wounding twelve Rakkasans. The convoy closed at Cu Chi at 2300. For the next ten days, the battalion marshaled and outloaded from Phouc Vinh to the Hue–Phu Bai airstrip.

On 11 October, the 3d of the 187th began its four hundred-mile move to northern South Vietnam to rejoin the 101st with the flight of advanced parties to the Hue–Phu Bai strip. By 18 October, all elements of the battalion had closed in. General Zais was on hand to welcome the Rakkasans. Sheets reported that his battalion was ready for combat. For the next two days, the battalion concentrated on settling into the new base and getting ready for more combat. On the morning of the twentieth, the battalion started into a new area of operations. For three days, the officers and NCOs got familiar with the new terrain and conducted some small-unit moves.

For the next week, the battalion moved about its area, found and destroyed an NVA base camp with some 104 bunkers and eight huts, and picked up a small number of mortars, machine guns, and rifles. On 29 October, Sheets received orders to move north to Camp Eagle, south of the Imperial City of Hue, the major base of the 101st Airborne Division, and operate in a new AO (area of operations). At 1630 on the first of November, the battalion left Camp Eagle, closed in to Camp

Evans, and took over the control of three firebases in their AO. The battalion had four missions: secure Camp Evans, keep surveillance on the enemy rocket belt and Song Bo River, recon in force to keep the enemy out of the base area, and reconstruct three firebases—Miguel, Long, and Helen.

During the early weeks of December, contact with the VC and/or the NVA was light. On Christmas Day, 1968, the Rakkasans observed the twenty-four-hour truce. The firebases were about 90 percent complete. But on the twenty-ninth, a platoon from A Company fought a VC force along the Song Bo River. On 31 December, C Company made contact and was hit by heavy fire. The company commander called in an air strike and artillery and forced the enemy to withdraw. Unfortunately, 1st Lt. Douglas A. Dugger and Pfc. Robert M. Sullivan were KIA.

During 1968, the 3d of the 187th had fought small and large battles in all four tactical zones, sent 48 troopers home in body bags, and suffered 149 WIA. The battalion's men were awarded, among other decorations, 65 Silver Stars and 201 Purple Hearts. For the Rakkasans in Vietnam, there was far more yet to come.

### Vitenam—1969

On New Year's Day, 1969, the 3d of the 187th found itself supporting the 101st Operation Nevada Eagle, securing and constructing firebases and reconnoitering in force (RIF) in the mountains southwest of Camp Evans, home base of the 3d Brigade, fourteen miles northeast of Hue. A Company operated out of Firebase Long with one platoon at Firebase Helen; B and C Companies RIFed around the Song Bo River and along the so-called "Rocket Ridge;" D Company worked on Firebase Rakkasan. Occasional contacts with the enemy were with small, elusive groups. As 1969 wore on, however, the Rakkasans would become involved in violent, bloody, hand-to-hand combat on a series of craggy, jungle-covered, isolated mountains.

In the next few months, the battalion would fight two almost entirely different enemy forces in two different environments. Large NVA units were deployed in the relatively unpopulated mountain areas bordering the A Shau Valley. Smaller Viet Cong local units and infrastructure operated in the populated lowlands northwest of Hue. The terrain was as varied as the enemy. From the northern border on the Song O Lau River to the main road, QL-l, the terrain is flat with fine-grain sand, fertile soil, trees and other vegetation along the finger lakes and along the east and west river boundaries. To the southwest, the rolling hills merge with the jungle-covered hills known as "Rocket Ridge." Beyond Rocket Ridge are the Annamese Mountains, with rugged cliffs and triple jungle canopy. Across the mountains to the southwest, the hills drop into the flat, single-canopied A Shau Valley. Beyond the valley, the mountains rise again toward the Laotian border.

On 10 January, the 3d of the 187th changed commanders: "Barracuda," Lt. Col. George M. Sheets, passed the battalion's colors to "Black Jack," Lt. Col. Weldon F. "Tiger" Honeycutt, 37. He was well known to General Westmoreland, who wrote of him in *A Soldier Reports,* "I had sent [him] as a corporal to Officer Candidate School and [he] had later served as my aide. Honeycutt was a competent, experienced commander."

Samuel Zaffiri, in *Hamburger Hill,* had other words for Lt. Col. Honeycutt. He wrote, "A profane, outspoken, fiercely competitive man, Honeycutt was the prototype of the hard-nosed commander. . . .

"In five short years he moved from private to captain and with the start of the Korean War was commanding a company with the 187th Regimental Combat Team, then under the command of Gen. William Westmoreland. When two other companies in the 187th had failed to take a key hill from the Chinese during fighting along the DMZ, Honeycutt had led a third assault, overrun the hill, and driven off the Chinese. Westmoreland was so impressed with his young captain's aggressiveness that he had nicknamed him 'Tiger.' The name had stuck, and thereafter most of Honeycutt's army superiors had called him simply Tiger Honeycutt. . . .

"Always a controversial figure, the colonel was considered by some fellow officers as one of the best young commanders in the army and by others as nothing more than a hothead and egomaniac. In a way, Honeycutt seemed to thrive on controversy and revel in the strong feelings others had about him." Whatever his personality, in the next few months he was to prove himself in one of the war's more controversial battles.

On the twenty-fourth of January, the 3d Brigade, commanded by Col. Joseph B. Conmy Jr., USMA January 1943, a gallant, inspiring officer who was awarded Purple Hearts in World War II, Korea, and in Vietnam, began Operation Ohio Rapids, a campaign to block NVA units' access to the populated lowlands, particularly the Imperial City of Hue during Tet '69. Captain Luther L. Sanders airlifted his D Company, 3d of the 187th, into Firebase Mexico; Capt. Barry Robinson III flew his B Company into Firebase Barbara. Honeycutt's battalion set up blocks to prevent the NVA regiments from infiltrating from the A Shau Valley into the lowlands of the Phong Dien and Hai Long Districts. For the next few days, the Rakkasans in the firebases took some incoming rockets, artillery, sniper fire, and hand grenades but, fortunately, suffered few casualties.

For the next three weeks, the battalion manned its firebases and patrolled its AO. On the fifteenth of February, one of Capt. Gerald R. Harkins's A Company platoons made contact with four NVA three thousand meters outside Firebase Mexico. The platoon killed three of them, wounded and medevaced one NVA, and found a number of AK-47s, machine guns, and assorted uniforms and medical gear. A Company searched the area and turned up more equipment abandoned by the fleeing NVA.

On the nineteenth of February, Honeycutt and his battalion came under the opcon of the 1st Brigade in Operation Spokane Rapids. Robinson took his B Company through a one-day stand-down at Camp Evans. Next day, the company airlifted into Firebase Brick. On the twenty-fourth, after a five-day stand-down, the rest of the battalion combat-assaulted into LZ Diana to reconnoiter the area in force. Between 24 February and 2 March, contact was sporadic and scattered.

At the beginning of March, the battalion returned to Camp Evans and back under the opcon of Col. Joe Conmy. General Zais launched the 101st into Operation Kentucky Jumper on 1 March. In support of this operation, Capt. Walter Griswold, his C Company, and other elements of the 3d of the 187th were airlifted into Firebases T-Bone and Long. A and B Companies combat-assaulted into LZs nine klicks south of Firebase Helen in the vicinity of the Song Bo River. D Company moved to Firebase Rakkasan. For the next two weeks, the Rakkasans patrolled outside their firebases, killed several NVA, and uncovered numerous caches of weapons. As the 101st moved to the west, it was getting closer and closer to the A Shau Valley.

"A Shau Valley . . . points like a spear at a throat toward the cities of Hue and Danang," wrote General Westmoreland in *A Soldier Reports.*

"The enemy long controlled the valley after March 1966, when two North Vietnamese regiments attacked a lone CIDG [Civilian Irregular Defense Group]–Special Forces camp there. Although normal practice when the enemy hit an outpost was to reinforce or counterattack, I simply lacked the forces in early 1966 to hold the valley against determined attack, so I withdrew the troops and abandoned the camp. With sufficient forces available in the spring of 1968, I directed a sweep back through the valley to end the threat it posed to Hue and Danang, and my successor, Gen. Creighton C. Abrams, continued to conduct sweeps to deny enemy passage through the valley."

For the rest of March and the first three weeks of April, the companies of 3/187th continued their patrols, ambushes, and searches of the area, made contact with small teams of the NVA, and found weapons and increasingly larger ammo caches as they pushed closer and closer to the A Shau Valley. But in just a few days, the Rakkasans would find huge caches of NVA weapons, food, and ammunition and would be engaged in a fight that would severely test their skills and determination.

During the early morning hours of the twenty-second of April, a FAC plane on a normal recon mission over the northern A Shau spotted some bamboo huts on a ridgeline about two thousand meters below the peak of Dong Ngai in the northwestern corner of the A Shau Valley. The 101st's intelligence team was already aware that the area, called the "warehouse," contained an abundance of NVA supplies. On the morning of the twenty-second, fighter bombers blasted the area with 250- and 500-pound bombs. On the twenty-third, B-52s carpeted the area with hundreds of 1000-pound bombs, creating huge secondary explosions. After the air strikes, a platoon of the 2/17 Cav Air assaulted into a hot DZ in a single CH-47 Chinook. As it hovered over the LZ, the troops slid down rope ladders through a hole in the canopy. Ground fire hit the helicopter, and it crashed through the tops of hundred-foot trees, killing seven men. The troops who escaped formed a perimeter and fought off a platoon-sized NVA unit but lost another five men. The platoon leader called for reinforcements. As two platoons started to land, the helicopters were hit by ground fire and lost two more choppers. The men expanded the perimeter but came under increasingly heavier enemy attacks.

Back at Camp Eagle, Honeycutt met with General Zais, who ordered him to relieve the 2/17 Cav on Dong Ngai and then clean out the bunkers and supply dumps on the mountain. When Honeycutt heard that 2/17 Cav had suffered another forty casualties, he decided the best course of action was to land his troops on the top of the mountain and attack down toward the 2/17th's perimeter, putting the NVA in a vise, rather than landing in the 2/17 Cav's "hot" LZ. Honeycutt ordered Capt. Barry Robinson to lead the assault, followed by Capt. Sanders's D Company. He told them that the air force had already carved out an LZ on the top of the mountain. On the morning of the twenty-fifth, B Company moved to Firebase Blaze and got ready to combat air assault onto Dong Ngai. Robinson met with his four platoon leaders, Lts. Frank Boccia, Marshall Eward, James Dickey, and Charles Denholm, and briefed them on the tight situation in which the 2/17 Cav found itself. He was blunt about its casualties and its beleaguered situation.

At 1530, Boccia loaded his men aboard six lift-ships for the short, fifteen-minute flight to the LZ. "At 1600, Bravo Company arrived over the upper LZ," wrote Fred Waterhouse. "The Rakkasans could see enemy bunkers and spider holes below. Lieutenant Frank Boccia rode in the lead ship along with Sp4s Dennis Helms, Tim Logan, Nate Hyde, Doug Walton, and Terry St. Onge. Pfc. Jon Fleagane, door gunner, spotted muzzle flashes coming from the right of the LZ. The copilot, Capt. David W. Watson, screamed into his intercom, 'Get that machine gun working.' Fleagane was already raking the trees below. At sixty meters and closing, the enemy found the range and the ship was hit by a torrent of fire. With bullets still hitting the ship, the pilot, Major Daugherty, eased into a hover about ten feet above the ground. In quick succession, Logan, St. Onge, Helms, Hyde and Walton leaped from the ship and scrambled into the surrounding jungle. Lieutenant Boccia's gas mask had hung up on an eye bolt. With the ship still taking fire, Boccia pulled madly on his mask. The ship lurched, and Boccia fell out and tumbled about fifteen feet down a steep ridge.

"Above, Daugherty started the ship up again and Fleagane stayed on the gun. An RPG hit the ship just under the pilot's seat. The explosion blew off Captain Watson's left arm, splattering the cockpit with blood. The ship dropped like a rock, its blades slashing wildly through the trees before snapping off and careening through the jungle like huge knives. The ship hit the ground with such force that its skids buckled and the transmission broke through the back wall and shattered Fleagane's left arm.

"The door gunner, stunned, sat there on the floor of the ship for a long moment and then saw something that would haunt him for the rest of his life. Though bleeding profusely, Captain Watson pulled a machete out from under his seat and charged up the ridge toward the enemy position. He had not covered fifteen feet and was only a foot or two from Rakkasan Terry St. Onge, who was standing behind a tree, when an RPG struck the captain in the chest. The explosion blew him and St. Onge into pieces all over the area."

In the downed helicopter, Fleagane pulled Major Daugherty out of his seat, but a sniper hit Daugherty in the knee. Fleagane and Daugherty scrambled onto the ground and tried to hide behind a log, but the same sniper hit Daugherty in the back.

Boccia had moved his men to the LZ and formed a perimeter, managed to medevac Daugherty and Fleagane, and called for gunships to strafe the area. The NVA were not suppressed. Seven more helicopters brought in the rest of B Company, but, in the action, four crashed after being hit by enemy fire. Honeycutt was hovering in his command ship above the mountain. When he saw the crashes, he called off further landings on the upper DZ. During the night, the enemy hit Boccia's perimeter but were driven off with machine-gun fire.

At first light the next morning, the rest of B Company and two platoons from A Company combat-assaulted into the lower LZ, the area held by the 2/17 Cav. After the Rakkasans secured the perimeter and helped get out the 2/17 Cav dead and wounded, the two companies sent squad-sized RIFs [reconnaissance in force] up the mountain toward Boccia's perimeter. Honeycutt brought in fighter-bombers and gunships to pound the area around Boccia's position and then sent Sanders and his Company to reinforce Boccia. Five of Sanders's ships got in, but the last two were shot down, cluttering and blocking the LZ with a total of six downed choppers.

The next day, Honeycutt sent Captain Harkins, CO of A Company, to the upper LZ to take charge. Harkins organized the various units into platoons, expanded the perimeter, and ordered Boccia and his own 3d Platoon leader, Lt. Daniel Bresnahan, to attack straight down the mountain.

In the lower LZ, Honeycutt ordered three platoons from B, A, and D Companies to attack up the mountain after first plastering the area with a "massive air-strike," creating a number of secondary blasts. Going up the mountain, two hundred meters from the lower LZ, D Company's platoon found more than 10,000 Chicom rifle grenades and 20,000 rounds of small-arms ammo. Lieutenant Denholm and his platoon from B Company found an equally large cache nearby but were halted shortly thereafter by an NVA reinforced platoon in some fifteen bunkers. Air strikes had little effect, but after a long artillery preparation, Denholm's platoon assaulted the bunker line with 90mm recoilless rifles and overran the bunkers in less than an hour. Attacking up the east side of the mountain, Lt. George Bennitt's platoon from A Company overran ten bunkers and another large ammo dump. The three platoons attacking up the mountain stopped at dark about two hundred meters from the upper LZ. At dawn the next morning, the twenty-eighth, after an hour of heavy air strikes and pummeling artillery, the Rakkasans started up the mountain, and a platoon from the upper LZ started down. The vise caught forty NVA soldiers in the middle. Late in the afternoon, the Rakkasans joined up, clearing the area around the upper LZ for some two to three hundred meters.

Honeycutt brought in an Engineer detachment to build a firebase on top of Dong Ngai. The Engineers worked around the clock for twenty-four hours, and by the afternoon of the twenty-ninth, three howitzer batteries were in the incomplete firebase. The Rakkasans continued to sniff out the enemy. D Company routed an enemy platoon on the afternoon of the thirtieth and found a supply dump of twenty tons of rice and hundreds of 122mm rockets and RPG rounds. For the next four days, D Company fought "small groups of NVA snipers and trail watchers," wrote Zaffiri. "On the morning of May 4, however, while the company was riffing northeast toward the peak of Dong Ngai, they ran head-on into an NVA bunker complex defended by a company of infantry with heavy weapons.

"Sanders's men managed to take out a number of the bunkers with recoilless-rifle fire, but had three ground assaults thrown back. After the third assault failed, Sanders called in mortars, gunships, and, finally, air strikes on the bunkers. The mortars and gunships had little effect on the deep bunkers, but the air strikes did the job. Using pinpoint bombing, the fighter planes hit the bunker complex with nearly thirty napalm bombs and turned it into a huge bonfire.

"As soon as the air strikes ended, Delta's men charged up the mountain and swept into the NVA positions. They were not met by rifle fire, but by the nauseous smell of burning flesh. In the bunkers and trenches, they discovered the bodies of fifteen enemy soldiers, many of them still burning. Delta moved through the position quickly in pursuit of the rest of the NVA company, but most of the enemy escaped, carrying with them many of their dead tied to bamboo poles."

Despite the intensity of the 3/187th's fight for Dong Ngai, its losses were less than might have been expected: five KIA and fifty-four WIA. But the NVA losses were far heavier: more than one hundred soldiers killed, tons of supplies lost, and one of its major bases in the A Shau Valley destroyed. The victory of 3/187th at Dong Ngai won for it the Valorous Unit Citation.

But Colonel Honeycutt and his battalion had not seen the last of the A Shau Valley on 8 May when the 3/187th was airlifted out of Firebase Airborne for a flight to Camp Evans, its home base, to prepare for Operation Apache Snow, slated to begin two days later. The Battalion would be back—to fight a battle, the results of which would echo through the halls of Congress. General Westmoreland wrote that "among the more intemperate critics was Senator Edward M. Kennedy, who on the floor of the Senate called the action 'senseless and irresponsible' and implied that American commanders had ordered the assaults and 'sacrificed' American lives only to assuage 'military pride.' That kind of criticism ignored reality and the purpose of the operations in the A Shau Valley."

For 3/187th, the ferocious battle of Ap Bia Mountain, redubbed "Hamburger Hill" by the media, who likened it to a "meat grinder," was its next bloody challenge.

# 10: The Battle for Dong Ap Bia

**Hamburger Hill**

During the widely reported and often misanalyzed Tet Offensive of 1968, the NVA had staged, through the A Shau Valley, an entire NVA division and other VC forces for its massive attacks on Hue and Danang. In the battle for Hue alone, the NVA lost over five thousand men. By early 1969, it was becoming apparent to the MACV [Military Assistance Command Vietnam] and XXIV Corps staffs that the A Shau Valley was once again an area of high NVA activity, logistically and strategically, and an important terminus for the Ho Chi Minh Trail. The 3/187th's battle for Dong Ngai and the discovery of mammoth supply depots in the area served to accentuate that point.

XXIV Corps, the U.S. command operating in the northern corps area of South Vietnam (I Corps), was commanded by the brilliant and indefatigable Lt. Gen. Richard G. Stilwell, 52, USMA '38, a man who prided himself on working twenty-hour days with about three hours reserved for sleep—usually from 0200 to 0500—when he wasn't busy. He planned to clear out the A Shau Valley using ten battalions of infantry, including the 9th Marine Regiment, the 3d ARVN Regiment, the 3/5th Cavalry, and three air assault battalions: 1/506th, 2/501st, and 3/187th. The overall plan of attack called for the marines and the 3/5th Cav to combat-assault into the valley and RIF [reconnaissance in force] toward the Laotian border while the ARVN units cut the highway through the base of the valley. The 501st and the 506th mission was to destroy the enemy in their AOs and block escape routes into Laos.

The 3/187th drew what turned out to be the toughest part of the operation: Clear and occupy Dong Ap Bia, a mountain that rose to 970 meters at its highest point with ridgelines at 800, 900, 916, and 937 meters high. In the rather cryptic words of one army historian: "3/187th Inf would combat-assault into LZ 2, 2,000 meters northwest of Dong Ap Bia and 1,500 meters west of the Laotian border. The order of movement would be D, A, C; B Company would act as the brigade reserve until released and then combat-assault into LZ 2. D Company would secure the LZ until replaced by A Company and then RIF to the high ground 500 meters to the northwest. C Company would secure the LZ until the

Headquarters element reached the LZ and then move 500 meters to the southwest. The Headquarters group would move to link up with C Company, riffing toward Dong Ap Bia. When B Company was released from standby status it would be combat-assaulted into LZ 2 and then proceed to the southwest to a ridgeline running from Hill 937.

The terrain in the area favored the defenders. The mountains they were to defend and their ridges were along the Trung Pham River on the Laotian border. The area was covered with a tropical, double- and triple-canopied jungle. The land beneath the trees was a tangled mass of saw-toothed elephant grass, thick stands of bamboo, and other tough vines that inhibited foot movement, even without an enemy presence. The hills gave way to ridgelines, cut with deep ravines, saddles, draws, and smaller hills. It was an area long occupied by the NVA and fortified with bunkers, spider holes, deep tunnels, trenches, and underground shelters for aid stations, CPs, and storage depots. And this time, the NVA intended to stay their ground.

Operation Apache Snow was scheduled to launch on 10 May 1969.

### 10 May 1969

Firebase Blaze, five hundred by a thousand meters, was twenty kilos south of Ap Bia Mountain. In the early morning hours, eighteen hundred men from five battalions—1/506th, 2/501st, and 3/187th from the 101st, and 4/1 and 2/1 ARVN—were assembled there to await liftoff. In the predawn hours, the troopers lounged about the area, napping, smoking, talking, wiping off sweat from the early-morning heat, cleaning weapons. Pilots and door gunners stood by some of the sixty-five Hueys, already at Firebase Blaze, that would air-assault the troops into the battle area. The men were poised to launch the largest air mobile assault in the Vietnam war. Ten artillery batteries were laid and ready to fire from Firebases Bradley, Airborne, Currahee, Berchtesgaden, and Cannon, having been moved in to their firing positions only sixteen hours before the invasion.

H-Hour was 0730. In the hour before the helicopter launch, fighter-bombers had bombed the LZs for fifty minutes; the artillery followed with a fifteen-minute barrage. Then came aerial rocket artillery helicopters for a one-minute "frosting on the cake." The troops could hear their bombs blasting the enemy defenses—and, they hoped, cutting down their losses later. At 0649, the TAC-Air prep stopped and the troops prepared to "saddle up." The lift helicopters, UH-1Ds, began to arrive at Firebase Blaze in groups of sixteen, for a total of sixty-four. At 0730, H-Hour, the sixty-four Hueys and the first four hundred men and the lead companies of 1/506th and 3/187th, covered by Cobra gunships, were on the way to the northern A Shau Valley. The Hueys flew to the south across the A Shau Valley, and then, using the walls of the valley as a screen, turned to the north along the Laotian border to their LZs.

By 0800, D Company, then A and C, landed on LZ 2 without opposition. Ten minutes later, the troops were moving toward their assigned locations and setting up defensive positions. As planned, Capt. Dean L. Johnson and his C Company secured the LZ. Captain Gerald R. Harkins and his A Company moved out toward the Laotian border. Captain Luther L. Sanders led his D Company to the south-southeast, passed through the battalion CP on LZ 2, and headed up the ridge protruding to the northwest of Dong Ap Bia. At 0945, Honeycutt and his command ship landed on LZ 2. Honeycutt relieved Capt. Dean Johnson of LZ security, and Johnson and C Company moved out toward the border. Then Honeycutt and part of his staff began to move up the mountain ridge behind D Company and, at about 1100, linked up with Sanders about a thousand meters from the top of the mountain. Helicopters hovering slowly overhead reported enemy trails, campsites, supply dumps, and bunkers. The signs of the enemy were becoming ominous. Honeycutt began to sense the enemy around him and radioed Colonel Conmy to release B Company to him. Conmy readily agreed, and B Company arrived at LZ 2 about 1430. B Company was commanded by Capt. Charles L. Littman, who had taken over from Captain Robinson on 8 May and would command the company for only twelve days. At about 1530, B Company reached Honeycutt's CP. Honeycutt ordered Littman to move his company up the mountain. "I doubt if you'll make it tonight," Honeycutt told him, "but sometime late tomorrow morning I want to move the CP up there."

"That shouldn't be any problem," Littman replied.

"And be careful."

"Don't worry, Colonel." Littman and B Company were on the way.

"After reaching the uppermost portion of the ridge, the company moved several hundred meters to the northeast and then proceeded south along a second ridge," wrote an Army historian. "As the company moved, the enemy's presence could be felt. Lookout towers high in the boughs of the canopy were passed. Jointed sections of bamboo, freshly cut for their water content, were strewn about. Spider holes and punji pits were encountered. B Company moved slowly, hoping to make the summit before dusk. The sound of artillery impacting on the hill, the ridges, and in the valleys and ravines was pleasing to the ear. The faint ping of mortar fire, coming from the battalion CP at D Company's location, was reassuring. A round whined overhead, then another. Contact! Small-arms fire began to pour in and then RPGs. The second platoon, led by Lt. Marshall Edwards, dispersed and returned fire. The bushes, the trees, the jagged rocks all seemed steeped with the violence of armed combat. The smell of cordite hung low over the anxious troops. Artillery was adjusted to within 25 meters of the platoon with shrapnel falling into friendly positions. The firing subsided, then flared again as the Rakkasans moved forward. . . . When more HE was poured into enemy positions, the fire lessened and then stopped; sweep teams found four enemy bodies and four AK-47's. . . . Artillery pounded the area throughout the night." Honeycutt ordered Littman to dig in and establish an NDP.

### 11 May 1969

Just prior to dawn, the Rakkasans in NDPs [night defensive position] launched a "mad minute," heavy machine-gun and automatic-rifle fire out of the perimeter into the enemy positions. Cobra gunships were on station overhead. At 0750, B Company, with Lieutenant Denholm's 4th Platoon in the lead, moved out. As the platoon made its way up the denuded ridge, the men found bloody trails, weapons, gear, and eight enemy KIAs. Throughout the late morning and early afternoon, the other three companies slugged on, finding fresh bunkers, commo wire, and other NVA gear. At about 1600, Denholm's men hit the enemy head-on. An enemy soldier sprang from a hole and shot Sp4 Aaron Rosenstreich in the chest. Sp4 John McCarrell was blown to bits by an NVA rocket. Rosenstreich died moments later. Denholm was blown down the trail, but, even deaf and stunned, he called for a machine gun. Sp4 Terry Larson rushed forward and was shot through the head. Sp4 Donald Mills rushed forward with an M60 and was shot through the chest. Seconds later, he got up, charged, and emptied his weapon into the sniper. In a bind, the B Company men grenaded the area around them and pulled back, carrying their dead and wounded with them. Honeycutt called in artillery and air strikes. At 1730, gunships flew over the area. During one strike, a gunship misfired and hit Honeycutt's CP with rockets. He was hit and two of his men killed. Thirty-five men were wounded, including battalion Sgt. Maj. Bernie Meehan. Honeycutt got on his radio and demanded that all aircraft check with his CP before launching strikes and halt all ARA [aerial rocket artillery] until friendly positions were marked more clearly.

Later that day, from documents found on an NVA soldier and translated by his Kit Carson scout, Honeycutt and the Brigade intelligence officer, Captain Fredericks, estimated that the 29th NVA Regiment was on the mountain with a strength of between twelve and eighteen hundred men, heavily reinforced with weapons. The 29th mission, according to the documents, was to infiltrate down to the plains and attack Hue.

A Company moved east toward the border. C Company moved to the southeast and at 0913 reported its location as three hundred meters southeast of the battalion CP that was on the hill's northeastern ridge for the remainder of the operation.

With the new intelligence, Honeycutt realized that his enemy was a major force and one ready and able to fight. He ordered Captain Johnson to move his C Company east toward the Ap Bia Mountain. He directed Harkins to move A Company back up the ridge to the battalion CP to relieve D Company. He told Sanders to use D Company to clear a ravine to the northeast, and then attack up the mountain from that position.

### 12 May 1969

During the day, eight air strikes pummeled the enemy positions, the last one at 1734. The strikes included high drag bombs, napalm, and five-hundred- and one-thousand-pound bombs with delay fuses. As the gunships left, artillery fire—105s, 155s, and 8-inch—blasted the area with great accuracy. B Company started up the ridge when the fire lifted. The bombing and napalm had opened trails in the jungle and the men saw enemy bunkers that they blasted with recoilless rifles. The fire caused the NVA soldiers to spring from their spider holes. They rolled grenades down on the Rakkasans, wounding six men. Littman moved his company back down the ridge, carrying the wounded with them. Helicopter gunships and fighter-bombers returned to cover the area with "snake and nape" (20mm cannon fire and napalm).

In the D Company area, Sanders was having trouble. As the single lines of men moved slowly and cautiously through the ravines and dense jungle, they were hit from three directions by many snipers high in the trees. The D Company troopers raked the trees with gunfire, but progress was slow. They could hear the enemy all around them.

Honeycutt wanted another LZ near B Company. One of the helicopters bringing in the engineers and their equipment was hit by enemy fire and crashed. But most of the engineers landed safely, rescued their gear, and, with B Company help, by 1500 had completed the lower LZ. Honeycutt had another LZ carved out 100 meters north of his CP— known as the upper LZ. By evening, C Company, after being ambushed in late afternoon when rocket-propelled grenades hit the trees above them and suffering eight wounded, was in an NDP 500 meters southeast of the lower LZ. B Company's NDP was located 350 meters northeast of the lower LZ. D Company was 500 meters to the north of the lower LZ. A Company and the battalion command post remained at the blocking position next to the upper LZ. During the night, the NVA probed all the NDPs and, at midnight, hit the NDPs with accurate mortar fire.

### 13 May 1969

At 0656, the forward air controller (FAC), arrived on station and directed ten air strikes against the known enemy fortifications. The Phantom jets used delayed-action ordnance to penetrate the canopy and explode in depth in the bunkers, trenches, and spider holes. The Rakkasans were well aware that the enemy troops ducked into the tunnels and bunkers at the sound of the jets and came out as soon as they left the area.

After the early-morning air strikes, B and C Companies resumed their treacherous climb up the ridge toward the enemy's dug-in positions and suffered a withering attack from a nest of snipers and small arms, RPGs and grenades. More and more wounded 3/187th soldiers from B and C Companies made their way back down the trails. Other Rakkasans, carrying cans of ammo and grenades, passed them on the way up. In the

C Company CP area, two men were killed and five wounded by an NVA attack into their security perimeter. The artillery FO called for fire and broke up the attack.

D Company was having an equally difficult time about six hundred meters from the battalion command post, wading through a river, climbing up the sides of a ravine, and then attacking toward the top of Ap Bia. The NVA hit with rocket-propelled grenades, badly wounding three men. Across the river, another RPG hit the 3d Platoon, wounding five men, and blowing Lieutenant Mattioli off the ridge and into the river.

"Delta Company, with platoons on both banks of the ravine, returned the fire with every available weapon and called for gunships," wrote Fred Waterhouse. "They also called for a medevac helicopter, which arrived on the scene at 1510 hours. As the Rakkasans were hoisting the wounded into the hovering helicopter, an RPG slammed into it. It crashed down on Pfc. George Pickel, killing him instantly. One of its whirling blades killed Sp4 William Springfield and wounded Miguel Moreno. Captain Luther Sanders watched in agony. He now had seven wounded and seven dead. His company would have to carry all of them out by litter. Delta Company started back up the mountain through the river bottom. At places, they climbed sheer cliffs and took one hour to move a hundred yards."

By late afternoon, the 3d Platoon of A Company reached the beleaguered D Company and the column started moving again, struggling up the steep cliffs at about thirty feet in half an hour. Then the rain came in torrents. Sanders halted his column and set up an NDP and called in artillery to surround his perimeter with close-in, constant shelling throughout the night. Just after midnight, the NVA, from the shelter of Laos, hit the Rakkasan positions with mortars. Honeycutt called in the "Spooky" gunship, a C-47 equipped with rapid-fire Gatling guns, to spray the area. The NVA did not attack that night. Meanwhile, Colonel Conmy ordered the 1/506th to change its mission and reinforce the 3/187th attack on the mountain.

## 14 May 1969

At 0646, the FAC reported in to Honeycutt's CP and directed thirteen air strikes—napalm, thousand-pound bombs—on the mountain throughout the day. The artillery from the nearby firebases blasted the area constantly. "The first concentrated attack on the summit began at 0756," wrote an Army historian. "C Company moved east from its NDP location up a small finger (Finger 1). B Company moved to the east from its NDP location up a small finger about 150 meters north of C Company (Finger 2). Both companies came into contact immediately but pressed on, with C Company reaching the military crest of the hill at 0843. Mutually supporting bunkers were encountered. Chicom claymores were set up in the trees. Heavy mortar, RPG, and small-arms fire continued to harass the Rakkasans."

On ridge finger 2, C Company found itself in a ferocious fight when the NVA pummeled them with small-arms fire, RPGs, and grenades, rolled down the sides of hills. In Lt. James Goff's 3d Platoon, six men were badly wounded. The troops kept moving forward, but the NVA came out of their holes, firing AK-47s. Goff's men were hit from all sides. Two were killed and fifteen wounded. The other platoons of C Company were nailed against the side of the mountain.

Sfc. Louis Garza led a platoon from B Company in three unsuccessful assaults up the hill to help B Company, and had seven men wounded. On his fourth attempt, Garza moved through the NVA bunker line and found NVA bodies throughout the area. The enemy in a second row of bunkers opened fire and wounded six more troopers. The lead platoons of B and C Companies began to fall back under heavy NVA fire. Sp4 John Comerford crawled up with an M60 machine gun and sprayed the bunkers. But it was not enough. Honeycutt sent a platoon from A Company to cover the withdrawal. Unfortunately, as it moved up, it was hit by helicopter gunships firing rockets that killed Sp4 Edward Brooks and badly wounded three other men. Lieutenant Donald Sullivan and his 2d Platoon of C Company tried to help the fallback but was hit with RPGs that wiped out a four-man litter team, blew his radio operator, Sp4 Ron Swanson, down the hill, and killed Rakkasan Willie Chapman. C Company now had a total of fifty-two men killed and wounded.

By 1700, the Rakkasans were in NDPs and Honeycutt asked for a sit rep [situation report]. He learned that he had lost twelve KIA and eighty badly wounded men. By 1920, though, he had medevaced out of the area all his dead and wounded. At 2000, a Spooky arrived on station and, throughout the night, laced the area west of the Rakkasan position toward the Laotian border.

**15 May 1969**

During the morning hours, the gunships and ten artillery firebases repeated their almost incessant bombing of the enemy positions as they had done the previous days, reducing the mountain and ridgelines to smoldering piles of blackened and smoking tree stumps, churned-up earth, denuded of vegetation.

At 1200, A and B Companies attacked the same two fingers that they had assaulted the previous day. Sfc. Louis Garza led his 4th Platoon from B Company over the same ground, and two claymore mines hit and wounded his two point men. Garza called for air support. After the strike with 250 pound bombs, Garza and his platoon moved forward, firing their machine guns and M16s, overran the bunkers, and killed eight NVAs. But sniper and machine-gun fire halted his advance. He marked the enemy position with smoke and called for helicopter gunships. Unfortunately, the first gunship salvoed an entire rack of rockets into B Company's CP, killing Pfc. Joseph Price and wounding fifteen others, including the CO, Capt. Charles Littman. He was replaced by Capt. John C. "Butch" Chappelle. Higher up the trail, Garza and his men were hit with an NVA counterattack that Pfcs. Snyder and Maryniewski drove off with machine-gun fire.

Lieutenant Frank McGreevy and his 1st Platoon of A Company were stopped in front of a line of bunkers. He tried to move forward but a machine-gun team, led by Sp4 Michael Lyden laying down covering fire, was hit by return fire that killed Lyden. McGreevy's platoon was now cut in half, and he ordered a withdrawal. Honeycutt called off the attack and told B and C Companies to set up a joint NDP. He also called in his artillery liaison officer and gave him a message to get back to the division staff. "I want you to make sure that everybody gets this. And I mean the artillery people and the gunship pilots and the liaison officers . . . everybody. I don't want any more ARA out here if they can't shoot the enemy instead of us. I'm tired of taking more casualties from friendlies than from the enemy. The next goddamn sonofabitch who comes out here and shoots us up, we're gonna shoot his fuckin' ass down. And that's final. Now you go back and tell 'em that."

During the night, NVA sappers out of Laos moved up the draw and tried to hit C Company and the battalion CP. A "Shadow" gunship, a C-119 armed with three miniguns, took them under fire. That evening the CO of 1/506th reported to Honeycutt that he was within 1,200 meters southeast of the lower LZ.

### 16 May 1969

A first-light check by C Company found fourteen NVA bodies in their area. The day began just like the previous six days: saturation bombing, air strikes, and ceaseless artillery volleys onto the known or suspected enemy locations. Honeycutt told Sanders to stop finding an avenue to the top of the mountain, realizing that D Company's three brutal days in the ravine was enough. He ordered D Company back up the ridge to secure B Company's LZ. Honeycutt planned his attack on the mountain with A Company in the lead, supported by a flanking attack by 1/506th. But the 1/506th was in trouble in its area. One NVA platoon hit the lead elements of the battalion that was receiving heavy fire from Hills 800, 900, and 916. The NVA attacks prevented the 1/506th from getting to the mountain in time to support the 3/187th's assault. Honeycutt called off the attack for the sixteenth. Colonel Conmy did not want 3/187th to attack without the help of 1/506th. Honeycutt was frustrated. He thought that 1/506th was taking too long, and he sensed that the NVA was bringing up reinforcements from Laos to beef up the mountain.

### 17 May 1969

Honeycutt put the day "on hold" and had his men prepare for the assault the next day by stockpiling supplies, passing out new protective gas masks, and bringing up concussion grenades for use against the dug-in NVA in bunkers. 1/506th, fighting up the mountain crest and taking casualties, had still not arrived in a support position. There was little contact during the hours of darkness.

### 18 May 1969

Early in the morning, the usual "prep" fires of air and artillery pounded the mountaintop. The first CS gas rounds, however, landed in the middle of A Company, and division made the decision to call off the CS attack. At 1025, A and D Companies moved out and, for the first time in the Ap Bia assault, every man in the attacking companies wore a flak jacket and most of the riflemen carried about forty rounds of M16 ammo and some as many as ten grenades. Honeycutt's plan had A and D Companies moving up the two fingers, proven to be the only accessible routes to the top.

On A Company's point was Lieutenant McGreevy and his 1st Platoon, followed by the 2d and 3d Platoons. As usual, the enemy fire increased with the appearance of the Rakkasans. McGreevy was hit and had to be evacuated. By 1215, the assault companies had to halt in place and wait for a heavy concentration of fire—gunships, artillery, mortars, napalm, and all the small-arms fire that the infantrymen could bring to bear: machine guns, M-79s, light antitank weapons and 90mm recoilless rifles.

In D Company's area on the flank of A Company, Lt. Thomas Lipscomb and his 3d Platoon were in the lead. At a bunker line, the enemy fire was heavy. Three men went down, and Lipscomb yelled for his men to move up.

"Keep moving," Sanders yelled to Lipscomb.

"They've got claymores all over up here," he yelled back. "If we try to move, they'll blow 'em on us."

"You've got to move, claymores or not. Shoot them if you have to, but you've got to get those men up that hill. That's our only chance. If we stay here, they'll kill us all."

Lipscomb charged a trench line with two other men while three of his men laid down covering fire. A grenade exploded at Lipscomb's feet, blowing him back down the hill and killing him instantly. Pfc. Paul Bellino rushed forward but he, too, was killed by a sniper.

Sanders realized that he had to get moving or, standing still, lose more men. He ordered Lt. Jerry Walden and his 1st Platoon to continue the attack. Shortly thereafter, Sanders was shot in the arm, and Lieutenant Walden took over the company. He called Honeycutt and called for more ammo. Helicopters arrived shortly, hovering a few feet over the ground, while the crew threw out boxes of ammo.

"Walden told the colonel his Rakkasans were not going to back off," wrote Fred Waterhouse. "Walden moved his men up in a skirmish line. They leapfrogged from log to log and crater to crater. NVA grenades flew through the air. Sp4s Howard Harris and Jack Little blazed away with an M60 machine gun. Harris was shot in the neck. Private First Class Roy Mathew moved up as assistant gunner. Seconds later he was killed, shot in the throat. Nearby, Pfc. Steve Korovesis, a new replacement, was hit by shrapnel and evacuated. He had been in Vietnam for one month and lasted ten minutes in his first battle.

"Lieutenant Walden moved up and down the line, steadying his men. They began taking flanking fire. Two Rakkasans tried to rush forward. They were both shot down. Private First Class Willie Kirkland, 1st Platoon medic, moved up to give aid. He was hit five times in the chest. While Pfc. Roger Murray laid down covering fire, Sgt. Tom McGall and Pfc. Michael Rocklen ran up and pulled Kirkland into a bomb crater. Kirkland died a few minutes later."

South of D Company, A Company moved to the attack. Lieutenant Daniel Bresnahan's 3d Platoon led the assault up a thirty-degree slope, overran the first line of bunkers, killed about ten NVA, and moved toward the second line of bunkers. Back at his CP, Honeycutt was receiving optimistic reports from his commanders. 1/506th, however, had moved only about a hundred meters against strong opposition.

At 1137, Lieutenant Walden reported to Honeycutt that he was within seventy-five meters of the top. But minutes later, Walden and 1st Sgt. Thomas Sterns were hit by shrapnel. D Company was without officers, and all platoons were running low on ammunition. Honeycutt told them to hold fast, that he would send help. He contacted Captain Johnson and ordered him to move C Company up the hill to reinforce what was left of A and D Companies, to take all the ammo they could carry, and to take over D Company as well as his own men.

Honeycutt realized the gravity of his situation in spite of some previous optimism. C Company had to fight up the hill and took fire from the southeast where, from a helicopter, he saw that the NVA were also in force in that direction. He also found out that 1/506th was in no condition to assist his final assault on the mountain. He called Colonel Conmy, briefed him on his very difficult situation, and asked for another company, a "fully intact air assault company." Conmy told him that it would be airborne in minutes. But that became open to discussion later.

From 1251 until 1330, all units held in place as jets raked the smoldering hill with "snake and nape." When Johnson reached the remnants of D Company, he told Lt. Joel Trautman, his 1st Platoon commander, to move up the small finger ridge. The men rushed forward in bounds. They could see the crest of the mountain only a hundred meters above them. Trautman was hit in the thigh by machine-gun fire and went down, losing consciousness. Honeycutt was overhead in a command chopper, directing air strikes and artillery fire. Finally, he felt that his men were going to take the mountain after the bloody fighting of the past nine days. He landed and started climbing up the mountain. At B Company's old LZ, his men were hit by small-arms fire, and Honeycutt shot an NVA soldier. As he started up the hill again, the sky became black, the wind gusted, lightning streaked through the sky, and a torrential rainstorm began. Visibility was limited to twenty meters. Honeycutt radioed all companies to hold fast until the rain stopped. The heavy rains continued until bomb craters were small ponds, the mud was thick and slippery on the slopes, and forward movement was almost impossible. Honeycutt checked with Colonel Conmy and decided to withdraw. C Company held to cover the withdrawal of A and D Companies. By 1530, all three companies had moved back.

Honeycutt had been expecting another company to help him take Ap Bia, but, unknown to him, General Zais, deeply concerned about the Rakkasan casualties, had stopped the reinforcing company from joining the battle. At 1700, General Zais arrived at Honeycutt's CP. The Rakkasans were a battered battalion. During the day, A and C Companies had lost nine men each, B had lost four, and Delta thirty-nine. Zais wanted to know if Honeycutt could fight on. Honeycutt said that he would need just one company more. Zais was hesitant. Honeycutt was adamant.

"General, if there is anybody that deserves to take that sonofabitch, it's the Rakkasans—and you know that as well as I do. And there is just no goddamn way in hell that I want to see Sherron and 2/506th come in here and take that mountain after all we've been through. And if it ain't gonna be that way, then you just fire my ass right now. Right this minute!"

Zais paced around the CP for about a minute and then said, "Okay, you can have your company."

"Thank you, General," said Honeycutt.

At 1830, A Company, 2/506th, began to land by helicopter on the upper LZ. That night, the company remained with B/3/187th in a blocking position while A, C, and D Companies set up NDPs within a few hundred meters of the lower LZ (one hundred meters north of the battalion command post).

**19 May 1969**

At 0630, the jets arrived and pounded the enemy positions with seven air strikes using bombs, napalm, and rockets. For some reason, the NVA popped purple smoke grenades. No friendly forces used "grape," so the jets had some accurately marked targets to hit. During the morning, D Company and A/2/506th moved to the lower LZ. Honeycutt worked on his final plan of attack on the mountain, slated for the morning of the twentieth. Other units moved into locations for the final assault. 2/3d ARVN moved by helicopter from Hue to an LZ a thousand meters south of Ap Bia and then climbed northwest to an assault position five hundred meters from the top of Hill 900. Three companies of 2/501st were airlifted from Firebase Airborne to an LZ eight hundred meters northeast of Ap Bia and then walked to within four hundred meters of the base of Hill 937. 1/506th attacked south of the mountain.

Honeycutt's plan of attack called for A/2/506th to move up the northern face (Finger 2); C Company to move up Finger 1; A Company to move to the south from the lower LZ and then proceed up the southern ridge; 2/3d ARVN to assault the eastern ridge; 2/501st to assault to the southwest from its position near the base of Hill 937. By dark, all units were in their assault positions around the mountain.

Over a captured radio, Honeycutt got a message from the NVA. "Black Jack, we are going to kill all of your men tomorrow. When you come up the mountain in the morning, Black Jack, we will be waiting for you. All of your men are going to die. Can you hear me, Black Jack? All will die!"

"We'll see who dies tomorrow, asshole," Honeycutt barked.

**20 May 1969**

For two hours, beginning around dawn, the air force jet and Skyraider pilots bombed all four sides of Ap Bia with every type of armament they could "scarf up" at their bases. Like the sequence of the previous ten days, when the pairs of planes left the area, the artillery blasted the NVA positions with tons of 105mm, 155mm, and 8-inch artillery rounds. At 1000, the four infantry battalions assaulted the burning, scoured, denuded mountaintop. In 3/187th area, the lineup had A Company on the right, C Company in the center, and A/2/506th on the left. When the troops reached the base of the mountain, they formed long skirmish lines and began to move cautiously up the slopes. They were surprised when they were not fired on with the usual heavy bursts of fire at close range.

The hill was eerily silent. And in ten minutes, the three companies had reached the first bunker line—now seemingly deserted. As a precaution, the troopers destroyed the bunkers with grenades and satchel charges. Twenty minutes later, their lines were just a hundred meters from the military crest of Ap Bia and closing in on the second bunker line.

The mountain was quiet for ten minutes. Then, at about 1040, when the skirmish lines were just seventy-five meters from the top, the bunkers came alive with a rain of RPGs at point-blank range. Ten to fifteen NVA hit C Company, wounded seven Rakkasans, and continued the fight by rolling grenades down the slope. Sp4 Tyrone Campbell and his assistant gunner rushed forward with a 90mm recoilless rifle and scored a direct hit on one bunker and, a moment later, another.

On the right flank of C Company, Sp4 Edward Merjil, 2d Platoon, was a one-man commando team. He knocked out two bunkers with a grenade launcher, and then, "with his squad on both sides laying down covering fire, rushed a third," wrote Samuel Zaffiri. "While his men poured fire on the bunker, pinning down the enemy soldiers inside, Merjil took careful aim from ten meters away and shot a grenade right into the aperture, killing the two NVA soldiers huddled inside.

"Merjil reloaded quickly, then rushed forward with the rest of his squad up the steep side of the mountain. Ten meters later, the men topped the mountain. They did not realize it at the time, but they were the first Americans to set foot on Dong Ap Bia. The time was 1145, exactly nine days and five hours after Bravo Company first made contact on the mountain.

"Still, Merjil and his men had taken only a few square feet of the mountain. The NVA were still dug in all over the top of it, and before the squad could move any farther, they were pinned down by fire coming from a half-dozen enemy positions."

Behind them, Lt. Donald Sullivan was pushing his 2d Platoon as hard a he could. To his left, Sp4 Lionel Mata and another squad moved up. Mata laid down a base of grazing fire with his machine gun, and within fifteen minutes, his squad had moved around the area and knocked out ten bunkers with smoke and frag grenades taped together. Then, C Company, two or three men at a time, reached the top of the mountain. The NVA deserted their bunkers and ran down the west face of the mountain in the draw between Hills 900 and 910 toward Laos. Overhead, Honeycutt directed 81mm mortar fire into the draw while B/1/506th sent a force below the draw and waited for the NVA to emerge. When they did, they ran into a wall of fire. But the NVA was aggressive: two platoons of B/1/506th fought hand-to-hand with the fleeing NVA.

On the western face of the mountain, C/187th set up a perimeter. Honeycutt ordered Captain Harkins to move his A Company up the mountain to reinforce C Company. A Company was fighting a hard battle just below the crest of Ap Bia, in which Harkins had already lost Lt. George Bennitt and fifteen men. Harkins rallied his troops and moved up. About thirty meters from the top, Harkins took a shot through his neck that lodged in his back. He staggered a few feet and fell into a shell hole. Overhead, Honeycutt urged him on even after Harkins told him that he had been wounded. "I've been hit bad," Harkins told him. Honeycutt said, "I know you've been hit, but you still gotta keep pushing." A medic bandaged Harkins, and Harkins staggered almost blindly ahead, holding on to his RTO's backpack.

The NVA in the last bunker line refused to give up, pinned down A Company's troops, and rolled grenades down on them. At the same time, an NVA squad hit C Company's right flank.

"Pinned down on the far right side of Alpha's skirmish line," wrote Samuel Zaffiri, "Sp4 Johnny Jackson, a machine gunner in the 3d Platoon, huddled behind a log and thought: *Here we go again.* Another attack failed. As he cowered there, though, he suddenly remembered what he had boastfully told a friend earlier in the morning. 'I'll tell you what,' he had said, 'if we go up that sonofabitch this time, I'm staying up. I ain't gonna be run down again and let those assholes shoot me in the back. I'm through with this retreating bullshit.'

"He kept thinking of his words now, and then on impulse stood up and shouted out loud so everyone in the 3d Platoon could hear him, 'Fuck this bullshit!' With a fluid motion, Jackson brought his M60 up to his chest and raked the enemy position above, then charged up the side of the mountain, wildly spraying bullets from side to side."

On his way to the top, Jackson stumbled into a spider hole occupied by two enemy soldiers. Before they could grab their weapons, Jackson sprayed them with his M60. Then he raced upward and found himself looking into the aperture of another bunker. He fired into it and scrambled up the remaining twenty or so meters to the top of the mountain.

Below him, his friend, Sp4 Michael Vallone, frightened but inspired by Jackson's charge, yelled, "Follow me," fired short bursts from his M16, and led his squad, then the platoon, and then the rest of A Company, up the mountain. At the top, A Company rolled over the last bunker line and made it to the top. The wounded Captain Harkins set up a perimeter defense tied in to C Company, turned the company over to Lt. Gordie Atcheson, and then began his laborious trek down the mountain.

To the southwest, B/1/506th was in a tough battle. The 3d Platoon attacked up Hill 900 but, about a hundred meters from the top, met a grim fate. Claymore mines hidden in trees blasted the point squad, killing the point man and wounding seven others. Two platoons of NVA, firing satchel charges, roared down the hill through the shattered platoon, then raced back up through it again. Fighting was close and brutal. Fifteen minutes later, the 3d Platoon had ten dead and was surrounded by a pile of NVA KIAs. Lieutenant Colonel John Bowers, CO of 1/506th, ordered Capt. William Stymiest, C Company CO, to send a force up the hill to relieve the battered 3d Platoon. In a two hour fight, C Company made it to the top, where sixty-five dead NVA littered the area.

By the end of the day, most of the troops of the 29th NVA Regiment had been killed or were trying to escape across the border to Laos. From his helicopter, Honeycutt could see the NVA running in all directions off the mountain. B/1/506th was still in a blocking position to cover the southwestern draw. Honeycutt brought in two fighter-bombers to strafe up and down the draw and then brought in artillery fire.

The Rakkasans on the top and slopes of Dong Ap Bia found a landscape that resembled what they imagined hell must be like. Throughout the area, they found NVA pith helmets, AK-47s, stick grenades, bloody bandages, and RPGs. In the center of Hill 937, a line of Rakkasans came across a group of fifteen NVAs who were apparently shell-shocked. Without waiting, the Rakkasans killed them all. Four of the NVA had been chained to trees. All of them wore patches that read: "Kill the Americans."

Honeycutt began the mop-up operation at about 1500. One POW, eighteen-year-old Pham Van Hai, told his interrogators that 80 percent of his hundred-man company and the 29th NVA Regiment's 7th and 8th Battalions had been nearly wiped out. Later, Sp4 Johnny Jackson and his squad, searching the top of the mountain, found an underground room containing the stripped and stacked bodies of more than forty NVA soldiers. Other Rakkasans searching the mountaintop discovered in its sides deep tunnels, a huge hospital, a regimental CP, and many storage areas containing 152 individual and 25 crew-served weapons, 75,000 rounds of ammo, thousands of mortar and RPG rounds, and over ten tons of rice.

The 3d Battalion of the 187th suffered 39 killed in action and 290 wounded. The total casualties of the American taking of Dong Ap Bia was 70 dead and 372 wounded.

The losses inflicted on the NVA in the Dong Ap Bia battle are debatable. The G2 Section of the 101st estimated the NVA dead at 633, based upon actual body count. But no one could count the NVA running off the mountain, those killed by artillery and air strikes, the wounded and dead carried into Laos, or the dead buried alive in bunkers and tunnels.

The 3/187th's battle for Dong Ap Bia was over. For the next seventeen days, the other three battalions would continue to mop up the mountain. But on 21 May, the Rakkasans were evacuated from the area to Camp Evans for a stand-down at Eagle Beach.

While the other battalions were policing the Dong Ap Bia battlefield, one imaginative soldier found a piece of a cardboard C-ration box, wrote on it, "Hamburger Hill," and nailed it to a charred tree trunk. Shortly thereafter, another, perhaps more practical and blunt soldier, had added beneath the sign, "Was it worth it?"

His question would be debated in the Congress, in the administration, in the media, and in many a gathering of military officers and men for months to come. Shortly after the battle, a spokesman for Gen. Creighton Abrams, Gen. Westmoreland's successor as COMUSMACV, said, "We are not fighting for terrain as such. We are going after the enemy." General Zais said, "The hill was in my area of operations. That was where the enemy was and that was where I attacked him." When some-one asked him why he didn't blast the hill with B-52s and spare the in-fantry assault, General Zais said, with some rancor, "I don't know how many wars we have to go through to convince people that aerial bom-bardment alone cannot do the job."

But the debate about the value of Hamburger Hill was far from over.

# 11: Vietnamization

The bloody battle for Dong Ap Bia may actually have triggered an important shift in the strategy of the Vietnam War. Shortly after the battle, the 27 June issue of *Life* magazine published an article showing the pictures of 241 men who had been killed in Vietnam in the preceding week. Although only five were of soldiers killed at Dong Ap Bia, the article seemed to imply that all 241 men had been killed storming Dong Ap Bia. Shelby Stanton, a Vietnam historian, felt that the *Life* article and the 1968 Tet offensive were major turning points in the American acceptance of the U.S. part in the war. General Abrams, COMUSMACV, received orders to "avoid such large-scale battles," according to Col. Harry S. Summers. "Protective reaction" was apparently the name of the new U.S.–Vietnam tactics.

And to carry out this revised strategy, President Nixon ordered the secretary of defense to withdraw 25,000 U.S. troops by 8 July 1969 and another 35,000 by early December. Such a plan—avoiding large battles and withdrawal of U.S. forces—"dramatically reduced the allies' capability to conduct operations beyond the outer fringes of the populated areas," said General Stilwell on his departure from command of XXIV Corps. He had already turned over the Corps to Lt. Gen. Melvin Zais, the former 101st commander. The new plan also inherently required that the South Vietnamese take up the fight to an increasingly larger degree. The result was the "Vietnamization" of the war.

On 27 September, all units returned to Camp Evans for a "standdown," seven days of training in preparation for the upcoming division Operation Republic Square, and the beginning of a new phase of their Vietnam experience.

The seven days of training taught the combat-oriented troopers a new type of warfare—pacification and Vietnamization. In the pacification phase, they learned that the term meant that the local governments had the responsibility for the military, social, political, and economic processes of their own people. That included sustained security of their territory, the destruction of the enemy's underground government, and the initiation of self-supporting and expandable economic and social programs. Vietnamization, they found out, meant that the U.S. would turn over to ARVN increasing responsibility for fighting the war, including its small and large battles.

On 29 September, Operation Republic Square began. Training was completed on 5 October, and on the following day, 3/187th moved into Phong Dien District as a "dedicated battalion," dedicated to turning over to the Vietnamese the control of their country. In Republic Square, the battalion's mission was "to conduct offensive operations emphasizing reconnaissance and ambushes to deny the enemy access to the populated areas and support the GVN [government of Vietnam] in accelerating pacification while improving the local GVN forces through intensified training and combined operations." That meant that the Rakkasans would work with the local villagers to restore the governments of the districts and hamlets, and would train the popular force militia (PF) and the People's Self-Defense Forces (PSDF) to root out the local VC leaders.

The first step in the process was to link up with the locals. To do so, the Rakkasans built a combined TOC [tactical operations center] in district headquarters with work areas for the district's chief, S3, duty officer, and the net control station. The Rakkasan and the district staffs planned combined and unilateral tactical operations in detail. The joint staffs held daily joint briefings to keep all key officers abreast of the district's changing tactical situation. Artillery grid coordinates were cleared by both staffs with little delay. Because the MACV district team was only twenty-five meters away, coordination with that office was simple.

On 6 October, A Company's Capt. David O. Treadwell, with the approval of the district chief, moved his 2d Platoon to the hamlet of the Uu Thong to conduct short-term civic action projects, hold limited medcaps, and train the local PF and PSDF. Initially, there was some friction and distrust between the two groups, but, as the days wore on, they developed a mutual understanding. On several occasions, some of the 2d Platoon left pieces of equipment at the training sites. In all cases, the hamlet people returned the items. The platoon left in December, but a ten-man civic action team stayed behind. Shortly thereafter, C Company formed a second civic action team.

In mid-November, Lt. Col. William A. Steinberg, "Tiger" Honeycutt's successor as CO of the Rakkasans, initiated his combat training program with the local militia. He moved his companies to field sites co-located with six RF [regional forces] companies. The battalion trained the RF companies intensely, including combined night ambushes and daylight recon patrols. This particular training ended on 31 December 1969.

The Rakkasan S2 section faced the problem of unearthing intelligence on four different enemy groups: the C-113 Local Force Company; district, village, and hamlet guerrillas; Viet Cong infrastructure; and NVA main line units. The Rakkasan S2 got help from the Vietnamese S2 and the MACV DIOCC advisor (District Intelligence Operations Coordinating Center). The S2 made charts showing the suspected VC in the district, villages, and hamlets. Then the S3 planned patrols to ferret the known VC. The battalion S5 position also took on new significance. He designed civic action projects to improve the living standards of the civilian population, projects that included building schools, dams, markets, and so on. He also distributed surplus food, soap, and other commodities. For the Rakkasans, the war was taking on a radically new look.

B Company made the first contact during Republic Square on 14 October, ambushing six VC several thousand meters northwest of the district headquarters and south of the main road, QL-1. Lieutenant John B. Moseman, during his first night in the field, was with the squad of his platoon that made the contact. The platoon killed five of the VC: a company commander, two squad leaders, a medic, and a rifleman, all of whom were members of the C-113 local company. The man captured was the company adjutant. He told Moseman that the company was understrength and that the key leaders were NVA. Similar missions, including the combined cordon-and-search operations of the Rakkasans and the local militia, put heavy pressure on the VC, curtailed their movements, and cut them off from their source of supplies and support.

On 27 January 1970, one of the Eagle flights met with disaster. Twelve men from A Company were aboard when the flight spotted some VC in a valley. The Rakkasans landed, attacked, and killed two VC. Unfortunately, the C and C (command and control) ship, the second helicopter, was hit by small-arms fire, killing the artillery liaison officer, Capt. Everett D. Herren, and critically wounding the battalion S3.

During the first five months of 1970, the Rakkasans continued their pacification program to include the use of psychological operations (Psyops, in the vernacular of the troops). Psyops methods included leaflet drops, roving loudspeaker teams, distribution of handbills, and payment to the locals for VC weapons and for information on VC locations, weapons, and booby traps.

In May, 3/187th began to conduct operations separate from the ARVN forces. On 11 May, the battalion deployed to an AO north of Highway QL-1 and extending to the south to include the most southern and western portions of Phong Dien District. The battalion made extensive use of the previously successful ambush technique and encountered scattered enemy opposition throughout the AO. By June, only eight mobile training teams remained in the lowlands around Phong Dien. The battalion continued to conduct operations from Firebase Rakkasan.

With the end of the rainy season in May, the VC stepped up their activities in the Phong Dien District. On 30 May, the battalion had its heaviest contact of the year. Captain Joseph T. Flatley had his B Company spread out in an NDP, and at 0348, small-arms fire and ten to twelve satchel charges hit the 1st Platoon. The platoon returned fire, but in the firefight in the black of the early morning, five Rakkasans were KIAs and four WIAs. At 0509, a "Dustoff" lifted the wounded out of the area. At 0840, a second "Dustoff," hovering into the area, was hit and forced down. Two crewman were wounded. A third "Dustoff" landed safely and took out the crew of the second ship and the remaining B Company wounded.

"During this period, the pacification program in Phong Dien District had surpassed all expectations," wrote an Army historian. "The combination of responsive district and province governments and the self-confidence that the Territorial Forces had acquired, both from their training and tactical successes, were all that were needed to encourage the former residents of the 'Street Without Joy.' By the end of May, all forms of refugee camps in Phong Dien District were completely closed while the people, no longer refugees, continued their lives in their own homes, on what was their own land. The unofficial designation, 'Street Without Joy,' translated from '*La Rue sans Joie*,' which French soldiers who had convoyed the area prior to their fall in 1954 had bestowed upon it, was now a misnomer."

On 25 June, command of the Rakkasans shifted to Lt. Col. Ivan C. Bland. His command post remained at Firebase Rakkasan, where his troops continued to build up the firebase while at the same time conducting limited combat operations—patrols and ambushes.

During July and August, the Rakkasans continued aggressive patrolling throughout their area of operations, set up night ambushes, and deployed sniper teams. On 3 August, Bland moved his CP back to the battalion rear at Camp Evans to conduct security operations in the immediate area. Bland sent his troops out in platoon-sized units, making maximum use of ambushes to thwart the enemy. During this period, there was little contact, partly because the monsoons hit the area in October, washing out bridges and roads, grounding aircraft, and limiting foot patrols. Low ceilings made aerial resupply very difficult. The enemy was also severely hampered.

On 15 October 1970, the command of the battalion changed once again when Lt. Col. Bryan J. Sutton took over. During October and early November, the battalion continued its patrols, ambushes, and air assaults. Sergeant John S. Fako was killed and four other men wounded on 15 October when a trooper from D Company activated a booby trap when he stepped from a chopper. On 7 November, an outpost in A Company was hit by twelve to fourteen RPG rounds, killing Pfc. Andrew S. Pierce Jr. and wounding two other men. One enemy soldier penetrated the perimeter and hit a Rakkasan on the head with his rocket launcher. Not to be outdone, the Rakkasan killed the enemy soldier with his M16. That night, 3/187th returned to Camp Evans for a seven-day stand-down.

The stand-down procedure included the usual refitting, reequipping, integration of new men, and refresher training on such subjects as CBR [chemical, biological, radiological], communications security, personal hygiene, defense against sappers, rules of engagement, mines and booby traps, drug abuse, use of TAC [tactical air command] Air, marksmanship, fire discipline, and even "Why Vietnam?"

After the stand-down, Sutton took his battalion back to his AO to search out the enemy under the mountainous jungle canopy of northern Nam Hoa District. The monsoons continued to hamper even small units' forays. The troops found some booby traps, but not as many as they found in the lowlands.

During November, platoon-sized units searched and attacked the enemy wherever they could be located. Often, a firefight would start after the enemy fired into a platoon NDP or perimeter. The Rakkasans responded with artillery from nearby firebases, their own rifles, grenades, and mortars, and then would sweep the area around their bases. To celebrate Thanksgiving and eat the traditional meal, Colonel Sutton rotated the battalion to Camp Evans, one company at a time. On Thanksgiving Day, the battalion hosted the Tin Tanh Orphanage of Quang Tri for a religious service and turkey dinner.

Colonel Sutton did his best to keep his battalion as healthy and as comfortable as the severe rain and combat conditions would allow. He sent his men back to Camp Evans, a small unit at a time. At Evans, the men received a thorough physical check by the battalion medics as soon as the choppers landed and were given medical treatment and then a hot shower. Then the S4 team issued each man a clean, dry uniform and took back unserviceable gear. For the rest of the day, the troops could go to the PX, the barber, have a few cold beers, and see a movie before they flew back to the wet mountain slopes under the dripping, saturated jungle canopy. One very successful result of the one-day stand-down was the significant reduction of immersion foot-fungus and other wet-weather illnesses. The battalion area at Camp Evans got a face-lift during this period, with new buildings, stall showers, signs, and sidewalks.

The cold monsoon rains continued into December. The tactical situation in the Rakkasan area remained essentially the same—sporadic contact with small groups of enemy troops and discovery of carefully concealed booby traps, claymore mines, and RPGs. After contacts, the Rakkasans put a heavy volume of fire on the areas where they saw the enemy or suspected him, then swept the area, uncovering bunkers, weapons, caches of various sizes, and spider holes. During these almost daily contacts, the Rakkasans had eleven men wounded. The operational area was obviously swarming with small units of the enemy that would hit and then fade, only to be followed and tracked down to the maximum extent possible.

During 1970, the new tactics of the war were evident by the limited extent of casualties 3/187th inflicted on the enemy: 37 KIA, 4 POWs, 48 individual and 4 crew-served weapons captured, and 189 bunkers destroyed. During 1970, the Rakkasans were awarded 81 Purple Hearts.

Early in January 1971, the entire battalion moved back to Camp Evans for refresher training in preparation for Operation Dewey Canyon II, shortly thereafter renamed "Lam Son 719." The Rakkasans were about

to enter yet another phase in their Vietnam experience: support of the
South Vietnamese Army in its attack across the border into Laos.

### ARVN into Laos—Lam Son 719

By the fall of 1970, President Nixon was under heavy pressure from the
public and the Congress to end the war in Vietnam. His national security advisor, Henry Kissinger, had already met with the North Vietnamese in Paris a number of times. In October of 1970, Kissinger and
Xuan Thuy, a high-ranking North Vietnamese diplomat, met again to
discuss a "cease-fire" agreement. Kissinger was pessimistic about its
chances because the North Vietnamese refused to pull their troops out
of the South even though Nixon had already brought home 165,000
troops and would bring home another 90,000 in the spring of 1972. In
a speech to the nation on 7 October 1970, Nixon unveiled his "standstill cease-fire" idea. Even the *Wall Street Journal* praised the approach as
"so appealing and so sane that only the most unreasonable critics could
object to it." But the North viewed the proposal as a "trick." There were
other complications in the negotiations, resulting in a continuation of
the war.

Prior to the operation, a MACV intelligence team had pieced together a picture of the strength of the NVA in Laos. First, it concluded,
the NVA maintained two large logistic base camp areas along the Ho Chi
Minh Trail—"611" to the south and ten thousand meters from Highway
QL-9 inside Laos; and "604" northwest of QL-9 and completely inside
Laos. The NVA used the Xe Pon River and the Namxe Samou River and
their tributaries as major infiltration routes to the two bases. Second,
there were three NVA battle-tested infantry regiments in the area and
twenty antiaircraft battalions—a total of 22,000 enemy troops. In addition, within two weeks, eight NVA Main Force infantry regiments and
artillery could move into the objective area. Third, from "604" the NVA
could fire 122mm and 130mm artillery against Khe Sanh. And fourth,
the objectives of the NVA were to interdict and sever QL-9 and bombard
Khe Sanh and other U.S. forward bases with artillery from Laos. The operational area of Lam Son 719 was about thirty-five by sixty kilometers.

On 23 December 1970, President Nixon approved a plan to use
ARVN ground forces, supported by U.S. air and artillery, to cut the Ho
Chi Minh trail by an incursion into Laos. General Abrams, COMUS-

MACV, proposed a "bold and risky plan of four phases," wrote Lt. Gen. Phillip B. Davidson, in *Vietnam at War.* "In Phase I (to start on 30 January), U.S. troops along the DMZ would clear the area to the Vietnam/Laos border and reactivate Khe Sanh as a base of operations. In Phase II, ARVN would launch a three-pronged assault from South Vietnam astride Highway 9 to Tchepone. The central column, consisting of the ARVN Airborne Division reinforced by the 1st Armored Brigade, would attack down Highway 9 by heliborne assault and ground movement to A Luoi. From there, the airborne division would air-assault into Tchepone while the armored brigade attacked overland."

The XXIV Corps, now under Lt. Gen. James W. Sutherland, would support the ARVN attack by helicopter lifts, air strikes, and artillery from South Vietnam. Critical to the success of the operation was the fact that the U.S. advisors, artillery FOs, and air controllers could not accompany their ARVN units across the border. Coordination between U.S. and ARVN thus became difficult and extremely detrimental to the success of the operation.

General Sutherland gave to Maj. Gen. Thomas M. Tarpley, now the commander of the 101st Airborne Division (Air Mobile), the mission of providing support and assistance to the U.S. and ARVN forces participating in Lam Son 719 in western Quang Tri Province and in Laos. He also assigned the 101st two other missions: the operational and security responsibility of the areas along the DMZ previously covered by the 1st ARVN Division, and the conduct of diversionary operations from the Hue area into the A Shau Valley along Route 547.

The 101st's "support mission" included the key role of aviation support to the ARVN forces. One of the key U.S. commanders during Lam Son 719 thus became Brig. Gen. Sidney B. Berry Jr., the ADC of the 101st. He commanded an aviation task force built around the structure of the 101st, supplemented with aviation and air cavalry troops from other divisions, the 1st Aviation Brigade, and from units scheduled for deactivation or redeployment.

The 101st began Operation Dewey Canyon II, its part in Lam Son 719, on 30 January when the 3d Brigade of the 101st, led by the Rakkasans, combat-assaulted into an area four miles southeast of Khe Sanh to secure Firebase Sheppard and, by "search and clear operations" in their AO, support the ARVN forces who would assault into Laos. This action marked the first return of Allies into this portion of western Quang Tri Province since the monsoons of 1970. After 3/187th secured the area, division engineers came in to rebuild and prepare the "battered fortress of Khe Sanh for a staging base."

During the first few weeks of February, the Rakkasans patrolled their area, searched for the enemy and his installations, found numerous bunkers and evidence of heavy NVA traffic in the area, and took a number of KIAs and WIAs. On 8 February, the Rakkasans found a huge bunker complex with thirty-seven new bunkers and considerable amounts of NVA gear. On 14 February, B Company found thirteen more bunkers. In this action, two men, Sp4 John M. Howell and Pfc. Richard B. Rinehart, were killed by heavy small-arms fire.

On 11 February, the 4th Battalion, 3d Infantry, 23d Division (shortly to be commanded by a former Korean Rakkasan, Maj. Gen. Fritz Kroesen), air-assaulted from the Vandergrift helipad to the "Rockpile," a critical, jungle-covered mountain adjacent to Khe Sanh and Route 9. The area was infested with NVA, who attacked the U.S. mechanized light infantry company already in the area. To reinforce that unit, 4/3d landed on a "hot" LZ and lost two helicopters to enemy fire. Over the next seven days, 4/3d was mauled by NVA mortar and artillery fire, nightly sapper attacks, and small-arms fire.

On 18 February, 3/187th air-assaulted into the Rockpile to replace 4/3d. A recon force went into the area first, landing below the mountain. Then Capt. Thomas A. Rogers landed his C Company on top of the Rockpile amid heavy mortar fire. The company helped 4/3d recover its KIAs and evacuate its wounded while putting suppressive fires around the hill's perimeter. During one NVA artillery attack, Maj. Ronald D. Scharnberg, the Rakkasan S3, was hit by shrapnel and evacuated. Unfortunately, he would return in a few days. Four other Rakassans from C Company were wounded. Rogers and his men called the Rockpile "Purple Heart Hill." Later on the eighteenth, Capt. Charles Matts landed his B Company just to the north of Purple Heart Hill. In that action, Sp4 Wade H. Rollins was KIA. That night, the NVA probed B Company's NDP and hit the recon platoon with a mortar barrage. The next day, Capt. Robert W. Edwards Jr. brought his D Company onto Purple Heart Hill to relieve C Company.

The Rakkasans continued to suffer casualties from the NVA probes and mortar and artillery fire. On the 20th, C Company and the battalion CP were hit by "incoming." Sp4 Edward F. Downey was KIA and twenty other Rakkasans were wounded.

On the twenty-sixth, Colonel Sutton moved his Rakkasan CP to Ca Lu, an abandoned forward base named Vandergrift, an FB last held by the Marines in 1968. In the AO, Capt. John M. Bobadilla's A Company found fifty enemy bunkers, including a mess hall, hospital, and 1,800 pounds of rice. On the twenty-seventh, A Company found an adjoining portion of the bunker complex it had found the previous day. In the complex, the company found another 2,400 pounds of rice, and a large supply of ammunition. A Company destroyed the complex with 800 pounds of demolitions. In early March, D Company found eighty-nine bunkers in three complexes and more rice and mortar rounds and rockets. On the sixth, B Company also found a series of bunkers and stockpiles of supplies.

The Rakkasans lost its commander, Lt. Col. Bryan J. Sutton, and its S3, Maj. Ronald D. Scharnberg, on 17 March when, for causes unknown, their observation helicopter crashed west of Khe Sanh. Colonel Sutton was replaced by Lt. Col. James R. Steverson, from the 1st Brigade, 5th Mechanized Infantry; Major Scharnberg's replacement was Maj. Chester Garret. The battalion received a new mission: A Company remained in the AO while the remainder of the battalion moved to begin operations in AO Panther, located west of Khe Sanh on the Laotian border.

The 1st Platoon of C Company was patrolling northwest of Khe Sanh on 22 March and uncovered four bunkers, each with front and rear entrances. That night, twenty to twenty-five NVA attacked the platoon's NDP with grenades and small arms and overran it. The platoon recovered and, in hand-to-hand combat, drove off the enemy. At 0200 and 0300, the NVA hit C Company again. At dawn, the enemy blasted the perimeter with satchel charges. Helicopter gunships drove off the enemy. A sweep in the morning found seven dead NVA, but C Company suffered the loss of five troopers: Pfc. Roger Stahl, Pfc. William S. Glenn, Pfc. John W. McLemore, Pfc. Reginald Abernathy, and Sp4 William H. Fells.

By 1 April, the Rakkasans' part in Lam Son 719 was drawing to a close. Colonel Steverson moved his CP from Khe Sanh to Hill 492 in preparation to closing the bases. The ARVN units involved in Lam Son 719 were moving back across the border from Laos.

Was Lam Son 719 a success? On the U.S. side, the total helicopter loss was 107 aircraft—an extremely large number. But, according to Lt. Gen. John Tolson in *Air Mobility, 1961–1971,* "Lam Son 719 would never have been undertaken, much less successfully completed, without the support of thousands of helicopter sorties. And for every thousand sorties, the loss rate was only one quarter of one percent. Granted, every helicopter loss was regrettable; however, this ratio does show a very high rate of accomplishment versus attrition."

During their operations in support of Lam Son 719, the Rakkasans secured Highway QL-9 and the Khe Sanh base, the vital pipeline of supply and the route of advance for ARVN forces into Laos. They were the first unit of the 101st into Khe Sanh and the last ones out. They succeeded in disrupting the NVA supply routes over a two-month period and destroyed base areas and great quantities of food, medical, and combat supplies. But the operation cost the Rakkassans dearly: nineteen men killed and forty-nine wounded in action. On 7 April, 3/187th returned to Camp Evans.

The drawdown of U.S. forces in Vietnam continued in 1971. The 1st Infantry Division returned to Fort Riley, Kansas; the 25th Division returned to Schofield Barracks in Hawaii; the 199th Light Infantry Brigade returned to Fort Benning; the 1st Brigade of the 9th Division returned to Fort Lewis, Washington; the 7th and 26th Marines moved to Panama; the 173d Airborne Brigade, the first combat unit into Vietnam in 1965, returned to Fort Campbell for deactivation. Later, many of its troopers would become Rakkasans.

From 7 April until 3 August, 3/187th resumed Operation Jefferson Glen, concentrating on operation in the lowlands in Phong Diem District of Thua Thien Province, to deny NVA access to the populated areas stretching from Highway QL-1 to the South China Sea. The Rakkasans also had the mission of upgrading the regional forces in the district. To do so, Colonel Steverson cross-attached two of his companies with the RF companies and thereafter formed combined U.S.-Vietnamese teams down to the squad level. Each RF company cycled through the training for a two-week period. The training was so effective that eventually RF companies operated in the Rakkasan area of operations with U.S. advisors.

On 27 April an oddity of the Vietnam war struck home to the 2d Platoon of Capt. Charles W. Lykins's A Company. On two occasions, men of the 2d Platoon spotted some VC, armed with M16s, in the open. Because of a lack of "political clearance," the men were forbidden to fire. Later, on 9 May, Sp4 Lawrence R. Dance, D Company, was hit by a sniper. He died six days later.

On 10 May, Capt. Harry D. Grace's B Company came under the opcon of 2/506th Infantry for what was supposed to be a three-day raid, the last U.S. incursion along the west border of the A Shau Valley. Contact during the operation was infrequent, but throughout the next forty-one—not three—days, the teams found large quantities of NVA supplies in hundreds of NVA bunker complexes. One complex of ninety-eight bunkers included woven-fiber sleeping pallets, pit latrines, tree-shaded patios complete with hand-built tables and benches, and a thirty-seat classroom with instructors' platforms. The U.S. Air Force later bombed and destroyed much of the NVA bases. On 23 June, Grace brought his company back to Camp Evans.

The Rakkasans continued to take losses in their area sweeps. On 28 May, Sp4 Donald R. Mathis, A Company, and on 3 June, Pfc. Jose A. Sanchez, B Company, were killed. On 9 June, D Company uncovered two NVA bunkers. "They were constructed so as to be protected from artillery," wrote an army historian. "Some medical and culinary supplies were found, and preparations were being made to destroy them when, at 1024 hours, an 82mm HE pressure-type booby trap was detonated outside one of the bunkers, killing two U.S. soldiers, (Lt. Michael M. Dalton and Sp4 Steven K. Madsen) and wounding three." On the same day, 2nd Platoon had six men WIA when the platoon was hit by rocket-propelled grenades and small-arms fire.

On 29 July, 1/506th took over opcon of FSB [Forward Supply Base] Firestone, from which 3/187th had been operating. The Rakkasans returned to Camp Evans to prepare for yet another type of mission peculiar to the war in Vietnam.

On 4 August, Colonel Steverson received new orders: move to Cam Ranh Bay to replace 4/503d Infantry of the 173d brigade and conduct defensive operations in the "rocket belt" around the Cam Ranh Bay Peninsula. Over the next three days. Steverson moved his battalion by

C-130s six hundred miles to the south. Once there, the battalion picked up the 2/319th Artillery as its direct support artillery and began operations as an independent infantry combat team under the opcon of the Cam Ranh Bay Support Command.

Throughout the period and the AO, the Rakkasans encountered few sightings of the enemy as compared to the first months of 1971. However, on 25 August, the relative calm at Cam Ranh Bay was shattered when sappers crept into the area of the Tri-Service Ammunition Storage Area on the Cam Ranh Bay Peninsula and left delayed-action satchel charges on some stored explosives. The three tremendous explosions caused widespread damage to the ammo storage area, but fortunately, caused few casualties. One air force soldier and three Rakkasans from a recon team, three hundred meters from the blast, were wounded. Intelligence later confirmed that the sappers were from the K510 Sapper Battalion.

In late August, B, C, and D Companies, patrolling their areas on and near the "Rocket Belt" found and destroyed rocket sites. Sometime later, B Company discovered some rocket sites that were oriented toward the Bay area. In the evening of 14 September, Rakkasan Recon Team 5 made one of the strongest contacts during 3/187th's stay in Cam Ranh Bay. The team spotted four or five men moving about a hundred meters from its NDP. Shortly thereafter, the team was hit with small-arms fire. The team searched the area and found more enemy trying to close in. The team brought in artillery and gunships and scattered the NVA.

The Rakkasans not only swept their AOs but also built firebases to support their operations. From 2 September to 7 October, the Rakkasans plus D Company, 299th Engineer Battalion, and B Battery, 2/319th Artillery, constructed two firebases on "defensible terrain" from which they could support all AOs occupied by the defensive forces of the CRB Support Command. The forward bases were named Sutton and Scharnberg in honor of 3/187th's CO and S3. The well-built FBs, requiring land clearing, excavation, prefabrication, and equipment installation, became a model of FB construction for the ARVN forces. Between 4 and 7 October, the Rakkasans shuttled back to Camp Evans in C-130s to renew operations in their old AO [Area of Operations], now half the size.

One of the most memorable days in the Vietnamese story of the Rakassans was 20 November 1971 when Colonel Steverson received orders to pull out of his AO and prepare to redeploy the Rakkasans to the Land of the Big PX. On 21 November, he ordered all companies back to Camp Evans, where they turned in their combat gear.

Shortly thereafter, the Rakkasan color guard furled the battalion's colors, draped proudly with campaign streamers. Two were Vietnamese Cross of Gallantry Awards, one Meritorious Unit Award, two American Valorous Unit Awards, and one Civil Action Medal Award. There were also two Presidential Unit Citations embroidered "Trang Bang" and "Dong Ap Bia Mountain." The honor guard placed the furled colors on a plane bound for Fort Campbell, Kentucky. Silently noted and long remembered by the departing Rakkasans were their Vietnamese casualties: 239 killed in action and 615 wounded in battle. With the Nixon drawdown, the Rakkasans were going home.

# 12: Between the Wars

In late 1971 and early 1972, the 101st Airborne Division (Air Assault) completed its deployment from Vietnam—the last U.S. division to leave the troubled and increasingly embattled area. On 6 April 1972 at Fort Campbell, Kentucky, Vice President Spiro Agnew and Gen. William C. Westmoreland, the army chief of staff and the former commander of the 101st and former COMUSMACV, greeted the division on its official homecoming ceremony. The Rakkasans were represented by 3/187th, the only unit of the regiment in the division at the time. Over the next few years, the Rakkasans would swell and shrink, dependent upon the DA's mode and budget.

In post–Vietnam War days, the command structure of the Defense Department went through some significant changes that were designed to permit the rapid deployment of ready forces, of which the Rakkasans would become a part, to trouble spots around the world. In March of 1980, the Rapid Deployment Joint Task Force (RDJTF) came to life at MacDill Air Force Base in Florida. The staffers of the task force were army, navy, air force, and marines. The RDJTF has no troop units as such under its command in normal times. Its peacetime mission was to develop plans for the rapid deployment of joint forces to any emergency around the globe. On 1 January 1983, the U.S. Central Command, a four-star billet, replaced the RDJTF. Like the RDJTF, CENTCOM was a planning headquarters, responsible for joint operations in Southwest Asia and the Middle East, but with no troops under its command until an emergency arose and the Defense Department gave it orders to proceed. CENTCOM would later gain deserved fame under Gen. H. Norman Schwarzkopf in the Gulf War.

The U.S. XVIIIth Airborne Corps at Fort Bragg was the senior U.S. Army Command with affiliations to CENTCOM. And within XVIIIth Airborne Corps were the 82d and 101st Airborne Divisions. The 101st, of course, was the army's only air assault division—the 82d the army's only "airborne" division, capable of massive entry into combat by parachute.

During the eighteen years between its return from Vietnam and its commitment to the Gulf War, the 101st was a fully-manned air assault division, one of a kind in any army. A quick glance at its Table of Organization and Equipment (T O and E) reveals what looks like a standard U.S. Army division: three infantry brigades, a division artillery, and a four-battalion support command. But its difference is radical in its combat aviation brigade of some 450 helicopters divided into three assault helicopter battalions, two attack helicopter battalions, a medium assault battalion, a combat aviation battalion, and an air reconnaissance squadron. The 101st also has paratroopers: a company-sized long-range surveillance detachment and a sixty-man pathfinder detachment in the aviation brigade headquarters company.

In those eighteen years, the 101st went through reorganizations, trained in the air mobile concept, sent units to Europe in Reforger 76, deployed units near Cairo, Egypt, in Exercise Bright Star, assisted in the summer training of the National Guard and the Army Reserves, deployed battalions to the Sinai desert for six-month tours of duty with the Multinational Force and Observers (MFO), and dispatched units for training exercises throughout the United States and in Germany and Honduras. The Rakkasans took part in all of the exercises.

During 1983, the 187th Regiment took on new life. On 1 October, the Department of the Army reactivated the 1st and 2d Battalions of the 187th and assigned them to the 193d Infantry Brigade in Panama. The 1st Battalion was stationed at Fort Clayton, some 250 yards from the Panama Canal; the 2d Battalion was posted to Fort Kobbe, adjacent to Howard Air Force Base. Also on 1 October, the 4th Battalion of the 187th came to life at Fort Campbell. And over a year later, DA activated the 5th Battalion of the 187th and also assigned it to the 101st at Fort Campbell. In the recent annals of the army, the 187th must have been the only U.S. Army regiment with five concurrently active battalions. The three battalions of the 187th at Campbell were the elements of the 3d Brigade of the 101st.

In November of 1984, 2/187th at Fort Kobbe went on jump status. The two 187th battalions thus formed a unique rapid-reaction force in Panama—1/187th with its helicopter assault capability and 2/187th with its parachuting potential. The paratroopers of 2/187th frequently dropped onto the Gatun Drop Zone and routinely deployed to the Honduran and Panamanian jump schools in training exercises. Both battalions centered their training on the squad and platoon, using the

Empire Range complex for live-fire exercises and small-unit operations. The battalions also trained and maneuvered with the U.S. Army Jungle Warfare School and were often sent to Costa Rica, Peru, and Puerto Rico for training operations.

By 1987, though, the time had come again for DA to alter the structure of the army—and the 187th was no exception. DA deactivated the 1st and 2d Battalions in Panama and redesignated the 4th and 5th Battalions at Campbell as the 1st and 2d. Thus, the 3d Brigade of the 101st was now composed of the 1st, 2d, and 3d Battalions of the 187th Infantry Regiment—not paratroopers but air mobile troops or "air assaulters."

One of the many missions of the 101st was to send battalions for six-month tours into the Sinai Peninsula to monitor the terms of the peace treaty signed by President Anwar Sadat of Egypt and Prime Minister Menachem Begin of Israel at Camp David on 26 March 1979. The treaty was brokered by President Jimmy Carter in an effort to halt the skirmishes after the Yom Kippur War of 1973 between the Egyptian forces and the occupying Israelis. The terms of the treaty required the signatories to request that the UN assemble and deploy a peacekeeping force in the Sinai to observe the Israeli withdrawal. In July 1979, the Charter of the UN Emergency Force, which had been monitoring the Israeli withdrawal from the Sinai, expired. From July 1979 until August 1981, a U.S. field mission observed the provisions of the treaty. Then, on 3 August 1981, Egypt and Israel signed a protocol to the peace treaty that created a Multinational Force and Observers (MFO) to monitor both nations' compliance with the terms of the treaty. On 25 April 1982, the MFO began operations and the Israelis withdrew the last of their troops from the Sinai.

The MFO is a rotating peacekeeping observer force of three battalions: one each from Colombia, Fiji, and the U.S. The MFO mission is to observe, report, and verify that Egypt and Israel comply with the troop and equipment restrictions within their area of operations.

In early April 1989, 1/187th was relieved of its MFO mission in the Sinai by TF 3/9th Infantry from Fort Ord, California. On 12 April 1989, 1/187th completed its redeployment to Fort Campbell and began an intense training period to hone its primary skills as an air assault infantry battalion.

But by the summer of 1990, across the world in an area known to few Rakkasans, an arrogant dictator was forcing his unwanted attention in the form of massive armored forces on a small, almost militarily undefended but oil-rich neighbor in the Middle East. The tempers of the peacekeeping nations of the world grew short. On Sunday afternoon, 5 August 1990, the leader of one of those nations, President George S. Bush, said of Iraq's invasion of Kuwait, "This will not stand. This will not stand, this aggression against Kuwait."

The Rakkasans' next clash with its destiny was about to begin.

# DESERT STORM

# 13: The Outbreak of the Persian Gulf War

In late July 1990, Saddam Hussein, the dictator of Iraq, had been assembling his forces along the Iraqi-Kuwaiti border. This massing of armored forces, including his elite Republican Guards, had not gone undetected by the U.S. intelligence agencies. Shortly before the invasion, a U.S. KH-11 spy satellite had tracked the massing of Saddam's armor almost tank by tank. In a few days prior to launching his attack, he had tripled his forces on the border to over one hundred thousand men. Satellite photos picked up the buildup and his logistics trains to the rear of the front-line forces, an almost certain sign of an imminent invasion across the border.

Saddam's motive was cash. Iraq's eight-year war with Iran had cost Saddam $80 billion. He saw a simple solution to his desperate money problem: seize the vast oil supplies of Kuwait, the super-rich, lightly defended, tiny neighbor to his southeast. And if that were a success, the oil of Saudi Arabia might also be his for the taking. Then he would be afloat in U.S. dollars.

Saddam blamed the United States for a lot of his problems. At a meeting of the Arab Cooperation Council in Amman on 24 February 1990, he claimed that the U.S. was the culprit in the problems of the region, that the U.S. wanted to dominate the Gulf, build up Israel, and humiliate the Arabs, who could no longer look to the deteriorating USSR for backing. At the Council, he ranted and raved against the U.S. naval forces in the Gulf and pleaded with his Arab cohorts to weaken the pro-Israeli American influence in the area.

Even though Saddam had a hundred thousand troops massed on Kuwait's border, Washington was still not convinced that an invasion was either impending or probable. One distraction had been talks between President Bush and Hosni Mubarak, the president of Egypt, and between President Bush and King Hussein of Jordan. Each man had assured President Bush that Iraq would not invade, that Saddam would negotiate with Kuwait. But by the evening of 1 August 1990, Saddam had completed massing on his border with Kuwait the hundred thousand troops, amply supported by tanks, APCs [armored personnel carriers], artillery, logistics, and communications. Saddam outnumbered the forces of Kuwait by five to one.

As late as the afternoon of 1 August, Iraqi Ambassador Mohammad al-Mashat, in a meeting with Assistant Secretary of State for Near Eastern and South Asian Affairs John Kelly, said, "You don't need to worry. We are not going to move against anybody."

One man who did not believe that lie was retired Army Col. Walter P. "Pat" Lang Jr., a former defense attaché in Saudi Arabia and now a Middle East and South Asia intelligence analyst in the Defense Intelligence Agency. During Saddam's buildup, he had meticulously analyzed raw intelligence data and had carefully plotted the movement of Saddam's forces from the very beginning of the buildup. On Monday, 30 July, he had reported to his boss, Lt. Gen. Harry E. Royster, that Iraqi artillery, aircraft, and logistics were on the move and added, "I do not believe he is bluffing. I have looked at his personality profile. He doesn't know how to bluff."

At about 0600, on Wednesday, 1 August, Lang arrived in his Pentagon office. His night staff showed him the latest photos of the Iraqi troop movements along the Kuwaiti border. He saw a portrait of a corps-sized armored force obviously deployed for an assault. Three Iraqi armored divisions had spread out in an attack posture, with tanks fifty to seventy-five yards apart, within three miles of the Kuwaiti border. The "Hammurabi" and "In God We Trust" Divisions had moved near the main, six-lane highway leading directly into Kuwait City, thirty-seven air miles away. The "Medina Luminous" Division was on line to the west. Some eighty helicopters were positioned close to the border. Lang flashed his estimate: The Iraqis will attack on the night of 1 August or early the next morning.

Other U.S. intelligence agencies were not that certain. The CIA, the Defense Intelligence Agency, and the State Department Bureau of Intelligence and Research had been predicting: (a) that Saddam was bluffing or (b) that he would seize only the islands of Warba and Bubiyan and a part of the disputed Rumaila oil fields that abut Iraq and Kuwait and then withdraw the bulk of his forces.

That afternoon, Schwarzkopf briefed the Joint Chiefs and secretary of defense, Richard Cheney, in the Pentagon "Tank," a secure briefing and conference room. In his briefing, he concluded that Saddam had a number of "courses of action" with his hundred thousand troops, to include the invasion of Kuwait. Schwarzkopf, at the time, did not so predict.

Schwarzkopf also summarized his contingency plan—Operations Plan 90-1002—loosely referred to as "ten-oh-two"—an old plan developed in the early eighties. The plan required a thirty-day advance notice to begin troop movement to the area; it was not until Day 27 that tanks would move into the area, and "ten-oh-two" would take three to four months to build up a force of a hundred thousand troops. The meeting ended with no specific decision, even though General Powell was leaning toward the "invasion option" and felt that the administration should take some positive steps.

At 0200 on the second of August, the tanks of Saddam's Republican Guards swarmed across the border of Kuwait, past the customs building and a gas station at Abdali, and roared down the six-lane highway toward Kuwait City, some eighty miles away. Three and a half hours later, Saddam's tanks were in Kuwait City. As the tanks circled the royal palace, the emir loaded his family onto his helicopter and flew off to a preplanned safe haven in Saudi Arabia. By nightfall of 2 August, all of the Emirate of Kuwait and its two million people were under the control of the Iraqi armed forces. The plunder and the rape of Kuwait had begun.

After a series of meetings with his national security advisors and, later, on the morning of 4 August at a meeting at Camp David, President Bush became convinced of the need to send a large U.S. forces to Saudi Arabia. General Powell insisted that whether the mission was to defend Saudi Arabia or drive the Iraqis out of Kuwait, the U.S. must send enough forces "to do the job" rapidly. After lengthy discussions with King Fahd Ibn Abdul Aziz, his brother, and members of the government, it was agreed that U.S. troops could deploy to Saudi Arabia provided (a) that they would leave as soon as the threat to Saudi Arabia was over and (b) that the U.S. would not launch a war without the king's approval. Thus began the buildup for the Gulf War.

On 7 August, the Pentagon alerted the first U.S. units for deployment. Two squadrons of F-15 Eagles, forty-eight aircraft, from Langley Air Force Base in Virginia received orders to move to airfields near Riyadh and Dhahran. Deployed in the giant C5As of the First Tactical Wing was the Division Ready Brigade of the 82d Airborne Division, some 2,300 soldiers, later dubbed "the trip wire" or the "bump in the road." The brigade, plus staff elements from XVIIIth Airborne Corps, arrived on

8 and 9 August and were the first U.S. ground troops to arrive in Saudi Arabia. The first U.S. soldier, a member of the 82d, was on the ground in Saudi Arabia within thirty-one hours of the time the 82d CO, Maj. Gen. James H. Johnson Jr., had received the initial alert.

The summer of 1990 at Fort Campbell was a time of intensified training and numerous commitments in support of the National Guard, the Reserves, and the cadets at West Point. "It was business as usual," said Brig. Gen. Henry H. "Hugh" Shelton, the assistant division commander of the 101st. "A very busy time frame."

Lieutenant Colonel Andy Berdy and his 2/187th Rakkasans were at the Jungle Operations Training Center in Panama undergoing an intensive period of training in the heat and humidity of Panama's jungles. Lieutenant Colonel Gary Bridges had his 3/327th at West Point's basic training site, Camp Natural Bridge, about ten miles from the West Point campus, where Bridges and his men trained some 1,200 cadets of the class of 1993 in "soldier" skills—rifle marksmanship, infantry-squad tactics, artillery-crew drills, map reading, patrolling, and weapons identification. Lieutenant Colonel Joe Chesley was preparing his 2/502d for a six months' deployment to the Sinai as part of the MFO. Other units were at Fort Knox, Fort Bragg, and one group from 3/101st Aviation Brigade was assisting a U.S. Reserve unit during its summer training at Gagetown, Canada.

One of the most significant training exercises that summer was a CENTCOM-sponsored CPX [command post exercise], "Internal Look," at Fort Bragg from 23 to 29 July. It was significant because the scenario of the CPX, developed by CENTCOM commander and his staff, was fortunately based on an imagined hostile Iraqi raid into Saudi Arabia. The staffs of XVIIIth Airborne Corps, the 82d and 101st Airborne Divisions, and the 7th Light Infantry Division set up their tents, communications, and computers in the woods at Fort Bragg. The CENTCOM staff "hunched over their terminals at Eglin Air Force Base in the Florida panhandle." Other units taking part were Headquarters, Third U.S. Army, and marine and navy commands. The exercise provided the 101st Division staff and other participants with a look at the entire Persian Gulf region, particularly the geography of Saudi Arabia, with which the 101st and the Rakkasans would become painfully familiar in a few short weeks. Of the exercise, General Schwarzkopf wrote in *It Doesn't Take a*

*Hero,* "I spent the week uneasily, with one foot in the realm of the exercise and the other in the realm of fact, where the real crisis had started to build."

"When the word came to deploy," wrote the division historian, Capt. Ida M. McGrath, "it seemed that every sinew and fiber at the installation began to perform its individual function with an end result of a tremendously effective and smooth deployment for the force."

The first and most important necessity was to reassemble the division at Fort Campbell. Lieutenant Colonel Berdy, for example, brought his 2/187th Task Force back from the Jungle Training Center in Panama by C-141s, C-5s, and commercial air as soon as the 3d Brigade (the 187th Infantry) commander, Colonel John MacDonald, alerted him.

Besides reassembling his division from far-flung summer commitments, Gen. J. H. Binford Peay had also to fill up the division. When he was alerted to move out, the division was at 86 percent Table of Organization and Equipment strength. Two weeks later, fillers of all ranks, not just privates and pfcs., began to arrive at Fort Campbell and had to be trained and assimilated into the ranks.

In preparation for the deployment, the commanders in the 187th briefed their troops on the rules of engagement and some facts on the culture of Saudi Arabia—basic dos and don'ts. The Rakkasans learned early on that alcohol in any form was strictly forbidden and that women play a far different role in Saudi Arabian life than do the women in the U.S. One advantage enjoyed by the 101st was that for a number of years the division had focused on that part of the globe. "Our division had a Southwest Asia focus as one of our many war plans that we have," General Peay said. "So over a number of years we have trained for the high intensity of the Southwest Asia environment."

While they waited to deploy, Colonel MacDonald had his brigade and battalion staffs war-game possible Saudi/Iraq/Kuwait situations using maps, aerial photos, satellite photos, and intelligence updated from such sources as the G2 of XVIIIth Airborne Corps and some even from CNN. The commanders and staffs tried from all sources to paint a portrait of the Iraqi war machine, its morale, its weapons, its tactics in the Iran-Iraqi War, its training under the Soviets, and its potential for using chemical weapons.

By the tenth of August, 101st Headquarters was beginning to receive the airflow data. "That was when we realized this was 'no kidding—we're going to war,' once that airflow started coming in," remembered Hugh Shelton.

The first two aircraft to depart Fort Campbell were C-5s carrying six Apache helicopters each; General Shelton; Col. Tom Garrett, the Aviation Brigade commander; Lt. Col. Dick Cody, the Apache Battalion commander; and 144 soldiers. The planes left at 0500 on the seventeenth and landed at Dhahran Airport at noon on the eighteenth. The temperature was 128 degrees. "When I walked off the airplane," remembered Shelton, "I'll be very frank. When I got off I thought I was standing in an engine backwash. As I walked across the ramp, Major Huber met me on the ramp, and, as I walked away from the plane, I noticed that the backwash did not go away."

Back at Campbell, the preparations for the deployment of the 101st were in a "full court press" mode.

### Deployment from Fort Campbell

Once Gen. Edwin Burba, commander of Forces Command (FORSCOM), at Fort McPherson, Georgia, had told General Shelton, "You guys are going," General Peay and his division staff were bombarded with phone calls, directives, air and ship flow data, and visits by staff officers from higher headquarters with yet more information and advice.

As the plan grew clearer in the 101st command post, it became obvious to General Peay that (a) he was going to deploy his entire division and (b) he would have to send most of his troops by air and the bulk of his equipment by sea. His staff sorted out who and what would go by which means. General Peay and his staff shortly realized that higher headquarters was giving him enough airflow to send out his Division Ready brigade and his aviation brigade by air and that the bulk of his troops would fly on commercial aircraft and that the rest of the division's equipment would go by ship.

The 101st's Emergency Operations Center (EOC), set up in the basement of Building T95 at Fort Campbell, two blocks from the division CP, became the hub for the deployment. It became operational at noon on the seventh of August and remained in operation twenty-four hours per day. Staffers from the 101st general and special staff sections manned the EOC. "For the next several weeks," wrote Captain McGrath, "these people working together would push out thousands of personnel, tons of equipment and supplies, and manage to do so pretty smoothly."

Within a few days, Colonel McDonald, the Rakkasan commander, moved his troops and their vehicles to the ready line to prepare them for shipment. "Trucks, engineer equipment, weapons systems, and people were everywhere," wrote Captain McGrath. "Relatives started coming in to see their loved ones because many thought that the division would be gone in a week. Satellite dishes from local and national networks established themselves across the street from Gate 4. At any time, people expected the units to depart for Saudi Arabia. The PX and commissary were swamped as soldiers did their last-minute shopping. The auto shops were busy as spouses did tune-ups and maintenance checks on their POVs [privately owned vehicles]. Local restaurants did a booming business due to the influx of people in the area. Both Clarksville and Hopkinsville saw an increase in the issuance of wedding licenses."

At 1930 on the thirteenth, the Military Traffic Management Command (MTMC) notified the EOC that two ships, the first of ten, the *American Eagle* and the *Cape Lobos,* were available for loading on the seventeenth at Blount Island Terminal in Jacksonville, Florida. The first movement of troops from Campbell started at 0700 on the fifteenth, where a large convoy of vehicles from the 187th started out on the 787-mile trip to Jacksonville. "There were 650 vehicles in all," wrote Maj. Jerry Bolzak. "The Rakkasans involved in the convoy will never forget the trip. Literally thousands of our fellow citizens turned out along the highway to wish us well. Hundreds of flags lined the route.

"The Rakkasans were cheered as they drove past. Banners proclaimed, GOD BLESS YOU, WE LOVE YOU, AND KICK BUTT. At one rest stop, children sang 'God Bless America' to a Rakkasan soldier. . . .

"The Rakkasan advance party finally flew away from Fort Campbell on 8 September 1990, followed by the main body on the eleventh. En route to Saudi Arabia, part of the main body was delayed in the United Kingdom and spent a day at Greenham Common—where other 101st soldiers waited for their 'Rendezvous with Destiny' almost fifty years ago."

First Lieutenant Joe Nadolski, Headquarters and Headquarters Company, 2/187th, wrote that "he and his men departed Fort Campbell, Kentucky, on a Northwest Airline 747 bound for Dhahran International Airport in Saudi Arabia. The flight crews were great to us. My troops were cold. I asked for blankets and newspapers. Our flight crews changed at New York, and at Rhein Main, Germany. We arrived at Dhahran on 12 September."

The landing in Dhahran was traumatic for the Rakkasans. One soldier recorded his initial reaction: "When the C-5A came to a halt on the airfield at Dhahran, soldiers gathered their weapons and personal gear and began the long climb down the ladders and to the front of the aircraft. As the huge nose of the aircraft slowly lifted toward the sky, soldiers began to experience the heat.

"As the forces rapidly moved from the plane and secured their rucksacks, they began to search for sunglasses to protect against the brightness of the sun. Soldiers then strapped on their rucks and began a half-mile road march to some very large tents to await transportation.

"Even for the well-conditioned soldiers, the march was torture and uniforms were soaked with sweat when the march had ended. Boxes of water were consumed before the buses finally arrived. The plastic bottles were everywhere and no soldier went anywhere without them.

"The ride to King Fahd Airport (thirty-five miles north of Dhahran) was torture and a mad rush to the latrines by a newly arriving busload of soldiers was a common sight. The next twenty-four hours for soldiers was spent in the parking garage on a cot on an air mattress simply drinking water. The aviation brigade troops bunked in the parking ramp for the duration because the ramp was close to where their aircraft were based."

The airlift deployment of the Rakkasans involved the flight of 13,500 men in C-5As, C-141s, 747s, and L1011s along various routes that traversed the air lanes from Campbell Army Air Field to Gander, Newfoundland, to Paris, to Cairo, and to Dhahran during the period 18 August to 25 September. The sealift from Jacksonville to the Suez Canal to the Red Sea to the Strait of Hormuz to the Persian Gulf started on 19 August. The ten ships in the sealift included ROROs (Roll On Roll Off) and LASHs (Lighter Aboard Ships) and carried 296 helicopters, 650 vehicles, 40 Conex containers, a total of 5,258 pieces of equipment. The equipment was moved to the port of Ad Dammam in 46 days. On the sixth of October, the 101st became the first division to totally close in Saudi Arabia.

Since his arrival in Saudi Arabia, General Shelton and a skeleton staff had been preparing for the arrival of the division. After a great deal of negotiations with other U.S. commanders, General Shelton found space at the only partially complete King Fahd Airport and, with the division's 326th Engineer Battalion, prepared a camp for housing (rather, "tenting") the division troops. Camp Eagle II was the result.

Camp Eagle II was a two-by-three-mile array of five thousand tents completely surrounded by sand dunes. One soldier said that "Camp Eagle II resembled nothing so much as a Civil War era's massive fields of white tents." Shelton and his engineers built the camp on a hardstand so tough that the engineers had to use large power drills to dig holes for tent stakes or drive them in with sledgehammers. Each 187th battalion area was a rectangle of tents, accurately lined up in rows of double tents surrounded by sandbagged walls half as high as the sides of the tents. The troops filled millions of sandbags for the walls. Latrines and showers bordered the ends of the streets between battalion areas. Hundreds of rolls of concertina wire encircled the camp area.

One of the troopers said that eventually the camp became "a first-class installation" but "never let it be said that Camp Eagle II was a nice place to live or even visit. Mosquitoes, sand vipers, scorpions, and spiders also shared the camp. The heat was miserable, and the dust got into everything. The laundry service was superior to washing your own clothes in a bucket if you didn't mind getting back some other soldier's underwear."

By late September, the deployment of the division was complete and the 101st was established and operational at Camp Eagle II. General Peay was now faced with the tactical phase of his reason for being in the desert of Saudi Arabia.

"The 101st Airborne Division (Air Assault) is a unique division—the only one of its kind in existence," I wrote in *Lightning: The 101st in the Gulf War.* "Other units may use helicopters to transport some of their units into relatively secure areas, and after the insertion of the ground troops, the helicopters depart the area and the infantrymen move out of the landing zone. This is the 'Air Mobility' concept, essentially the movement of troops and equipment by helicopter from one secure area to another.

"The Air Assault Division, on the other hand, totally merges and integrates its ground and aviation units and can land mission-tailored combat forces directly onto an objective or into the main battle area, under hostile conditions. The division conducts combat operations at a high tempo and has firepower intensity with, in addition to its organic artillery battalions, two attack helicopter battalions and an air cavalry squadron."

Basically, General Peay had at his disposal, for direct action, nine infantry battalions, and 330 helicopters included in three assault battalions with UH-60 Blackhawks; two attack battalions with AH-64 Apaches and OH-58C Kiowa Scouts; a medium battalion with CH-47D Chinooks; a command aviation battalion with UH-1 Hueys; an air recon Squadron armed with AH-1F Cobras and OH-58C Kiowas; and the attached 2/229th Aviation Regiment equipped with Apaches, Kiowas, and Blackhawks.

Forces continued to build up in-country. Much to the surprise of a number of U.S. high-level planners and intelligence experts, Saddam had not ventured out of Kuwait even when his only significant U.S. opposition was the 2,300-man Ready Brigade of the 82d—known among the troops as the desert "speed bump."

Schwarzkopf was taking this time to plan the deployment of his forces, increasing significantly daily. Initially, his forces were thin and he was faced with covering and defending vast areas of desert with lightly armed airborne and air assault troops against an overwhelming force equipped with thousands of heavy tanks, APCs, and scores of artillery pieces. The Scud and chemical warfare potentials were ever-present threats that compounded the defensive posture of the Allied forces. But more and more U.S. and Allied forces arrived daily.

Egypt sent its 15,000-man 4th Infantry Division; Saudi Arabia had 67,000 soldiers on the ground; England sent the 6,000-man 7th Armored Brigade; Syria sent 4,000 men and agreed to send an additional 10,000 men and 300 tanks; France deployed 13,000 soldiers. By 25 September, over 150,000 U.S. troops, including the 101st, the 82d, and the 24th Infantry Division plus marines, air force, Special Forces, rangers, and navy Seal teams were on the Saudi desert floor. Many more were yet to come. General Powell felt that if the U.S. took on the mission, it should have ample forces to get the job done with minimum casualties. That meant massing overwhelming forces.

The 101st and the Rakkasans continued to train and await their mission. It would come shortly.

# 14: Covering Force Mission—Desert Shield

General Schwarzkopf and his CENTCOM planners were faced with the dilemma that confronts every commander in every war and battle: What is the enemy going to do? Where? When? How? What will I do? CENTCOM did know that Saddam's land forces consisted of 900,000 men in sixty-three divisions, only eight of which were the elite Republican Guards. But, nonetheless, Saddam did have 5,747 tanks, 1,072 of which were Soviet T-72s, most of which were in Kuwait. He also had 10,000 light armored vehicles, about 3,500 artillery pieces, and 3,000 heavy equipment transporters for moving tanks. Schwarzkopf had concluded early on, and so briefed the president at a Camp David meeting on the morning of 4 August, that "we would not have to worry about the air force after a fairly short period. The navy's not a problem." He summed up by saying that the Iraqi strengths were obviously the size of their land force and their chemical weapons, which they had used in the Iran-Iraq War and in 1988 against some of their own citizens, Kurdish rebels in northern Iraq. But his ground forces were a definite threat and could be launched into Saudi Arabia at any moment.

General Peay arrived at King Fahd airport on 29 August and immediately went to XVIIIth Airborne Corps headquarters at Dragon City between Dhahran and the airport. He met with Lt. Gen. Gary Luck, the corps commander, and Brig. Gen. Ed Scholes, his chief of staff. Luck already had the corps mission: "On order, establish a defense in sector to defeat attacking Iraqi forces; defend approaches and critical oil facilities vicinity Abqaiq–al-Hufuf; defend the approaches to Ad Dammam-Dhahran enclave; ensure the integrity of MARCENT'S (Marine Central Command) western flank and facilitate transition to offensive operations."

Before President Bush ordered the second buildup of forces in late October, the major army unit in theater was the XVIIIth Airborne Corps composed of the 82d Airborne Division, the 24th Mechanized Division, the 3d Armored Cavalry Regiment, the 12th Combat Aviation Brigade, the 101st Airborne Division, and the 1st Cavalry Division, which had closed in theater on 22 October.

General Luck gave General Peay his mission. In field manual militarese: "101st conducts covering force operations in sector; provides helicopter support and fire support to eastern province area command forces to disrupt and delay Iraqi forces, and assists in passage of lines of EPAC (Eastern Province Area Command) forces; on order, guards in sector to protect the western flank of XVIII Airborne Corps and provides a brigade to the XVIII Airborne Corps as theater reserve for contingency operations; prepares for and conducts future operations as required." General Peay met with General Schwarzkopf shortly after he arrived in theater. "I think I saw General Schwarzkopf within a week to ten days, as I recall, after closing into country," he remembered. "I conducted some initial briefings with him, he passed on some of his early-on concepts, because our division was given the covering force mission, which I thought was one of the great missions to have early on in terms of learning, adapting to the desert, the harshness of it, and the ability then to refine our operating procedures and work with distances, and to work with other forces during that maturation period, that, I think, was very valuable in the Desert Storm part of it."

The development of the initial mission for the 101st flowed down the chain. "General Schwarzkopf and his staff laid out the initial mission," General Peay said. "General Luck then took that mission and developed the corps plan. . . . Internal to the mission given the 101st, we developed our plan within the corps commander's intent." The plan to defend Saudi Arabia, the covering force mission, took shape. It was called "Desert Shield."

For his covering force mission, General Peay had a number of potent attachments: the 3d Armored Cavalry Regiment from Fort Bliss with 123 Abrams tanks, 116 Bradleys, 26 Cobras, and 24 155mm SP [self-propelled] artillery howitzers; the 12th Combat Aviation Brigade, with 101 aircraft of various configurations; two artillery brigades, the 75th and the 212th, with M109 155mm SP howitzers and M110 SP 8-inch howitzers; the 2/229th Attack Helicopter Battalion from Fort Rucker with 91 assorted helicopters.

In Desert Shield, the 101st's covering force mission was to defend an area known as Area of Operations (AO) Normandy, about 103 kilometers northwest of Camp Eagle II and 85 kilometers south of the Kuwaiti border. AO Normandy was an area 50 by 30 kilometers spread across the corps area of operations. To defend the area, General Peay had to establish a forward operating base (FOB) within the AO. Initially, when a small force from the 82d Airborne Division was there, Corps had named the base FOB Essex. On 2 September, Luck told Peay that he could change the name to FOB Bastogne. It was 195 kilometers from Camp Eagle II to FOB Bastogne—a fifty-two-minute flight in a Blackhawk helicopter or three and a half hours by ground vehicle along MSR [main supply route] Audi. Peay set up another FOB in the western part of Normandy at FOB Oasis, 305 kilometers northwest of Camp Eagle II.

In FOB Bastogne, the division engineers renovated several existing buildings in a deserted ARAMCO oil compound for use as a CP and medical and maintenance facilities. An abandoned dirt airstrip outside of town was transformed into a massive logistics base stocked with fuel, ammo, food, and spare and repair parts. Tapline (Trans Arabian Pipeline) Road ran through AO Normandy from northwest to southeast. The Rakkasans who drove along this road, "a one-lane superhighway," according to General Peay, referred to it as "Suicide Alley," because of the heavy civilian traffic, buses, trucks, and cars, driven by locals with no traffic regulations. Accidents were frequent and massive.

FOB Bastogne gradually developed into a fairly livable operational support center. But it was not easy. Some of the Rakkasans who arrived early found hundreds of camel and sheep carcasses in the desert surrounding the FOB. Black flies swarmed everywhere and were so oppressive that the troops dubbed them the national bird of Saudi Arabia. The division surgeon investigated. One report said that "it was the Saudi custom to take an old or diseased animal into the desert, tie its front legs, and leave it to die." Soldiers, including the Rakkasans, built bunkers and fighting positions in the animal graveyard to the north of the city and waited for the attack that never came.

To the north, between AO Normandy and the Kuwaiti border, there was a thin line of Saudi troops. To the east, the U.S. Marines were deployed in a covering force role. To the west were Arab and other Saudi forces. The U.S. 24th Division was in a pocket in the southwestern quadrant of the corps sector behind the 101st that was to the north and west. The 82d Airborne and the 1st Infantry Divisions (Mech) were in the southern part of the corps zone behind the 24th. The corps sector was roughly the size of the New Hampshire and Vermont combined. In the event that the Iraqis attacked south from Kuwait, the 101st would take the brunt of the offensive, because AO Normandy was across the front of the corps sector.

The 101st officially assumed control of FOB Bastogne from the 82d Airborne Division of 4 September. The mission included an aviation screen in AO Apache to the north.

An-Nuriya was the town around which FOB Bastogne was based. By the time the Rakkasans had arrived at Bastogne, An-Nuriya had swelled with thousands of Kuwaiti refugees. The tales of rape, plunder, and murder told by the refugees raised the Rakkasans' level of hatred of Saddam to a high degree. The Rakkasans, however, had been thoroughly indoctrinated with the need for security and were careful of the refugees. As one of them put it, "With the promise of terrorist attacks by Saddam Hussein, almost everyone in the civilian communities was suspect."

General Peay divided AO Normandy into five sectors. The two aviation brigades patrolled in the northeast sector; the 1st Brigade had the northwest sector; the 3d Armored Cavalry Regiment had responsibility for the southeast corner; the 2d Brigade and 2/17th Cav Squadron, operating out of FOB Oasis, covered the southwest sector; and the Rakkasans had the area between the 2d Brigade and the 3d ACR. Colonel McDonald established a brigade logistics base, "Sukchon," to the rear of the Rakkasans' position. Colonel Tom Hill, the CO of the 1st Brigade, said later, "Had the whole scheme unfolded the way we thought it would, I would have been the first American unit engaged in ground combat." The Rakkasans were right beside him.

AO Normandy was across the front of the planned main battle position. General Peay explained the situation and the plan of battle if the Iraqis chose to attack Saudi Arabia: "The two Iraqi divisions would come directly south across Tapline Road. . . . Actually, we were postured to the north of Tapline Road, with the 24th Division in the main battle area to our south. . . . The concept was that we'd fight the covering force down south and pass through the 24th . . . to the main battle area. The third (Iraqi) division (mechanized), though, was going to come from the northwest and then cut to the southeast, down Tapline Road on our flank. We had 180 Humvee (high mobility, multipurpose, wheeled vehicles) TOWs, and we task-organized one company of infantry with one company of TOWs so that we had the security capability for the TOW team. We had enough infantry in there to also assist in the labor required with the ammunition. We put in those positions with great detail and rehearsed and rehearsed and rehearsed these plans. And, in addition, it was not the Humvee fight alone. It was a combined arms fight using the U.S. Air Force, four battalions of Apaches, and one battalion of Cobras plus our cav squadron Cobras. So we basically had six battalions of aviation. We also had two full heavy field artillery brigades from Fort Sill and we had the Armored Cav Regiment from Fort Bliss. So it was much more than just a Humvee TOW fight."

Along with the Apaches, the 180 TOWs mounted on the HMMWVs were the division's primary antitank and antimechanized counterpunch. The division engineers dug between seven hundred and one thousand fighting positions for the HMMWVs. Each TOW company, paired with an infantry company, had three fighting positions, located about five hundred meters apart. "If the Iraqis attacked," said one trooper, "the TOWs would hold them off as long as possible from the primary position before retreating to the secondary and tertiary positions."

To formalize its plan for the defense of Saudi Arabia, the 101st staff developed OPLAN 90-3, divided into five phases. In Phase I, the division would deploy fully to its preassigned positions in AO Normandy. Normally, two brigades and the 3d ACR were in AO Normandy at the same time. Phase II would start with the Iraqi attack out of Kuwait. The 101st would remain in sector as long as possible fighting with the Apaches and TOWs and then hand off the battle to the 24th Division. The 101st would then defend the 24th's western flank. During Phase III, the 101st would pass through the lines of the 24th and move to the west to guard positions in AO Carentan, on the west flank of the corps sector. In Phase IV, the 101st would occupy its guard positions with the Rakkasans in the south, 1st in the center, and the 2d to the north. The Rakkasans would be prepared to become XVIII Airborne Corps reserve. Phase V was a counterattack against the Iraqi second-echelon forces. The 101st would support the 1st Cavalry Division that was the main effort for the counterattack. In October, the division conducted a training exercise down to company level to rehearse fully the passage of lines spelled out in OPLAN 90-3.

The Rakkasans who moved in and out of AO Normandy during October, November, and December of 1990 were getting used to the climate, the desert, and the sometimes bizarre conditions they found in the area. At FOB Bastogne, they could see in one section a control tower, covered with camouflage netting, rising out of the sand. Two men in the tower controlled the positioning of helicopters at a refueling point. In another area, an Apache rolled into a refueling point and got a "hot" refuel in the newly constructed pad in the sand while another rolled in behind it. Around the perimeter, Rakkasans and other soldiers manned their dug-in machine-gun positions. A Chinook, with its massive rotor blades sagging, sat on a pad after a resupply run from Camp Eagle II. Outside the FOB, Rakkasans ran out of helicopters and hit the sand in training exercises. Vulcan (machine gun) positions surrounded the FOB, deeply dug into the desert sand, covered with camouflage nets. Air defense artillerymen, mortarmen, infantrymen, all in desert camouflage uniforms and deep holes, awaited the attack.

The Saudis were reluctant to permit live-fire exercises. But eventually General Peay got his way. "Despite the challenges," he said, "during the last three months of 1990, the division got in some of the best live-fire training we've ever had." On 6 November, Lt. Col. Thomas Greco and his 3/187th test-fired their small arms on the King Faisal Range Complex.

During November, General Peay ran the division through a second field training exercise rehearsal. This FTX tested the division chain of command on the critical phases of the defensive plan. During this training and rehearsing, the division staff improved and adapted many air assault techniques—"a farsightedness," wrote one officer, "that would prove beneficial in the actual battle yet to come."

Even in a combat situation, brigade and battalion changes of command took place. On 7 November, Col. Robert T. Clark took over command of the Rakkasans from Col. John MacDonald, who received his just desserts—assignment to the Pentagon, and a Legion of Merit from General Peay.

From August through December, the Iraqis continued to build up their forces in Kuwait and literally dug in. They constructed a multi-belted, hardened defense in the eastern part of the Kuwaiti Theater of Operations (KTO). The CENTCOM intelligence gatherers predicted that the Iraqis would develop strong-point defenses in the west in the vicinity of as-Salman and an-Nasiriyah. And in reserve for the entire KTO were the Republican Guards.

By 3 December, all of the 187th units were in the brigade sector in AO Normandy. "From 5 December to 27 December," wrote Fred Waterhouse, "the brigade concentrated on offensive scenarios focusing on air assaults behind enemy lines and linkup with a converging friendly unit."

For the Rakkasans, the constant training in all aspects of their duties paid off. They became more confident in themselves, their buddies, and their brigade. Their expert infantry badge (EIB) rate and skill qualifications rose through the fall. In an interview with the *Boston Globe* published on 18 October, Lt. Col. Andy Berdy, CO of 2/187th, said, "Our mission, for now, remains defensive. That is the emphasis in field training. We have no specific plans to go on the offensive. . . . I don't think it is boasting to say that if Saddam sticks his nose across the border, we will tear his head off. Defensewise, we are one hundred percent."

During the Christmas holidays, VIPs, one after another, from the president, to Secretary of the Army Stone, to General Powell, made appearances. Entertainers, such as the indefatigable Bob Hope, Johnny Bench, Jay Leno, and Steve Martin made the rounds, including visits to the Rakkasans. They ate well at Christmas, a lavish meal reminiscent of home. And as the division historian put it, "The holidays passed rapidly as the division began to prepare for the inevitable attack into Iraq."

During the fall, Schwarzkopf built up his forces to a strength sufficient to defend Saudi Arabia. But, by then, Washington was beginning to push for an offensive to drive Saddam out of Kuwait. Schwarzkopf's staff began planning in earnest for an offensive. But according to his thinking, he needed far more troops—armored units. On 21 October, Powell flew to Saudi Arabia to meet with Schwarzkopf. CENTCOM staff briefed Powell on the current situation. Following the briefing, the two four-stars agreed that, given the heavily dug-in defensive positions of the massive Iraqi forces and their armored strength, the U.S. had to "think big." That, they reasoned, meant adding another two hundred thousand U.S. troops between early November and mid-January, including, according to Schwarzkopf, the VII Corps from Europe. Powell suggested adding the 1st Infantry Division (Mechanized) from Fort Riley. Schwarzkopf agreed and concluded that if the president were serious about a winning offensive, he had to have VII Corps.

Back in the States on Halloween, Cheney and Powell presented the plan to the president; he bought it. Because of the Gulf weather—wet and cold in the spring—Bush agreed that a massive, decisive winter campaign, before the onset of the miserable spring weather, would be in order with an air campaign beginning in January and the ground campaign blasting off in February. The "good to go" date for the campaign was 15 January. Bush reasoned that when Saddam saw the massive buildup of forces, he would finally realize that the U.S. was not "bluffing."

In late November, Schwarzkopf briefed his senior commanders, including Lt. Gen. Frederick Franks, the VII Corps commander, who had flown into Dhahran with his principal staff officers. Schwarzkopf did not set a rigid timetable but suggested that the air force might take fourteen days for the strategic air campaign and three weeks for the tactical phase. "We are not going to attack into Kuwait," said Schwarzkopf. "We are not going into the teeth of this. We are going to hit him out here on the wing. Our objective will be to avoid the Iraqi main forces and go after his center of gravity." Schwarzkopf put his hand on the map where the Republican Guards were located. "We are going to destroy him. We're going to push them back against the Persian Gulf and the Euphrates River, and we're going to kill them in there."

After the briefing, some of the commanders discussed among themselves the sense and meaning of what they had just heard. General Peay was philosophical. "If we can bomb them to 50 percent in three weeks, why don't we take another three weeks and get the other 50 percent for good measure? Once the ground attack began, it would be a true air-land battle, with troops covered by air all the time." The plan for close air support provided six fresh sorties of air cover over each division every twenty minutes. Schwarzkopf had said that there would be "lots of air."

The logistics support for the buildup of U.S. forces in Saudi Arabia was phenomenal. In the first eighty days, more than 170,000 troops and more than 160,000 tons of cargo were moved to Saudi Arabia by air. By the time the allied forces began the offensive on 17 January, the U.S. had shipped some 460,000 tons of ammunition, 300,000 desert camouflage uniforms, 200,000 tires, and 150 million military meals to sustain 540,000 soldiers, sailors, airmen, and marines.

By early January, all the troops that Schwarzkopf had requested were in theater and combat ready. With the backing of the United Nations and the U.S. Congress, Desert Shield was about to become Desert

Storm. But first, Norman Schwarzkopf had to say a "Hail Mary." It may be that, even though he is not a Catholic, he ended up saying the whole Rosary.

## The Move West

As 1990 was coming to a close, the staffs from CENTCOM down the line were planning resolutely to shift from the role of defending Saudi Arabia to throwing Saddam and his forces out of Kuwait. By mid-November, Schwarzkopf's famous battle plan, the "Hail Mary" shift, was the accepted theater offensive strategy. It had to be planned in minute detail by every unit to squad level, briefed down the line and back-briefed up the line. According to Schwarzkopf, his strategy was "to suck [Saddam] into the desert as far as I could. Then I'd pound the living hell out of him. Finally, I'd engulf him and police him up." General Colin Powell said of the Iraqi Army, "First, we are going to cut it off, then we are going to kill it."

Schwarzkopf's plan of attack called for a major shift of forces to the west in Saudi Arabia, south of and along Iraqi border; next an alignment of forces; and then a sweeping attack that "stormed" to the north and then to the east. Schwarzkopf's plan was designed to trap the Iraqi forces in a vise between attacking elements, cut their lines of communications, and pummel them by air and ground attacks into surrender.

On 27 December, Secretary Cheney and General Powell were briefed on the concept by Schwarzkopf in Riyadh. "After General Schwarzkopf explained his 'end-run concept,' the commanders from the two army corps, the marines, the air force, and the 22d Support Command presented their respective plans, in broad conceptual terms, to support the flanking movement," wrote Lt. Gen. William G. "Gus" Pagonis, Schwarzkopf's brilliant, hardworking logistician. "The logistical plans paid particular attention to the crossing of the two corps and the building of forward logistical bases to the west."

General Peay, members of his staff, and his commanders made three trips to King Khalid Military City (KKMC) and reported to ARCENT headquarters. ARCENT was the senior army headquarters for the Gulf War. On the second visit, General Peay and his brigade commanders reconnoitered the area that the division might ultimately occupy before the jump-off into Iraq.

XVIII Airborne Corps's mission, one of the flanking sweeps, was to penetrate Iraqi forward defenses and to interdict Iraqi lines of communications along the Euphrates River to block Iraqi reinforcements or the escape of Iraqi forces to the west from Kuwait. On order, the corps would attack east to assist in the destruction of the Republican Guard Forces Corps (RGFC).

The 101st mission was this: "When directed, the 101st Airborne Division (Air Assault) moves by air and ground to Tactical Assembly Area Campbell and prepares for offensive operations; commencing G-Day, conducts air assault to establish FOB Cobra and attacks to interdict, block, and defeat enemy forces operating in and through EA [engagement area] Eagle; on order, conducts attacks to the east to assist in the defeat of the RGFC forces."

General Peay and his staff worked long hours to develop two plans to carry out the division mission. The first was OPLAN 90-4, Desert Rendezvous One. After deliberations with General Luck at Corps, although both thought the plan feasible, they decided to shelve it because the division went too far to the west and might even have involved house-to-house fighting. "Rendezvous One had us going into built-up areas and destroying bridges and stuff in some of the larger towns," said Lt. Col. Bob VanAntwerp, the division engineer. "That would have been a very risky mission for us."

Desert Rendezvous Two, or OPLAN 90-5, was the plan Luck and Peay finally decided on. It had four maneuver phases. Phase I was the logistics buildup to support a short-duration, high-tempo ground offensive. In Phase II, the division moved from Camp Eagle II and the covering force area into a tactical assembly area southeast of Rafha, Saudi Arabia. In Phase III, 1st Brigade would seize FOB Cobra, deep in Iraq, and the Division Support Command would build up Cobra to a "robust" level for further air assaults into AO Eagle. Also in Phase III, Col. Bob Clark and his Rakkasans would air-assault into AO Eagle on the second day of the ground war. The Rakkasans' role was to cut Saddam's LOC [line of communications] along the Euphrates. Next, the 2d Brigade would attack Objective Strike, the Tallil airfield, on the fourth day of the ground war. In Phase IV of OPLAN 90-5, the division would prepare for further attacks.

In early January, Col. Bob Clark ran his Rakkasans through scenarios that emphasized air assaults behind the Iraqi lines and then linking up with other 101st units. Clark ran the exercises in the covering force area in Q-town. "We did some very aggressive live-fire training with all the echelons from squad up through the battalion level . . . live-fire maneuvers day and night . . . and the confidence that the soldiers got going through that really paid great dividends when we launched into the Euphrates. One battalion made an attack of an Iraqi bunker trench line complex that we built with our engineers on the desert floor patterned after photographs that had been taken of the trench line the Iraqis had built in Kuwait taken from aerial photos, satellite imagery. We did a very credible job of replicating their actual defenses."

The 15 January deadline drew closer and closer with no blinking by Saddam. "On 15 January, a relaxed and confident President Bush summoned Secretary of Defense Dick Cheney to the Oval Office," wrote one of *Time*'s writers, "and as commande in chief, signed the National Security directive ordering his troops to battle. He gave Saddam one full day's grace for face, so the Iraqi could explain, perhaps to himself, that he had not caved in to a deadline. Then the skies over Baghdad erupted."

Surprisingly, the first shots of the war were not fired by the air force but by two teams of eight AH-64 Apache helicopters from 1/101st, part of the 101st Aviation Brigade, led by the battalion's commander, Lt. Col. Richard A. "Commander" Cody, at 0238 on the black, moonless morning of 17 January. The targets of Task Force Normandy were two Iraqi radar sites, about 50 miles apart, that were linked to four Iraqi fighter bases and the Intelligence Operations Center in Baghdad. Each radar site was a complex of at least a dozen targets—three ZPU-4s; a troposcatter radar; generator buildings; Spoon Rest, Squateye, and Flatface dish antennas; and a barracks.

Twenty-two minutes after the "Expect No Mercy" pilots of the 1/101st had knocked out the radar sites, one hundred Allied planes roared through the "deaf, dumb, and blind" alley that the Apaches had paved for them inside Iraq. Desert Storm was under way. After the war, Cody, reminiscing, said that "the Apache is the finest combat helicopter ever produced—bar none."

At the start of the air-war portion of Desert Storm, Col. Bob Clark was holding down the fort at Camp Eagle II with his Rakkasans. "I found out just before it started being executed," he remembered after the war. "Heard it on the radio. The mood in CE II was very serious. There was no bravado, no chest-thumping, no wild-eyed enthusiasm. Very serious. Everybody put their war faces on. I'll tell you, the morning after it started, every radio in tent city was tuned in to Armed Forces Radio. When the initial reports started being heard by the soldiers, there was just great enthusiasm. I could hear soldiers in their tents when a major bombing run was made on a certain facility. I could hear them whooping it up. It was quite an emotional high. After the first couple of days, though, I think we came to the realization this thing had a long way to go and air power alone wasn't going to do it. Most of us who had been around for a while were quite aware of that, but the young folks, the troops, I think it dawned on them. The common phrase in our brigade was 'The road home goes through Iraq.'"

Specialist First Class Paul F. Williams was on duty as the shift NCO at the 101st's main command post, a maintenance building, part of the KFIA [King Fahd International Airport] complex, at Camp Eagle II, on the night of 16–17 January. Just before 0200 on the seventeenth, he received a phone call from Major Martin, an XVIII Airborne Corps G3 staffer. He passed on to Williams two crucial messages: the U.S. Navy had just launched one hundred Tomahawk missiles toward Iraqi targets, and ARCENT had declared that "Operation Desert Storm" was in effect. Williams quickly passed the message to General Peay and the other staff sections and relayed the message to the subordinate commanders in the 101st. Five months of waiting, planning, sweating, praying, and training, were over.

Lieutenant Colonel Thomas J. Costello was the CO of 3/320th FA Battalion, the direct support artillery battalion for the Rakkasans. "We knew, of course, that planning for the move against the Iraqis had been ongoing for months," he wrote later. "While the plans were top secret, and very closely held, few of us had been given some insights into what was in store. . . . We had been assuming that the offensive would focus on Kuwait, and might possibly range as far west as the Wadi al Batin. 1/187th, under the command of Lt. Col. Hank Kinnison, had been tasked with developing and rehearsing tactics for an air-assault mission into Kuwait while the other two battalions of the brigade were focusing on the covering force mission in October and November, and Hank and his guys had developed many useful lessons learned. The underlying assumption, nonetheless, was that the air assault would be as 'deep' as forty or fifty kilometers, and would be against one of the softer, but highly lucrative, Iraqi targets in Kuwait itself. In fact, until the hostages were released in December, the possibility of a hostage rescue was on the menu of potential missions.

"When we returned to Camp Eagle II at the end of December, Colonel Clark assembled his task-force commanders and staff, and revealed our planned missions to us. To say that we were dumbstruck would be something of an understatement. Up until that time, no one that I knew of had envisioned anything as bold as the move well to the west and the planned air assault into the Euphrates River. The scope of the operation was breathtaking, and the depth of the assault intimidating. From the inception of the division's planning, the Rakkasans of the 3d Brigade were given the Euphrates Valley mission, but the exact objectives and parameters of the mission underwent a series of changes and modifications. Initially, we were to seize bridges over the Euphrates in the city of as-Samawah, hand the area off to a follow-on brigade, and then air-assault to the east and seize the bridges in the city of an-Nasiriyah. (Jim Mathis told me, after hearing this, that he wrote home to have his wife, Nadine, mail his copy of *A Bridge Too Far*.)

"As time went on, that particular plan underwent revision after revision, finally being scrapped for several reasons: The bridges were targeted by the air force enough times that there was a high degree of confidence that they would be dropped by the time the ground campaign commenced; the NCA [National Command Authority] was uneasy about the prospects of U.S. troops getting sucked into one or more urban fights; the probability of collateral damage and unacceptable civilian casualties was too high; and so forth. The plan eventually focused on interdicting Highway 8, the main road paralleling the Euphrates, linking Basra and Baghdad on the south side of the river. Whether the bridges remained standing or not, Highway 8 was certain to be a critical route of withdrawal for Iraqi forces, particularly the Republican Guard (in this case, the road became even more critical if the bridges to the east were down, since this would then become the best route of withdrawal), and it offered the potential of being a major supply and reinforcement route into the Kuwaiti theatre of operations, if the battle offered the Iraqis that opportunity."

The day after Colonel Cody and his highly successful TF Normandy returned to Camp Eagle II, the 101st began its massive move to the northwest. It was a major challenge for the 101st's commanders and logisticians.

"We were given an air and ground movement plan by Corps," wrote General Shelton, "which assigned ground routes and gave us 'block' times that we could be on our assigned routes. . . . We were anxious to get started, and departed the second we were cleared by Corps to move north (o/a 17 Jan—the day the air war commenced.) We (ASSLT CP) launched in two ESSS [External stores sub-system]-equipped UH-60s heavily loaded with command-and-control equipment early that morning for the four-hundred-or-so mile trip. I remember as we headed north that morning thinking, as we skimmed across the desert floor at 120 knots, 'Here we come, you bastard; I hope you know what you've asked for.' About an hour into the flight, the missile-warning light/audio activated and we went into evasive maneuvers. Still don't know what made it activate, but the pilot's immediate response reinforced a key point that was to be repeated many times in the next forty-five days—the way you train is the way you fight—the pilot's reaction was at this point instinctive."

At Camp Eagle II, the Rakkasans and the other troops of the 101st got ready for the move to TAA [Tactical Assembly Area] Campbell. They broke down the tents and picked up their ammunition. They crammed their gear into their duffel bags and rucksacks; NCOs supervised the loading of allocated vehicles; unit commanders made plans—when, where, how many, loading restraints—for the transportation they were going to use—C-130s, helicopters, trucks, organic vehicles.

The movement of the two corps to the northwest was a spectacular military operation. According to General Pagonis, "For eighteen critical days, eighteen-wheelers were transporting combat equipment and materiel, passing one point on the westward road every minute, every hour, twenty-four hours a day. The movement was staggering. By 24 February, each of the corps was in position and the logistical forward bases stocked to the necessary levels."

Between 18 January and 7 February, XVIII Airborne Corps moved from the vicinity of Dhahran, northwest to the Iraqi border, leapfrogging well past VII Corps. The 101st's destination in the "great shift" was TAA Campbell, about nine hundred kilometers from Camp Eagle II, approximately seventy-five kilometers southeast of the Saudi town of Rahfa, and ten kilometers southwest of the Iraqi border. TAA Campbell was a massive area—about 3,200 square kilometers. On D-Day, 17 January, the 101st Assault CP—General Shelton and a small staff—arrived in Campbell. The main body of the division began to move on 18 January, Phase II of OPLAN 90-5. The first ground convoy, twenty-four vehicles, left Camp Eagle II on the eighteenth. The route from Camp Eagle II to TAA Campbell was 615 miles long. The Rakkasans closed into TAA Campbell on 23 January.

The rest of the division continued to move northwest by aircraft and ground vehicles for the next several days. The division moved a total of 350 aircraft, 4,000-plus vehicles, three battalions of 105mm howitzers, and 17,132 soldiers by air and ground. The majority of the soldiers moved from KFIA to the Rahfa airport by C-130. Two-and-a-half-ton trucks and larger vehicles moved by ground convoys along a southern route through the Saudi capital of Riyadh. The bulk of the Rakkasans, 2,500 soldiers, moved in 137 C-130 sorties.

According to General Shelton, "The move . . . went amazingly smoothly without substantial problems. This is particularly astonishing considering the length of the route (seven hundred miles) and the fact that transportation units came from all over the world. . . . The 3d Brigade and the 1st Brigade arrived at the airfield, and we had two-and-a-half-tons carry them up to the Saudi-Iraqi border, where they went into defensive positions. . . . Rain was falling and the temperature was bitter. Nevertheless, we were all glad to be there."

In TAA Campbell, General Peay assumed responsibility for screening along Phase Line Razor, a line that ran northwest to southeast, north of and roughly parallel to the Tapline Road. General Peay assigned Colonel Hill and his 1st Brigade positions on the left and Colonel Clark and his Rakkasans positions on the right. Colonel Clark's mission was to reconnoiter in his zone from Phase Line Razor to the border, to provide security for the rest of the division, to gather intelligence and locate and report targets of opportunity, and, on order, to destroy all Iraqi forces along the border in the brigade sector. The disputed and largely unmarked border between Iraq and Saudi Arabia, along which were actual Saudi and Iraqi guard posts, was about ten klicks to the north. The XVIII Airborne Corps line of departure ran roughly along the border.

TAA Campbell was 3,200 square kilometers of flat, open, desolate, barren desert. Viewed from the air, the division's unit positions were little clusters of pale tents, tan vehicles, camouflage nets covering weapons, communications centers, command posts, with plain desert separating one cluster from another. The main terrain features of TAA Campbell were Tapline Road and the oil pipeline from which the road took its name. To the troops, Tapline Road was "Suicide Alley" due to the volume of traffic and the weaving driving tactics of the local drivers through troop convoys.

Once the 101st closed into TAA Campbell, the emphasis was on digging in, securing the area, and refining the plans for the offensive into Iraq. Once most of the 101st was in place, the screens out to the front, the troops dug in, and CPs, communication vans, howitzers, Humvees, and supply points camouflaged, General Peay focused on preparing to attack into Iraq by his airborne assault force—and preparing to make military history.

### Campbell to Cobra—The Move North

In TAA Campbell, General Peay, his staff, and his major subordinate commander spent a lot of time "fine-tuning" OPLAN 90-5. The First Brigade would still lead the assault into Iraq and establish FOB Cobra. Then the Rakkasans would air-assault directly from TAA Campbell into blocking positions along the Euphrates River. The air assaults into Iraq would, of necessity, be preceded by several days of aerial reconnaissance.

In TAA Campbell, the Rakkasan brigade and battalion staffs refined their plans and perfected the details of their anticipated actions on G-Day. They calculated vehicle and howitzer load configurations and war-gamed the exact equipment they would need for their long air assault to the Euphrates. Lieutenant Colonel Costello and other Rakkasan battalion commanders slimmed down their TOCs [tactical operations center], so that they had "lean teams" riding in on the first choppers.

"The target kept moving," wrote Lieutenant Colonel Costello, "as the Chinook pilots updated their estimates on fuel requirements and load capacity. A landing site, called LZ Sand, was selected at the point the aviators felt they could reach, some forty kilometers or so short of AO Eagle. The plan was for us to fly in the day of G plus 1, land, reorganize, and move by ground to a point just short of AO Eagle, there to await the arrival of the infantry assault. Traveling by Blackhawk, they would be able to fly directly into Eagle, and would make their assault after dark on the evening of G plus 1. We continued to plan, rehearse, back-brief, and wait, as the Powers That Be deliberated on when G-Day would be."

During the training in TAA Campbell, unit commanders put emphasis on common task skills, including range firing. In addition, as far as they were able, they perfected NBC [nuclear, biological, chemical] defense and decontamination skills. *Saddam has chemical weapons,* they remembered. Unit supply teams issued each soldier PB pills to help build up a tolerance against nerve agents and valium injectors to mitigate harmful effects of atropine, which was used as a nerve-agent antidote. General Peay tied all of the plans together with daily staff meetings and frequent updates for brigade and separate battalion commanders. The second in the series of unit back-briefs to General Peay was conducted in early February.

The Rakkasans dug into the desert as deep as they could—a few feet—before reaching hard rock. Then they built up their bunkers with walls of sandbags. The longer they stayed, the higher the walls. TAA Campbell was no Camp Eagle II. At Campbell, the Rakkasans were ready to repulse an Iraqi attack. Out on the perimeter, the troops lived in holes in the ground, covered with tarps behind sandbagged revetments. The temperatures were far lower than in CE II, with highs in the upper sixties during the day and into the thirties at night. Sleeping bags were useful. One big problem was the blowing sand that required much preventive maintenance, especially on the division's trademarks—its helicopters. Blowing sand could also cut visibility from seven miles to less than half a mile. In any event, the troops on the perimeter could sense combat getting closer.

Until 14 February, General Luck had not authorized General Peay to send any troops beyond the FLOT [forward line of own troops]. But on 14 February, even though there was still no official date for G-Day, Luck authorized Peay to send troops across the border. Peay could then initiate his "G minus 7" plan. On the night of 14 February, 101st helicopters flew recon missions across the border for the second time. "We flew principally three times during the day, first light, midday, and last light," recalled Lt. Col. John Hamlin, USMA '72, CO of the 2/17th Cav, the division's air recon squadron. "One was to pick up any troop movements along the border, between us and the Iraqi border; the second was also picking up trends of local population's moves—for instance, the Bedouin camps, civilian vehicles, tractors, anything that would give us an indication that something was changing—as well as the basic combat patrol to pick up any infiltrators and so forth that came in across the border."

Early on the morning of 16 February, a team of Apaches from Cody's 1-101 AATK [attack aviation battalion] flew up to the area that General Peay and his 101st Aviation Brigade commander, Col. Tom Garrett, had selected for FOB Cobra, ninety-three miles inside Iraq. On the seventeenth, Colonel Garrett flew up to the area. "This recon was a critical turning point in the decision-making process," said Colonel Garrett, "as it identified a potential target along the flight route to Cobra, but confirmed that the Cobra area itself was virtually undefended." He knew that the site selection was "critical to the success of the division's plan to conduct an air assault to the Euphrates River." The forward operating base had to be big enough to hold an infantry brigade, a DISCOM [division support command] logistics cell, up to five separate FARPs [forward arming and refuel point], laager sites for up to five aviation battalions, and a heavy PZ for landing external loads from heavy lift helicopters. Colonel Garrett had studied all available photo imagery and maps and made a personal recon of the area. He concluded that in spite of a "dust problem," the primary area was suitable for the FOB.

On the seventeenth, Apaches from Lt. Col. Bill Bryan's 2/229th Attack Helicopter Battalion were flying a route recon of MSR Newmarket, a road into Iraq to feed into FOB Cobra, along which the Cav Squadron had found some enemy bunkers. When the Apaches from the 2/229th went into the area, they took some fire from the bunkers. The Apaches attacked the bunkers with 30mm cannon. Ten Iraqi soldiers emerged from the bunkers waving white flags and surrendered. Hamlin's men went in with the Blackhawks and picked up the ten Iraqis. These were the first Iraqi troops captured by the 101st. Shortly thereafter, a group of forty Iraqis came out of a second bunker and attempted to surrender to the Apaches, an unusual arrangement. A company of Blackhawks with an infantry platoon quickly flew in and pick up the EPWs [enemy prisoners of war].

At 0810 on 20 February, Colonel Garrett committed Lt. Col. Mark Curran's 3/101 AVN to attack Objective TOAD. Then 2/229th AATK entered the battle. Garrett finally decided that "enemy resistance was virtually nonexistent, yet neither did any Iraqi infantrymen show any sign of surrender." General Peay set up a loudspeaker team on a UH-60 to try to talk the Iraqis into surrendering. The 311th MI Battalion also dropped leaflets in Arabic. A few Iraqis came out of the bunkers, but most of them stayed inside.

General Peay then committed Capt. Thomas Jardine's B Company of 1/187th from the standby battalion commanded by Lt. Col. Henry Kinnison. Jardine and his men went under the command of Colonel Garrett with the mission to secure the area, round up the Iraqis, and sweep the area for maps and other intelligence data. Jardine and his company landed on Objective TOAD and swept from one bunker to the next, prying out the Iraqis. Most surrendered immediately but about forty did not want to give up without a fight and fired some small arms at the Rakkasans. None was wounded. "Those hard-core guys . . . clearly did not want to surrender, and it could have easily swung the other way," remembered Colonel Kinnison.

General Peay then sent in Capt. Joseph Buche's A Company of 1/187th to help sweep the area. With both companies on the ground and with the support of 2/229th and the Aviation Brigade assets, including CH-47s to help haul out the EPWs, Kinnison and his men cleared Objective TOAD by the evening of the twentieth. Some 406 Iraqis surrendered, including the battalion commander, eight other officers, and one warrant officer.

"It was an unexpected windfall," said Colonel Garrett, "yielding an entire infantry battalion. . . . The Iraqi commander was captured along with all of his maps, orders, and classified documents. Additionally, 101st soldiers captured or destroyed a huge cache of Iraqi weapons and ammunition, to include ZPU-4 ADA guns that were never fired at the attacking U.S. aircraft. Most important, it was discovered that this battalion consisted mainly of border troops and new conscripts, and was part of the 49th Infantry Division. Morale, foodstuffs, and well-trained troops were in short supply. The makeup of the battalion and its division confirmed U.S. suspicions that the western flank of the KTO was lightly defended and would not pose a major obstacle to the advance of XVIII Airborne Corps."

"When we captured those prisoners, some very telling things came out," said General Peay after the war. "We found those prisoners wellgroomed, we found that they had brand-new weaponry; they were hungry but they were not starving. To a man, they despised Saddam. We learned through the interrogation process where his air defense was, where some of his other ground infantry was. All that told me to take more risks, to go quicker; it allowed us to solidify our plan."

A few days before G-Day, General Schwarzkopf flew into TAA Campbell for a quick briefing and a few words of advice to General Peay. "He wanted to be sure that the leaders were competent," recalled General Peay, "that they were aggressive, understood their mission, and would want to move."

The 101st and the Rakkasans were trained, briefed, and combat ready for the ground war. The last man in the last squad knew what he was supposed to do and when he was to do it. The 101st was about to make military history again—this time in the attack—not defense.

# 15: Cobra to the Euphrates

"23 Feb 91 D+37

1500 Phoncon with MG Peay, 101st Air Assault Division. The CINC (General Schwarzkopf) wished him Godspeed in the upcoming attack." (From CENTCOM Log.)

On the night of 23 February, G minus 1, four long-range surveillance detachments (LRSD) attached to the 2/17 Cav initiated the occupation of FOB Cobra by flying into the area and reporting back any enemy activity near Cobra or reinforcements coming along the other side. After the reports from the LRSDs, Col. Tom Hill's 1st Brigade was ready to launch the 101st's assault into Iraq. According to Colonel Hills he had the mission of "attacking across the Saudi Arabian border at H-Hour G-Day by air assault and ground to seize and secure an FOB, code-named Cobra, in order to facilitate future division operations in the Euphrates River Valley. FOB Cobra was a piece of desert, located approximately eighty miles within Iraq and about thirty-five kilometers southeast of as-Salman, the main objective of the French armored attack, also to occur on G-Day."

Colonel Hill's plan involved air-assaulting four infantry battalions under cover of darkness into FOB Cobra. Once there, the brigade would secure an airhead line and set up a perimeter defense of an area about fifteen kilometers long and twelve kilometers wide. In addition to the four battalions of infantry, Hill would also use forty-seven Chinooks to fly in fifty TOW HMMWVs with crews, necessary command and control vehicles, two 105mm batteries, and four battalion aid stations. By H plus 2, Colonel Hill hoped to begin air-landing enough equipment and fuel to set up a rapid refuel point (RRP).

The weather in Saudi Arabia varies widely. February 1991 was no exception. H-hour on G-Day was numbingly cold, wet, and so thickly fogged that General Peay was forced to postpone H-Hour (time of landing in Cobra) two hours—to 0800. After the delay, the troops, in TAA Campbell, heavily loaded with packs, rucks, weapons, and ammunition, climbed clumsily aboard scores of helicopters—sixty-seven Blackhawks, thirty Chinooks, and ten UH-1 Hueys. Once loaded, the choppers revved up their engines, created a huge dust storm, and took off at 0720 for the forty-or-so-minute flight to Cobra.

The lead company in the 1st Brigade's assault was Capt. John Russell's A Company, 1/327th Infantry. Forty-one minutes after taking off, the four Blackhawks carrying him and fifty-nine of his men landed in Cobra. Russell was surprised that there were no Iraqis firing at his men as they landed. "I really thought the LZ would be hot. It wasn't," he remembered.

The rest of Hill's men continued to land in Cobra amid the churning dust and loud rumble of the many choppers landing or hovering above the LZ. Lieutenant Colonel Frank Hancock's 1/327th, the lead element of the 1st Brigade, was on the ground at 0825. An Iraqi infantry battalion, huddled in bunkers, was securing the road next to the area where the battalion was landing. "For the next one and a half hours, we called in the 105mm artillery on the objective, along with two sorties of F-16s and two sorties of A-10s," recalled Hancock. "At around 1030 hours, the first group of Iraqis started to come out of their bunkers. I sent my D Company commander, Captain Gill, along with my scouts to accept surrender. We initially thought there were perhaps fifty prisoners." After additional attacks by helicopters, a total of 339 Iraqis surrendered, turning over 775 RPGs, 600 rifles, 4 heavy machine guns, 4 mortars, 2 AA weapons, 8 tons of ammunition, and $5,000 worth of Iraqi money.

Hill and his men continued to clear and set up Cobra and at 1029 reported back to General Peay that Cobra was secure. The 96 aircraft used to deliver the first lift flew back to Campbell and ferried in the second lift by 1156. At the same time, a convoy of 632 wheeled vehicles and 2,000 soldiers was rumbling north along the very dusty MSR Newmarket.

After Hill's men had arrived and cleared Cobra, it was Col. Ted Purdom's turn to bring his 2d Brigade into the FOB. Because of fog, wind, and rain, he could not move his entire brigade on G-Day. But by the morning of the twenty-fifth, G plus 1, he had his entire task force in Cobra.

By the end of G-Day, Cobra was a very active FOB. Its establishment involved the largest helicopter-borne assault ever conducted in a single day. Major Grigson, the 101st's public affairs officer, called the air assault a "bold and bodacious action." To establish Cobra, an area of two hundred square kilometers, the Blackhawks and Chinooks had each made the 180-mile round trip three times. They had delivered five forward-area refuel points, some forty separate refueling stations, and 200,000 gallons of fuel. Some 370 helicopters, including all of the recon, assault, and transport aircraft, had made 1,046 sorties on G-Day. To support the massive number of aircraft that would be needed to haul the Rakkasans to the Euphrates, Lt. Col. Bob VanAntwerp's 326th Engineer Battalion had built in TAA Campbell a 750,000-gallon-capacity aviation refuel point. His Task Force Grader had also worked during the night of G-Day to make MSR Newmarket navigable.

By nightfall of G-Day, FOB Cobra was equipped to support the Rakkasans' northward thrust to cut off the Iraqis who might attempt to escape along Highway 8 from Kuwait and place the Rakkasans in a tactical position to threaten Baghdad itself. Most of the 1st and 2d Brigades were deployed to Cobra, and support elements of the division went about readying the refuel points. Back in TAA Campbell, Colonel Clark and the Rakkasans were preparing to launch to the Euphrates—the most combat-oriented phase of the 101st's assault into Iraq.

Colonel Clark's objective was AO Eagle, an area 155 miles north of TAA Campbell, 85 miles northeast of FOB Cobra, and 145 miles southeast of Baghdad. East-west Highway 8 ran through the middle of AO Eagle, from as-Samawah in the west to Basra in the east. General Peay's plan was to air-assault all three Rakkasan infantry battalions into three LZs in AO Eagle, just south of the Euphrates, near the town of Al Khidr on the night of the twenty-fifth.

"A bridge over a major canal on the west and an overpass over the Iraqi State Railway in the east (of Al Khidr) offered two superb places to cut the highway, and the area was far enough away from any major cities to enable us to engage in major combat operations without the constraints of a major civilian populace," wrote Lieutenant Colonel Costello. "A major pipeline traversed the area from the southeast to the northwest, with a major pumping station that posed an obvious objective at the southeastern corner of what was named AO Eagle."

As one officer observed, "This air assault would jump the Rakkasans in a couple of hours over as much terrain as an armored division or mech division could move in a day or more."

Colonel Clark decided that, after the infantry battalions had landed, he would send Lt. Col. Andy Berdy and his 2/187th to the right flank as the brigade's main effort with the mission of cutting the Baghdad-Basra railroad intersection and blocking Iraqi forces coming from the east.

Lieutenant Colonel Hank Kinnison's 1/187th would be to the rear of 2/187th, facing east against any Iraqi forces and "seizing what we had determined to be key terrain within AO Eagle, the Darraji pump station along the pipelines leading from the Rumaila fields to refineries in as-Samawah," wrote Lt. Col. Peter C. Kinney, the brigade S3. "Darraji offered a small airstrip that would benefit logistic buildup for future operations and save helicopter wear and tear in the sand. . . .

"Third Bat would be on 2d's left flank facing west up Highway 8 toward Baghdad and engage primarily Iraqi logistic traffic bound for Kuwait. Third Bat was commanded by Lt. Col. Tom Greco, who commanded Task Force Rakkasan, all the wheeled assets of the brigade coming into LZ Sand on CH-47s. Sand was forty kilometers shy of the Euphrates due to the range limitation of the CH-47 versus the UH-60. Tom's XO, Maj. Jerry Balzack, fought the 3d Bat for its first twenty-four hours on Highway 8 until the linkup with TF Rakkasan."

The 101st Aviation Brigade helped to prep the AO prior to the 3d Brigade's air assault. In that operation, the 2/229th AATK and the 2/17th Cav reconned the area from 1330 to 1800 on G-Day, the twenty-fourth. Through the night of the twenty-fourth, the 1/101st AATK and one company from the 2/229th reconned along the MSR, pinpointed the 3d Brigade's LZ, located the road into AO Eagle, and scouted for the enemy. Neither mission reported any enemy contact.

Colonel Clark needed to know the type of terrain in AO Eagle. On G-Day, he inserted his scouts and four LRSDs. On the afternoon of G-Day, he sent Lt. Jerry Biller and his scout platoon from 3/187th into LZ Sand, forty kilometers south of AO Eagle. LZ Sand would be the LZ for the heavy lift Chinooks that lacked the range to make a full round trip to AO Eagle.

Biller's "Team Jerry" flew into LZ Sand in a driving rain. Biller's mission was to mark the LZ for the heavy choppers and to check the ground route, 41A, that led up to AO Eagle from Sand. (41A was not an Iraqi designation; 41A was so dubbed by a staff officer with a sense of humor to remind them of the Kentucky highway that ran past Fort Campbell.) The heavy downpour turned the soil into a quagmire of thick, clinging, clayey mud.

Biller and his men unloaded their gear, including motorcycles, some of which got stuck in the mud when they tried to drive off. Off-road vehicular traffic was almost impossible. Biller quickly realized that he could not set up LZ Sand in that area and, with the initiative of a bright young lieutenant, moved to LZ ten kilometers to the west. That night the skies cleared and the temperature dropped to near freezing. In TAA Campbell, the LRSD teams reported to Colonel Clark that the area was a series of rolling hills pockmarked with shallow wadis and standing water pools and that their helicopters sank a full foot into the mud.

Originally, General Peay had planned to launch the 3d Brigade into AO Eagle during the hours of darkness on the night of the twenty-fifth, because, reasoned General Peay, "Nighttime gives us more protection from any possible air defense that they might have."

Colonel Clark got a call from General Peay on the morning of G plus 1. As he remembered it, General Peay said, "The weather forecast for tonight is bad. You need to make the call to go early in daylight to beat the weather, or wait. I opted to go early."

### On to the Euphrates

Basically, the 3d Brigade's air assault out of TAA Campbell was two huge lifts. The first was Task Force Rakkasan, the heavy elements, in sixty CH-47 sorties. It was made up of two artillery batteries from 3/320th FA [field artillery], three antitank companies, two mounted rifle companies, and four engineer vehicles. Lieutenant Colonel Tom Greco, CO 3/187th, was in command of TF Rakkasan. At 1100 on G plus 1, the first choppers of TF Rakkasan lifted out of TAA Campbell and began landing in LZ Sand at 1216. General Peay remembered that "it was a long assault, 'on the deck' at full speed to avoid air defenses. Soldiers and equipment were crammed into the helicopters like sardines." The first choppers of TF Rakkasan were four CH-47s, each with two HMMWVs. Three more put six TOW vehicles from 1/187th on the ground. The rest of the task force followed into LZ Sand for the next six hours.

After he landed, Lieutenant Smith led his platoon from D Company, 3/187th up Highway 41A to Checkpoint CP 25. There he captured twelve Iraqis and two vehicles, one of which was a tank and pump unit used to refuel Iraqi vehicles moving up 41A.

Lieutenant Colonel Tom Costello, CO of 3/320th, remembered his last hours in TAA Campbell before flying into PZ Sand. "On Sunday morning, the twenty-fourth, we could see the dust from the 1st Brigade's lift, from the PZ we would be using the next day, into FOB Cobra. It sounds trite, but grim determination is the best phrase I can use to describe the atmosphere in the TOC. (I was scared, but tried not to show it. I imagine everyone else was as scared as I was. Grim determination is a good cover for fear. . . .)

"By late afternoon of G-Day, 1st Brigade's lift was completed, and we were able to go into PZ posture. We positioned and rigged the loads, gave some last-minute instructions, and settled for a few hours' sleep. Our lifts began the next morning, and would be an all-day affair. As each CH-47 completed its first turn and refueled, it returned for another load. . . . Our turn finally came, and we loaded into the Chinook for the hour-plus flight. We took off in sunshine, and flew into gray skies as we went north. We crossed the border into Iraq almost immediately, and it looked no different than Saudi Arabia. About halfway into the flight we passed over FOB Cobra, and were reassured to see that it was already a significant presence. The skies got darker as we went along, and we landed in a drizzle, to be met by Capt. Jim Waring, who was now my assistant S3. We got into the position on the ground as we had rehearsed. . . ."

Greco met Costello on the LZ. Greco decided to send ahead to AO Eagle the first three serials of Task Force Rakkasan and put his S3, Major Glover, in charge. Just as Glover and his vehicles were leaving, Greco got word from Colonel Clark, who was on the ground in AO Eagle, to stay put for the night, that the trafficability in the AO was terrible and the ground elements barely able to move. Glover and his serial had just left Sand. Fortunately, at 2200 on the night of G plus 1, Glover and Captain Dejarnette, CO of D Company, 3/187th, one of the antitank companies that had landed on Sand, linked together along 41A and moved on to AO Eagle.

Colonel Clark flew in the command-and-control plane of Task Force Rakkasan and then flew back to TAA Campbell to brief his infantry battalion commanders "on the ground." At 1500, he flew out again in the

command-and-control "bird" for the flight of the infantry elements to
AO Eagle. "By the time we got deep into Iraq," he recalled, "cloud cover
was low, it was raining and very windy, and we went in on final into the
Euphrates." The first wave of some thousand infantrymen rode north
in sixty-six Blackhawks. The flight time was about an hour and seventeen minutes; the distance 150 miles. The LZs in AO Eagle were dubbed
Chester, Festus, and Crockett.

Major Steve Chester was the Brigade S5 and was in the third Blackhawk of the first serial into LZ Chester. He remembered, "For any combat air assault the seats are removed from the aircraft and the troops are
terribly laden. . . . I think that the required load list, coupled with a combat load of rations and ammunition, and the extras that many troops
carried against all directives and common sense, resulted in personal
loads that went beyond reason. Several of the people required the assistance of two others to ruck up and get off the ground. I really felt for
the people with M60s or Dragons. You can also imagine what this did to
foot mobility at the far end.

"I carried my share of the common gear, two fragmentation and two
smoke grenades, a hundred rounds for my 9mm, a combat lifesaver kit,
sleeping bag, ground roll, wet weather suit, poncho, one change of
clothes, a hygiene kit, and a small radio. One thing I've always found is
that the thirst for information is almost overpowering when you are in
the middle of something and isolated from the big picture. The BBC
and VOA broadcasts were a godsend, even if not always accurate. Even
with the spare load I was carrying, I was at about 80-pound load, so I
would guess that some of the loads went to 150 pounds."

His description of the flight from Campbell to AO Eagle was typical
of the flight of each of the Rakkasans flying into combat.

"Our lift of sixty-six birds took off, if I remember correctly, at 1500
on the twenty-fifth. I spent the flight with a knee in one kidney, a rifle
muzzle in the other, and a large air assault trooper on my skinny lap,
gas mask squarely pressed into my bladder for the entire hour-and-forty-
five-minute flight. No one seemed frightened, but a couple of the
younger kids seemed a little tense. It amazed me at that point how young
they looked. The only thing that was universally felt was a strong desire
to get out of that UH-60. We flew a low-altitude, high-speed profile that
took us over FOB Cobra in a large flock. It was nice to see the guys at

Cobra waving flags at us as we flew over. The whole flight, the weather got worse, and I spent most of the time mentally preparing for the wonderful feeling of cold water running down my neck. I *hate* that. One minute out, the troops locked and loaded and the doors were open in an icy blast of wind and rain. The standard chorus came up from every throat—'Oh shit!' The landing was every bit as pleasant as expected—rain, high winds, forty degree temperature, and a quagmire of some of the most tenaciously clinging mud I've ever seen in my life. We had several people who fell and suffered sprained legs and backs.

"As an aside, we landed virtually on top of some Iraqi in his car. He took off running, falling several times. He left his car running, windows open, and lights on. We left it that way, figuring he'd get himself in trouble with a full tank of gas."

Staff Sergeant Sean M. O'Brian was the leader of the first squad, 1st Platoon, in Capt. Tim Fahy's C Company, 1/187th. The company landed late in the afternoon of G plus 1. O'Brian carried a typical heavy load: two claymore mines, two 60mm mortar rounds, two hand grenades, three smoke grenades, two star clusters, ten magazines of 5.56 ball ammo, six quarts of water, nine MREs, a poncho, a liner, pen and paper, fifty sandbags, extra socks, one IV (intravenous) set, and other first-aid supplies. He crammed into his rucksack a few toilet articles and three cartons of cigarettes. He also carried a MOPP (mission-oriented protective posture) suit, load-bearing equipment, protective vest, Kevlar helmet, and, of course, his individual weapon. The Blackhawk carrying O'Brian and his squad was so overloaded with fuel, troops, and gear that the pilot had to use a rolling takeoff.

At the end of the flight to AO Eagle, the choppers began their descent. "We landed flat and we seemed to slide forever," said O'Brian. "The bird on one side slid by us as we slowed to a stop, and the bird on the other side slid by. I was waiting for the next bird to slide into us."

"The weather conditions were abysmal," recalled Colonel Clark. "We had mud up to our knees, soldiers were carrying very heavy rucksacks, mobility was very hampered, just moving. You talk about a mobility problem. Things were a little tense that first night."

On landing in AO Eagle on LZ Crockett, Lt. Col. Hank Kinnison and his 1/187th had the mission of securing Objective Boston, a pump station and airstrip. O'Brian's Blackhawk landed about a thousand meters from Boston. In about fifteen minutes, Fahy's C Company reached the compound, breached the perimeter, and scrambled through a hole in the fence with Lt. David A. Priatko's platoon in the lead. His men found about twenty buildings of various sorts scattered throughout the area. C Company moved carefully through the pump station, alternating "covering and clearing." After searching each building carefully, they found no Iraqis, but they knew from the condition of the buildings and the meals still on the tables that the Iraqis had just left. The uniforms they found identified the Iraqis as militia.

Shortly before dusk, O'Brian's men heard a burst of automatic weapons fire from a bunker within the compound. He and his squad got the mission to clear the bunker. "As an infantryman, I can't think of anything I would less rather do than go into a bunker," said Lieutenant Colonel Kinnison later.

"I was scared, no other way to put it, scared for me and my guys," O'Brian said. "It was raining, foggy, a moonless night." O'Brian and his men put on night-vision goggles and used laser sighting devices when clearing the bunkers, moving from one to another carefully. It took the squad about forty-five minutes. "We never did find the guys who were shooting," said O'Brian. "We were disappointed about that on one hand and relieved on the other." Clearing the bunker complex meant that Objective Boston was secure.

Major Jerry Bolzak, temporarily in command of 3/187th, and the battalion landed on LZ Chester along with the Brigade Tactical Command Post (TACCP). After landing and moving to the highway, Capt. James G. Rodger's A Company destroyed fourteen enemy vehicles and killed one soldier and wounded two. Capt. Richard A. Carlson's C Company destroyed twelve vehicles and killed one Iraqi. That evening, the TACCP moved south to set up communications. That night at about 2200, 3/187th and 2/187th cut Highway 8. Lieutenant Sullivan from C/326th Engineers blew the bridge in B Company's sector.

"I think one of the most remarkable facets of the fight on the Euphrates," wrote Colonel Kinney, "was the fact that Colonel Clark only got half of his brigade on the ground for the first twenty-four hours because weather prevented the planned turnaround of the sixty-six UH-60s for the second lift into AO Eagle. What that amounted to was a brigade of only six companies supported by 81mm mortars and a few ground-mounted TOWs for the first twenty-four hours of combat. Those six companies carried the fight till the night of G plus 2 when Task Force Rakkasan arrived with our artillery from 3/320th Field Artillery, our mounted TOWs, and the engineer demo required to cut Highway 8. "I don't believe the Iraqis ever figured us out till too late. We took some small-arms fire from the local militia just off the landing zones in the 3d Bat sector, but they were brushed away quickly and never bothered us again. First Bat surprised the forces in the Darraji pump station, who ran when they heard the thunder of so many helos, leaving their warm supper on the table inside the pump station; negligible contact there. The real story was on Highway 8, where Capt. Richard A. Carlson's C/3/187th on the left and Capt. Michael S. McBridge's B/2/187th on the right, separated by about eight kilometers, began a busy three days ambushing Iraqi trucks. . . . Every vehicle shot by 2d Bat contained contraband stolen from Kuwaiti homes. TV sets, VCRs, bicycles, tea sets, silverware, and women's and children's clothing seemed to be Iraqi looters' priorities. It was clear the second day that we weren't facing a beaten army, but a bunch of thieves."

If the Iraqis had had an armored force of tanks and APCs in the area, they could have seriously battered the lightly armed Rakkasans along Highway 8. But they had no such force. Nonetheless, lightly armed, the Rakkasans were still able to destroy Iraqi vehicles on the highway that night. In a firefight in EA [engagement area] Yankee, McBridge's B Company, 2/187th, killed two Iraqis, wounded seventeen, and evacuated the wounded to the battalion aid station. There, Major Bonneville, the battalion surgeon, and Lieutenant Golden, the medical platoon leader, worked on the Iraqis and saved all of them.

On the night of G plus 2, the Rakkasan second "light" lift, which had flown into Cobra the day before, landed in AO Eagle, raising Colonel Clark's strength to 2,200 infantrymen.

At early light on the morning of G plus 2, TF Rakkasan began moving north along Highway 41A toward AO Eagle and closed in the area by 1400. The trip had not been easy. "At about 0300 on G plus 2, I was called to a meeting at Greco's command post at which we discussed plans for the morning," wrote Colonel Costello. "He had arranged, via TAC-SAT, for the Chinooks to return, after dropping off at Cobra, and lift the remaining elements of TF Rakkasan into the area of operations, thus bypassing the road. At first light, we assumed PZ posture again, but the winds and visibility precluded aircraft operations. Glover's element had still not closed Eagle, although it was getting close now. The light elements of the brigade were up there with no heavy weapons, and only their mortars for support. They had not been heavily engaged as yet, but we knew that Highway 8 would be a key withdrawal route for the Iraqi forces; for all we knew, the entire Republican Guard could be on its way up the road, and there were no TOWs, artillery, or, due to the weather, attack helicopters to stop them. In fact, the demolition materials intended for use in cutting the highway were still with us. It was time to get up there. . . .

"We made the trip fairly uneventfully in the end, covering the distance in about six hours, and encountering no problems negotiating the route with the howitzers, notwithstanding their heavy loads."

In AO Eagle, the Rakkasans were busy blocking traffic, blowing craters and bridges. Captain John Christensen and his team blew a highway bridge along the highway, and attack helicopters of 1/101st AHB blew up a bridge at Al Khidr with Hellfire missiles.

In the *New York Post*, the Associated Press published a story about the exploits of the 3d Brigade. "'I still can't believe we got this far, this fast,' said Lt. Col. Hank Kinnison, a forty-two-year-old from Lubbock, Texas. Commanding the 1st Battalion, 187th Infantry, Kinnison spoke as he leaned against a ten-foot-high portrait of President Saddam Hussein. 'Nice ties,' he said. The portrait showed the Iraqi leader in a pink necktie. 'I've always admired Saddam's ties,' Kinnison said. Some 1st Battalion Rakkasans did some artwork on the portrait of Saddam Hussein. . . . Since Tuesday, Rakkasans of the 187th Infantry have been attacking fleeing enemy troops along the highway northwest of the provincial capital of Nasiriyah and just south of the Euphrates River. Later that day the Rakkasans hit a convoy of trucks fleeing from the strategic city of Basra, wounding fourteen soldiers and capturing an additional seven unscathed.

"'We were the first guys to ask them to lay down their weapons and they did,' said Rakkasan Col. Robert Clark, commander of the 101st's 3d Brigade, the 187th Infantry. 'It took just a little convincing.' The colonel was speaking from his command post near the Euphrates River more than 100 miles from Saudi Arabia and less than 150 miles from Baghdad.

"Along the highway, dozens of ragged-looking Iraqi civilians looted one burned-out truck that had been carting flour. Women turned from the looting to expose a single breast to American soldiers and pointed to their mouths in a sign troops interpreted to mean they had babies to feed. Iraqi men also pointed to their mouths and cursed Saddam Hussein in broken English."

By the evening of G plus 2, 26 February, the Rakkasans were astride Highway 8, deployed in a defense configured to block Highway 8 to any Iraqi traffic, east or west, reinforcements or fleeing vehicles. One writer in *Triumph Without Victory* observed, "As Iraqi military convoys attempted to crash through the American roadblocks, they were fired upon by soldiers from Clark's 3d Brigade of the 101st Airborne. Most deadly were the wire-guided TOW missiles fired from launchers mounted on Humvees. Seeing the carnage, some Iraqi soldiers turned their vehicles and fled. General Binford Peay's soldiers had seized and secured Highway 8. Nothing moved on the road without his permission."

In the rest of the 101st's area, the 1st Brigade improved the capabilities of FOB Cobra, cleared the main supply route, linked up with the 197th Infantry Brigade of the 24th Infantry Division on MSR [main supply route] Virginia, and contacted the 82d Airborne Division on the division's western border. The 2d Brigade continued to fly into FOB Cobra from TAA Campbell. General Peay moved his assault command post to FOB Cobra on G-Day. From there, he directed Colonels Purdom and Garrett to be ready to move the 2d Brigade to the east to the new forward operating base—Viper. The 101st was ready to continue the attack to the east, part of the wide envelopment, the climax of the "Hail Mary" plan, that Schwarzkopf and his staff had mapped out.

By the night of G plus 2, the coalition forces had moved ahead along the entire front with unexpected speed. By Tuesday morning, U.S. forces were at the Kuwait International Airport, where the U.S. Marines fought the Republican Guards in a tank battle. By nightfall, the marines were at the airport. That same night, a Scud missile hit a U.S. Army barracks at al-Khobar, Saudi Arabia, killing twenty-eight American soldiers. At his midmorning press conference, Brig. Gen. Richard Neal, one of Schwarzkopf's staffers, briefing the press, said that the Allies had stopped counting the Iraqi EPWs at fifty thousand. Late Tuesday night, lead elements of marines and Kuwaiti forces entered Kuwait City and found that the city's hotels and government buildings had been massively destroyed, the U.S. Embassy had been booby-trapped, and thousands of hostages had been seized by the retreating Iraqis. Surrendering Iraqi soldiers reported that many of their officers had fled north in stolen cars.

On the twenty-sixth, General Luck told General Peay that the entire coalition force was reorienting east "in order to cut off the enemy's escape routes north of Basra." The 101st's new direction of attack was north of the 24th in order "to further interdict Iraqi escape routes."

General Peay decided to establish a new forward operating base ninety-three miles to the east of Cobra, from which he could launch helicopter attacks to the northeast. He ordered Colonel Purdom to air-assault his 2d Brigade into FOB Viper and told Colonel Garrett to move four attack helicopter battalions to Viper, from where he would be prepared to attack Iraqi columns escaping north from the Kuwait area.

The rains stopped on the twenty-sixth but were replaced by sandstorms that made some ground and air movements impossible. In an interview after the war, General Peay said that the storms on G plus 1 and G plus 2 were like storms that he had never before seen. "We had been through *shamals* but never anything like this. These troopers flew in and around it. They were enormously proficient aviators. It is almost miraculous to think that we covered the kind of distances we did in this war." By the end of the day on the twenty-seventh, General Peay had his 1st Brigade at Cobra, the 2d and most of the Aviation Brigade at FOB Viper, and the Rakkasans completely blocking traffic along Highway 8.

"The night of 26–27 February passed quietly for us," wrote Lieutenant Colonel Costello about activities in AO Campbell. "There was some small-arms activity along the road, but no artillery business. It was evident that things were going very, very well. The marines and coalition forces were on the outskirts of Kuwait City, and the VII Corps was turning on the flanks of the Republican Guard. Colonel Clark cautioned against carelessness and told the infantry battalion commanders that he wanted more use of artillery (truly a gifted soldier!). His intent was to create a big signature, to discourage anyone from messing with us. After the brigade meeting, I walked back to the TOC and had a BC [battery commander] and staff call on my own to pass on the data I had collected at the brigade meeting."

In AO Eagle, in a cinder-block building he called the Alamo, Major Chester processed POWs, refugees, and stragglers. "In general, the prisoners who came in were filthy, half starved, ill trained, illiterate, and wanted nothing to do with Saddam's war," he wrote later. "In spite of the propaganda they had been subjected to, most had no qualms about being captured and several expressed hopes they could stay in Saudi Arabia . . . the prisoners scarfed up MREs at a tremendous rate and cared not if pork were involved. A common comment was that they appreciated how accurate the U.S. bombing was, since the Brits and French were a little less discriminating and had hit a fair number of civilian targets. I had never heard of anyone thanking someone for bombing their nation before."

By the evening of G plus 3 the Rakkasans' blockade of Highway 8 was in full force. "I think the most dramatic moments for me were on G plus 3 when in the morning I overflew Highway 8 with the commander of 3/101 Attack Aviation, Lt. Col. Mark Kern," wrote Lieutenant Colonel Kinney, "and viewed the devastation wrought by the two infantry battalions, and later that night when we brought two batteries from 3/320 Field Artillery to bear on some trucks skirting our kill zones.

"The scene on Highway 8 was right out of a movie as we hovered east above the Iraqi dead. Their bodies had been removed from the GAZ-66 command cars they were driving, laid on the ground with arms and legs crossed, signifying that they had been searched. Farther ahead was a burning Mercedes truck towing an antiaircraft gun with the crew bodies hanging out the doors. "The artillery made its mark that night. If there was any thought in the local Iraqi commander's head of counterattacking our airhead, it probably ended that night when the King of Battle spoke. Second Bat's S3 called me late that night and reported that two Iraqi trucks had bypassed the roadblocks and were following the railroad embankment cross-country. His TOW gunners had them only briefly in their thermal sights and couldn't get a shot as they ducked along behind the embankment and over irrigation dikes next to the Euphrates. The brigade FSO did a great job computing the movement of the targets. . . . Minutes later sixty rounds of 105mm HE/VT caught their two trucks as the valley echoed and reechoed with their concussion and the flashes of impact illuminated the whole area of operations. We were literally jumping up and down in our holes and cheering that display of raw power. I was never as impressed with the power of the U.S. Army or as proud to be one of her soldiers as I was on the twenty-seventh of February 1991.

"As for the Iraqi soldiers we faced on Highway 8, I feel pity for them now—I didn't then. They never knew what hit them and were never smart enough to warn others of our presence until after the cease-fire. We encountered few officers, mostly NCOs of the Republican Guard units who told us that their officers had abandoned them by helicopter on the twentieth of February and told the troops to find their way home the best they could. Leadership as befits a bunch of thieves. Of the POWs that were taken, most were genuinely surprised that as soon as we'd shoot them (with medical shots, that is), they'd be medevaced to our rear and/or fed. All the POWs were very cooperative, even friendly, once they knew we weren't going to treat them to the same standard they probably would have given us. . . . In the words of the battalion commander of the 841st Infantry who surrendered to the 1st Bat: 'You Americans don't fight fair.' Fair to him as a veteran of the Iran-Iraq war was mowing down Iranian children in his minefields. What we did to them was beyond their comprehension."

The Rakkasans continued to cut off Highway 8. To get out of Kuwait, the Iraqis could only go north from Basra. General Peay set up engagement area Thomas about 120 miles to the northeast of FOB Viper, and assigned Colonel Garrett and his four battalions of attack helicopters the mission of attacking the Iraqi armored and motorized forces trying to escape to the north through EA Thomas. Colonel Garrett wrote later, "This mission change was a direct result of the success of the 3d Brigade's establishment of a blocking position on Highway 8. Intelligence showed that the Iraqi withdrawal, which was channeled both north through Basra and west up Highway 8, suddenly turned exclusively to the northern route as word spread among the Iraqis that the U.S. had cut off the western escape route. The turning of the Iraqi Army created an impossible bottleneck at the few surviving bridges crossing the Euphrates, resulting in a classic kill-box to be exploited by the Allied forces."

At about 1000 on the twenty-seventh, General Shelton received a "frag order" that assigned the 12th and 101st Aviation Brigades to attack the Iraqi traffic moving north out of Basra. By noon on the twenty-seventh, four AAH [assault helicopter] battalions were in Viper—two from the 12th and two from the 101st. That afternoon, General Shelton and Colonel Garrett briefed the AAH battalion commanders on the plan. "The aviation brigade mission," wrote Colonel Garrett, "was to conduct deep attacks on withdrawing Iraqi forces in the vicinity of a causeway which crossed the Euphrates. The first AH-64 company from 1/101st departed Viper at 1430 hours and encountered numerous targets en route to the target area and in the target area, with most of the traffic on the causeway having already been engaged by the air force. A second AH-64 company from 2/229th launched to conduct a battle handover with 1/101st and continue the attack."

By the afternoon of the twenty-seventh, the oil-well fires ignited by the departing Iraqis had created a smoke screen and reduced visibility considerably. At the beginning of the flight, the weather was reasonably good, but near the causeway, the fires from the wells and burning vehicles cut down the visibility to about three hundred meters.

"It was like going into darkness," said Lt. Col. Bill Bryan, CO 2/229th. "There were just so many oil fires there from the burning oil wells north of Basra and Kuwait. Plus the vehicles that had already been destroyed were burning. As we approached the causeway, we had to go from Day TV to FLIR to be able to see." When he arrived at the battle site, Bryan said that it was "Hammer Time, and we were launching everything we had—2.75s, Hellfires, and 30mm depending on the target and the range. . . . This was purely a helicopter fight. In my mind, first of all, the air force had nothing they could fly and fight in three-hundred-meter visibility and there is no other piece of equipment that can fly that distance, that fast, and certainly it would have taken an armored division a day to get there. So this was clearly a classical armed-helicopter mission, especially with the FLIR system. You will have to get in there and fight with reduced visibility. This was basically in the daytime. So, we get up there, there are many fires everywhere, there are fires in front of us and most of them are burning vehicles, some of them are actual oil wells, but it is dark, occasionally you will see a flame through the smoke and the poor visibility will come in again, but the fires are all in front of us, and everybody is pretty much servicing targets. There were enough of them out there. They were hovering over this citadel complex, bunkers, and vehicles. At one point, I looked down and on the right side of me was a 57mm that I could spit on, and on the left side was a 23mm."

In the "Battle of the Causeway," the 101st and 12th Aviation Brigades destroyed fourteen Iraqi armored personnel carriers, eight BM-21 multiple rocket launchers, four M-16 helicopters, fifty-six trucks, and two SA-6 radars, and seriously damaged a bridge across the Euphrates.

On the evening of 27 February, General Schwarzkopf called General Powell. "Here's what I propose," he said. "I want the air force to keep bombing those convoys backed up at the Euphrates where the bridges are blown. I want to continue the ground attack tomorrow; drive them into the sea, and totally destroy everything in our path. That's the way we wrote the plan for Desert Storm, and in one more day we'll be done."

But Schwarzkopf was not to get that "one more day."

On 27 February, General Schwarzkopf held a press conference. He said that it was not the coalition force's intent to destroy Iraq. "When we were here," he said, pointing to the Rakkasans in AO Eagle along Highway 8, "we were 150 miles from Baghdad. If it had been our intention to take Iraq, to overrun the country, we could have done it unopposed for all intents and purposes."

On the twenty-seventh, Generals Schwarzkopf and Powell had additional phone conversations. Powell told Schwarzkopf that aides to President Bush were suggesting a cease-fire at 0800 on the twenty-eighth, but, thinking no doubt about a "Hundred Hour War," suggested termination at 0500 and a cease-fire at 0800. Schwarzkopf said, "I don't have any problem with it. . . . I'll check with my commanders, but unless they've hit some snag I don't know about, we can stop."

Schwarzkopf checked with his major commanders and found no difficulties. "Then," he wrote, "a few hours later Powell called to confirm: 'We'll cease offensive operations, but there's been a change. The president will make his announcement at nine o'clock, but we won't actually stop until midnight (Washington time). That makes it a hundred-hour war.' I had to hand it to them; they really knew how to package a historic event. President Bush and Secretary Cheney each came on the line to offer congratulations. Finally Powell came back on and said, 'Okay, that's it. Cease fire at eight o'clock local time tomorrow morning.'"

# 16: Cease Fire—The Road Home

Throughout the battle area, the word went out: Cease fire at 0500 local time.

To the (Rakkasan) troopers who had been away from Fort Campbell for upward of five months, the CEASE-FIRE (spelled in capital letters in their minds) meant one thing: HOME (and that was spelled in Technicolor and neon lights).

Home meant spouses and children and girlfriends and daily showers and clean uniforms and home-cooked meals and temperate climates and an occasional beer and a full night's uninterrupted sleep and a car and ladies in American-style clothes. It meant an end to the rain and sandstorms, torrid heat, MREs, daily gallons of water in plastic bottles, mud-filled holes, dust, Saudi nonwaterproof tents, sand dunes, sandbags, camels, sheep, Bedouins, chemical warfare threats, Scud alerts, noisy, bumpy flights in crammed helicopters, box latrines, slit trenches, hand-washed clothes in buckets or basins, irregular mail, long lines at rare telephones, scant goodies at mobile PXs, and Iraqi soldiers with black mustaches. It meant, most of all that going home— the "real world," the land of the big PX—was a definite possibility. But when?

"It always takes a lot longer to clean up than you think," mused Lt. Col. Hank Kinnison. "We got some more time here in this wonderful country sucking sand."

In AO Eagle, the night of the twenty-seventh, the Rakkasans continued their blockade of Highway 8. Costello's artillery fired a series of concentrations against Iraqi convoys trying to negotiate the highway.

But the Rakkasans, strung out along the highway, had a problem unique to the 101st: handling hundreds of Iraqi refugees who were fleeing from cities retaken by the Republican Guards. The refugees were in a pitiful state. "Many from Dirvaiyah," wrote Maj. Steve Chester, "had been beaten or burned with lengths of reinforcing bars. One man had his eyes, tongue, and ears hacked out and fingers cut off. . . . The Kuwaiti refugees ran the gamut from the fat cats and collaborators trying to sneak home to burned, tortured prisoners."

After the cease-fire, the Rakkasans maintained their positions along Highway 8 and processed refugees. With the cease-fire, some Iraqis rebelled, opposed to the brutality of the Saddam dictatorship. "Essentially, the entire Euphrates valley and Kurdistan rose up just before the cease-fire," wrote Major Chester. "Iraq is an artificial entity, like all of the Middle Eastern countries, comprised of Shiites, Sunnis, Kurds, Christians. . . . As the rebellion occurred, the official U.S. policy was one of noninvolvement. This continued even as reports of incredible brutality came out of the areas being retaken. We were told, 'Hands off'. . . . As the rebellion grew, the leadership came repeatedly to our area to beg help, and armed bands appeared constantly around the area. At one point, I was holding meetings with thirteen of the sixteen emirs, who wanted military, medical, and food assistance. . . . The best I could do was keep sending messages explaining the situation, and tell the rebels, 'I can't help, but I will tell my superiors'. . . . The bottom line was that the 3d Brigade was dropped into a sea of chaos for a month."

After the cease-fire, "it was really a matter of waiting," wrote Lt. Col. Tom Costello. "The cease-fire held, of course, and the POWs were returned on schedule. We were careful not to get too optimistic, knowing full well what the Iraqis were capable of, and not trusting them for a minute. We were hard pressed to believe that they would be so thoroughly beaten so quickly, and could not believe our good fortune in their failure to employ chemicals. There were a couple of false alarms and intel reports of imminent surprise chemical attacks over the ensuing few days, but things remained peaceful."

On the twelfth of March, the Rakkasans finally packed up and flew out of AO Eagle back to FOB Cobra. But on the thirteenth came a reversal: General Luck told General Peay to send the Rakkasans back to the Euphrates area "to maintain a presence of force in support of the cease-fire negotiations." Two battalions of the Rakkasans, 1/187th and 2/187th, flew back to Eagle, spread out, and reassumed their defensive positions centered on the Darraji pump station and the airstrip nearby. Although they had been gone for about twenty-four hours, when they got back to the area they found that some of the buildings they had left—the water-purification plant and the electricity-generating plant, for example—had been completely trashed by people in the area.

On 24 March, the Rakkasans again left AO Eagle when the 2d
Armored Cavalry Regiment rumbled into the area to take over its
defense. For the next three days, starting on the twenty-fifth, the
Rakkasans choppered back to the airport at Rafha. From Rafha, the
Rakkasans flew by C-130 back to King Fahd International Airport and
the well-remembered Camp Eagle II. Between 28 March and 5 April,
the Rakkasans cleaned equipment and vehicles in preparation for the
move back to Campbell—the real one.

The first 101st troops to leave Saudi Arabia were 905 men from the
2d Brigade who flew out of FOB Viper to TAA Campbell and, on the
eighth, boarded commercial aircraft in Dhahran and flew to Fort
Campbell via Frankfurt, Germany, and JFK in New York.

"Very hushed up, very hurried," remembered Col. Ted Purdom, CO
of the 2d Brigade. "There were three flights from Frankfurt into JFK
and the first indication I had was at JFK when basically the aircraft were
met, as we taxied down the runway, by fire trucks, by police cars, sirens.
We got into JFK International Airport and everybody was clapping and
applauding, what have you. Then when we came back to Fort Campbell, there's a thousand people out there on the tarmac and the bands
are playing and the flags are waving. It was an emotional experience
that was very uplifting. The soldiers were glad to be home. Basically,
that welcome was given to every aircraft that came in."

Back in Saudi Arabia, according to General Peay, the rest of the division, including the Rakkasans, "cleared the war zone, washed vehicles,
checked gear, and went through innumerable customs inspections."
The cleaning of vehicles and equipment went on for twenty-four hours
a day. The inspections were "white glove standards," said General Peay
after the war. "It was very difficult and time-consuming work but the
troops worked hard because they were going home. To keep up the
morale of the troops who were working so hard, the division moved in
hamburger stands and other conveniences at the wash-up sites."

In late March, General Schwarzkopf made a visit to the 101st at
Camp Eagle. General Peay assembled the brigade and battalion
commanders, sergeants major, and the division staff in a room at the
water-treatment plant that General Peay used as a command post.
After a briefing on the combat operations of the division, General
Schwarzkopf made a few comments. In a letter dated 19 October 1993,
he told me, "What I actually said was that while the air force and

armored forces were the thunder in Desert Storm, the 101st Airborne Division was the lightning of Desert Storm."

Most of the 101st returned to Campbell Army Airfield on civilian planes between 3 and 15 April. The Rakkasans returned between 7 and 9 April. After they debarked, and with a National Guard band playing, the troops moved to buses for a ride to their troop areas, where they turned in weapons, gas masks, and other issued equipment and readied themselves for a long-awaited two-week leave.

At 1410 on 13 April, General Peay and some four hundred troopers arrived at Campbell aboard a Boeing 747. General Peay brought with him the 101st colors, symbolizing the return of the division to its home base. "A joyful crowd of family members and guests cheered the desert-weary troops as they stepped off the plane," wrote Bettina Tilson of the *Leaf Chronicle* staff. "The sea of colorful homemade banners, flags, and balloons was in sharp contrast to the 'chocolate chip' brown desert uniforms of the soldiers as the two groups stood facing one another, anxious for the ceremony to end so they could be reunited."

"Last August upon our rapid deployment, I wrote you that the Eagle was in full flight," General Peay told the crowd. "Today the Eagle has officially returned to this nest as represented by these splendid soldiers and the division colors. . . . The soldiers of the 101st returned desert-hardened, broader, wiser, and more mature."

In an interview with General Peay after the war, he said that he felt the greatest success of the 101st was, first, an "ability to gain operational positioning and to go deep and cut the Iraqi line of communications at the Euphrates. It bothered the enemy psychologically that the division could go so far so fast and so deep." A second success, he said, was the ability to "operate the division in a covering role during the first six months of the campaign in an area the size of the state of Montana." He was disappointed that the 101st was not given the mission to exploit its deep penetration of Iraq and air-assault near Baghdad.

In the sixties and seventies, the army's top tacticians had thought about, written about, tested, and then cast into permanent tactical doctrine the "air-assault concept," a departure from the air-mobility concept practiced and honed during the Vietnam War. The 101st's establishment of FOB Cobra and then the Rakkasans' bold, deep penetration into hostile terrain all the way to the Euphrates and the buildup therein of an active area of operations solidified the "air-assault concept" and proved the value of the doctrine. And had the opportunity arisen, the 101st and the Rakkasans could have exploited their thrust into the enemy territory. They were loaded and ready.

They proved that lightning can strike unexpectedly anywhere in a vast area.

Well, that's the story of the Rakkasans, sometimes a regiment, sometimes a regimental combat team, sometimes only a battalion.

But the Rakkasans are a unique part of the U.S. Army—the only regiment whose history ranges through many radical changes in the developing tactics and doctrine of the U.S. Army and covers four wars in the last fifty-plus years. The 187th started out as a glider regiment in the 11th Airborne Division in the Philippines in World War II; it performed heroically as a separate parachute regimental combat team with, among other things, two combat jumps in the Korean War; it endured the unnecessary and fortunately short-lived switch from the triangular concept to the ill-conceived pentomic idea; one of its battalions made 115 helicopter assaults and fought valiantly as an air mobile unit in the Vietnam War; finally, it demonstrated the wisdom of the "air-assault concept" when it made the longest and largest combat air assault in military history, air-assaulting from Saudi Arabia to the Euphrates.

During its four wars, the Rakkasans have earned four Medals of Honor; 26 Distinguished Service Crosses; 411 Silver Stars; 3,841 Purple Hearts; 917 of its brave soldiers have died as a result of combat. The Rakkasans proudly display twenty-three Battle Streamers, fifteen combat citations, including five American and three foreign Presidential Unit Citations.

Back home at Fort Campbell, Kentucky, the 3d Brigade of the 101st Airborne Division (Air Assault) readies itself for its next mission, training rigorously, updating its ever more sophisticated equipment and personal gear, and standing combat-ready—a singular part of the best army the United States has ever fielded.

As the Rakkasans, veterans and recruits, officers and men, say and feel:

AIRBORNE ALWAYS ALL WAYS

# Bibliography

## Books

Alexander, Bevin. *Korea—The First War We Lost.* New York: Hippocrene Books, 1986.

Anderson, Jack, and Dale Van Atta. *Stormin' Norman.* New York: Kensington Publishing Corp., 1991.

Appleman, Roy E. *South to the Naktong, North to the Yalu.* Washington. D.C.: Government Printing Office, 1961.

Blair, Clay. *The Forgotten War.* New York: Random House, Inc., 1987.

Bowman, John S., Ed. *The Vietnam War: An Almanac.* New York: World Almanac Publications, 1985.

Breuer, William B. *Geronimo.* New York: St. Martin's Press, 1989.

Davidson, Lt. Gen. Phillip B. *Vietnam at War.* Novato, Calif.: Presidio Press, 1988.

Devlin, Gerard M. *Paratrooper.* New York: St. Martin's Press, 1979.

Editors of Time. *Desert Storm: The War in the Persian Gulf.* New York: Time Warner Publishing, Inc., 1991.

Editors of *U.S. News and World Report. Triumph Without Victory.* New York: Times Books, Random House, 1992.

Fehrenbach, T. R. *This Kind of War.* New York: Macmillan, 1963.

Flanagan, Lt. Gen. Edward M., Jr. *Lightning.* McLean, Va.: Brassey's, Inc., 1993.

Flanagan, Major Edward M., Jr. *The Angels.* Washington, D.C.: Infantry Journal Press, 1946.

Furgurson, Ernest B. *Westmoreland, the Inevitable General.* Boston: Little Brown and Co., 1968.

Goulden, Joseph C. *Korea—The Untold Story of the War.* New York: Times Books, 1982.

Grigson, Maj. Dan. (Concept) *North to the Euphrates.* Clarksville, Tenn.: Kentucky Chapter, AUSA, 1991.

Hoyt, Edwin P. *On to the Yalu.* New York: Military Heritage Press, 1984.

Hoyt, Edwin P. *The Bloody Road to Panmunjom.* New York: Military Heritage Press, 1985.

Jones, Col. Robert. *101st Airborne Division: U.S. Airborne, 50th Anniversary Book.* Paducah, Ky.: Turner Publishing Co., 1990.

Karnow, Stanley. *Vietnam—A History.* New York: The Viking Press, 1983.

MacArthur, Gen. Douglas. *Reminiscences.* New York: Da Capo Press, 1964.

Manchester, William. *American Caesar.* Boston: Little Brown and Co., 1978.

Palmer, Gen. Bruce J. *The 25-Year War.* New York: Simon and Schuster, 1984.

Ridgway, Gen. Matthew B. *Soldier—The Memoirs of Matthew B. Ridgway.* New York: Harper and Brothers, 1956.

Roberts, Arch E. *Rakkasans!* Nashville: Tenn.: Battery Press, 1984.

Ryan, Cornelius. *A Bridge Too Far.* New York: Simon and Schuster, 1974.

Schwarzkopf, Gen. H. Norman. *It Doesn't Take a Hero.* New York: Bantam Books, 1992.

Special Report: *The U.S. Army in Desert Storm.* Arlington, Va.: Institute of Land Warfare, AUSA, June 1991.

Waterhouse, Fred J. *The Rakkasans.* Paducah, Ky.: Turner Publishing Co., 1991.

Westmoreland, Gen. William C. *A Soldier Reports.* New York: Doubleday and Co., 1976.

Woodward, Bob. *The Commanders.* New York: Simon and Schuster, 1991.

Zaffiri, Samuel. *Hamburger Hill.* Novato, Calif.: Presidio Press, 1988.

Zaffiri, Samuel. *Westmoreland.* New York: William Morrow and Co., 1994.

### Army Times Interviews

Berdy, Lt. Col. Andy, Commander, 2d Battalion, 187th Infantry.

Clark, Col. Robert, Commander, 187th Infantry.

Garrett, Col. Tom, Commander, 101st Aviation Brigade.

Peay, Maj. Gen. H. Binford, III, Commanding General, 101st Airborne Division, (Air Assault).

### Author Interviews

Bradin, Col. James, Beaufort, SC, 14 July 1993.

Peay, Gen. H. Binford, III, Fort Bragg, NC, 7 and 16 July, 20 August 1993; telephone interview on 20 August 1993.

Peck, Lt. Col. Terry, Fort Bragg, NC, 4 November 1992.

Scholes, Maj. Gen. Edison E., Fort Bragg, NC, 4 November 1992.

Shelton, Lt. Gen. Hugh H., Fort Bragg, NC, 30 August 1991, 3 August 1993.

**Private Papers, Letters, and Personal Communications**

Bernheim, Col. Eli D., Jr., letters dated 6 September and 4 December 1989.

Boyle, Col. William J., letters dated 16 May 1995 and September 1995.

Charles, Col. A. K., letter dated 15 September 1995.

Chester, Maj. Steve, 3rd Brigade, 101st, S5, letter dated 18 October 1992.

Cleland, Maj. Gen. John R., letters dated 12 March 1989 and 10 March 1995.

Costello, Lt. Col. Thomas, CO 3/320th FA Bn, letter dated 23 February 1992.

Crawford, Capt. W. T., Interview of Colonel G. H. Gerhart, Taegu, Korea, 8 April 1952.

Detlie, Lt. Col. Douglas S., letter dated 25 April 1989.

Furris, Lt. Col. Phillip A., letter dated 13 June 1995.

Gorwitz, Brig. Gen. Bertram Hall, two letters, 20 July 1989 and 19 June 1995.

Hennessey, Gen. J. J., letter dated 9 June 1989.

Higgins, Earl, letter dated 4 September 1990.

Johnson, Mace, letters dated 22 April and 6 May 1990.

Kinnard, Lt. Gen. H. W. O., undated in 1995.

Klepeis, Maj. Walter, four letters from 18 September 1991 to 18 April 1994.

Kroesen, Gen. Frederick J., letters dated 28 August and 25 September.

Liell, William J., letter dated 14 June 1990.

Mackmull, Lt. Gen. Jack V., detailed, comprehensive account of the origin of the air-assault concept, letter, 18 July 1993.

Miley, Col. William E., letter including a well-documented, personal account of battle on Mount Macolod, Luzon.

Munson, Brig. Gen. Delbert E., two letters dated 21 and 23 June 1995.

Parks, Dr. Donald A., letter dated 7 November 1990.

Peay, Gen. H. Binford, III, letters dated 14 May 1991, 14 June 1991, 30 July 1991, 27 February 1992.

Peck, Lt. Col. Terry, two letters, 27 October and 27 November 1992.

Pugh, Dr. Charles E., letter dated 18 April 1989.

Scholes, Maj. Gen. Edison E., letter dated 26 April 1991.

Schusteff, Bob, letter dated 6 November 1990.

Shelton, Lt. Gen. Hugh H., letters dated 10 October 1992, 22 November 1992, and a tape dated July 1993.

Spiller, Roger J., Command and General Staff College, letter dated 18 April 1987.

Stoff, Brig. Gen. William A., DA Chief of Military History, letter dated 19 April 1989.

Thomas, Lt. Col. Charles G., five letters from 23 January 1992 to 28 May 1992.

Trapnell, Lt. Gen. T. J. H., letter dated 3 April 1989.

Ward, Jim, letter dated 10 August 1989.

Waterhouse, Fred J., letters dated 14 June 1989, 18 October 1989, and 7 May 1994.

Weber, Col. William E., six letters from 9 March 1989 to 17 March 1995 and one letter, 29 November 1995, enclosing maps and photos.

Westmoreland, Gen. William C., letter dated 19 April 1989.

Woelful, Lou, undated letter.

### Magazines and Newspapers

Brown, Russ. "DSC and Silver Star Same Day." *Rakkasan Shimbun*, Summer 1989.

Casines, Art. "Rakkasans Played Role in 1958 Mideast Crisis." *Rakkasan Shimbun*, Spring 1989.

Donnelly, Tom. "The Generals' War." *Army Times*, 2 March 1992. "From the Top." *Army Times*, 24 February 1992. "Road to Baghdad." *Army Times*, 25 January 1993.

Editors, Newsweek. "America at War." *Newsweek*, Commemorative Edition, Spring/Summer 1991.

Editors, "Wings of Eagles: A Desert Storm Scrapbook." The *Leaf Chronicle*, (Clarksville, TN), 15 January 1992.

Esper, George. "Hamburger Hill Falls to GIs in Bloody Fight." *Stars and Stripes*, 21 May 1969.

Levy, Al. "Rakkasan Attack on Compound 76 Restored Order." *Rakkasan Shimbun*, Winter 1988.

Naylor, Sean D. "Flight of Eagles." *Army Times*, 22 July 1991.

Patrick, MSgt. Raymond W. "Koje Do." *Rakkasan Shimbun,* Summer 1989.

Simmons, Ron. "Koje Do." *Rakkasan Shimbun,* Summer 1994.

Spears, Col. John H. "Historical Reflections of the 187th Infantry." *Rakkasan Shimbun,* Spring 1988.

Steele, Dennis. "155 Miles Into Iraq: The 101st Strikes Deep." *Army,* August 1991.

Thompson, Capt. A. G. "Reds Ran But They Couldn't Hide." *Rakkasan Shimbun,* April 1988.

Tilson, Bettina. "It Begins." *Leaf Chronicle* Supplement, (Clarksville, TN), 16 January 1992.

Waterhouse, Fred. "Koje Do Remembered." *Rakkasan Shimbun,* Winter 1988.

**Military Documents**

Annual Historical Summary, Headquarters DA, 3/187th, 101st Airborne Division, 1 January 1968–31 December 1968.

Bolt, Col. William J. "Command Report: 101st Airborne Division (Air Assault) for Operation Desert Shield and Desert Storm, 2 August 1990 through 1 May 1991." 1 July 1991.

Cannon, M. Hamlin. *Leyte: The Return to the Philipines,* Washington, D.C.: U.S. Army, Office of the Chief of Military History, U.S. Government Printing Office, 1987.

Command Briefing, 101st Airborne Division, with maps and charts.

Guerrilla Operations Outline, 1952, Hqs, FECOM Liaison Detachment, 11 April 1952.

History of 1st Abn BG, 187th Infantry, undated (approximately 1960).

History of 2d Abn BG, 187th Infantry, 1961.

Key Korean War Battles, 8th Army Staff Historian, March 1972.

Lippard, 1st Lt. Clifford M. "101st Airborne Division (Air Assault), History for Operation Desert Shield/Desert Storm," 1 July 1991.

McGrath, Capt. Ida M. unpublished manuscript, "Desert Shield, 7 August 1990 to 15 January 1991," undated.

Officer Rosters, Hqs 187th Abn RCT, APO 51, SF, CA, 28 December 1950 through 22 August 1952.

ROTCM 145-20, *American Military History, 1607–1953.* Washington, D.C.: DA, July 1956.

Scholes, Maj. Gen. Edison E. XVIII Airborne Corps Staff Paper, "Repositioning of XVIII Airborne Corps." Fort Bragg, NC. Undated.

Smith, Robert Ross. *Triumph in the Philippines.* Washington, D.C.: DA, Office of the Chief of Military History, Government Printing Office, 1963.

Staff Paper, "The Battle of Sukchon-Sunchon," C & GSC, Ft. Leavenworth, KS.

The Third Battalion,(Airborne), 187th Infantry, Histories of 1968, 1969, 1970, 1971, dated 10 May 1973.

Tolson, Lt. Gen. John J. *Vietnam Studies—Airmobility 1961–1971.* Washington, D.C.: DA, U.S. Government Printing Office, 1973.

Unit History, unpublished.

**Monographs**

Bernheim, Col. Eli D., Jr. letter to author, March 1988, including an unpublished, detailed history of the 187th GIR in World War II, author unknown.

Giordano, Maj. Joseph B. "Opn of G Co 187th GIR—Ormoc." The Infantry School, 1948.

Hoppenstein, Maj. Isaac. "The Opns of the 187th Glider Infantry Regiment in the Landing at Nasugbu, Luzon." The Infantry School, 1948.

Klepeis, Maj. Walter. Series of unpublished monographs: "I and R Platoon Tracks the Enemy"; "Cpl Lester Hammond, CMH Winner"; "Needed: An Aggressive FO Team"; "Only God Can Lift a Jeep"; "A Night Combat Patrol"; "How Accurate Were 105mm Recoilless Rifles?"; "*Parlez-Vous Français, mon Colonel?*"; "To Capture a Prisoner."

Leister, Capt. Albert F. "Opns of 11th Abn Div from Nasugbu to Manila," The Infantry School, 1950.

Merritt, Capt. Harrison J. "The Opn of Co. G, 187th GIR in Attack on Nichols Field, Luzon." The Infantry School, 1948.

Roskey, William. "Koje Island: The 1952 Korean Hostage Crisis." Arlington, Va.: The Institute of Land Warfare, AUSA, September 1994.

# Index

Abernathy, Pfc. Reginald, 311
Abrams, Gen. Creighton C., 278, 300, 308
Acheson, Dean, 148
Adams, Lt. Col. Hank,195
Agee, Capt. Thomas H., 200
Agnew, Spiro, 316
Air Assault Concept, 261–62
Alamo Report, 32, 33
Albade, Capt. Wells, 31
Alexander, Sgt. W.B., 198
Allen, Brig. Gen. Frank, 166
Allen, Lt. Gabe, 84
Allen, Maj. Richard J., 139
Almond, Maj. Gen. Edward M., 152, 173, 211, 212, 214, 220
Anzerone, Lt. 115
Area of Operations (AO) Campbell, 366, 369, 370, 371, 372
Area of Operations (AO) Eagle, 355, 359, 363
Area of Operations (AO) Normandy, 334–35
Arellano, Pfc., 218
Argylls, 165
Atcheson, Lt. Gordie, 299
Atwater, Capt. Jack, 31

Baier, Pfc. Arnold L., 109
Bailey, Sfc. Fred Jr., 155
Ballard, Lt., 273
Balzack, Maj. Jerry, 356, 361
Barriger, Maj. Gen. William L., 249
Barsanti, Maj. Gen. Olinto M., 270
Basham, Capt. Eldon O., 241, 242
Bashore, Capt. Paul G., 35, 113
Battle of the Airfields, 30–49
Beatty, Lt. Col. George S. Jr., 249
Beightler, Maj. Gen. Robert, 123
Belford, Maj. Jack, 251
Bellows, Capt. Charles, 41
Belton, MSgt. George, 174

Bench, Johnny, 339
Bennit, Lt. George, 281, 298
Berdy, Lt. Col. Andy, 326, 327, 339, 356
Bernheim, Eli, 16, 17, 28, 29, 56, 82, 94, 99, 103, 104, 110, 111, 113, 132–33
Berry, Brig. Gen. Sidney B. Jr., 309
Biller, Lt. Jerry, 356, 357
Billingsley, Pfc., 219
"Biscuit Bombers," 49
Bito Beach, Leyte, 23; and withdrawal from, 64
Blackjack Bastion, 252
Bland, Lt. Col. Iran C., 305, 306
Blessing, Lt. Jack, 41
Boatner, Brig. Gen. Hayden L., 227, 230
Bobadilla, Capt. John M., 311
Boccia, Lt. Frank, 279, 280
*Bock's Car,* 124
Bolte, Gen. Charles, 148
Bonasso, Lt. Col. Russell P., 261
Bondie, Cpl., 237
Bonneville, Maj., 362
Borg, Pfc. B. H., 219
Bowen, Brig. Gen. Frank, 154, 157, 159, 160, 161, 170, 172, 173, 177, 192, 195, 199, 204, 213, 214, 215; and assumption of command of 187th, 143; and alert to jump near Chunchon, 191
Bowen, Pvt. Mason F., 240
Bowers, Lt. Col. John, 299
Bowers, Maj. William S., 127
Bowie, MSgt. James, 232
Boyle, Lt. Col. William J., 157, 161, 170
Bradford, Pfc. Clark, 155
Bridges, Lt. Col. Gary, 326, 327
British 27th Commonwealth Brigade, 152, 165

Brooks, Sp4 Edward, 290
Brooks, Capt. Waldo W., 164
Brough, Lt. Walter L., 32
Brown, Lt. Francis, 242
Brown, Brig. Gen. Wyburn D., 8
Brubaker, Lt. Col. Eldridge, 213
Bruce, Maj. Gen. A. D., 59
Brucker, Secretary of the Army Wilbur, 257
Bryan, Maj. Gen. "Babe," 208
Bryan, Lt. Col. Bill, 350, 368
Bucha, Capt. Paul W., 270, 271
Buche, Capt. Joseph, 351
Bulkeley, Lt. John D., 18
Burba, Gen. Edwin H. Jr., 329
Burgess, Lt. Col. Henry, 32, 35, 39, 40, 46, 123
Bush, President George S., 319, 325, 339, 340, 343, 369

Calcasieu Swamp, 13
Campbell, Pvt., 115
Campbell, Sp4 Tyrone, 297
Camp Eagle II, 331, 335, 346, 372
Camp Mackall, NC 3, 4, 9, 12
Camp Stoneman, CA., 13, 14
Carlson, Capt. Richard A., 361
Carlson, Lt., 44
Carnahan, Maj. Davy, 41, 103, 109, 113, 119
Carolus, Cpl. Charles H., 136
Carter, Capt. Glen, 113, 129
Casey, Col. Maurice F. Jr., 227
Cavanaugh, Capt. Steve, 87
Cease Fire in Gulf War, 369, 370, 371
Chapman, Maj. Gen. E. G. Jr., 5, 9
Chapman, Willie, 290
Chappelle, Capt. John C. "Butch," 291
Chase, Brig. Gen. William C., 88
Cheney, Richard, 324, 339, 341, 343, 369
Chesley, Lt. Col. Joe, 326
Chester, Maj. Steve, 359–60, 366, 370, 371
Chiesa, Pfc. John, 62
Chinese Communist Forces (CCF)

167; and renewed attack, 168; and massive invasion of South Korea, 176; and attack near Hoengsong, 181; and renewed major assault, 208–11
Christensen, Capt. John, 363
Ciceri, Maj. John, 117
Clark, Gen. Mark, and successor to Gen. Ridgway, 227
Clark, Col. Robert T., 338, 342, 343, 344, 345, 347, 355, 356, 357, 358, 362, 363, 364, 365
Clark, SSgt. Vernon W., 70, 71
Clark, Lt. William A., 114
Clayman, Col. Donald C., 259
Cleland, Lt. John R. D., 188, 189
Clift, Lt. Jack T., 32
Coad, Brig. Basil J., 65
Cody, Lt. Col. Dick, "Commander", 329, 343, 346
Coe, Col. Rinaldo, 84
Cohn, Capt. Hans, 41
Coleman, Lt. Robert B., 181
Collins, Gen. J. Lawton, 174
Colson, Brig. Gen. Charles F., 227
Comerford, Sp4 John, 290
Conable, Maj. John, 16, 120, 136
Conmy, Col. J. B., 273, 276, 285, 289, 292, 294, 295
Connally, Senator Tom, 149
Connor, Lt. Col. John P. "Poopy," 170, 184, 186, 195, 201, 203, 213, 217
Conrad, Lt. Michael J., 259
Cook, Capt. James D., 182, 187, 188
Coplen, Sgt. Donald D., 111
Corbett, Pius, 84
Corregidor, 17, 18
Costello, Lt. Col. Thomas J., 344–45, 358, 362, 365, 370, 371
Coune, Capt. Felix, 41
Crawford, Lt. Col. Bill, 23, 74
Crawford, Capt., 199, 203, 204
CPX Internal Look, 326
Crete, 11
Curran, Lt. Col. Mark, 351

Dalton, Lt. Michael M., 313

D'Amato, Cpl. Joseph, 240
Dance, Sp4 Lawrence R., 313
Darrigo, Capt. Joseph, 149–50
Daugherty, Maj., 279, 280
Davis, Lt. Col. Douglas C., 31, 42, 43
Dean, Maj. Gen. William F., 151
Dejarnette, Capt., 358
Denholm. Lt. Charles, 279, 280, 286
Dependents and arrival in Japan,
  137; and departure, 138–39
Desert Storm and initial deploy-
  ments, 325–26
Dickerson, Lt. Robert L., 7, 71
Dickey, Lt. James, 279
Disney, Cpl. Robert A., 241
Dodd, Brig. Gen. Francis T., 226
Domitrovits, Bob, 255, 257
Dong Ap Bia, 283
Downey, Sp4 Edward, 311
Dreyer, Pfc. Howard L., 219
Dugger, Lt. Douglas A., 275

Echols, SSgt. Edwin A., 110
Edwards, Sgt., 237
Edwards, Lt. Marshall, 285
Edwards, Capt. Robert W. Jr., 310
Eichelberger, Lt. Gen. Robert L.,
  64, 67, 69, 70, 71, 73, 76, 78, 81,
  82, 84, 85–88, 92, 95, 130, 131,
  137, 138
Eisenhower, Gen. Dwight D., 11
Ellis, SSgt., 111
Enola Gay, 1 24
Epps, Lt. J. N., 183, 187, 188, 200,
  201, 202, 203, 217, 219
Ermatinger, Capt. Ralph E., 131
Estes, Gen. Howell M. Jr., 270
Eward, Lt. Marshall, 279
Ewing, Maj. Nat, "Bud", 61, 111, 120

Fahy, Capt. Tim, 360, 361
Fako, Sgt. John S., 306
Farnsworth, Lt. Clayton B., 44–45
Farrell, Brig. Gen. Francis W., 84;
  and artillery plan for Malepunyo,
  117
Farren, Lt. Col. James, 42
Fechteler, RAdm. William M., 68

Felix, Maj. Russell, 240
Fells, Sp4 William H., 311
Fengstadt, Pvt. Gordon O., 155
Ferguson, Sgt. Charles, 204
Ferrelly, Capt., 29
Fiore, Anthony S., 227, 229, 250,
  251
Flatley, Capt. Joseph T., 305
Fleagan, Pfc. Jon, 279, 280
Forrest, Lt. Col. John F., 270
Fort McKinley and 11th Airborne
  Division attack of, 95, 100–01
Forward Operating Base (FOB)
  Bastogne, 335, 336, 338
Forward Operating Base (FOB)
  Cobra, 342, 350, 354, 355, 358,
  362, 364, 365, 371, 373
Foss, Lt. John W. II, 259
Foster, Cpl. Charles E., 242
Franks, Lt. Gen. Frederick M. Jr.,
  340
Fredericks, Capt., 287
Frogner, Cpl., 219
Fuji Heiden, 118
Fujishige, Col. Masatoshi, 72, 80,
  108; and capture and interroga-
  tion of, 116
Fullerton, Pfc. Norman, 204
Fye, Capt. John H., 237, 240

Gallagher, Lt. Col. Dan, 249, 251
Gardner, Cpl. Lawrence N., 202
Garret, Maj. Chester, 311
Garrett, Capt. O. G., 232, 241
Garrett, Col. Thomas, 328, 350, 351,
  364, 365, 367, 368
Garvin, Lt. Robert M., 181
Garza, Sfc. Louis, 290, 291
Gasperini, Spc. Edward R., 158, 164,
  166
Gavin, Lt. Gen. James M., 262
Genko Line, 89, 90, 93; and descrip-
  tion of, 91–92, 98, 193
Gerhart, Lt. Col. George H., 160,
  170, 197
Gerhart Task Force, 213
Gill, Capt., 354
Giordano, Lt. Joseph, 56, 57, 58

Giraud, Gen. Henri, 9
Glenn, Pfc. William F., 311
Glider pay, 15
Glover, Maj. 358, 363
Goff, Lt. James, 290
Golden, Lt., 362
Goltra, MSgt. Richard V., 202
Gormlie, Maj. George F., 197
Gorwitz, Capt. Bertram K.,"Igor,"
220, 264
Grace, Capt. Henry D., 313
Greco, Lt. Col. Tom, 356, 357, 358,
359, 362
Greene, Lt. Col. Charles H., 165
Grigson, Maj., 354
Griswold, Lt. Gen. Oscar, 100, 105,
116, 117
Griswold, Capt. Walter, 277
Grones, Lt. Col. Dow S., 235
Gutierrez, Pvt. Jesse C., 241
Gypsy Task Force, 123–24

Hacksaw Ridge, 56
"Hail Mary" shift of forces, 341
Halsey, Admiral William F. "Bull,"
20
Hamburger Hill, 282
Hamlin, Lt. James E., 241
Hamlin, Lt. Col. John, 350
Hammer, Sgt. Carl A., 251
Hammond, Cpl. Lester, 238, 239,
240
Hammond, Lt. Robert D., 200, 259
Hammrick, Pfc. Carl M., 218–19
Hancock, Lt. Col. Frank, 354
Hanna, Capt., 84
Hanna, Lt., 3 7
Hanson, Cpl. Robert L., 213
Harkink, Pvt., 114
Harkins, Capt. Gerald R., 277, 280,
285, 287, 298, 299
Harrell, Pfc. Cleo, 52
Harris, Sp4 Howard, 293
Haugen, Col. Orin D., "Hardrock",
4, 25, 30, 57, 85; and death of, 94
Hawkins, SSgt. Travis B., 113
Haywood, Sfc., 183, 189
Helms, Sp4 Dennis, 279

Henderson, MSgt. Philander, 239
Henebry, Brig. Gen. John P.,"Jack,"
192, 193, 194
Hernandez, Cpl. Rudy, 218–19
Herren, Capt. Everett D., 304
Herrick, Col. Curtis J., and assump-
tion of command 187th, 254, 255
Hewitt, Lt. R. D., 189
Hildebrand, Col. Harry D., 7, 26,
55, 81, 88, 107
Hill, Col. Tom, 336, 347, 353
Hockman, MSgt. Charles, 250
Hodge, Maj. Gen. John R., 21, 24, 35
Hoffman, N. C., 3, 10
Holcombe, Lt. Col. Frank S.,
"Hacksaw," 57, 86
Holland, Maj. C. M. "Mike," 219, 235
Hollandia Operation, 16
Honeycutt, Lt. Col. Weldon F,
"Tiger," 277, 278, 279, 280, 281,
282, 285, 286, 287, 288, 289,
290–300; and assumes command
3/187, 276,
Hope, Bob, 339
Hoppenstein, Maj., 72, 80
Hoska, Lt. Col. Lucas E. Jr., 7, 26,
41, 79, 92
Howell, Sp4 John M., 310
Howze Board, 262–63
Howze, Lt. Gen. Hamilton H., 262
Huber, Maj., 29
Hudson, CWO John, 166
"Hundred Hour War," 369
Hurster, Lt. John G., 48
Hyatt, Edward, 2, 16
Hyde, Sp4 Nate, 79

Ignatz, Sfc. William, 159, 193,
214–15
Il, Lt. Gen. Nam, 223, 224
Iraqi forces and deployment of,
333, 335
Iwabuchi, RAdm. Sonji, 66, 91

Jablonsky, Col. Harvey J., 141; and
assumption of command of 187th,
139
Jackson, Sp4 Johnny, 298, 299, 290

Japanese defense of Manila, 90–91;
    and Genko Line, 93–94
Japanese Forces; 3d Parachute
    Regiment,40; 8th Division, 79;
    16th Division, 33, 36; 17th
    Infantry Regiment, 108; 26th
    Division, 56; 37th Infantry
    Division, 123; 115th Fishing
    Battalion, 108; Fuji Force,108
Japanese parachute attack on Leyte
    airstrips, 27, 40
Jardine, Capt. Thomas, 351
Jarrell, Sgt. Robert E., 242
Jenkins, Lt. Gen. Reuben E., 242
Johnson, Capt. Dean, 285, 287, 294
Johnson, Maj. Gen. James H. Jr., 326
Johnson, Lt. Col. Robert L., 112
Jones, Col. George, 69
Jones, Sfc. Robert L., 218
Joy, VAdm C. Turner. 223
Joyce, Cpl. Coleman, V, 138

Kalamas, Michael J., 38, 39
Kawabe, Gen., Torashiro, 128
Keleher, Lt. Col. W.P., 183
Kelly, Maj. Peter L., "Spider," 233
Kelly, Pvt. Ova A., 46
Kennedy, Senator Edward M., 282
Kern, Lt. Col. Mark, 366
King, Adm. Ernest J., 19
Kinnard, Maj. Gen. Harry W.O.,
    263, 264, 265
Kinney, Lt. Col. Peter C., 356, 361,
    366–67
Kinnison, Lt. Col. Henry, 344, 351,
    356, 360, 361, 363, 370
Kirkland, Pfc. Willie, 294
Kirksey, Pfc.,161
Kirksey, Sgt. Aaron D., 177–78
Kissinger, Henry, 308
Klepeis, Lt. Walter, 237, 238, 239,
    240, 241
Kneebone, Lt., 51
Knollwood Maneuver, 12
Koje-do and description of and con-
    ditions in, 224–27
Korean Military Advisory Group,
    148–49

Korean War and start of, 147
Korn, Maj. David, 234
Korovesis, Pfc. Steve, 293
Kouts, Capt. William C., 237, 239
Kozlowski, Lt. Chester J., 31
Kroesen, Maj. Gen. Frederick J.,
    249, 250, 310
Krueger, Lt. Gen. Walter, 20, 24, 76,
    86, 107, 119, 123
Krupa, Sfc. Leo, 203

Lackey, Col. John, 123
LaFlamme, Lt. Col. Ernie, 30, 74, 77
Lahti, Col. Edward H., 86, 118, 132;
    and interrogation of Fujishige,
    116
Lambert, Lt. Col. Harry F., 161, 165
Lang, Col. Walter P. "Pat" Jr., 324
Larson, Sp4 Terry, 286
Lasala, Sgt. Frank J., 1, 11
Lear, Lt. Gen. Ben, 9
Lee, Col. Hak Ku, 226, 230, 234
Lee, Capt. Raymond, 79, 80
Leister, Capt. Albert F., 78, 81
Leno, Jay. 339
Leyte, invasion of, 20, 21, 22
Liell, Cpl. William, 240
Lindquist, Brig. Gen. Roy E., and
    assumption of command of 187th,
    252, 254
Lindsey, MSgt. Jake, 199
Lipa airborne school, 122–23
Lipscomb, Lt. Thomas, 293
Little, Sp4 Jack, 293
Littman, Capt. Charles L., 285, 288,
    291
Loewis, Maj. "Jungle Jim," 109, 110,
    111, 112
Logan, Sp4 Tim, 279
Logistical support in Saudi Arabia,
    340
Luck, Lt. Gen. Gary E., 333, 334,
    335, 342, 349, 365
Lundt, Pvt. Gustav W., 110
Lyden, Sp4 Michael, 291
Lykins, Capt. Charles W., 313
Lynch, Capt. Mike, 193
Lyman, Capt. William, 84

MacArthur, Gen. Douglas A., 17, 21, 64, 76, 86, 169; and trip to Australia, 18–19; and return to the Philippines, 19; and landing on Leyte, 21; and capture of Manila, 88; and plan to invade Japan, 119–20; and arrival in Japan, 131–32; and surrender aboard Missouri, 133–34; and visit to Seoul, 150; and belief in airborne concept, 156; and plan to drop 187th in North Korea, 157–58; and comment on Sukchon drop, 162; and belief that Korean War was won, 167; and orders to cross 38th Parallel, 193; and relief from command, 205
MacCleave, Lt. Col. Bob, 68
MacDonald, Col. John, 327, 329, 338
MacKall, Pvt. John T. "Tommy", 9
Madsen, Sp4 Steven K., 313
Mahonag, 54, 55, 56
Makino, Gen., 33
Malik, Jacob, 222, 223
Maloney, Lt. Edward J., 193, 216
Mamula, 2d Lt. Rudolf, 43
Manarawat, 32
Mancil, Sgt. Edward C., 153
Manila and description of in the war years, 90
Manila Hotel Annex, 86
Mann, Lt. Col. Tommy, 61, 62, 84
March, Gen. Peyton C., 66
Marcuso, Sgt., 161
Maria, Sfc. Antonio G., 177
Marshall, Gen. George C., 11
Martin, Maj., 344
Martin, Steve, 339
Maryniewski, Pfc., 291
Massad, Lt. Col. Ernie, 4, 79, 81, 98, 106
Massey, Lt. William S., 11
Mata, Sp4 Lionel, 297
Mathis, Sp4 Donald R., 313
Mathis, Jim, 345
Matthews, Pfc. Roy, 293
Mattioli, Lt., 289

Matts, Capt. Charles, 310
Mausert, Maj. Rye, 142, 172, 180, 194, 214, 215, 216, 217
McBridge, Capt. Michael S., 362
McCarrell, Sp4 John, 286
McCarthy, Maj. Gen. Chester F., 227
McCoy, Pfc. Francis T., 111
McDonald, Lt. Col. Donald D., 149
McEntee, Col. Ducat, 124
McGall, Sgt. Tom, 294
McGonagle, Sfc. Joseph, 242
McGowan, Lt. Col. Glen J. "Chief," 23
McGrath, Capt. Ida M., 327, 328, 329
McGreevy, Lt. Frank, 291, 293
McGrew, Pfc., Delbert R., 114
McKenna, Sgt., 44, 46
McLemore, Pfc. John W., 311
McLeod, Capt. John H., 82
McNair, Lt. Gen. Leslie, 7, 11, 12
McNamara, Robert S., 262
McNider, Brig. Gen. Hanford, 107
Meehan, Sgt. Maj. Bernie, 287
Merjil, Sp4 Edward, 297
Merritt, Capt. Harrison, 53, 95, 96, 97, 98, 109
Mesereau, Maj. Tom, 30, 129, 130
Milburn, Maj. Gen. Frank W., 169, 208
Miley, Capt. Jack, 199, 200
Miley, Capt. William M., "Buzz," 110, 115, 116
Miley, Maj. Gen. William "Bud," 139
Miller, Pvt., 44
Miller, Pfc. Archie, and fifth Purple Heart, 115
Miller, Sfc. Robert E., 218
Miller, Pfc. Warren, 111
Mills, Sp4 Donald, 286
Miyagi Task Force, 136
Mobato Point and description of, 101–02; and battle for, 103–04
Moore, Sp5 Dennis, 271
Moore, William "Fuzzy", 196
Moreno, Col., 114
Moreno, Miguel, 289
Morris, Sgt. Daniel R., 115

Morrison, Pfc, 189
Mount Macolod and description of, 108; and end of battle, 116
Mount Malepunyo and description of, 116–17
Muccio, Ambassador John J., 148
Mueller, Col. Arndt L., 260
Muldoon, MSgt. Ervin L., 200
Muller, Lt. Col. Henry, 9, 50, 51, 70, 72, 74, 87, 105, 118; and interrogation of Fujishige, 116
Munsan-ni, 190
Munson, Lt. Col. Delbert, 154–15, 160, 161, 163, 170, 179, 184, 195, 214
Murray, Pfc. Roger, 294
Muse, Lt. Samuel, 200, 201

Nadolski, Lt. Joe, 329–30
Neal, Brig. Gen. Richard, 364
Nelson, CWO William G., 28, 36, 47, 50, 54, 61
Nesbit, Capt. Sterling R., 35
Nichols Field and 11th Airborne attack of, 94, 95
Nicholson, Lt. John W., 259
Nimitz, Admiral Chester, 19, 20, 134
Nixon, President Richard, 308
Nolan, Lt. William J., 201
Norstad, Lt. Gen. Lauris, 141
Norton, Col. John, 262
Nyquist, Lt. J. B., 165

O'Brian, SSgt. Sean M., 360, 361
Okaboyashi, Col. Junkichi, 63
O'Kane, Lt. Col. Mortimer J., 84
Olsen, Lt. Charles "Pop," 29, 30, 60
O'Meara, Brig. Gen. Andrew P., 248
Operation Coronet, 119
Operation Courageous, 192
Operation Dauntless, 208
Operation Dewey Canyon II, 309–10
Operation Feint, 242
Operation Gypsy, 256
Operation Husky, 11
Operation Jefferson Glen, 312
Operation Kentucky Jumper, 277

Operation Killer, 189–90
Operation King II, 22
Operation Lam Son 719, 307–12
Operation Mike VI, 69, 70
Operation Nightmare Alley, 183
Operation Ohio Rapids, 277
Operation Olympic, 119
Operation Piledriver, 221
Operation Plan, 90–02, 325
Operation Ripper, 190–91
Operation Rugged, 205
Operation Thunderbolt, 181
Operation Tomahawk, 192
Ori, Capt. George, 51
Osmena, Philippine President Sergio, 21

Pacific War Strategy, 19–20
Pagonis, Lt. Gen. William G., 346
Palfrey, Pvt. Julian C., 113
Parachute Pay, 15
Parkinson, Lt. Thomas V., 238, 240
Patrick, MSgt. Raymond W., 231
Patterson, Robert, 12
Payne, Sgt. Samuel, 240
Pearson, Lt. Col. George, 26, 29, 30, 35, 36, 37, 43, 45, 46, 47, 53, 61, 68, 101, 103, 107, 109, 110, 112, 114, 126, 130, 132, 136; and assumes command of 187th, 107; and plan of attack on Malepunyo, 118; and resumption of command of 187th, 138
Pearson, Brig. Gen. Willard, 269
Peay, Maj. Gen. J. H. Binford III, 327, 328, 331, 332, 333, 334, 335, 336, 337, 338, 340, 341, 344, 347, 348, 349, 359, 351, 352, 353, 354, 355, 357, 364, 365, 367, 373; and 101st battle plan in Desert Shield, 335–36,
Pentomic reorganization, 255, 257
Percival, Lt. Gen. Sir Arthur, 133, 134
Pergamo, Lt. Paul J., 41
Perkins, Pfc. Warren G., 46
Persian Gulf War and outbreak of, 323–25

Piao, Gen. Lin, 170, 189
Pickel, Lt., 43
Pickel, Pfc. George, 289
Pierce, Pfc. Andrew S. Jr., 306
Pierson, Brig. Gen. Albert, 6, 7, 11, 49, 74, 77, 127, 130, 136
Pierson Task Force, 99, 102
Piscione, Pfc., 217
Polka, Lt. Jim, 61
Powell, Gen. Colin L., 325, 339, 341, 369
Powell, Gen. Herbert B., 262
Priatko, Capt. Richard A., 361
Price, Pfc. Joseph, 291
Pulver, Pfc. Olaf P., 189
Purcell, Paddy, 196
Purdon, Col. Ted, 354, 364, 365, 371, 373
"Purple Heart Hill," 51, 60, 62, 63

Quandt, Lt. Col. Douglass P., 8, 31, 35, 49, 56, 100, 127

Rangarai, Lt. Col. A.G., 196
Rangaswami, Capt. V., 196
Rangel, Pfc. Joe E., 41
Reenan, Sgt. Francis, 174
Reynolds, Col. Norman G., 257
Rhee, President Syngman, 152
Rich, Cpl. Clyde, 240
Ridgway, Gen. Matthew B., 12, 120, 189, 193, 219, 221, 223, 226; and assumption of command, 175, 176; and withdrawal, 176–77; and holding Wonju, 183–84; and drop at Munsan-ni, 197; and successor to MacArthur, 205, 211, 212
Richards, Louis M., 186
Rinehart, Pfc. Richard B., 310
Roberts, Capt. Arch, 160, 161, 254
Roberts, Col. Elvy, 265
Roberts, Lt. James W., 99, 111, 201
Roberts, Brig. Gen. W.L., 148
Robinson, Capt. Barry, 277, 279, 285
Roche, Col. John W., 192
Rocklen, Pfc. Michael, 294
Rockwell, Lt. Col. L. H., 150

Rogers, Lt. Gen. Gordon B.,2 61
Rogers, Capt. James, 361
Rogers, Capt. Thomas A., 310
Rollins, Sp4 Wade H., 310
Roosevelt, Franklin D., 19
Rosenstreich, Sp4 Aaron, 286
Ross, MSgt. Al, 216
Royster, Lt. Gen. Harry E., 324
Russ, Col. Joseph R., 235
Russell, Capt. John, 354
Rutherford, Lt. Andrew P., 242
Ryals, MSgt. Willard W., 164–65, 193, 195–96
Ryan, Maj. Gen. William O., 128, 129
Ryneska, Col. Joseph F., and assumption of command 187th, 255, 256
Sachers, Lt. Henry S., 239, 240
Sadler, Cpl. John F., 232, 233
Sanchez, Pfc. Jose A., 313
Sanders, Capt. Harry, 231, 242
Sanders, Capt. Luther L., 277, 279, 280, 281, 285, 287, 288, 289, 292, 293
Saudi Arabia and buildup of forces in, 332–33
Saunier, Pfc, 217
Scharnberg, Maj. Ronald D., 310, 311
Schimmelpfennig, Col. Irving R., 75
Schmidt, Lt. Carl, 220
Scholes, Brig. Gen. Edson E., 333
Schommer, Capt. Cletus N., 112
Schusteff, Robert, 198
Schwarzkof, Gen. H. Norman, 259–60, 324–25, 332, 333, 334, 339, 340, 353, 364, 369, 372; and plan of attack, 341
Seaton, Lt. Col. Stuart M., 235
Seifert, Lt. Leo, 202
Shadden, Pvt. 53
Shanahan, Capt. Jack B., 199
Shaneyfelt, Maj. Stanley, 271, 272
Sharkey, Lt. Col. Thomas, 258, 259
Sharp, B. G. William F., 18
Sheets, Lt. Col. George M., 272, 273, 274, 276

Shelton, Brig. Gen. Henry H.
"Hugh," 326, 328, 330, 331, 346,
347, 367, 368
Sherburne, Maj. Gen. T.L., 257
Sherrill, Lt., Jim, 271
Shigemitsu, Mamoru, 133
Shipley, Lt. Col. Norman, 28, 50
Shorty Ridge, 78, 83, 84, 85, 87
Sibert, Maj. Gen. Franklin C., 20
Sidenberg, Pfc. Joe R., 120–21
Siegel, Lt., 54
Simkins, Lt., 165–66
Simmons, Ron, 228, 231, 233
Simpkins, Sgt. Carl A., 251
Skau, Lt. George, 87
Smith, Lt., 357
Smith, Lt. Col. Charles B., 151
Snyder, Pfc., 291
Soule, Col. Robert H.,"Shorty," 7,
76–79, 83, 84, 88
Spellman, Lt. David B., 181
Sperduto, Sgt. L. F., 189
Springfield, Sp4 William, 289
Stadtherr, Lt. Col. Nick, 31
Stahl, Pfc. Roger, 311
Stanchuk, Sgt, 219
Steinberg, Lt. Col. William A., 303
Step, Capt. Leslie, 244
Sterns, Sgt. Thomas, 294
Stevenson, Sgt. Kenneth E., 155
Steverson, Lt. Col. James R., 311
Stewart, Cpl. Henry, 187–88
Stilwell, Lt. Gen. Richard G., 283,
302
St. Onge, Sp4 Terry, 279, 280
Stringham, Sgt. Ernie, 56
Strong, Lt. Col. John L., 102
Strover, Capt. John E., 161
Stymiest, Capt. William, 299
Sullivan, Lt. Donald, 290, 297, 361
Sullivan, Pfc. Robert M., 275
Sutherland, Lt. Gen. James W., 309
Sutherland, Maj. Gen. Richard K.,
128
Sutton, Lt. Col. Bryan J., 306, 307,
311
Suzuki, Lt. Gen. Sosaku, 26, 33
Swanson, Sp4 Ron, 290

Swarmer Exercise, 141–42
Swing, Maj. Gen. Joseph M., 6, 8, 9,
11, 12, 13, 16, 24, 28, 29, 30, 31,
35, 36, 42, 46, 53, 55, 56, 59, 67,
70, 71, 73, 74, 75, 76, 78, 79, 84,
85, 86, 87; and new mission in
Southern Luzon,105; and attack
plans for Southern Luzon, 105;
and attack on Mt. Malepunyo,
117, 118; and invasion of Japan,
119; and orders to move the 11th
to Okinawa, 124–25; and possible
combat jump near Tokyo, 128;
and departure from 11th Airborne
Division, 112, 139; and new mission in Southern Luzon, 105; and
plan and attack of Mt. Malepunyo,
117; and 11th Airborne Honor
Guard, 129; and touch down at
Atsugi, 130
Swing Board, 11
"Swing Session,",8

Tactical Assembly Area (TAA)
Campbell, 346, 358
Tagaytay Ridge and jump on, 84–87
Tarpley, Maj. Gen. Thomas M., 309
Task Force Growdon, 198
Task Force Hawkins, 198
Task Force Normandy, 343, 346
Task Force Rakkasan, 356, 357, 358,
362
Task Force Smith, 151
Taylor, Sfc. Ira, 187
Taylor, Gen. Maxwell D., 247, 257
Tipton, Col. Norman E., 68, 82, 96,
100, 101, 109, 132
Tolson. Lt. Gen. John J., 261, 262,
270
Tomochika, Gen., 63, 64
Trapnell, Brig. Gen. Thomas J.H.,
217, 230, 233, 234; and assump-
tion of command of 187th, 222
Trautman, Lt. Joel, 294
Treadwell, Capt. David O., 303
Truman, President Harry, 150; and
relief of MacArthur, 205
Tulley, Capt. Robert B., 216

Tynor, Lt. Col. Layton C., 174

Umezu, Gen. Yoshijiro, 133
United States Air Force units; 5th
Air Force Headquarters, 46, 47;
5th Bomber Command, 34; 21st
Troop Carrier Wing, 159; 54th
Troop Carrier Wing, 15, 126;
314th Troop Carrier Wing, 159,
192; 315th Air Division, 192, 227;
437th Troop Carrier Wing, 192
United States Army units Eighth
Army, 157, 169, 170, 171; and situation at start of Korean War, 151,
152
Corps; I Corps, 65, 165; IX Corps,
21, 152, 169; X Corps, 21, 168,
169, 173; XIV Corps, 65, 105;
XVIII Airborne Corps, 254, 316;
and Desert Storm mission, 342;
XXIV Corps, 21, 24, 34, 35, 283
Divisions, Americal, 135; 1st Cavalry,
20, 25, 88, 101, 117, 151, 156, 157,
167, 168, 265; 2d Infantry, 152,
167, 171; 7th Infantry, 24, 25, 26,
151, 152, 170; 11th Air Assault and
reorganization, 263, 264; 11th
Airborne, 3, 10, 12 and activation,
5; and strength, 6, and combat on
Leyte, 22, 24–26; and orders for
attack on Luzon, 66; and 1945
reorganization, 119; and move to
Okinawa, 126–28; and move to
Japan, 129–30; and arrival in
Japan, 132; and move to occupation zone, 135, 137; 17th
Airborne, 12; 24th Infantry, 20, 25,
151, 165, 247; 25th Infantry, 151,
247; 37th Infantry, 88; 77th
Infantry, 34, 48, 58, 59, 60, 137;
96th Infantry, 24, 25; 101st Air
Assault (Airborne), 317; and
deployment from Fort Campbell,
328–30; and mission in Desert
Shield/Desert Storm, 334; and
plans, 342
Regiments; 1st Brigade, 101st AA
Divison and move to Viet Nam,

269; 158th Infantry, 105, 106, 107,
109; 187th (Glider, Parachute,
Airborne) Infantry, 3, 6, 10, 12,
13, 61; and activation, 5; and
strength and equipment, 7; and
basic training, 8; and arrival in
New Guinea, 14; and New Guinea
build-up, 15; and load-up for the
Philippines,16; and move to Leyte,
17; and landing on Bito Beach, 23,
24; and Leyte combat, 25, 30; and
plans for Luzon invasion, 71; and
security of the MSR, 88; and movement to Tagaytay Ridge, 104; and
reunion as a regiment, 106; and
relieved by 1st Cavalry, 107; and
movement to Cuenca, 109; and
attack on Mount Macolod,
109–18; and conversion to Para-
Glider Infantry Regiment, 119;
and garrison of Manila, 122; and
move to Okinawa, 127–28; and
occupation area in Japan, 135,
137; and paratrooper fill-up, 136;
and departure from Japan,
139–40, and arrival at Fort
Campbell, Ky., 140; and reorganization as an airborne infantry regiment,141; and participation in
Exercise Swarmer, 142–43; and
departure from Campbell, 154;
and deployment to Korea, 153;
and arrival in Japan, 154–55; and
first combat in Korea, 155–56; and
jump at Sukchon-Sunchon, 159;
and equipment drop, 162; and
return to theatre reserve, 167; and
operations near Pyongyang, 170;
and Eighth Army reserve, 171; and
move north, 172–73; and alert to
move to Suwon, 177; and assignment to X Corps, 179; and
defense of Punji Pass, 179–80; and
battle of the hills, 184–87; and
assembly near Taegu, 189, 192;
and plan to jump at Munsan-ni,
192–93; and jump on Munsan-ni,
193–99; and move back to Taegu,

204; and use in a "ground" role, 212; and attack to Hoengsong, 212–19; and move to Wonju, 221; and move to Japan, 222, and life in Japan, 222–24; and movement to Koje-do, 227–28; and set-up on Koje-do, 228–30; and opertions at Koje-do, 230–34; and return to Taegu, 234; and move to the "Iron Triangle," 236; and "Blackjack" nickname, 236; and return to Seoul, 243; and return to and life in Japan, 245–47; and return to Korea, 247–48; and move to Kumwha area, 247–48; and return to Japan, 252; and return to the U.S., 253–54; and assignment to XVIII Airborne Corps, 255; and move to Fort Campbell, 256; and reorganization and reassignment to Germany, 257–58; and movement to Beirut as 1st Airborne Battle Group, 187th, 258–59; and return to Fort Bragg, 258, 259, 264; and reorganization of, 317–18, and Sinai Peninsula mission, 318; and deployment during summer 1990, 326–29; and deployment in AO Normandy, 339; and plan to air assault to the Euphrates, 345–46; and closure in TAA Campbell, 347; and return to Fort Campbell, 373; and personal and unit awards, 374; 2d Airborne Battle Group,187th, 257, 259, 260, 264; and reorganization, 263, 264; 3d Airborne Battle Group, 187th, 263, 264; 188th Glider Infantry, 7, 25, 55, 75, 76, 77, 78, 81, 83, 83, 84, 87, 106; 199th Light Infantry Brigade, 272; 501st Parachute Infantry, 11; 503d Parachute Infantry, 29, 156; 508th Airborne RCT, 253; 511th Parachute Infantry, 4, 9, 25, 28, 48, 52, 59, 67, 81, 82, 85, 86; and march on Manila, 87–90; and Genko Line, 90, 92, 93, 106; 541st Parachute Infantry, 12, 124

Battalions; 1st/149th Infantry, 46, 47; 1st/187th Infantry, 34, 45, 46, 53, 59, 62, 75–79, 83, 84, 87, 102, 103, 115, 162; 2d/187th Infantry, 52, 53, 54, 55, 56, 82, 95–01, 113, 161, 162; 3d/187th Airborne Infantry, 161, 266; and fight at Yongyu, 163, 165; and Task Force, 167; and move to Viet Nam, 270–71; and "Nomad Battalion, 274; and Dong Ap Bia, 283–84, 300; and Vietnamization, 303; and Cam Ranh Bay mission, 313–14; and return from Viet Nam, 315; 2d/188th Glider Infantry, 61, 62; 2d/511th Parachute, 34, 56, 59; 3d/511th Parachute, 102; 3d/306th Infantry, 34; 44th Tank, 109; 85th Chemical, 110; 127th Airborne Engineer, 5, 23, 41, 77, 109; 152d AntiAircraft, 42, 53; 287th Field Artillery Observation, 34; 457th Parachute Field Artillery, 8, 12, 85, 102; 674th (Glider Parachute) Field Artillery, 7, 10, 13, 25, 42, 75, 84, 85, 92, 112, 153, 160–61, 248; 675th Glider Field Artillery, 25, 84, 85, 98, 106, 109; 767th Tank, 43
Companies and Batteries; A Battery, 82d Airborne AA Battalion, 153; A Company, 127th Engineers, 153; 2d Ranger Company, 192; 4th Ranger Company, 192, 196; 48th Quartermaster, 41; 511th Signal, 31, 51, 130; 221st Airborne Medical, 32; 711th Ordnance, 41
Other U.S. ground forces; 1st Marine Brigade, 152; 1st Marine Division, 152, 168; 44th Field Hospital, 48
Urich, Pvt. Earl, 110
U.S. forces in Vietnam and drawdown, 1971, 312, 315

Valent, Sgt. "Jumpy," 189
Vallone, Sp4 Michael, 299
VanAntwerp, Lt. Col. Bob, 342, 355
Vandergast, Sfc. James A., 200

Vanderpool, Maj. Jay D., 102
Van Fleet, Lt. Gen. James A., 219, 221, 226, 225; and successor to Ridgway, 205; and assumption of command, 207–11
Vietnamization, 302

Wade, Capt. Jim, 242
Wainwright, Lt. Gen. Jonathan M., 17, 18, 133, 134
Walden, Lt. Jerry, 293, 294
Walker, Lt. Gen. Walton W., 151, 158, 169, 170, 171; and death of, 174
Walton, Sp4 Douglas, 279
Waring, Capt. Jim, 358
Watson, Capt. David W., 279, 280
Weber, Lt. William E., 155, 173; and attack on Hill, 362, 184–86
West, Lt. Arvid E., 259
Westmoreland, Gen. William C., "Westy," 235, 236, 239, 240, 241, 243, 252, 276, 282, 316; and assumption of command of the 187th, 234; and promotion to brigadier general, 245; and argument with Maj. Gen. Barriger, 249–50; and opposition to pentomic concept, 260, 263; and assumption of command of XVIII Airborne Corps, 263
West Point Class 1915 and famous names, 6
Whetstone, Lt. Col. Russell E., 228, 232, 235, 239
White, Lt. S. J.,187, 189
Whitehead, Gen. Ennis C., 25
Whitney, Maj. Gen. Courtney, 131
Wilkes, MSgt. Philip J., 183
Williams, Col. Alex, 130
Williams, Lt. Charles L., 218, 219
Williams, Sfc. Paul F., 344
Willoughby, Maj. Gen. Charles A., 167, 168
Wilson, Lt. Col. Arthur H. "Harry", 28, 50, 51, 53, 56, 58, 68, 75, 78, 84, 102, 107, 109, 160, 161, 170, 180, 194, 195, 208; and assumes

command of 187th, 137; and resumes command of 187th, 142, 154
Wilson, Pfc. Lemone, 218
Wilson, Pfc. Richard G., 163, 166
Wooley, Lt. Earl K., 201, 203

Yamashita, Gen. Tomoyuki, 22, 26, 33, 51, 39, 65, 66, 67
Yates, Pfc. Billy B., 219
Young, Capt. Blaine F., 217
Yup, Col. Paik Sun, 150

Zais, Gen. Melvin, 257, 274, 277, 278, 295, 300, 301
Zrenchak, Pvt. Andrew, 110